THE FALL OF
CHARLES I

THE FALL OF CHARLES I

JANE HAYTER-HAMES

AMBERLEY

First published 2022

Amberley Publishing
The Hill, Stroud
Gloucestershire, GL5 4EP

www.amberley-books.com

British Library Cataloguing in Publication Data.
A catalogue record for this book is available from the British Library.

ISBN 978 1 3981 0808 0 (hardback)
ISBN 978 1 3981 0809 7 (ebook)

1 2 3 4 5 6 7 8 9 10

Map design by John Plumer of JP Map Graphics Ltd.

Typeset in 10pt on 13pt Sabon.
Typesetting by SJmagic DESIGN SERVICES, India.
Printed in the UK.

Contents

Appendices

Selected documents of negotiation or constitutional
change, the main points of:

List of Maps

List of Illustrations

List of Characters

Abbot, George	Archbishop of Canterbury
Allen, Mr	Agitator to the army
Ashburnham, John, MP	Attendant gentleman to Charles I at Hampton Court
Barrington, Sir Thomas	MP, relative of Oliver Cromwell
Bastwick, John	Puritan writer, imprisoned for libel
Baxter, Richard	Presbyterian author
Bellievre, Pompone de	French ambassador. Mazarin's negotiator for Charles I
Berkeley, Sir John	Adviser to Charles I
Birkenhead, Sir John	Publisher of *Mercurius Aulicus*
Bodin, Jean	French jurist and political philosopher
Bouchier, Elizabeth	Wife of Oliver Cromwell
Boyle, Richard, 1st Earl of Cork	Munster landowner and Lord Justice of Ireland
Boyle, Richard, 2nd Earl of Cork	Eldest son of 1st Earl of Cork, Royalist
Boyle, Roger, 1st Viscount Broghill	Third son of Richard, 1st Earl of Cork. Protestant military commander in Munster, Ireland
Bradshaw, John	Chief Justice of Chester, President of the High Court of Justice to try Charles I
Bramhall, John	Bishop of Derry, Chaplain to Sir Thomas Wentworth
Brooke, Lord	Puritan and general in parliamentarian army
Burke, Richard, Earl of Clanricard	Leading peer from Connaught
Butler, Elizabeth (neé Preston), Countess of Ormond	Inherited Butler estate and married James, 12th Earl and 1st Duke of Ormond

Butler, James, 12th Earl and 1st Duke of Ormond	Royalist and Lord Lieutenant of Ireland
Butler, Thomas, 10th Earl of Ormond, 'Black Tom'	Great-uncle of 1st Duke
Butler, Walter, 11th Earl of Ormond, Catholic	Grandfather of the 1st Duke
Campbell, Archibald, 7th Earl of Argyll	'Gillesbuig Grumach', Catholic
Campbell, Archibald, Lord Lorne, 8th Earl and 1st Marquis of Argyll	Scottish privy councillor, Covenanter
Carr, Robert, Earl of Somerset	Favourite of James I & VI
Castlehaven, James Touchet, Earl of	Confederate military commander in Ireland
Cecil, Robert, Earl of Salisbury	Chief Minister to James I
Chichester, Sir Arthur	Lord Deputy of Ireland
Clarke, William	Secretary to the New Model Army
Clotworthy, Sir John, MP	Ulster planter from Devonshire family, Presbyterian
Coke, Sir Edward	Judge and jurist, constitutional theorist
Cook, John	Lawyer, radical and Independent, led the prosecution of Charles I. Regicide
Conway, Lord	Led Charles I's army against the Scots
Coote, Sir Charles	Planter in Connaught, took troops to Wicklow to put down rebellion
Cottington, Sir Francis	Chancellor of the Exchequer of England
Cranfield, Lionel	Lord High Treasurer of England
Cromwell, Bridget	Oliver Cromwell's daughter, married Henry Ireton and then Charles Fleetwood
Cromwell, Oliver	MP, Lord Protector, Lord Lieutenant of Ireland, General and commander-in-chief
Cromwell, Sir Oliver of Hinchinbrook, Huntingdon	Courtier and host to James I, Oliver Cromwell's uncle
Davies, Sir John	Attorney General of Ireland

Denbigh, Lord	Led deputation from army to Charles I December 1648
Devereux, Robert, 3rd Earl of Essex	Commander of the parliamentarian army 1642–45
Dillon, Lord	Led Irish parliamentary deputation to Charles I regarding 'the Graces'
Eliot, Sir John	MP and radical
Fairfax, Lady	Wife of Sir Thomas, Presbyterian
Fairfax, Sir Thomas	Commander-in-Chief of the New Model Army
Falkland, Lord	Lord Deputy of Ireland 1622–29
Fiennes, Nathaniel, MP	Son of William, radical and parliamentarian officer
Fiennes, William, 1st Viscount Saye and Sele	Puritan peer, ally of the Earl of Bedford in the Lords
Finch, John, 1st Baron	Judge, Keeper of the Great Seal of England
Fleetwood, Charles	Parliamentarian officer, Lord Deputy of Ireland
Goffe, Lt-Colonel	Officer in the New Model Army
Gordon, George, 2nd Marquess of Huntly	Scottish nobleman from Aberdeenshire, royalist
Goring, Lord	Royalist commander
Graham, James, 5th Earl and 1st Marquis of Montrose	Appointed as Charles I's Captain General in Scotland
Graves, Colonel	Commander of the garrison at Holmby
Grenville, Sir Richard	Royalist commander
Grey, Lord, of Warke	Parliamentary commander
Grotius, Hugo	Dutch jurist, theory of natural law
Hamilton, James, 1st Duke of Hamilton	Scottish nobleman, Privy Councillor and royalist commander
Hamilton, Thomas, 1st Earl of Haddington, 'Tam o' the Cowgate'	Lawyer, Privy Councillor of Scotland
Hammond, Colonel Robert	Commander of Carisbrooke Castle, Isle of Wight
Hampden, John	MP, radical and parliamentarian officer
Harrison, Thomas	Army officer, religious radical

Hazelrig, Sir Arthur	MP, republican and Governor of Newcastle 1647
Henderson, Alexander	Minister of the Kirk, leader of Covenanters
Hobbes, Thomas	Political philosopher, author of *Leviathan*
Holland, Earl of	Favourite of Henrietta-Maria
Holles, Denzil	MP, Presbyterian
Home, George, 1st Earl of Dunbar	James VI & I's principal minister in Scotland
Hopton, Sir Ralph, MP	Royalist commander in the west
Hyde, Edward, Earl of Clarendon	Councillor to Prince Charles, historian, Lord Chancellor
Ireton, Henry	Commissary General in the New Model Army, Lord Deputy of Ireland
Johnston of Warriston, Archibald	Presbyterian, lawyer and judge, Scottish MP. Co-author of Covenant and leader of the Covenanting movement
Jones, Michael, Colonel	Army officer, commander of Dublin Castle
Joyce, Cornet	Officer in the New Model Army
Juxon, William	Bishop of London, Lord Treasurer of England
Knox, John	Calvinist and leader of the Scottish Reformation
Lambert, John	Major General in the New Model Army
Langdale, Marmaduke, 1st Baron	Royalist army commander
Laud, William	Archbishop of Canterbury
Lauderdale, John Maitland, 1st Duke	Scottish nobleman and statesman
Leicester, Robert Sidney, 2nd Earl	Lord Lieutenant of Ireland
Lenthall, William	Speaker to the House of Commons
Leslie, Alexander, 1st Earl of Leven	Served under Gustavus Adolphus, General of Scottish Covenanting army
Lilburne, John	Leveller leader, radical pamphleteer and constitutional protestor
Loftus, Adam, 1st Viscount Loftus	Lord Justice of Ireland

Ludlow, Edmund	MP, parliamentary officer, Independent, republican
MacDonald, Sir Alasdair MacColla	Son of the laird of Colonsay, led Irish forces in Scotland, fought alongside Montrose
MacDonnell, Randal, 1st Marquis of Antrim	Irish peer from Ulster, supported Charles I, member of the council of the Confederate Catholics
Machiavelli, Niccolo	Italian Renaissance diplomat and author
Maguire, Conor, 2nd Baron of Enniskillen	Leader of Irish rebellion in 1641
Mainwaring, Sir Phillip	Secretary to Sir Thomas Wentworth
Mansfeld, Philipp von	Commander in the Thirty Years War
Marten, Henry	MP, lawyer, republican
Marvell, Andrew	Poet, civil servant and MP
Massey, General	Parliamentarian officer and Presbyterian
Mazarin, Jules	Cardinal, chief minister to Louis XIV
Milton, John	Poet, secretary to the Commonwealth
Monck, George, General	Army commander under Charles I and parliament
Monro, Robert	Highlander, fought in Swedish army, officer of Covenanter army, commander in Ulster
Montagu, Edward, 2nd Earl of Manchester	Parliamentarian officer
Montrieul, Jean de	French agent to Charles I
Mountnorris, Francis Annesley, Baron	Vice treasurer of Ireland
Nedham, Marchamont	Journalist and editor, physician
Newcastle, William Cavendish, Earl of	Royalist commander
O'Brien, Murrough, 1st Earl of Inchiquin	Commander of crown forces in Munster, Lord President of Munster
O'More, Rory	Leader of Irish rebellion
O'Neill, Hugh, Earl of Tyrone	Commander of Irish nationalist forces from Ulster against Queen Elizabeth I
O'Neill, Owen Roe	Commander of Confederate forces in Ulster

List of Characters

O'Neill, Sir Phelim	Leader of the 1641 rebellion in Ireland
Overton, Richard	Leveller and pamphleteer
Parker, Henry	Political theorist
Pembroke, Earl of	Privy Councillor
Petty, Mr	Agitator to the army
Poyntz, Sydnam	Commander of the parliamentarian army in the North
Preston, Richard	Scottish gentleman, married to the heiress of the Butlers by James I
Preston, Thomas	Commander of Leinster army of Irish Confederacy
Pride, Colonel	Army officer who commanded the purge of parliament December 1648
Prynne, William	Puritan lawyer imprisoned and mutilated under Laud
Pym, John	MP, radical, ally in the Commons of the Earl of Bedford
Rainsborough, Colonel	New Model Army officer, speaker at the Putney debates
Rich, Richard, Earl of Warwick	Parliamentarian commander
Rinuccini, Giovanni Battista	Papal nuncio to Ireland
Rous, Francis	MP, radical
Rushworth, John	Secretary to the New Model Army
Russell, Francis, 4th Earl of Bedford	Radical peer and leader of the opposition to Charles I
Sexby, Edward	Agitator to the army, follower of Lilburne, republican
Skippon, Philip	Officer in parliamentarian army, commanded London trained bands
Spottiswoode, John	Archbishop of St Andrews
St John, Oliver	MP and radical
St Leger, Sir William	Lord President of Munster
Stapleton, Sir Philip	MP, Presbyterian, Colonel of Horse in parliamentarian army
Taafe, Theobald, 2nd Viscount	Confederate and commander of forces in Munster

Temple, Sir John	Wrote an account of the Irish rebellion, published 1646
Traquair, Earl of	Treasurer of Scotland
Ussher, James	Archbishop of Armagh
Vane, Sir Henry the younger, MP	MP, vice treasurer of the navy
Villiers, George, 1st Duke of Buckingham	Favourite of James I, Master of the King's Horse and Admiral of the Fleet
Villiers, Katherine (née Manners)	Duchess of Buckingham, Countess of Antrim
Waller, Sir William	Parliamentary commander
Walwyn, William	Pamphleteer, Leveller
Wandesford, Christopher	Friend of Wentworth, MP, Privy Councillor and Lord Deputy of Ireland
Wentworth, Thomas, Earl of Strafford	President of the Council of the North, Lord Lieutenant of Ireland
Weston, Richard, Earl of Portland	Chancellor of the Exchequer and Lord Treasurer of England
Wharton, Philip, Lord	Puritan and parliamentarian officer
Whitelocke, Bulstrode	Lawyer, parliamentarian, diarist, Keeper of the Great Seal under the Protectorate in 1653
Wildman, John	Soldier, Leveller and agitator to the army
Windebank, Sir Francis	MP, Secretary of State to Charles I, died a Catholic

Royals

Anne of Denmark	Wife of James I & VI, sister of King Christian IV of Denmark
Charles I	Second son of James VI & I, king of England, Scotland and Ireland
Charles Louis	Elector Palatinate, son of Frederick and Elizabeth of Bohemia
Charles II	Eldest son of Charles I, Prince of Wales, King Charles II of England, Scotland and Ireland
Christian IV	King of Denmark

List of Characters

Elizabeth, Queen of Bohemia	Daughter of James I & VI, married Frederick, Elector Palatine. The Winter Queen
Frederick V	Elector of the Palatinate, King of Bohemia
Gustavus Adolphus	King of Sweden
Henri IV	King of France, father of Henrietta-Maria, first Bourbon monarch
Henrietta-Maria	Queen of England, Scotland and Ireland, youngest daughter of Henri IV of France and wife of Charles I
Henriette-Anne	Youngest daughter of Charles I and Henrietta-Maria
Henry, Duke of Gloucester	Youngest son of Charles I and Henrietta-Maria
Henry, Prince of Wales	Eldest son of James I & VI and Queen Anne
James, Duke of York	James II, second son of Charles I and Henrietta-Maria
James VI and I	King James VI of Scotland, I of England and Ireland
Louis XIII	King of France, brother of Henrietta-Maria
Louis XIV	King of France, son of Louis XIII, nephew of Henrietta-Maria
Marie de Medici	Queen of France, mother of Louis XIII and of Henrietta-Maria
Mary, Princess of Orange	Eldest daughter of Charles I and Henrietta-Maria
Maurice of Nassau	Prince of Orange, uncle of William II of Orange
Maurice, Prince of the Rhine	Son of Frederick and Elizabeth of the Palatinate
Philip II	King of Spain, son of Charles V (Holy Roman Emperor and head of the House of Habsburg)
Rupert	Prince of the Rhine, son of Elizabeth and Frederick of the Palatinate and Bohemia
William II	Prince of Orange, son of Frederick Henry of Orange and husband of Princess Mary of England

1

On the Fault Line
of the Islands

Alasdair MacColla MacDonald was a huge man. Said to be half a head taller than other men, he had the build of a born warrior. Alasdair MacColla came from Colonsay, the most southerly of the Hebridean islands. His culture was Gaelic, a Scot from the Western Isles, free-spirited and a fighter of terrifying strength. Like his father, the chieftain of Colonsay, Alasdair could fight with either hand, hefting the heavy broadsword from right hand to left, or back again. He confounded his opponents who were trained to react to one hand and one angle of attack. When he lifted the sword with both hands and swung it down mightily, he was a destroyer and unbeatable.[1]

Alasdair was a MacDonald, from the line of men who ruled the Western Isles in late medieval times and who resisted the overlordship of the kings of Scotland. His nearest and most hated enemy was Archibald Campbell, Earl of Argyll, who had imprisoned his father and refused to let him free. It was an old feud, but when Alasdair grew to manhood early in the seventeenth century, it had become a crucial contest on a significant fault line.

Within the British Isles, there were two major movements of people at the beginning of the seventeenth century. In Ulster, the leaders of the great clans – or septs – had been beaten and when they left Ireland, their land was confiscated. Plantation then moved into Ulster large numbers of Presbyterian Scots, small farmers who settled on the land, while newly empowered aristocrats were able to enlarge their landholdings there and their power. This displacement of people across the North Channel caused political tension and a change of culture in Ulster; it was a sudden dislodgement across the crucial frontier between Scotland and Ireland.

The other movement was that of the Scots king, who went south to London, taking up two further crowns: those of England and Ireland. The big men of Scotland, who owed allegiance to the royal Stuart in Edinburgh, now owed it to the king of England who was resident in London. For the clansmen, who liked to challenge any claim whatsoever for their allegiance, this shifted old patterns of power.

So it was not surprising that when trouble started it began in Scotland and spread to Ulster.

The situation in Scotland will be a large part of our story, but for the moment let us gaze carefully at that key stretch of water between Scotland and Ireland. The North Channel is not wide; from the cliffs of Antrim one can see the southernmost islands of Scotland – Colonsay and Islay – and sometimes the peninsula of Kintyre. The colours are pale and misted, changing as the sea's humours alter, but the mauve and the faint pastel greens of land show easily against the cool waters, sometimes picked out by black lines of rock or white foam edges on the shoreline. From Islay the watcher can see the rise of Ulster, the slashes of white chalk on Antrim's coast and the long mound of its plateau.

For ancient men, living by sea among islands and peninsulas difficult to tame, the land masses were not separate countries but part of one world. The Irish Gaels had taken territory from the Picts and spread across Scotland, claiming its kingship. But the west remained separate from the emerging Scottish kingdom and even in the fifteenth century the Clan Donald held the Lordship of the Isles as an independent kingdom. Finally it fell and was absorbed into the kingdom of Scotland at the end of the fifteenth century, but the Clan Donald remained on Colonsay, on Islay, on Sleat and back where they had come from centuries before, in the Glens of Antrim in Ireland.[2]

In Ireland and Scotland, the Gaelic language lived alongside English as a living tongue. Gaelic culture was strong. Despite the greater organisation of feudal systems, Gaelic law suited the west of Britain and of Ireland, with its moorland and mountain, its cattle herders and seagoing people. The lowland kings had found these peoples hard to tame.

But taming their western fringes had become increasingly important. The world was changing fast in the early seventeenth century. Governments had more complex systems to manage. They aimed to centralise power and administration. It was not enough to have the supposed allegiance of men who lived on the remote fringes of their kingdoms if those leaders had their own policies and could mobilise thousands of men for war; what early modern kings demanded was that their countries should be coherent: one government, one military ruler and one rule of law.

The big men of the west had resisted. The Lordship of the Isles had been absorbed by the kingdom of Scotland, but Clan Donald still saw itself as independent, still kept up its old culture and old feuds. Viewed from the North Channel, King James VI of Scotland had already presented the MacDonalds and their allies with new challenges before he moved to England and acquired greater powers.

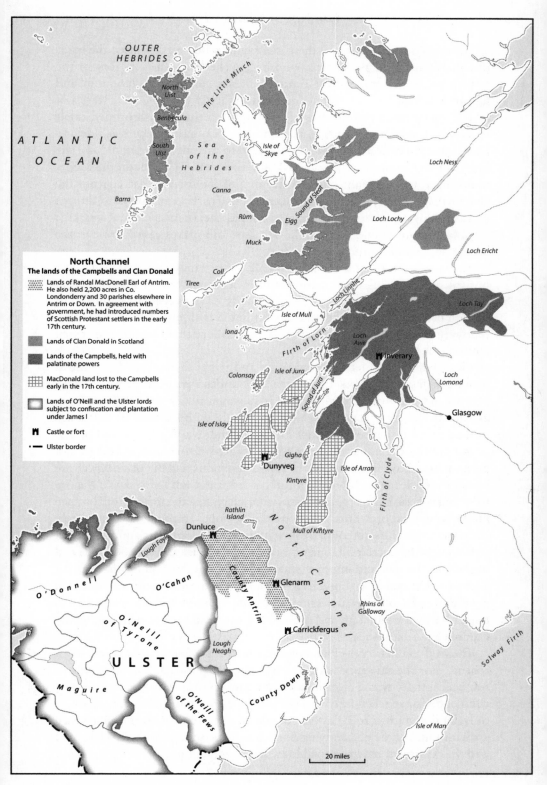

OUTER
HEBRIDES

*North
Uist*

Benbecula

*South
Uist*

The Little Minch

*Isle of
Skye*

Loch Ness

ATLANTIC

OCEAN

*Sea
of the
Hebrides*

Sound of Sleat

Barra

Canna

Rùm

Eigg

Loch Lochy

Muck

Loch Ericht

Coll

Tiree

Loch Linnhe

Loch Tay

Isle of Mull

Firth of Lorn

*Loch
Awe*

North Channel
The lands of the Campbells and Clan Donald

Lands of Randal MacDonell Earl of Antrim.
He also held 2,200 acres in Co.
Londonderry and 30 parishes elsewhere in
Antrim or Down. In agreement with
government, he had introduced numbers
of Scottish Protestant settlers in the early
17th century.

Lands of Clan Donald in Scotland

Lands of the Campbells, held with
palatinate powers

MacDonald land lost to the Campbells
early in the 17th century.

Lands of O'Neill and the Ulster lords
subject to confiscation and plantation
under James I

Castle or fort

Ulster border

Iona

Colonsay

Isle of Jura

Sound of Jura

Inverary

*Loch
Lomond*

Glasgow

Isle of Islay

Gigha

Isle of Arran

Dunyveg

Kintyre

Firth of Clyde

*Rathlin
Island*

Mull of Kintyre

Dunluce

North Channel

*Rhins of
Galloway*

County Antrim

Glenarm

O'Donnell

Lough Foyle

O'Cahan

Carrickfergus

*O'Neill
of Tyrone*

*Lough
Neagh*

ULSTER

Solway Firth

Maguire

*O'Neill
of the Fews*

County Down

Isle of Man

20 miles

The North Channel in the early seventeenth century.

For the old enemy was still there, the family who had colonised the lands of Clan Donald for the crown, who had pushed into the territory of the MacDonalds, undermined their independence, confiscated clan lands and finally overthrown them. That family was the Campbells, who were not Gaels, but of British origin from Strathclyde on the English border. Their name was Gaelic however; Cambeul meant wrymouth, which was how the locals described Colin, the first of the line to intrude into Argyll, and the head of their family was known as MacCailein Mór – great son of Colin – the head of Colin's clan. At the beginning of the seventeenth century the MacCailein Mór was Archibald Campbell, 7th Earl of Argyll – known as Gillesbuig Grumach, meaning Archibald the Grim. His son was also Archibald, who would become the 8th Earl and play a central role in the drama of the mid-century.

The Gaelic west had been under attack for centuries and was crumbling but still strangely vigorous, buoyant in its beliefs and bouncing back from defeats. But in human affairs, there is usually a long period of gestation or tension before some event triggers a shift in the fault lines between peoples. As the seventeenth century began, there was more than one area in which tension was building.

The Clan Donald had a heroic past and tribal memories of greatness. Among their ritual centres, the Southern Hebrides were especially important because of their position and fertility. Islay was significant: the old crowning ground at Finlaggan was there, high in the hills, within a lake. At the centre of that lake a tiny island lies half-hidden by the swaying reeds, and on the island are the remnants of a small fortress which for many centuries had been the ritual meeting place of the island chieftains and the place where the Lord of the Isles was crowned.[3] On the coast, the Clan Donald had a more modern fortress, Dunyveg, in construction much like the fortress of Dunluce on the wild coast of Antrim. These were MacDonald strongholds, intricately constructed on cliffs and outcrops to command the harbours and channels.

Islay was the ancestral home of the Lords of the Isles. When the last Lord of the Isles, beaten and impoverished, sold Islay to the Campbells in 1615, a great tribal memory shuddered and a valuable possession was lost. On neighbouring Colonsay, a second line of MacDonalds remained in place, but Colkitto, the chieftain and Alasdair's father, had been imprisoned by the Campbell laird in 1613.

The wild conflicts of the Highlands had not been quelled by the seventeenth century, nor the savagery with which they were pursued, but to Colkitto's son his captivity was a piece of wicked treachery. Alasdair MacColla was a child of five or so when Islay was lost and his father imprisoned. He was sent to Ireland and grew to be a warrior son of a gritty Highland father. Once grown to his full height, moving back and forth across the North Channel with his kinsmen, between the lands of McDonnell of Antrim and the old

MacDonald lands of Argyllshire and the Islands, Alasdair became a soldier by profession and a Gael of the old traditions by culture. He was nurtured on the enmity with the Campbells; his aim and focus was to pit himself against the MacCailein Mór, free his father and wrest back the ancestral lands on the Southern Hebrides.

The MacDonalds were Catholics. The rip tide of Reformation which had swept through Scotland had built a powerful culture from which the western peoples felt removed. The Campbells, servants of the crown, courtiers even, had dived into Calvinism like cormorants into a lake, but Alasdair MacColla and his powerful kinsman Randal MacDonell, Earl of Antrim, had remained traditional in their faith.

Their country was not fertile like the lowlands where the king rode, or the pastures of southern England to which the king had now migrated. But the air was fresh and the coast warm from the sea currents; the waterways were the known territory of the Gael. It was a windy place and they had in them that free-spirited wildness to match their homeland. So it was inevitable that a fighting man like Alasdair MacColla would keep alive his passionate hatred for the Earl of Argyll and everything he represented.

That island landscape, however, was the borderline between the two religious cultures of the archipelago. Around Britain and Ireland ran a spectrum of Christian practice like a circlet and the North Channel was the borderline of two extremes. At its mild heart was the Protestantism of the Established Church as Elizabeth I had left it. With a set of principles which acknowledged Calvin but with some of the old forms of service from the days of the Catholic Mass, it was a religious culture of compromise well suited to the temper of rural England. In East Anglia the hotter Protestants urged greater purity, greater Reformation, while in Scotland the Reformation had been convulsive and an even sterner Calvinism had taken hold. In Ireland, however, attempts to change the religious culture had failed and since the Elizabethan wars the Gaelic population had settled into stubborn Catholic resistance. To break that down, Irish land had been confiscated and resettled, with new Protestant planters brought in from Britain, but settling them in Ulster largely backfired. The new farmers who came from lowland Scotland were not only Calvinist but Presbyterian with a stubbornness all their own. They were not amenable to the church structures as set up by the crown.

It was here, between Ulster and Argyll, with the Hebridean islands between them, that the religious divide was stark. There was antagonism between the Gaelic Catholic masses and the incoming Protestant planters. On the seaboard, people went back and forth between lowland Ayrshire, Catholic Ulster and the unreformed islands; in these movements the Roman church and Calvinism met face to face. The earldom of Argyll, with its mountainous land and long sea lochs, was held for Protestantism and the crown by the MacCailein Mór. The portraits of Archibald Campbell, 8th Earl of Argyll, show a face made for Calvinism, in black robe and skullcap, whereas Randal MacDonnell, Earl of Antrim, was fair, with an open and mobile face, a changeable man of warm emotion who held onto an old culture and was used to the gilded rituals of the Mass.

They might have continued their raids and feuding, legal battles and savage imprisonments, but it was not just their contest around the shores of the North Channel that was at issue in the early decades of the seventeenth century. The North Channel might be a crucial place for religious conflict, but the seventeenth century was a pivotal moment in European development. A century of intense struggle was opening on the continent. During that critical century, the three kingdoms ruled by the Stuart dynasty went into crisis. They all emerged very changed. Ireland was irrevocably reconfigured, while Scotland and England were set on a new trajectory.

But as the century opened, the King of Scotland was still in Edinburgh, waiting for his great inheritance in England. When, and if, he inherited his cousin Elizabeth's two crowns, they would enrich him marvellously. So James thought, and his fellow countrymen in Scotland assumed the inheritance would also enrich the king's native land and them. As it turned out, that inheritance was the preliminary to challenge and conflict. And when it came, the war began in Scotland.

2

Inheriting Three Kingdoms

During the century in which the Tudors ruled England, the governing structures of Europe had been unlocked. King James was to inherit the consequences of that deep change. The Reformation was an event of vast significance. From the fall of the Roman Empire centuries before, popes had taken on a role which gave legal coherence to Europe, held together its culture and retained a common language for much of the continent. The Pope could confirm the legitimate claims of kings and sanction inheritance, while the church controlled vast swathes of property throughout western Europe. The church was educator and archive, the guardian of records and teacher of literacy; universities were church institutions. Church law was outside the scope of national law. The papacy was a supranational institution, so when it was challenged, the underlying structure of Europe began to shudder and fracture. The aim of the reformers was to reinvigorate their church, to cleanse it of corruption and return it to its original vision. As it turned out, of course, far more was at stake.

Europe's rulers were faced with profound decisions, for a religion is an administrative system and a culture, as well as a set of beliefs. Rulers had to reconcile their own spiritual understanding with the political realities of a swiftly changing world. Europe was already changing its shape. The Ottomans had conquered the Byzantine Empire and finally taken Constantinople in 1453. In western Europe, monarchs ran increasingly complex administrations with growing populations. Externally, the flows of trade and wealth were moving, so that merchants in Amsterdam, Antwerp and London had a new significance, while those in Venice and even Genoa were no longer pre-eminent. New opportunities appeared across the Atlantic, creating new conflicts.

Brave, clever and astute, Elizabeth I was nonetheless an indecisive woman but her management of these tides of change had been remarkably successful.

Perhaps her caution was a useful brake on the surging ambitions of the men in her ports and at her court. She would take risks, but she disliked extremes. Radical ideas, radical preaching, military commitment, even swift administrative changes all upset her. Her motto, which she inscribed on many of her letters, was *semper eadem* (always the same), a virtue she clearly prized; but although Elizabeth might try to maintain stability and constancy in herself, her world was quite the opposite.

She was also parsimonious but – against her instincts – she had fought several wars. Her famous victory over the great Catholic power of Spain was costly, but her most expensive war had been fought within her own kingdom of Ireland, a military conquest which had profound consequences after Elizabeth was dead.

The monarchs of England had claimed overlordship of Ireland since Henry II's conquest. The Irish lords had recognised the English monarch's suzerainty and Henry's claim had been confirmed by the Pope, but their rule was patchy and contested. The island became divided into the English and Gaelic lordships, with separate law and cultures. Henry VIII had altered his title to King of Ireland and had this confirmed by the Irish parliament; he had tried to amalgamate the two lordships but after a promising start, the policy was not completed and his heirs turned to military methods. Under Elizabeth, first the southern province of Munster rebelled, then Ulster went to war. The policy of plantation had been instigated by Queen Mary but after Elizabeth's armies quelled Munster, confiscation and plantation were enforced on an enormous scale. For crown officials, plantation had many objectives, among them to crush rebellion and to implant Protestants with English culture who would anglicise and 'civilise' the areas into which they moved. It was expected that Ireland would develop agriculturally and commercially, tax would be paid, trade increase and the island become more governable and financially viable. After the Munster rebellion, there was a period of around a decade before the great men of Ulster rose to defend their religion and national rights and they proved a formidable foe for Elizabeth. England embarked on a full conquest, which culminated in a Spanish fleet coming to the aid of O'Neill and his allies – but they were beaten at Kinsale in County Cork in 1601.

It was a brutal war, in which crops were deliberately burned, peasants butchered and people died of famine. But Kinsale did not end it and the cost to England was enormous, as troops succumbed to undernourishment and fever far more than mortal combat. In financial terms, the debt was said by Cecil, Elizabeth's chief minister, to be £2 million, whereas the Desmond rebellion in Munster had cost around a quarter of a million.

Warfare continued after Kinsale, no longer as pitched battles but destruction of castles, retreats to the woods and savagery towards local populations to break support for O'Neill. England could hardly bear the cost. William Cecil, Lord Burghley, had died and the queen was ageing, but her commanders in Ireland pressed on with full conquest. Meanwhile, negotiations began but when O'Neill finally made his submission to Mountjoy, he did not know that the old queen had already caught her final illness. By the time the Ulster chieftains surrendered, she was already dead. O'Neill wept, he said for sorrow but surely out of rage; with a new reign, negotiations might have been different.

Elizabeth died in March 1603. Her councillors had prepared for this moment; Robert Cecil, son of old Lord Burghley, was taking up the duties of his father and had corresponded with James VI of Scotland. The King of Scots must be sent for. Elizabeth's had been a reign of unusual stability and advantage; nothing must jeopardise all the gains which England had made.

As Elizabeth's body lay in her palace of Richmond, Sir John Carey was already riding helter-skelter to Edinburgh. Horses had been posted ready on the road and Carey galloped northwards across England, to be first with the news. He had a nasty fall on his journey, but he reached Holyrood Palace in Edinburgh in two and a half days of hard riding. It was night. Carey roused the household and knelt before James VI of Scotland, acknowledging him as the new King of England and Ireland. James asked what Carey wanted in recompense for this wonderful news and Sir John asked to be made a gentleman of the bedchamber, where access to the monarch was guaranteed. The request was granted.

James's journey to England was the opposite of Carey's. He set forth in early April on a long progress of welcomes, visits, rejoicings and entertainments. It took him a month to reach London. His queen, Anne of Denmark, left in June and travelled with her eldest children, Henry and Elizabeth, who had lived with aristocratic foster parents and only got to know each other on this journey. Queen Anne made visits off the highway as the prince and princess, aged nine and seven, progressed slowly down the road to London. The youngest child, Charles, was sickly and had weak legs. He was only sent south to join his parents the following summer.

Prince Henry was a sparkling child, clever and energetic. Princess Elizabeth was lively and attractive. She took her status calmly and even as a child presided over major ceremonies alone without problems. Charles was nervous, craved affection and lacked the vigour of his siblings, but he was diligent at study and learned easily.

The king was welcomed in London as James I of England. When the royal family were reunited at Windsor, James asked a courtier 'if he did not think his Annie looked passing well, and my little Bessie too' as he scooped the little girl up in his arms.[1] The court and people, used to the elderly virgin queen, were amused by James's homely style and the novelty of royal children. 'We have a King,' the pamphlet writers exclaimed, for a male monarch was in itself a novelty.

James had promised to return to Scotland every three years, but he only went back once. The Scots were initially proud of their king's great inheritance, but it soon became clear that the court had abandoned Edinburgh for good. James was delighted to get away. In Scotland, he had been taunted by clerics, and threatened and abducted by noblemen. The palaces were colder and smaller than the fine buildings which Elizabeth bequeathed to him. In England, courtiers were deferential and polite; they had different methods of pressurising their monarch, as he gradually came to realise. But James had been an effective Scottish ruler, learning from childhood how to manage the particular challenges of his native kingdom. Now he could rule it from a distance; of Scotland, James later boasted, 'This I may say, and may truly vaunt it; here I sit and govern it with my pen, I write and it is done, and by a clerk of the Council I govern Scotland now, which others could not do by the sword.'[2] He was writing from the heart. He had become king of Scotland as an infant and it had been a hair-raising business, but it had made him the man he was: wily, jovial and astute, clever at staying ahead of the problems the kingdom posed, although not always able to solve them. More feudal, more clannish and far less developed, Scotland and its rule was not much missed by the king, but Scottish political life continued despite his flourishes of pen.

James had had a strange childhood. With his mother in prison and with no siblings, he had been brought up by a stern regent and a brilliant but Calvinist tutor whom he feared. The boy spent little time with other children and in any case, he was already a king. In the schoolroom, he was a precocious child who learned extraordinary feats of academic skill. His peculiar upbringing produced a highly educated man who was confident and opinionated but he had unusual emotions. He was not taught manners and spent little time with women but he was a genuine scholar and wrote significant books, including *Basilikon Doron* and *The True Law of Free Monarchies*, both treaties on kingship.

James had a lively writing style with a unique voice. Both of his books were advice, one for his people and the other for his son. He stated clearly that God had invented the institution of kingship and that it was God who made individual kings. Men might not remove a king, even if he was tyrannical; that was a matter for God. But kings would be punished all right, 'for the highest bench is the sliddriest to sit upon'. He wrote that 'the kings were the authors and makers of the laws, and not the laws of the kings'.[3] *The True Law* was published in 1598, before James moved to London. In Edinburgh, he was seldom challenged by parliament and he believed in his divine rights and duties. After he moved to London and experienced English political life, his statements altered.

He was thirty-seven when he inherited the thrones of England and Ireland, with political habits and an understanding of his role formed in Scotland; but

England was a different polity. The way that James managed the transition had long-lasting effects, both for his kingdoms and for his descendants.

James lived at a crucial time when the medieval order was ending and the power of monarchs being analysed. The terms 'divine right of kings' and 'absolutism' can be misleading and complex. The divine right of kings was essentially a clerical concept, whereas 'absolute' referred to law or to sovereignty. Even if a king was made by God and held office by divine right, he might still be bound by the law. The term 'absolute' meant there was no higher power, for example a king who owed no sovereignty to another.[4] Some scholars argued that if kings were bound by law, they were not absolute. Each kingdom had its own traditions, as James was to learn, and in each, men of influence were trying to define their constitutions and adapt them to swiftly changing circumstance. James had matured in Scotland, whose constitution he understood but in England, the role of parliament and the Common Law were both very different. James discovered that his great inheritance did indeed bring greater power and riches but not the political ease he had envisaged; his reign was marked by bitter struggles with his English parliaments.

He was lucky in his chief minister. Sir Robert Cecil had been trained by his father, served under Elizabeth and had corresponded with James well in advance of his accession. Small, with a slightly hunched back, he was astute and capable. It was Cecil who smoothed James's passage onto the triple throne and who ran his government for the first decade of the new reign. Elevated as Earl of Salisbury and already Secretary of State, in 1608 Cecil also became Lord Treasurer. He bore the great burden of government tirelessly for the remainder of his life.

James was often out of London as he loved to hunt, taking his friends and attendants with him to the royal houses of Royston and Newmarket. Many were Scots, causing jealousy among the English courtiers, but James was extravagant now that he had English wealth at his disposal. He was generous, and not only to Scots; as a foreign king in a strange land, he wanted to keep all the men of influence well-affected.

Problems began to arise as the king's extravagance and his concept of kingship came into conflict with parliament and English law. Since the Commons controlled the right to tax, once royal income and credit were at a limit, the king was dependent on MPs. Where taxation had already been granted, there might still be disagreements about the terms, which then became a matter of law. James knew that an English monarch must act in conformity with law and he accepted the taxation powers of the Commons, but he also knew that he could call or dissolve parliaments, as well as appoint judges so that he controlled the very institutions which circumscribed his powers. However, although parliament made statute law, in England the Common Law had existed from antiquity and was not subject to the will of kings.

He was briefed on his powers when he arrived in London but James, who had an academic mind, could argue his position. In 1604, he told Salisbury 'that the common law be not made to fight against the king's authority'.[5] By 1610, after James had been in England for several years, he was more circumspect. His minister told the Commons that the king thought it dangerous to define the power of a king. The king 'had no power to make laws of himself, or to exact any subsidies de jure without the consent of his three estates', i.e., his parliament.[6]

In both Scotland and England, the king had prerogative powers over which his parliaments had no say, for example in foreign policy, which remains the case today. It was the boundary between those powers and the rights of parliament which the English Commons was already probing in 1610. Parliament had many roles: MPs were lawmakers and tax-givers, counsellors to the king and representatives of their localities, but they also protected and promoted their own institution.

In England, political experts generally agreed that their monarchy was a mixed one – government had elements of democracy, aristocracy, and monarchy. Great legal minds such as the Elizabethan Sir Thomas Smith and the Jacobean Sir Edward Coke had published works on the issue.[7]

In Dublin and Edinburgh, parliaments were less assertive than in London. Parliaments in Dublin were modelled on the English version and were called by the king's Lord Deputy but they were subject to the English Privy Council, which irked them. As Ireland contributed no tax to the royal household and could barely raise enough to cover government of a modest kind in the Pale or the English lordship, so naturally it had less power.

For the crown that was one of the big problems with Gaeldom: the Highlands and Islands of Scotland and the west of Ireland paid no tax. On top of that, the clansmen would not conform to the law of the land and were forever fighting, if not resisting crown agents then feuding and squabbling among themselves to the detriment of the people and the destruction of property. They also remained mainly Catholic. Elizabeth had fought the FitzGerald power in Munster and the O'Neill power in Ulster. James had used his great nobles Argyll and Huntly to keep down the Highlanders in the south-west and north-east of Scotland, but in the 1590s he and his ministers had attempted something more ambitious. Gaeldom had to be quelled and pacified. James spoke warmly on the topic; he thought it a disgrace that part of his kingdom was 'still possessed with such barbarous cannibals'.[8]

The Gaelic lords knew their way was threatened by both James and Elizabeth; an Irish bard warned his patron that 'The men of London, the warriors of Scotland/ are contending together,/ thou Chief of the noble host of Sioth Trium,/ in one compact mass about us.'[9] Once James held all three crowns, he controlled both islands and both shores of the North Channel; he could pursue a single policy towards the Gaels. He planned a radical policy to clear the natives and colonise the Highlands and Islands with Protestant Lowlanders. His bishop thought this too drastic and suggested that it was easier 'to induce them all, without hostility or opening of your highness' coffers to reduce them to a hasty reformation'.[10] It was better to negotiate with the Highlanders – so Lord Ochiltree was sent to try it. He invited the Highland chiefs onto a boat, kidnapped them and held them until they signed the Statutes of Iona of 1609, whereby their status would be recognised as long as they cooperated with government and educated their children in the Lowlands.

James went soft on the Highlanders because a better project had appeared in Ireland where the Gaelic aristocracy left of their own accord. Hugh O'Neill, Earl of Tyrone, beaten by Elizabeth in war, had been pardoned and regained his estates but the Ulster noblemen were still harassed by the Jacobean government. Summoned to London but fearful of imprisonment, they decided to flee, sailing from Lough Swilly in 1607. The 'Flight of the Earls' was not only a symbol of Gaeldom's decline; it allowed the crown to proclaim them traitors, confiscate their vast territories and reassign land in Ulster. Deputy Chichester advised King James to divide the land between loyal Irish leaders, only settling British incomers on what remained. However, the Attorney General, Sir John Davies, went to London with a more thorough plan, suggesting that the native Irish be removed altogether so that British settlers could move safely onto unbroken tracts of land. This scheme was adopted, and many Ulstermen were forced off their ancestral farms. Onto their land moved Protestants from Britain, mainly Lowland Scots who set about planting. With their seeds they sowed a lasting grievance that soon erupted.

The Ulster leaders had been supported by the Catholic powers but it was the king's policy to make peace with Spain. Elizabeth had all but bankrupted her government by the wars of her last years, leaving a debt of £400,000. Both she and James deplored war because of the costs, but James was personally afraid of fighting. Swords and military activity horrified him. This was to have important consequences too.

The first duty of government is defence of the realm, and in early modern times this was especially true. Rulers were war leaders – men remembered their monarchs leading armies into battle, and Elizabeth had cast herself as champion of her army. In Gaeldom, the head of the sept was chosen for his martial ability, while feudal law rested on the duty of nobles to bring out men for war. In Britain, too, great magnates could mobilise men on their estates, especially in the rural north and west, and it was aristocrats who led royal armies. So, James was an anomaly.

Peace with Spain made sense but James went further and undermined the established system for defending England which dated back centuries. The local militias had been modernised and reinvigorated under Elizabeth, when regular musters were instigated. The Lord Lieutenant of each county maintained an arsenal and muster rolls of suitable men. The results varied. In some districts the inhabitants were nervous of these gatherings of men with arms, and in other districts the men were said not to train but spend the day at the pub. Musters also interrupted the harvest and could not realistically be held during the summer until the crops were in. To augment the militias, especially in London, trained bands were given a more thorough grounding in modern fighting techniques and they at least posed some threat to the enemy. James, however, discontinued militia musters. This horrified many of his ministers and was a blow to men of military aspirations.

Gentlemen had always been taught swordplay. When James came to the throne, military arts were of keen interest. In Europe, the sixteenth century had been a time of war. Borders were changing, overlordships being contested, but the main driver was the Reformation. The wars of religion rippled through Europe for over a century. As the seventeenth century opened, ideas on warfare were altering and the musket was becoming a common weapon. Many Englishmen fought in the Netherlands, which gave them experience of European methods.

The seventeenth century was to be a period of warfare and intense upheaval. The wars of religion were only part of a much wider crisis as feudalism broke down and the church was challenged. At the same time, populations were growing but the climate deteriorated for much of the century. Governments had greater reach and responsibility but modernisation – for example in land-use – inevitably created tensions, both locally and between states. Many of these burst into conflict.

James cast himself as a peacemaker; in Scotland he had maintained peace, now he brought it to England. A treaty with Spain was signed in 1604. His new subjects were certainly relieved that the cost of war would end but as time passed, his foreign policy alarmed and dissatisfied many. Under Elizabeth, England had been an assertive power, challenging the great might of Spain, pushing out into the Atlantic and Americas, starting to rival the Dutch ports in banking and trade. James might lose England her advantage – so some thought. Nor was it possible to be both a champion of Protestantism – which James was – and an ally of the Catholic powers, which James increasingly appeared to promote.

However, the Prince of Wales gave ambitious men some hope. Prince Henry grew into a vigorous adolescent and was interested in the practical concerns of a prince, as his father was not. Bright and assertive, Henry studied architecture and was passionate about the new military arts. He was told off by James for not studying hard like his brother Charles, but Henry came out of one such interview with his father and told his tutor, 'I know what becomes a Prince. It is not necessary for me to be a professor, but a soldier and a man of the world.'[11] A coterie of men who had fought in Ireland and the Netherlands began to form around the young prince.

Conflict in Europe was increasingly defined by religion, but within James's three kingdoms there was divergence. As a result, men from the three kingdoms fought on opposing sides in Europe and learned warfare from the generals they served. In the Netherlands, Protestants struggled to throw off Spanish rule and during that war Irishmen served in the Spanish armies – men like Owen Roe O'Neill from the great Ulster house. Englishmen, however, learned warfare from Prince Maurice of Nassau, the Protestant champion of the Dutch. In the seventeenth century, Gustavus Adolphus of Sweden emerged as the great Protestant war leader and developed military strategies that were studied far and wide. Many Scotsmen served in his armies and would return to their native land with his skills and shining example in their minds. Alexander Leslie and Robert Monro both learned soldiering in the Dutch and Swedish armies. Young men who could not join the armies, but who thirsted for the skills and challenge of war, read books of strategy and analysis of battles. For them, Gustavus Adolphus became a hero and role model.

But while young men read of mighty deeds abroad, their king was dedicated to peace. For a decade after his accession, militia musters were almost entirely suspended. This 'militia vacation' was thought by older men a danger to the nation and by younger men a frustration to their development. Some Lord Lieutenants kept up the local training, despite James's repeal of the militia laws, but Prince Henry remained the great hope of aristocratic military circles.

Sir Walter Raleigh was in the Tower. Soldier, sailor, poet and a coloniser of the Americas, Raleigh represented all the aspirations of Elizabeth's England. He had been imprisoned on a charge of plotting against the accession of James, but Prince Henry took to visiting him in the Tower to learn from his ideas of exploration and his knowledge of war.

Painted with swords and armour, drawn practising with a pike, for the assertive and ambitious men of England Prince Henry showed great promise. His father, however, was a scholar and an idealist, poor at managing money and with odd personal tastes. However, on the vital subject of religion, the majority of English people found King James very sound.

3

The King James Version

Many years earlier, in 1590, Queen Elizabeth had written to her cousin King James about the Presbyterians, whom she saw as a serious threat: 'Let me warn you that there is risen, both in your Realm and mine, a sect of perilous consequence, such as would have no kings but a presbytery, and take our place while they enjoy our privilege.' These Presbyterians believed they heard God's word and only they could judge what was right. 'Yea look we well unto them,' Elizabeth warned the Scots king.[1]

James already had experience of Presbyterians. Andrew Melville, scholar and Presbyterian leader, had called the king 'God's silly vassal' and said that the kirk derived its power directly from God and was outside the power of the state. [2] Melville wrote that ministers teach 'and all godly princes and magistrates ought to hear and obey'.[3] Here was the resurgence of an old problem. The Roman church had been outside state control but the Reformation had allowed monarchs to assert their sovereignty; now Presbyterians were claiming to be above the secular rulers once more.

In Scotland, the Reformation had not been instigated by the crown but by the people who resented the wealth of their church and, led by Knox and other Geneva-educated preachers, overthrew Roman Catholicism. Scotland embraced a strict Calvinism, both in theology and in church structure. For Calvinists, civil government was only valid when it followed the Word of God. This gave the church a moral status on a par with the government, sometimes talking of the 'Twa Kingdoms' – their own and the king's.

The kirk had organised itself on the pattern created by the Swiss Reformers, with a tiered structure: at the bottom was the parish, where all male inhabitants could vote on religious issues, and at the top the General Assembly. These synods, or assemblies, were far more democratic than the parliaments called in those days, but for the state they posed two problems. One was their claim to power and decisions coming directly from God; this made them hard to challenge. The other was their ambition to manage not only church services, but also education and government policy. The kirk intended to create a godly realm and its ministers felt entitled to lecture the ruler or challenge the courts to achieve that. They had only a grudging respect for the institutions of the state. Scotland's institutions were not strong in the face of such a determined assault.

King James had been thoroughly educated in Calvinist theology and been taught an aversion to Catholicism, so his religion chimed with his people's, but he was not austere by nature; he enjoyed hunting, masques and wine. Brainy and intellectually confident, he had strong views on theology. By statute, the king of Scotland had supreme authority over all estates spiritual and temporal but asserting authority over the kirk posed a challenge. In Edinburgh he had survived the challenges of the Reformed clergy and after he moved to England, where there could be no more personal affronts, he still tried to manage the Scottish kirk. James thought a hierarchical structure essential in both church and state. 'No Bishop, no King' was his repeated aphorism. After he moved to England, he managed to insert bishops into the Scottish kirk as moderators of the synods with power to appoint the ministers. He also prevented General Assemblies from meeting and pushed through the Five Articles of Perth, which stipulated how to perform the sacraments. He hoped to assimilate the churches of Scotland and England but his attempts to alter Scottish church liturgy met such stiff resistance that he pulled back; he was too astute to go further.[4]

In England, the accession of James to Elizabeth's throne gave great hope to both Puritans and Catholics. Puritans expected a Scottish king to further purify the church, while Catholics had been wooed by James in case Elizabeth should look for an alternate heir; now they were disappointed. James steered down the ground between them. Soon after his accession he called a conference at Hampton Court for the following year, to review the policy and practice of the English church. When the theologians gathered, the king enthusiastically took part. His stern childhood education had given him a taste for academic debate; he loved to be the chief performer and was a competent theologian. At Hampton Court, it became clear that James would uphold the Elizabethan church settlement, with only small changes. Rejecting the Lambeth Articles and insisting on conformity to the Church of England, James brushed aside the demands of Puritans but did not see how determined they were, nor how bitter was their disappointment.

The Hampton Court Conference did, however, give birth to one of James's most enduring achievements. The King James Bible was put in hand, a new translation to supplant the inaccurate Bishops' Bible and the Genevan Bible that was currently very popular. James set in motion the project of translation and advised the scholars.

The new Bible was crucial. For Protestants everywhere, it was essential to read the Gospels to form a personal understanding of God's will and teaching. To achieve that, Melville had planned universal education in Scotland, although little had yet been achieved. But every church, and increasing numbers of families, had a Bible. Demand for education was increasing and the Reformation added an extra spur to literacy.[5] Widespread reading of the Bible had profound and sometimes explosive results. In it, the living god could be studied, his will known and therefore acted on. 'O most glorious and most gracious God,' John Donne wrote, 'into whose presence our own consciences make us afraid to come, and from whose presence we cannot hide ourselves.'[6] God was close and active in the world. Evangelical preaching had been discouraged by Elizabeth but wherever it continued, it excited people, causing discussion and controversy. The Bible itself was the vital source; no wonder James wanted to be the commissioning editor of the published text.

His consort, Queen Anne, had grown up a Lutheran in Denmark but converted to Catholicism in Scotland which vexed James a great deal. She refused to take Anglican communion at the coronation in London, encouraged the Catholic gentry and urged a Catholic marriage for Prince Henry.

James was mostly lenient towards Catholics, and Salisbury concurred, distinguishing between the quiet and the dangerous. The main concern of the state was loyalty, not private belief, and the recusancy laws had been applied most strictly when the state was threatened externally or by Catholic malcontents. Moreover, James had a vision of uniting Christendom and even put forward a proposal to the Pope but without success. Yet James, who was enraged by Presbyterian demands and was therefore strict with English Puritans, was now pushed by his counsellors into similar treatment of Catholics. The recusancy laws were to be enforced. Smarting with disappointment and knowing that peace with Spain meant no new armada would sail, a group of conspirators began plotting a radical solution – to blow up both king and parliament when the new session opened. The Gunpowder Plot of 1605 was aimed at the whole royal family except Princess Elizabeth, who could be kidnapped as a prospective heir. After that, a popular rising might install a Catholic reign. They convinced themselves that if they could exploit bones of contention – Catholicism, resentment against Scots and a union – to strike a spectacular blow at Westminster and foster general chaos, a new regime was possible.[7]

A peer was warned, the cellars below the House of Lords were searched and the gunpowder discovered. Even after the arrest of Guy Fawkes, co-conspirator Catesby and his associates continued with their plan but any support they had melted away. Several of the leaders died in a skirmish on 8 November, so only the testimony of the few who were captured was extracted. From it, the king and his ministers compiled a narrative which was reported to the nation and has lived on in national celebrations for five centuries.

The Gunpowder Plot aroused the animosity of a nervous Protestant nation and parliament insisted that Catholics not only go to communion but take the sacrament. Fines were increased, the threat of land confiscation was intensified, and a new oath was introduced. The immediate reaction of James was horror at the near approach of destruction, for kings were 'furnished with some sparkles of divinity'.[8] For some time he was melancholy and full of dread, for he was fearful of violence, but his policy did not greatly change; he was still inclined to leniency against loyal Catholics but Puritans dwelt angrily on the Catholic plot against king and parliament.

Europe was splitting between Catholic and Protestant states, but Protestants were divided between the followers of Luther or Calvin, the latter influencing Britain and Ireland. The influence of Geneva had potency not only in theology but in statecraft. After Geneva had thrown off rule by the Duke of Savoy, it became part of the Swiss Confederacy with a constitution moulded by Calvin. When the Netherlands struggled against Spain for independence, they too instigated Calvin's theology and a similar form of government, led by an elected leader known as the Stadholder, although the Prince of Orange was chosen. With elected presbyteries and heads of states, Geneva and the Netherlands were becoming oligarchic states, with a powerful merchant class, the separation of powers as endorsed by Calvin and elections in both church and state. Naturally, the model was influential.

The Genevan Bible too was a product of Calvin's time, translated into English by British exiles in Switzerland, with notes by Calvin himself and by Knox. Some marginal notes permitted disobedience to tyrannical kings, which roused King James, who pronounced these comments as 'partial, untrue, seditious and savouring of dangerous and traitorous conceits'.[9] James considered himself a godly king in the Genevan sense, father of his people who were in his care. He was also Head of the Church of England and of Ireland, which were solemn duties for a man learned in theology and philosophy.

The English church, which Elizabeth had settled early in her reign and refused to change any further despite much urging, was a compromise. Its articles of faith were Calvinist, including ideas of who might be saved; but it retained some Catholic ritual and forms of service. The aesthetic forms had pleased the elegant and musical queen, while it was hoped the rituals would mollify the Catholics, who were forced to conform. But hidden within the compromise was an intellectual tension which King James and his successors would have to manage.

Also influencing the public mood were deeper long-term changes. Population had grown and Europeans had reached the New World. The seventeenth century offered great challenges and opportunities yet, after the confidence and expansion of the Elizabethan age, the mood began to turn. The people of the early seventeenth century developed a sense of foreboding which was partly practical and partly metaphysical. Economic problems underlay much of the gloom; the boom of the sixteenth century was followed by a period of slower trade, flat prices and no further increase of population. Towards the middle of the century the climate deteriorated, the sun became very inactive and harvests were poor. But there seems more to people's mood than physical conditions as the seventeenth century progressed.[10]

'The long day of mankind draweth fast towards an evening and the world's tragedy and time are near an end,' wrote Raleigh.[11] Donne gave sermons of similar pessimism: 'The seasons of the year irregular and distempered; the sun fainter and languishing; men less in stature and shorter lived. No addition, but only every year new sorts, new species of worms and flies and sicknesses,' he wrote. 'This is the world's old age, it is declining.'[12] Dr Johnson later reported than in the time of John Milton 'there prevailed ... an opinion that the world was in decay ... It was suspected that the whole creation languished.'[13]

We cannot know how widespread these views were, but during James's reign they appeared in books published in both England and Germany. Discussion of the millennium became more active, that thousand-year period of happiness when the church would be purified and Christ would reign. Reforming the church had brought out the expectations of the early Christians once more – they felt that Christ's Kingdom would now come on earth. The question was when.

James saw himself as a peacemaker and bringer of union between his kingdoms and their religions. His overture to the Pope came to nothing and his hopes for a union of England with Scotland soon met resistance. On practical matters, James saw himself as a benign patriarch, tolerating Catholics more than many thought he should, and finding compromises with Scottish Presbyterians who had made a covenant with God a generation before and were not keen on compromise.

In Ireland, where his government was working hard to engineer a Protestant majority in parliament, the issue of religion was sharp and all-pervasive. Loyalty was a crucial issue; O'Neill had brought in a Spanish fleet. When an Irish delegation came to London in 1614, James spoke at length on both Catholicism and politics before scolding the delegation: 'Surely I have good reason for saying that you are only half-subjects of mine. For you give your soul to the pope, and to me only the body and even it, your bodily strength, you divide between me and the king of Spain ... Strive henceforth to become good subjects, that you may have *cor unum et viam unam* (one heart and one way), and then I shall respect you all alike.'[14]

The government watched suspiciously for any sign of interference, as the king's Catholic subjects went to France and Spain, to study or to join the Spanish armies.

So, the Bible that King James commissioned was more than a theological text – it would inform the outlook of future generations as they studied the word of God. The king set the instructions and approved the fifty-four translators who worked in groups at Westminster, Oxford and Cambridge. For James, the object was a clear translation using familiar words which his people could read and understand. The final text was reviewed by Bishop Bilson and Miles Smith, and after it was published in 1611 it became the text used regularly in parish churches.

For the royal family, religion was also a dynastic consideration. As they got older, his children's marriages became an increasingly important issue for the king. James was a substantial monarch among European princes and his children should marry into the great royal houses – but so few were Protestant. For his heir Prince Henry, feelers were put out to Spain, to Tuscany and Savoy, as well as to France – although all of these were Catholic houses. No decision had been reached when a negotiation for Princess Elizabeth brought brighter hopes, in the form of a Protestant suitor. Frederick V, Elector Palatine arrived in London in October 1612 to wed the sixteen-year-old princess.

Frederick had succeeded his father two years before but he was not a royal prince and Queen Anne was displeased, sneering at her daughter as 'Goodie Palsgrave' as if she were marrying a tradesman.[15] However, Frederick was a significant figure in Protestant Europe, ruler of the Palatinate from his castle in Heidelberg on a tributary of the Rhine and one of the only seven electors who chose the Habsburg emperor. He was pleasant and intelligent, a fitting husband for Princess Elizabeth.

Frederick was in London but the marriage had not been solemnised when tragedy overtook the royal family. Prince Henry had been unwell but his death in November from typhoid was sudden and unforeseen. Elizabeth adored her brother and was grief-stricken but she turned to Frederick for comfort. The king and queen withdrew into their separate households to grieve while the nation mourned the death of their promising prince. His would be a great loss.

A shadow fell over the wedding preparations, but James rallied and in February 1613 the wedding took place. Two months later, Frederick and Elizabeth left for the Palatinate. The king and queen accompanied them as far as Rochester where they parted, the young couple travelling on to Canterbury and sailing from Margate to the Netherlands, where they were the guests of Prince Maurice of Nassau, the Dutch soldier and Protestant champion, to whom Frederick was related. Here there were further celebrations of the marriage before they completed their journey, Elizabeth sailing up the River Rhine to her new home in Heidelberg, where she received a warm welcome. She was soon to experience an elevation in status followed by war, transforming her into the Winter Queen, one of Protestant Europe's icons.

At home in England, little Prince Charles became heir to the triple thrones.

4

Men of Influence

The crown worn by the monarch is far more than a mark of office; it is a symbol of the state and its power. It is the institution which brings cases in court and under which government is executed. James, the first Stuart monarch of England and Ireland, embodied that power. He had a strong sense of sovereignty but he underestimated English law, its antiquity, centrality and the respect in which it was held by the English elite.[1]

As head of government in all three kingdoms, the monarch was at the centre of concentric circles of powerful men and a few aristocratic women of influence.

The privy councillors who ran his government, civil service and the treasury could be considered the first circle. A very different group made up the Gentlemen of the Bedchamber, who could enter the king's private apartments and managed his domestic life. The third group, the men who sat in his parliaments, came together infrequently but they controlled how much tax he received and they had considerable influence.

However physically near to the king these men were, in Scotland and Ireland he had separate privy councils with significant powers. He also had parliaments in both countries. The Irish one was modelled on the English institution but without its lawmaking powers, while the Scottish one was a weak body with one chamber and no strong traditions.

Across these institutions cut the nobility. Some were privy councillors and all peers were members of the House of Lords. Noblemen came to court and many were friends of the king, hunting or dining with him, attending court masques or state occasions. In the bedchamber were courtiers, those whom the king liked or was willing to have close to him.

James was loyal to his friends, and his old Scots friends in particular were rewarded when he came into his grand inheritance. Personally, he was surrounded by Scots but several English nobles were promoted too;

however, there were few Irishmen at the court. There had been great changes in Ireland, where some of the leading families had been dispossessed, but, in any case, James was unfamiliar with the country.

James was thirty-seven and an experienced ruler when he came to England, but he was still coming to a country he hardly knew. It was important to deal carefully with the men of influence there, and Sir Robert Cecil was the most important of them. It was Cecil who had managed the offer of Elizabeth's thrones to the Scots king and James rewarded him with a peerage, as Earl of Salisbury. James never warmed to Salisbury, but he knew the man was indispensable. Before he came to England, James had agreed to keep all Elizabeth's councillors but he hoped to add as many Scots to the English Privy Council.[2] In the event, that proved too difficult. He brought in the English Howards, his chief Scottish minister Sir George Home and his cousin the Duke of Lennox with a few others, but Salisbury continued to run the English administration.

It was James's cherished aim to create a union of England and Scotland with 'one worship of God, one kingdom entirely governed, one uniformity of law'.[3] To his great annoyance, this union was firmly blocked by the English parliament. The House of Commons was highly resistant, would not compromise the laws of England and refused to call their country Great Britain in case that meant that English law would not hold. They strongly resisted the naturalisation of Scots as English citizens.[4] James reprimanded one particular English firebrand on this subject and accused him of prejudice against the Scots.

Prejudice against the Irish was ubiquitous. An 'Irish Masque' was performed at court whose theatrical effect rested on mocking the way Irish people spoke.[5] Spencer in Elizabeth's reign was only one of a chorus of official voices returning from Ireland to complain about the lack of civility and the appalling high-handedness of the aristocracy there. Yet the ability of Irish leaders to rise against English rule was feared. Officials there saw it as their duty to anglicise the country and tame its people. Because of prejudice and distance, but moreso because of cost, few Irishmen came to court. One or two had been raised in English households, like Donogh O'Brien, Earl of Thomond, who was court educated, and Richard Burke, Earl of Clanricard, who had grown up in Essex's household.[6] Both were considered English in their behaviour.

Scots, however, were the king's friends. Thwarted in his hopes of creating a full union and unable to make the Privy Council half Scots and half English, James contented himself by filling the bedchamber with his fellow countrymen. This created problems for Salisbury, who had no access to the intimate gatherings in the king's private apartments.

Outside the bedchamber, the next royal space was the privy chamber and here other men attended and records were kept, but the bedchamber was unregulated and exclusive. In Elizabeth's day, only women entered the queen's rooms but now there was a king, and how different it was. James taunted Salisbury that he was only used to a queen's court.[7]

The Gentlemen of the Bedchamber were sworn in as members and had specific jobs. They waited on the king at private meals, helped him dress, were guardians of the bedchamber and water closet, watched his health and were companions and friends. When James was away in the country hunting, he took these men with him. The bedchamber men were adept at acquiring titles and patronage. Soon the privy purse was controlled by the bedchamber, which handled large sums in cash. Salisbury had control of the sign manual, the papers signed by the king for business purposes, but the bedchamber men would get up warrants and have them signed by James privately.[8]

When James left for England, his cousin Lennox stood in for him in the Scottish parliament. George Home, Earl of Dunbar, chief minister for Scottish affairs, travelled frequently between the capitals and was influential in England where he controlled access to the king. In Scotland, the Privy Council was led by the Chancellor – a series of Scottish peers held the position. Thomas Hamilton, or Tam o' the Cowgate, was a lawyer and the most senior judge in Scotland, on whom the king often relied. When James boasted that he ran Scotland with a stroke of the pen it was through these men and his Privy Council in Edinburgh. James also had control of legislation, because he sent a list of those he wanted appointed to the Lords of the Articles, who in turn introduced legislation to parliament. So he had the Perth Articles confirmed by statute in 1621, although hostility was intense and they were not enforced. Scotland was still essentially feudal, with a weak parliament, but there was a vigorous political culture of an informal kind. When James lived in Scotland he was constantly in touch with his people at every level. The king knew all the nobles personally and met commoners when they assembled. The three estates who held land from the king – tenants-in-chief, clergy and burghs – sat in parliaments but a less formal gathering, a Convention of Estates, often met several times a year generally to pass tax. The king attended and a parliament often followed, in which legislation was passed. Issues were wrestled out in Edinburgh and at the heart of the discussions was King James. Once he left for England, he communicated frequently with his councillors but not with anyone else. He was assertive from afar: over the church which he disciplined, over the Highlanders who were brought to heel – often by imprisonment – and over the crown tenants who were more highly taxed. However, the estates were consulted less and less. After 1612, the Scottish parliament met only twice more during the reign and then to raise tax for James and for his daughter's wedding. Scotland, like Ireland beforehand, now had an absentee king; but unlike Ireland, it had no permanent viceroy or king's representative. The king's role was split between various ministers, none with full powers.[9]

Under Tudor rule, energetic Englishmen had arrived in Ireland to fill government posts and it was these men who composed James's Irish Privy Council; all were long-term servants of the crown, half were soldiers. Lord Deputy Sir Arthur Chichester, who represented the king and headed his government, was also a soldier. The uneasy relationship between landowners of Gaelic and Norman descent had been recently disturbed by the introduction of Tudor planters. As Chichester set about planting Ulster, yet another group moved in: Presbyterian Scots. For the old families of the Pale – the area around Dublin – who were of Norman descent and largely Catholic but accustomed to taking crown positions, a loss of income and prestige was underway as Elizabethan planters gained the official positions and their benefits. The Gaelic Irish, who had held old clan or sept lands from ancient times, had struggled to prove title to them under newly introduced English law. Many had taken advantage of a Tudor policy of surrender and regrant, by which they gained title deeds guaranteed by English law. As the Stuart administrations developed, even these turned out to be insecure. So, the Irish gentry were a disturbed group, with new settlers pressing forward and older grandees disgruntled or under threat. The rebels of the previous reign, however, had either fled, died or lost their lands.

The centre of court life and the London home of the sovereign was in Whitehall. Westminster Abbey had been originally founded on an island in the Thames and a palace built beside it, to which the magnificent Westminster Hall was added.[10] In this Palace of Westminster, medieval kings called their councils which evolved into two houses of parliament.[11] The nearby palace of Whitehall had been built by the Archbishop of York, extended by Wolsey and taken over by Henry VIII. He rebuilt it, creating a gallery overlooking the Thames but the Palace of Whitehall was a warren of buildings with grand rooms and higgledy-piggledy additions and apartments.

James I spent little time there, constantly escaping to his houses in Hertfordshire and East Anglia to hunt with his friends. Although in the early days of his marriage he was clearly fond of his wife, who bore him seven children, they now lived separate lives and Anne used the Palace of Greenwich or Somerset House. Queen Anne loved masques and there were festivities at court where James was delighted by the ladies' audacious attire. There are reports of him hugging gentlemen and kissing ladies, and after a favourite's wedding James visited the newly-weds in bed the following morning in his nightshirt.[12] He was a man of unpredictable but warm emotions, which gradually seemed to splay more widely.

There were serious problems with the funding of the state and James's lifestyle left him open to charges of extravagance. The number of his country houses grew and all were kept ready in case he should suddenly arrive. James lavished gifts on the nobility and on his friends. They were a worry to Salisbury, who managed to insert a few Englishmen into the bedchamber but it was the king who promoted the handsome young Scot Robert Carr, who had once been his page and who attracted his attention when he fell from his horse during a tilt in 1607. Soon James was doting on him, leaning on his arm, pinching his cheek and showering him with favours. The promotion of favourites was to have a dangerous effect on the public mood, both for James and for his heir.

The sudden rise and ennoblement of the favourite Robert Carr, later Earl of Somerset, was part of an emotional loosening of the reins which increased markedly in James as he got older. At the same time, he became more louche. Exactly what James wanted from the two handsome young men on whom he doted in his last years is unclear, but certainly affection and caresses were among them. Carr at first played along but subsequently could not control his distaste for the slobbering kisses of the unkempt king. George Villiers, who replaced him, played his part with consummate skill, which accelerated the tensions between the monarch and his people to a dangerous level.

The men who would bear the brunt of those rising tensions were, at that time, children and adolescents. In the merchant houses, the homes of the minor gentry and in cottages across the three kingdoms, children were scraping their knees and boys were learning their lessons or practising their swordplay, unaware of the shifting currents beneath the ship of state. Men and women from all backgrounds would be drawn into a conflict which, in the high days of Robert Carr and the early days of George Villiers, were not yet seriously felt. Young aristocrats were sent to court or brought to manhood on their estates, where the worries of their parents were about their inheritance and marriages, not the trials of loyalty and strength they would face. Much depended on their age. Robert Devereux, 3rd Earl of Essex was already fully grown when James leered at Robert Carr, but the heir to the Hamilton estates was a small child.

One of the great Irish houses was that of the Butlers; Thomas Butler, 10th Earl of Ormond was Queen Elizabeth's cousin and the most powerful nobleman in Ireland. Elizabeth had called him 'Black Tom' or 'my black husband', because of his hair and dark looks. His only child was his daughter Elizabeth, so his house was vulnerable and James meddled.

A story was told how, late in his life, when he was blind, Black Tom gathered his relatives to his house in Carrick-on-Suir for Christmas. Behind his chair a fair-haired child whipped his top and Black Tom asked the servant what the noise was.

'It's young Jemmy Butler a-whipping his gig,' the servant replied.

There were many James Butlers. 'And what Jemmy Butler is that?' the earl asked.

'It's Jemmy Butler of Kilcash,' he replied.

The old patriarch called the boy to him and prophesied that 'young Jemmy Butler of Kilcash' would restore his house after a time of much trouble.[13]

The earl had foresight. He died the following year and his Catholic nephew Walter inherited the earldom but James, who worried about the power of the Butlers, prevented Walter from inheriting the great Butler estates too; they went to Black Tom's daughter Lady Elizabeth, whose marriage the king then arranged. James was a great man for matchmaking and it pleased him to enrich his young men, so Lady Elizabeth was betrothed to one of the Gentlemen of the Bedchamber, a man named Richard Preston from Perthshire who was beneath her in status but given an earldom. When Earl Walter protested, he was imprisoned. Jemmy Butler of Kilcash was Walter's grandson and heir but his prospects seemed poor. Yet he did fulfil Black Tom's prediction and went on to play a decisive role in the affairs of at least two kingdoms.

King James made another marriage for young James Hamilton, son of his friend the Marquis of Hamilton, who came to court in 1620. Hamilton was the premier Scottish peer but the king obliged him to marry an Englishwoman of very inferior rank, the niece of George Villiers, Duke of Buckingham, who had become the royal favourite. Hamilton smarted over this all his life and was still angry about it just before his death.[14] Yet he remained a servant of the Stuarts and paid heavily for his loyalty.

King James tried some other matchmaking, and one elderly gentleman protested in alarm that he was far too old to marry when James was looking for a husband for some particularly unattractive widow.

The king, who had been an able and intellectual ruler, showed signs of losing his mental vigour. He became emotionally incontinent as he grew older, but he was always an exuberant man and liable to display his feelings in startling ways. He drank when he could no longer hold it, became dirty and bedraggled at court, and was more and more enamoured of his adored young man. But this was extremely dangerous. Throughout his reign James had been dogged by money woes, and had fought bitterly with his parliaments about it, so the shameless enriching of his last and most treasured favourite, Buckingham, infuriated the tax-paying people of England.

5

Money and Land

When he rode south to take up the crown of England, James believed he had inherited great wealth, far outstripping that of his Scottish crown. This was true – England had much greater resources – but debt had been growing in Elizabeth's later years and English crown finance needed careful management. Unfortunately, instead of bringing debt down, James greatly exacerbated it.

When the Tudors came to the throne, the monarch – like his noblemen – was expected to 'live of his own', to run his court and government from the income of his estates, although this was no longer possible. The crown also received the 'ancient customs' on wool and hides, while parliament could augment crown income by taxation. The Dissolution of the Monasteries had greatly enriched the crown but Henry VIII had largely squandered this new-found wealth on foreign wars.

Elizabeth I was a conservative woman; during her reign, government generally balanced the books. However, despite high inflation she and Burghley had not increased rents or tax rates, letting income fall behind. More importantly, from the 1580s England had fought costly wars which meant Elizabeth passed on a substantial debt to her successor.

When James arrived in London, the wars had ended and there was uncollected tax still to come in, so it was expected that debts would be reduced and that crown income and expenditure would once more be brought into balance, especially since Salisbury updated the customs rates. This was not what happened. It took James's ministers some years to realise that the new king was uncontrollably extravagant and that special measures would have to be used to balance the books.

The crown's primary income was from land, so a simple way to raise money was to sell part of the crown estate. Sales of unproductive assets were not serious but if continued, they led to a reduction in both the capital and income of the monarch. The king could ask parliament for taxation, and some tax could be collected without the Commons' consent. In earlier centuries the monarch had feudal rights and, as feudalism collapsed, inventive ways were devised to create revenue from those rights. The king's prerogative – his especial powers – could also be used to reduce expenditure.

Although the House of Commons had long-established rights over granting tax, it was the crown which collected it. The monarch might ask parliament for subsidies which were levied on wealth and so mainly on land, but this was in extraordinary circumstances such as war. There were other customs duties; parliament generally awarded tonnage and poundage to each new monarch for the duration of their reign and the Tudors had instigated impositions which were controversial and which parliament did not control. To get a steady income, the customs were often farmed out, with variable results.

To cover temporary cash-flow problems, the crown borrowed. Queen Elizabeth had dealt with an Italian financier and at first, James too borrowed from continental sources but increasingly the City of London could provide large sums.[1] Borrowing was not considered a problem; it was later in the reign, when the debts continued to rise and future tax revenues were promised against those debts, that the crown's finances became increasingly compromised.

The early years of James's reign showed great promise for national wealth. With the end of the war, markets reopened and customs figures show how swiftly external trade then grew. This was positive for the crown, which relied heavily on that revenue, but the whole economy benefitted as the Atlantic rim started a long-term period of advance.

The king's involvement in trade had wide effects. He was the grantor of patents and monopolies which gave rights to the grantee and might be awarded for a fee but were usually given as a favour, perhaps in lieu of some other royal expense. Company charters were more significant; they might benefit both the crown and the nation by increasing trade and developing overseas possessions such as the North American coast or trading routes to Asia. Increased trade brought increased customs, but the benefit to crown finance was often slow to materialise.

Elizabeth and Burghley had involved themselves in various profit-making schemes or projects, at which they had been largely successful. James too was open to suggestions of this kind; in fact more so than his predecessor, as he listened to a wide range of voices and suggestions for schemes. James was no fool, but he was more of an academic than a businessman and he lacked the Tudors' sharp instinct for judging character.

Projects worked differently to grants and charters. The monarch might take shares in a business venture and be paid when the profit came in. Often such projects had wide-ranging or social effects. It was argued that such schemes brought public gain, such as the New River scheme which brought water from Hertfordshire to supply London. The mixture of public good and private gain was possible in theory, but often conflicts arose between the two. When James made gifts of patents to his friends and favourites, the clear lines of crown finance might become blurred and ministers lose control. When James invested, there were often losses.[2]

All the same, the reign opened in a period of economic advance. Not only customs revenue, but the activities of London financiers showed the growing wealth of England. Whereas Elizabeth had an Italian banker, James increasingly raised funds in London, where financiers could mobilise capital from a variety of sources. Merchants, well-off citizens or their widows, even smaller traders had stored cash which they were willing to lend for profit.[3] James's government borrowed from the City of London but was increasingly found unreliable about repayment.[4] Later in his reign, James turned to successful merchant-financiers like Lionel Cranfield who had begun his career in the wool trade but became a customs collector and then a crown official. Cranfield impressed James and controlled fiscal policy from around 1618 but even he failed to cure the king's financial problems.

Inevitably, the accession of James changed the nature of the court, which was a significant part of crown expenditure. It was at court that the monarch kept up his style and display, but it was also the place where government did its business. Elizabeth had been clever at projecting the symbolism of monarchy; James was less formal but he was also a family man. The Virgin Queen had been a glamorous woman and dressed for show, but she was single and childless so her court had lower costs than James with his wife and three children, all of whom had establishments of their own.

The king's policies over the great trading companies show the commercial strengths and weaknesses of the reign. James exercised his right to grant patents, monopolies and charters to companies: the Merchant Adventurers, the East India Company, the Russia Company and others all owed their exclusive trading rights to the king. The monarch awarded these concessions and charters, which protected the trading companies as they built up capital and developed markets, but the system was widely criticised for restricting trade. The usual form for these enterprises had become joint-stock companies and most of the disparate groups who took concessions from the king to settle in North America used this structure too.

After two decades of war, peace with Spain came in 1604. England and France began colonising those areas of the Americas unclaimed by the Spanish. The earliest English colony was a merchant one in Virginia, but trading companies, religious groups and private individuals all applied for royal charters and were awarded tracts of American land to develop. Within certain bounds, they could establish local government on their own terms. Once companies were formed, investors might remain in England and adventure their capital, or become the undertakers who worked overseas to build up the colony. These concepts – undertaker, adventurer and joint-stock company – were developing as Britain extended its commercial interests. Motives and methods for American settlement varied: the *Mayflower* landed in 1620 to form a Puritan colony at Cape Cod but Sir Ferdinando Gorges attempted a vast aristocratic estate in New England which ultimately failed. From these diverse beginnings the English colonies developed along the North American coast and on the islands, offering an expansion of trade and scope for social experiment.

As trade in northern Europe grew, England had new opportunities. The glamorous days of the Mediterranean and the merchants of Venice had passed their peak; the new routes were in the Baltic, the North Sea and the Atlantic. From Russia came timber and furs, while grain was exported from around the Baltic rim. The time of the west and north was dawning and England's merchants were in the thick of it. In York, Norwich, Hull and Exeter bales of cloth and hide were loaded into creaking vessels, while in London trade of every kind slipped from the quays or came ashore to make a good loud clanking in the counting houses.

With increased trade came the expansion of banking and currency dealing. There were exchanges in major cities, so that merchants could get foreign currencies for their deals, and these grew into centres for currency speculation and banking. Gold and silver coins had a face value and a weight. As exchange rates altered, so the face value and the overseas metal value of the coins might diverge, leaving room for currency speculation.

The increasing use of paper money facilitated trade but it relied on reputation; a man who wrote a bill of exchange had to have sound credit. As trade grew in northern Europe, banking grew with it, drawing in cash from savers to lend out at profit and giving cash for paper bills at a discount. Antwerp had emerged as the main banking centre for the north, with Amsterdam the principal trading port, but London was growing as a centre of both trade and banking, hoping to rival the Dutch. The church had always condemned usury but Protestant thinking was less critical; Calvin sanctioned modest interest on capital. So, the Reformation had spawned a culture which was sympathetic to banking and investment.

The City of London, downriver from Whitehall and controlled by its own corporation, was becoming a financial centre under James. Here goldsmiths traded in metal and became bankers on a modest scale but here too were the great financiers who helped the crown with its cash-flow problems. Scriveners also worked in the City, writing conveyances, deeds and mortgage agreements; John Milton was born there in 1608, the son of a City scrivener. In the narrow and packed streets, members of the various guilds grouped themselves together, with the goldsmiths clustered near the Royal Exchange where foreign currency was traded.

If London and the ports had new trading opportunities, so too rural England was changing. Feudalism had withered away, and as it declined the landholding system which supported it was adapted. Changes in land use and improved agricultural skills made feudal farming methods inefficient. The system of strip fields which had been usual in lowland England was gradually reorganised and holdings consolidated. Often this was done by agreement, but there was also contention when farmers with common rights found them gradually extinguished. Population growth meant there was less wasteland to be cleared. Sheep farming on enclosed pasture created grievances too, which under Elizabeth had sometimes led to riots. However, serfdom had gone too and more yeomen farmers had emerged. So, the shape of farming changed and the terms of landholding adapted. Old manorial tenancies continued, handed on from father to son by copyhold but other small farmers lost their land and became labourers. People left the land to become artisans or moved to the growing towns for employment. The estates of the monasteries were now in the hands of an expanded gentry who were improving and enclosing their land. They would prove to be an assertive group as the century progressed but so would the merchants and professionals of the growing towns. In this seething change, government had to adapt to new needs and demands.

The crown was also adapting to the decay of feudalism, as the links between land and warfare were transformed into financial transactions. The most inflammatory of these was the way the crown managed wardship for landowners. Under feudal law, land had been held in return for military service. If the owner died leaving a child heir, the monarch could let that land to another warrior until the child grew up. By James's reign, that right had been commuted into a fine, collected when the son came of age. Many families struggled to pay, but the heir could not claim his estate until they did. Another grievance was purveyance, which gave the royal household a right to provisions, often huge quantities of food bought cheaply or barely paid for. In the regions, this right was turned into a cash demand. So, there were post-feudal grievances at both the lower and higher ends of society.

Now that James had ascended the throne, the people must meet their new monarch and, as was customary at the beginning of a reign, a parliament was called and elections organised. To vote, men had to hold property of a given but not uniform value so the members who hurried to London represented the propertied classes. Up from the shires came the landed gentry, greatly strengthened as a group since acquiring monastic land. The boroughs returned aldermen and merchants with a keen eye for business and there were always lawyers in the Commons, watchful over the passing of new laws and jealous of the privileges and traditions of parliament which had developed so carefully since its early medieval gatherings. The House of Lords was dominated by the great nobles who lived off income from their estates, although merchants and crown officials were often ennobled. Confident, assertive and highly protective of their traditions and rights, the English parliament soon startled the Scottish king.

James liked to speak in public, and the members listened attentively when he addressed them but had issues of their own they wished to discuss. Firstly, they challenged him over the election, then complained about feudal dues before turning to problems with religion. James was appalled.

Those in the House of Commons were pursuing issues unresolved from Elizabeth's reign – purveyance, wardship and monopolies – while testing their strength with the new king over his religious decisions.

Parliament therefore got off to a contentious start. James had meddled in the election of one member and when queried stated that MPs derived all their privileges from him. The members made it clear to their new king that he had been misinformed; they held their privileges as of right and election returns were not sent to Chancery but were dealt with by the house itself.

Then they turned to purveyance, wardship and religion. For the king, the main issue for the parliament was a union of England and Scotland. It was dear to his heart and he was keenly aware of the commercial benefits if the two nations became one, without trading restrictions. The Commons, however, had many objections and the most they would agree to was a commission to investigate such a union, as suggested by Salisbury. James planned to style himself King of Great Britain but Bacon asked, 'By what law shall this Britain be governed?'[5] Worried that the title might create legal anomalies before any terms were agreed, the Commons resisted. Then they tried to question the king's religious policy; many members held Puritan views and were dissatisfied with the Hampton Court conference. The crown needed parliamentary revenue and the Commons granted James tonnage and poundage for the duration of his reign, but despite urging by his ministers, the members were clearly unwilling to offer more subsidies. The Commons wanted to review the position of the chartered companies, which many felt acted as monopolies and were suppressing trade.

By now James was exasperated by his parliament. He came down to the House, harangued the members of the Commons and prorogued the parliament.

During the next meeting in 1605, the Gunpowder Plot to blow up parliament and kill the royal family was discovered. The conspirators were executed and the result, inevitably, was an intensification of the recusancy laws against Catholics. The parliament went on with its business and granted a subsidy to the king but immediately started their complaints about purveyance once more. It was already clear that James was extravagant; Salisbury had urged the king to retrench and James agreed heartily but continued to spend freely as before. The country houses were kept open for hunting and the gifts to friends continued. Parliament was prorogued and reassembled five times until it was dissolved in 1611. They were unhelpful about union, which was James's most cherished project. The complaints they made about prerogative rights were not met. So, the king's first experience of an English parliament was a sour one and meanwhile he was building up unmanageable debts.

During the first decade of James's reign, Salisbury made considerable headway in clearing the crown debt, by careful tax collection and the sale of unproductive land. However, it simply grew again as James maintained a lavish lifestyle and an extravagant court, but primarily because he showered gifts on his friends and favourites. His ministers agreed that a monarch must put on a show but privately begged the king to retrench. James was simply unable – he would prove as incontinent with money as he became with his affections.

His policies on trade also had mixed results. His concessions for America were taken up but, as yet, transatlantic trade was tiny. The important trade routes were into Europe. The great trading houses were those with royal charters of exclusive rights, which owned property and were building up share capital. Of these, the Merchant Adventurers were the oldest and best established, selling cloth to the Low Countries and northern Europe. Throughout both islands, wool was the principal export and mercers, or cloth merchants, played a major role in the trade networks. In England, there had been regular efforts to improve profits by dyeing and weaving wool before it was exported, but there was strong competition from other Europeans, especially in the Netherlands.

King James made a serious mistake when he agreed to Alderman Cockayne's proposal to ban all exports of undyed wool. Even if the ban had been successful, giving Cockayne a concession for dyeing caused ill will and when the Dutch refused to buy the finished cloth there was a crisis in the English woollen industry. Cloth was left unsold in warehouses throughout the land while European buyers found new suppliers of the undyed cloth which England had previously supplied. Men were laid off and the woollen industry declined rapidly. Although James rescinded the embargo, the industry had hardly recovered by the 1640s. Far from increasing trade and bringing income, the project alienated the vital industry.

The king's difficult financial position in England was made worse because neither Scotland nor Ireland was solvent.

For the Scottish Council the departure of the king made the books look better because all the costs for his households were now borne by the English. However, Scotland was a poor country and tax collection there was inefficient; nor was there a permanent Exchequer, but there were energetic treasurers so the paucity of revenue is remarkable. It was half of what was collected in Ireland, which was little enough. All the same, the Scots begrudged any subsidy and firmly believed that the king should live of his own, although to a great extent he was now living off the English. Crown tenants in Scotland were increasingly taxed on top of their rents and complained loudly. Perhaps the pensions bill explained the deficit: the Scottish revenue would barely pay it and at the end of the reign there was a debt of £1 million Scots, with heavy interest payments.

In Ireland, crown finance had been boosted by dissolving the monasteries but declined under Elizabeth as two devastating periods of war drained the Exchequer. The Tudors originally refused to subsidise government in Ireland but Elizabeth had to pay for the wars out of English revenue as the costs were enormous. Irish taxes followed the same pattern as the English ones but were not always collected. In some areas it was too difficult, and the big ports had received exemptions, saying they would collect it themselves.

So plantation was an attractive proposition for the crown. The main aim was to prevent rebellion and to anglicise Ireland in landholding, laws and manners. This in turn would root out Catholicism, or so the government fervently hoped. But it had the other great attraction that land grants could be sold and new proprietors – the undertakers – obliged to pay ground rents. Once anglicised, tax could be collected, trade would flourish and the Irish economy would develop.

To confirm plans for plantation an Irish parliament was needed, but when Chichester called it in 1611 the traditional Irish elite had a shock. The Palesmen had previously dominated parliaments but James had created so many new borough seats with Protestant MPs that the Palesmen were no longer in a majority. The ensuing objections and disputes were so intense that parliament was prorogued and a delegation set off for London where James lectured them about their loyalty to the Pope.

Nonetheless, it was unwise to alienate the loyal Catholics of old family who for so long had served the crown. James modified his tone and by 1614 subsidies had been granted and legislation passed. However, two dangers had arisen: parliament in Dublin had been polarised on sectarian lines, and plantation and an increase in government business were making new fortunes, creating temptation.

Where government produced profit there would be officials hovering around to take a cut. Chichester, who in most respects was a capable and responsible administrator, awarded himself a sizeable estate. Corrupt land practices became a recurrent pattern. But the crown itself succumbed to temptation. James saw that, with or without rebellion, plantation could be extended. If the crown could challenge land titles, more estates could be forfeited to the crown and those lands could be granted, sold or rented out. So began the dangerous practice of 'discovering titles', a practice which would extend into the next reign, creating insecurity, mistrust and ultimately rebellion.

In Ireland and Scotland, as in England, the terms of landownership were changing. The medieval systems, whether Norman or Gaelic, had similarities. In both, great men awarded land to their clients and kinsmen in return for goods and service in war. They had enormous power, but as government centralised and strengthened it was keen to whittle that power away. In all three kingdoms, some aristocrats ruled palatinates, or separate fiefdoms where they had political and legal control. James, like the Tudors, closed the net around the Gaelic leaders, supplanting their tribal titles by his own and insisting on inheritance by primogeniture. As the two islands modernised, the terms by which land was held dramatically altered and instead of military service payment was by money rents. This might suit the lowlands, but in the Highlands new problems developed. In Scotland, many clan leaders who had once been guardians of the clan's territory were transformed into the owners of vast tracts of land.[6]

This was against the crown policy of both Elizabeth and James. Both monarchs attempted to reduce the size of aristocratic estates and dissolve

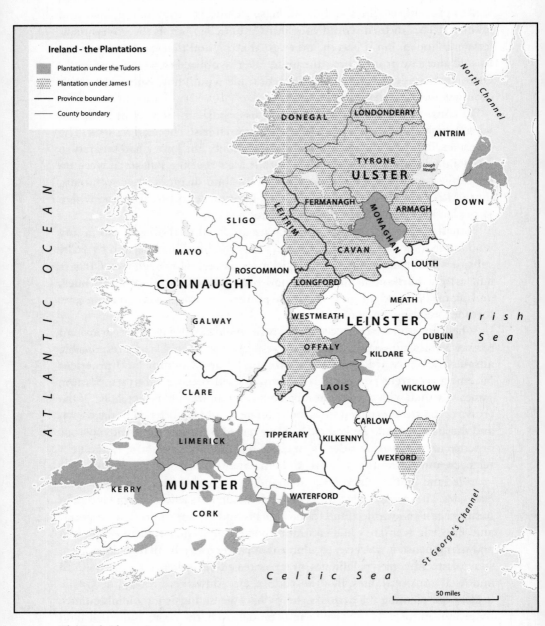

The Irish Plantations.

palatinate powers. When Irish land was awarded to undertakers, Elizabeth had capped the size of each plantation and stipulated that smaller farmers be brought in as tenants. James too attempted to control the Highlanders through the 1609 Statutes of Iona and Ulster through the plantations. His government wanted more and better tenant farmers. The power of the Highland chiefs was not so easily broken; the MacDonalds of Islay rebelled again in 1614 until forces were sent from Dublin to suppress them.[7] Nor were the aims of plantation met; the great Irish fiefdoms of the FitzGeralds and the O'Neills were broken up but new grandees managed to swell their holdings, men such as Richard Boyle, a sharp-witted Elizabethan lawyer who accumulated an enormous estate in Munster and was said to have the largest landowning income in the two islands;[8] or Randal MacDonnell, the head of the Irish branch of the MacDonalds, who accumulated around 340,000 acres in Antrim after the Ulster plantation.

Nor was the main aim of the Ulster plantations met. The plan was that undertakers would bring in settlers but many of the grantees never lived in Ireland or met their obligations. Instead, the original Irish landowners became tenants of absentee undertakers whom they bitterly resented. The City of London lost its concession for Derry – which was later re-awarded – as London failed to bring in settlers so the Irish inhabitants remained on the land.[9] Government policy was to develop the island and alter the culture. In counties Antrim and Down, where crown policy was enacted, large numbers of Irish farmers were dispossessed and many small Scottish farmers settled, but it was here that the grievances of the natives were most intense. On top of that, the Scottish settlers were Presbyterian, which caused different problems for the crown.[10]

Nonetheless, plantation weakened the Gaelic Irish and gave the government an increasing grip. As administration tightened, the crown found it easier to collect customs from all the ports. It also levied the feudal dues which the English Commons complained of so bitterly, but in Ireland wardship rules allowed the crown to appoint guardians for young heirs, so by placing them in Protestant households young Catholic noblemen were encouraged to change their religion. Under James, the crown increased its revenue in Ireland and England began to reduce its subsidy to the country, but the ownership of Irish land was not just insecure but becoming an explosive issue.

Despite the efforts of James's treasurers and tax collectors in Scotland and Ireland, England was still making subventions to both countries, and in England the Treasury was in trouble. Rather than struggle against a persistent tide, Salisbury tried a single and radical solution. The feudal and prerogative dues would be abolished in return for a fixed income of £200,000 a year. Parliament was duly reassembled to negotiate the Great Contract.

James's idea of kingship had already been battered in England. In Edinburgh, his nobles had been unruly and sometimes dangerous, but his parliaments there passed his statutes en bloc and without demur. There was prior discussion in the estates but parliament itself was docile. In London, the nobles were obsequious but the Commons contested every one of his rights. James was cross, wounded and perplexed. By 1610, parliamentarians had defeated all his hopes of union. But Salisbury persevered. The Great Contract was nearing completion when James's right to impositions ran into the Commons' right to freedom of speech and negotiations broke down. It would take the rest of the century for all its aims to be achieved. In spring of the following year, James's first parliament was finally dissolved. Soon afterwards Salisbury died and the Elizabethan order ended.

James became sour and antagonistic to parliaments altogether. He advised his son not to hold them and referred to the 1610 parliament as the 'house of hell'.[11] The subsequent parliaments of the reign were brief and called to raise money; the Addled Parliament of 1614 only sat for two months, voted no subsidies and became extremely acrimonious. James was so incensed with it that he had four members arrested for making violent speeches. He hoped never to call another one and began negotiating with the Spanish ambassador over a marriage for Prince Charles which would bring a large dowry. After all, said James, the Cortes of Castile is a small body whereas his Commons had five hundred members.[12]

James seemed unaware of the origin and growth of the English parliament. English Common Law and customs had their roots in Anglo-Saxon England and were cherished. The Norman and Plantagenet kings had developed them and instituted formal parliaments. The Tudors had taken their throne on the battlefield and had strengthened their legitimacy by clever use of their parliaments. The great changes of the Reformation had been taken to the Commons of both England and Ireland to be enshrined in statute. Henry VIII had told his 1543 parliament that 'we at no time stand so highly in our estate royal as in the time of parliament, wherein we as head and you as members are conjoined and knit together into one body politic'.[13] The concept of the 'king in parliament' as the conjoined powers of the realm was a current one.

James, however, came from a nation where Norman feudalism had been grafted onto Gaelic and Nordic rootstock; the shape of society was different. The Scottish parliament had developed during James's reign but it remained a weak institution that passed any legislation handed to it by the Lords of the Articles at the will of the king. The London parliament was quite different. When James looked at his fellow kings in France and Spain he saw puny national parliaments seldom called, not the assertive crowd who thronged the English Commons. Had he looked to the German principalities, the Netherlands or Poland, even the provinces of France and Spain, he might have noticed traditions more like those which had survived so long in England and which had strengthened under the Tudor monarchs.[14] Instead he was affronted by them and found other ways in which to raise money by developing the powers contained within his prerogative. The fight was on.

6

Multiple Kingdoms

When James inherited Elizabeth's two kingdoms, he had an opportunity to improve trade and administrative coordination across both islands. It was a chance that was largely missed. The king wanted to bring together the three churches and to unite Scotland with England but he was thwarted in both aims. With their different histories, laws and religious cultures, there were real structural obstacles to union and resistance from various groups. But the failure to solve these disjunctions left tensions which his successors inherited.[1]

Other European rulers had multiple kingdoms and tackled the problems in a variety of ways.[2] Most commonly, conquered and inherited territories were amalgamated; France gradually absorbed smaller principalities and imposed Catholicism over the whole territory. The Holy Roman Empire was a different type of polity, a group of Germanic states which all owed allegiance to a single emperor who was chosen by seven electors, four of them princes and three bishops. In practice, they always elected a Habsburg prince from the great Austrian dynasty. Held together by trade agreements and a careful system of currency exchange, the loose bonds of the Habsburg empire had worked well for generations – until religious differences disrupted it.

Wales had been amalgamated with England for government purposes; James now envisaged uniting that kingdom with Scotland. Such a union would allow free trade across the island, although some in both countries feared the competition. Such a union would also make James's role as monarch easier and more coherent. For him union was a blessing 'which God hath in my person bestowed upon you. Hath he not made us all in one island, compassed with one sea and of itself by nature indivisible?' He spoke in images taken from those of the church. 'What God hath conjoined let no man separate. I am the husband and all the whole isle is my lawful wife; I am the head and it is the body; I am the shepherd and it is my flock. I hope therefore that no man will think that I, a Christian King under the Gospel, should be a polygamist and husband to two wives.'[3]

James wanted a union with one king, one law and one church, but it was not a simple matter. Ireland was a conquered kingdom and subordinate to England but Scotland was unconquered and sovereign, owing no allegiance to a superior ruler or state. Kingdoms within multiple systems had to guard their sovereignty carefully, lest it become eroded. In the sixteenth century, the English had even talked of having an empire, the ultimate sovereign state which was independent of the Pope and all other princes.[4]

It seems that James failed to understand the high value that Englishmen placed on their law and parliamentary traditions. His proclamation that he should be styled King of Great Britain caused intense alarm and was squashed by the Commons, as it suggested that a new state had been created and might undermine English law.[5] The English had other fears: that Scotland might undercut England in trade, that Scots might become naturalised in England and fill all the offices of state in London. If the island of Britain was to be conjoined, which law would it use and which form for the church?

So, the king's desire for a union of England and Scotland was a challenge. By creating a commission to study the proposal and drawing out the discussions, the Commons gradually smothered the project but it had raised an issue which would have to be tackled: the true nature of the political relationship between the kingdoms. The English managed to prevent a union but the influence of the Scots continued to be felt in England.

Was it the mixture of race and culture which posed a problem, or the systems of government? Multiple kingdoms often had complex patterns of ethnicity. Across Britain and Ireland, waves of settlement from Europe had produced an ethnic map which cut across the borders of the kingdoms. In the west and north, the Gaelic peoples retained their culture, while in the east Scandinavian and Anglo-Saxon peoples made up most of the population. Norman influence and law had dominated all three kingdoms but not their languages – English and Scots were both essentially Germanic languages, whereas Gaelic was quite distinct. King James spoke Scots and had to moderate the way he spoke when he moved to London, but it was essentially the same tongue as English, with different pronunciation and some unique vocabulary. Gaelic speakers, however, retained a different culture with poets who knew their history, praised its heroes and stirred strong passions.

Although there had been a gradual melding of culture during the medieval period, in the sixteenth century society had been disrupted once more by upheavals in the church. Within Britain, the east was more Puritan and the west more Catholic, with an Anglican compromise in between, but with the church so central to forming social mores and maintaining obedience, and with the elite in all three kingdoms holding strong theological views, religious divergence posed problems for a ruler.

For James to rule the three kingdoms effectively, he needed skill and subtlety; he had both, but he was already middle-aged when he came south. England was a strange country to him, and, like his predecessors, he never went to Ireland.

Perhaps his job was made harder because he was the lynchpin which held the three kingdoms together; only the king had authority over all three governments. In each capital, his councillors were chosen separately and they reported to the king. In Edinburgh, the monarch had become an absentee but his ministers conferred with James in London. They were often at court but their influence over English issues was negligible. Equally, James did not discuss Scottish affairs with his English ministers and Privy Council. The Lord Lieutenant of Ireland was chosen by the king and reported to him, although the English Privy Council did have control over Irish legislation. There was therefore little coordinated government across the three realms; it was the person of the king which held them together.

Yet, the conflicts of the previous century had ended. The religious uprisings which had flamed in England under Henry VIII had died out and the wars of conquest in Ireland had ended. Even the terrible rivalries of the Scottish clans – between each other and with the crown – had been quelled. James craved peace and had good reason to expect it.

He was disappointed. Crisis erupted, not in his kingdoms but in Europe, and his daughter, Princess Elizabeth, was at the heart of it. Now in Heidelberg as wife of Frederick V, Elizabeth found herself in the midst of the growing religious tensions within the Empire.

Within that complex polity, religious difference had emerged but for two centuries the emperor had been a Habsburg, a family which now ruled some of the most important states of Europe and which remained Catholic. Two Habsburg brothers had inherited multiple kingdoms: one succeeded to the Holy Roman Empire and one to the crowns of Spain, Portugal, Sicily and Naples.

Spain had lost the Netherlands after a long war with a largely religious motive. In 1618, Ferdinand of Austria ran into similar problems. Bohemia was part of the Empire but it was largely Protestant and was treated with increasing severity by the Catholic emperor. Matters came to a head when a group of Bohemian nobles threw the imperial officials out of a window in the castle. This 'Defenestration of Prague' led to catharsis. The Bohemian Diet, or parliament, convened and, determined on a Protestant ruler, rejected the imperial heir and offered the crown of Bohemia to Frederick of the Palatinate. After a brief hesitation, Frederick and Elizabeth accepted and left Heidelberg with their children to take up the throne in Prague. The Habsburg emperor retaliated and the King of Spain prepared for action, the start of a long conflagration.

James was a peacemaker; he had made a treaty with Spain and peace remained his policy. But his son-in-law Frederick had precipitated this conflict, which was escalating alarmingly. In Britain, Princess Elizabeth was known as a staunch Protestant and a princess of the royal house; people of influence expected the crown to support her cause. The ensuing conflict, which began in 1618 and became known as the Thirty Years War, was one Britain could hardly evade, but James was personally afraid of fighting and philosophically opposed to war. He already had financial problems and any involvement would be ruinous. He tried to prevaricate, convincing himself that he could negotiate a settlement between the King of Spain and Frederick.

But King James was getting older. Even before Salisbury died the king had doted on one young man, but his second great favourite had a more profound effect on affairs of state. People heard that the king was fawning on some country boy with good looks and not much breeding, and people at court said the king was losing the run of himself. It was the relationship between the king, his favourite and the young heir that would shape the last years of his reign.

7

The Heir

Prince Charles Stuart was born at Dunfermline Castle on 19 November 1600. He was Queen Anne's third surviving child, but he was a small and sickly infant with weak legs, partly due to a bad diet. When his father became King of England and his parents moved south, they left him behind in Scotland. Charles was brought to join his family the following year.

The royal children had been raised separately, in different aristocratic households. Prince Henry only got to know his sister Elizabeth on the journey to London, when a strong bond grew up between them. Charles, who was small and less important, craved the attention and affection of his older brother. In England he was put into the care of the Careys, who were kind and attentive, but he grew slowly and continued to have trouble with his legs, possibly because of rickets, and found royal ceremonies perplexing. When his father insisted on him spending more time at court, Charles found the often crude behaviour there unpleasant. His sister, Princess Elizabeth, tried to stay away, although Prince Henry was assertive and tried to prevent bad language.

Charles was bookish, more so than his brother, but he struggled to learn the fencing, riding and hunting skills which befitted a prince. James played off one brother against the other, but Charles wanted only attention and approval from Henry. The heir's death in 1612 was a bitter loss. Two months later his sister married and went abroad, so Charles never saw her again. He was left as his parents' only son and as heir to his father's three kingdoms.

The prince's religious beliefs, later shown to be deeply held, were learned from his father and his father's divines, although growing up in England his experiences were different from the Scottish Calvinism in which James had been schooled. Of Queen Anne he saw less, although it was probably from her that he developed a taste for painting and theatre. Denmark was a developed country with a renaissance court, from which Anne brought ideas of architecture and the arts. James, however, was the principal influence on his son's ideas of kingship and statecraft. Those ideas had begun in Scotland and then developed in England in a different political culture when the king was losing the energy to adapt. They were instilled in Charles who would have to use them within the vehicle of his own personality, with his unique strengths and weaknesses.

He was a shy and fastidious boy, with a wilful or obstinate streak which was coupled with his pride, a need to stand on ceremony and a determination to be respected. This sense of vulnerable honour, of being open to humiliation, a fear of not being treated or obeyed as a royal prince should be, turned into a crippling weakness. But Charles had dignity and intelligence, a kind of sensitive nobility which won him friends.

Charles was a child when James became infatuated with Robert Carr, but by the time Carr fell from favour and the king transferred his affections to George Villiers the prince had lost his siblings and was a boy of sixteen. The new favourite began as an alarming rival in Charles's life but gradually a triple relationship developed until Charles and Buckingham became close friends.

George Villiers, later Duke of Buckingham, was an impossibly good-looking young man. Rubens glamorised and romanticised the subjects of his paintings but even so his portrait – indeed, every likeness – of George Villiers shows a vigorous, well-made man with classical looks, glowing eyes and rich auburn hair. He was graceful and athletic, and danced beautifully. Buckingham gained such ascendancy over the king that he was magnificently enriched, his family married into the highest nobility and eventually he gained control over state policy. He completely overshadowed the early years of Charles's manhood and the beginning of his reign.

James made George Villiers a Gentleman of the Bedchamber in 1615 and soon could not be without him. Titles came thick and fast: Master of Horse, Knight of the Garter, Earl of Buckingham and, by 1623, Duke of Buckingham. Buckingham was young when he met the king, around seventeen, so the blundering arrogance with which he pursued state policy largely reflects his youth and inexperience. Buckingham controlled patronage and owned York House on the Strand along with several magnificent country estates. His income was greater than that of Scotland.

From Ireland, Buckingham got wind of that heady smell of easy money which so allured him and to which his nose was so well attuned. He began an energetic policy of Irish commission business. The duke had agents and clients for many dealings and managed to take profits from almost all Irish exports as well as aiming for a large estate in Connaught. He had a very free hand but his interests were challenged by the Lord High Treasurer who was attempting to reduce government expenditure, such as pensions. Buckingham, however, proved untouchable.

George Villiers, 1st Duke of Buckingham.

James told his Council, 'I, James am neither a god nor an angel, but a man like any other. Therefore I act like a man, and confess to loving those dear to me more than other men. You may be sure than I love the Earl of Buckingham more than anyone else, and more than you who are here assembled. I wish to speak in my own behalf and not to have it thought to be a defect, for Jesus Christ did the same and therefore I cannot be blamed. Christ had his John, and I have my George.'[1]

Buckingham knew what he had to do to retain this enormous power and favour. 'I naturally so love your person, and adore all your other parts, which are more than ever one man had,' he wrote to the king.

Queen Anne called him 'dear dog' and treated him with placid scorn, but no one could cross or block Buckingham, and after the queen's death in 1619 he was an untouchable star held aloft by an ailing and besotted king. In 1619 the French ambassador wrote, 'It seems to me that the intelligence of this king has diminished. Not that he cannot act firmly and well at times and particularly when the peace of the kingdom is involved. But such efforts are not so continual as they once were. His mind uses its powers only for a short time, but in the long run he is cowardly.'[2] Several years later the Venetian ambassador reported, 'All good sentiments are clearly dead in the king. He is too blinded in disordered self-love and in his wish for quiet and pleasure.'[3]

The Duke of Buckingham had become lover, companion, mistress, wife and son in the muddled affections of the swiftly ageing king. Nonetheless, he made a good match for himself, bullying the Earl of Rutland into consent for a marriage to his daughter Lady Katherine Manners and extracting a huge dowry. The earl and his daughter were both Catholics but Catherine, under pressure from the king, converted. She was a devoted wife and bore Buckingham four children, loving him sweetly despite his infidelities. The king treated her as a daughter and fussed over her pregnancy – she must not ride fast in a carriage or eat too much fruit.

Naturally there were dangers in the promotion of Buckingham: jealousy, nepotism and awful policy-making. But the situation was made much worse because of the long-running dispute between the king and parliament over money, and also because the European powers were preparing for conflict.

Once war broke out in the Holy Roman Empire, James was in a terrible position. His money affairs were constantly under pressure and since the Addled Parliament of 1614 he had looked for other ways to raise money. One of these was the negotiation he was pursuing for a marriage between Prince Charles and the Infanta of Spain, which James believed would bring a magnificent dowry. Philip III of Spain had demanded major concessions to English Catholics: the laws against them must end, the Infanta must have her Catholic establishment and her children must have Catholic instruction. This had blocked the negotiations, as James knew the English would never accept such terms. The Reformation had been a hard-won change in England but once it was established the new faith was firmly held; Britain would not revert to the rule of Rome or even tolerate overt Catholic practices.

Nonetheless James persevered, constantly discussing the marriage with the Spanish ambassador Gondomar, to whom he became close – in fact, he increasingly relied upon the man. When James heard that his son-in-law Frederick had accepted the invitation from Bohemia, he was aghast. Before he had time to write, Frederick had accepted the crown and set off for Prague. Before Christmas 1619, Frederick and Elizabeth were crowned King and Queen of Bohemia. By the following August an imperial army had marched into the Palatinate and was soon supported by Spanish forces.

The crisis which ensued hung over the remainder of James's reign and wracked him. He must, he knew, support his daughter and son-in-law, as well as the religion he himself held so strongly. But he hated war; to send armies to Bohemia and against Spain was a betrayal of everything he had worked for as a king, and in any case he did not have the funds with which to pay them. He was determined to make peace through Spain, to persuade Frederick to admit his mistake, give up the throne of Bohemia and return to the Palatinate.

The English public, however, felt differently. Catholic troops, sent by Spain, were attacking their Princess Elizabeth, now Protestant Queen of Bohemia – this was appalling. In the days of Good Queen Bess there would not have been Spaniards conferring in the palace morning, noon and night. In those days, Englishmen had singèd the King of Spain's beard and beaten his armada. Voluntary contributions were collected towards an army to support Frederick, but the policy of the king remained negotiation.

In Europe, the princes of the Protestant Union tried to win James over to their side. The Dutch offered a dowry large enough to pay James's debts if the alliance with Spain was forgotten and Charles married Prince Maurice's daughter.[4]

A parliament was called but, distrustful of James, it granted too little money to mount a satisfactory military expedition. In England, military preparations were made and money was sent for Frederick, but his cause swiftly collapsed. Spanish troops invaded the Palatinate and Frederick suffered a total defeat at the Battle of the White Mountain outside Prague in November 1620. Frederick, Elizabeth and their children fled. The other princes turned against them and even James prevented his daughter coming to England, but Maurice, Prince of Orange offered them refuge in The Hague. Elizabeth had been Queen of Bohemia for less than a year; now she became known as the Winter Queen for that one winter in Bohemia and the long exile it earned for her.

However, the rout in Bohemia was the beginning of a religious struggle within the Empire which engulfed other powers; Spain, Denmark and Sweden took sides, and the Thirty Years War finally drew in France. The struggle continued until the Peace of Westphalia in 1648, when agreement was reached that rulers should choose the religion of their states and which gave each of them greater sovereignty, although they remained part of the structure of empire, using concepts which are still current in Europe, particularly subsidiarity.

But that was a long way in the future. In May 1621, James sent Ambassador Digby to Vienna to mediate with the Emperor for Frederick's restitution. However, the feelings of parliament had been roused and the members were in ill humour. They granted little money but sent a petition to the king asking for enforcement of anti-Catholic laws, war with Spain and that Prince Charles should marry a Protestant. James was enraged. Foreign policy and his family's marriages were so wholly within his power and outside the remit of parliament that he threatened the Commons with punishment. Now they roared. It was their established right to speak freely and any threat from the king was a threat to the privileges of parliament. They moderated their tone but sent in another petition.

Gondomar advised James to punish them and Buckingham urged him to dissolve them. His councillors begged him not to; he would be without money, with only Spain for support. James prevaricated but after Christmas he dissolved parliament.

Despite public feeling, James was still pursuing the Spanish marriage with Philip IV, although the Infanta herself said she would rather enter a nunnery than marry a heretic and the Pope would not give consent. Still James hoped that Frederick would regain the Palatinate, but Heidelberg fell and there seemed no way back. The couple had five children and Elizabeth was pregnant again. What was to become of the Winter Queen's baby sons?

James comforted himself with the company of Buckingham. He also lavished attention on his son, who was growing to manhood. Prince Charles had matured slowly into a quiet young man but as the father aged, he grew more affectionate to his heir. Charles craved his father's attention and approbation as he had previously needed his brother's. At first Buckingham was contemptuous of the boy but James wanted them to be reconciled and the favourite saw that befriending the heir would strengthen his own position. The prince was becoming a man and courtiers treated him as a person of consequence. Buckingham gave a feast of friendship for Charles. James was overjoyed and the two young men became companions and allies.

The curious love of the old king for the handsome young man took a new turn. James called Buckingham 'Steenie' because he looked like a picture of Saint Stephen. For years James had doted on Steenie and his family, writing to him as 'Only sweet and dear child', 'sweet heart', 'Sweet Steenie gossip', and 'Sweet child and wife'. James had been quixotic with his son, sometimes affectionate but often sarcastic, but as he aged, he became increasingly sentimental. Once the heir and the favourite were friends, he doted on them together and referred to the prince as 'Baby Charles'.

It was Buckingham who conceived the crazy notion of going to Spain to claim the Infanta in person. Buckingham was Lord Admiral and in that role he would accompany Prince Charles to claim his bride. Charles was twenty-three and trained for kingship, so he should have seen the perils of this adventure, but his father had sailed to Denmark in a storm to claim Anne for his wife so the journey seemed romantic, despite the marriage negotiations having stalled for so long and remaining unfinished. James informed his diplomat Cottington that 'Baby Charles and Steenie have a great mind to go by post to Spain to fetch home the Infanta'. They would travel incognito. What did he think? Cottington was aghast.[5]

They went. After a great reception in Madrid, they were kept at some distance as marriage negotiations dragged on. Charles hardly saw the Infanta and when he climbed into her garden she ran away screaming. The Spanish were polite, not knowing how to proceed. They were not keen on the marriage, but Charles was heir to three kingdoms. After several

Francis, Lord Cottington.

months James feared that his son was somehow captive. He wrote fussing letters: 'Alas! Sweethearts, as long as I want the sweet comfort of my boys' conversation, I am forced, yea, and delight to converse with them by long letters. God bless you both, my sweet boys, and send you, after a successful journey, a joyful happy return in the arms of your dear da.' He said he wore Steenie's picture 'next my heart'. To Charles he wrote, 'My sweet Baby, for God's sake, and your dad's, put not yourself in hazard by any violent exercise.'[6]

Buckingham grew impatient, but the religious demands of the Spanish increased. Charles had begun the adventure in the mood to fall in love, but by high summer even he was aware that the Spanish would never help his sister Elizabeth regain her position in the Palatinate and that impediments to his marriage were growing, not receding. He was being strung along.

In England there was grave disquiet. The heir to the throne was in Madrid at the mercy of the King of Spain when much of the political nation was all for fighting the Spaniards. The prince was accompanied by that peacock Buckingham, on whom the king showered largesse and who interfered in every state policy like an arrogant fool. They were demeaning themselves, making England an object of fun. James may have kept the peace and saved England from the terrible cost of war, but England was becoming weak, the pawn of Spain.

In the last reign, Englishmen had fought in the Low Countries to free its people from the claws of Catholic Spain. Now the royal prince was cavorting about in Madrid while the Netherlands emerged as a powerful nation. England had been its mentor but now the Dutch were outstripping England in commerce and trade. Ships from the Netherlands had viciously attacked English vessels in the East Indies; in fact the Netherlands had a trading fleet which rivalled if not outshone England's. They were expanding their trade with the backing of their great finance houses. Their books balanced too; they had a trade surplus. The Netherlands was streaking out ahead, right under the noses of the City of London. What had happened to the great days of Elizabeth, when English seamen had no rivals in daring and skill? What indeed.

At last Charles saw that the betrothal was a sham and set out for the Spanish coast. In Santander an English squadron collected the knights errant and delivered them to Portsmouth. They were welcomed back with rejoicing; bells were rung and tables spread in the streets of London. Safely home, the boys gladdened the king's heart. The three of them shut themselves up in James's chamber for hours while those outside heard gales of laughter and merry voices. But Buckingham had turned against Spain and so, gradually, Charles did too. James was prevaricating, but the tide had turned and as James's health deteriorated, so the young men became ascendant. When a parliament was called James addressed it, but Charles and Buckingham dominated its business. At their instigation, the Commons impeached Lionel Cranfield, the Treasurer. Then King James did rouse himself: 'By God Steenie, you are a fool,' he told the duke, warning the two young men that they might make themselves popular now but live to see popular opinion turn against them.[7]

The proposed Spanish marriage had had several purposes, so the return of the young men without the Infanta was a personal and political reverse. James had hoped for an alliance with Spain to recover the Palatinate for Frederick, a consort of the first rank for his son and a splendid dowry to augment his finances. He still hoped for a Spanish marriage, but Buckingham has turned against Spain and Charles felt jilted. Buckingham began to talk of war against Spain and a French marriage. James pointed out that all the great European monarchs were Catholic and would demand concessions in a marriage treaty. The three kingdoms deserved a premier princess but they were not Protestant. Buckingham was all for war with Spain and an alliance with France, its competitor. Charles vacillated but having been spurned as a lover, his deference to his father weakened and the influence of the duke won.

James was old and unwell; power was slipping away from the king to his son and favourite. They were able to override the king's policy, open negotiations for a French marriage and start building an alliance against Spain. The Spanish ambassador worked hard to poison the king's mind against Buckingham but late in 1624 James wrote inviting Steenie to Windsor at Christmas, 'as I desire only to live in this world for your sake, and that I had rather live banished in any part of the world with you, than live a sorrowful widow-life without you. And so God bless you, my sweet child and wife, and grant that ye may ever be a comfort to your dear dad and husband.'[8]

In December, a marriage contract was signed by which Charles was to marry the youngest daughter of the late King Henri IV of France. Undertakings about the Palatinate were vague. While the princess was allowed a Catholic chapel and priests, her family were to choose her household and her children were to be brought up by their mother until they were twelve. A secret codicil was also signed giving the utmost tolerance to English Catholics. Church bells were rung and Londoners given free wine and beer, but there was little enthusiasm in England for the marriage.

James died in one of his country houses at the end of March 1625. Charles was proclaimed king in London, Dublin and Edinburgh. Parliaments were generally called for a new reign, but in this case it was urgent because Charles wanted to raise money to go to war against Spain. The new king's finances were poor. His father had left large debts and even if many of those went unpaid, the crown still faced problems with funding. None of the three kingdoms were solvent, so mounting a war would be a challenge.

In England, or at least in London, the mood was for war. In Dublin however, feelings were different. The Lord Lieutenant heard reports that prayers were being said for 'our King Philip', as Catholics hoped for succour from the Spanish monarch. It became clear that if the crown planned war with Spain, it must first secure Ireland. The Lord Lieutenant knew that rebellion within might be supported by external attack; Ireland was vulnerable to Spanish forces. But many Irish Catholics were keen to prove their loyalty, especially the Old English who wanted to shore up their waning position. Here was an opportunity for the young king to cement that loyalty and make a new settlement with his Irish subjects.

8

The New Reign

When Charles became king, neither his people nor the courtiers knew much about him. He had become a healthy young man but he was small and slender. By vigorous exercise he had strengthened his legs and he stood well, but he spoke little; one ambassador surmised that he was either clever and circumspect, or else not very bright. Actually, Charles had a bad stammer, so he made short speeches, unlike his father who enjoyed speaking at length. As soon as he became king, Charles cleared up the court, removing crowds of supplicants and hangers-on, reinstating etiquette and keeping strict times for meals and prayers which he attended conscientiously. The drinking and swearing had to stop. Charles retained his father's ministers but created a new committee for foreign affairs. Buckingham was his close confidante and representative, a member of his council and his principal adviser.

Important decisions had already been taken. Charles was to marry a French princess; the negotiations had been hastily concluded before James I died and a marriage treaty signed the previous December. James had argued against concessions to Catholics, which were put in a separate document. Charles was impatient, and the Privy Council consented to the marriage treaty although parliament had not been consulted.

Charles was to marry the youngest child of the late King Henri IV. Henrietta-Maria's father had been a dynamic character with a great love for women. The first Bourbon king, he had changed his Huguenot religion for Catholicism to please the French when he ascended the throne. But Henri had been assassinated when the princess was a baby, and her brother was now Louis XIII of France. Cardinal Richelieu had recently become the young king's minister and would set French policy regarding Spain and the war within the Empire.

Henrietta-Maria was fifteen when she married. She was young and she was small; Charles was around 5 feet 4 inches tall, but his bride only came up to his shoulder. She was a vivacious brunette with a quick temper. The marriage was made by proxy and Buckingham was sent to Paris to fetch the bride, using the visit to press France into an anti-Habsburg alliance – but Richelieu resisted, unwilling to commit when there was danger of a Huguenot revolt. Henrietta-Maria was escorted north by her family and attendants to board an English ship. Now styled Queen of England, she would turn out to be one of the feistiest little creatures to take that title. She had her father's courage, which she would later need, but she could speak almost no English. She had been taught royal dignity and etiquette, lectured at length on her role as the patron of Catholicism in heretic England, but of statecraft, diplomacy and English history she knew nothing.

Charles met her in Dover when she arrived in June 1625. They attempted to get to know each other as he escorted her first to Canterbury, where they were married, and then to London. Both as king and as a husband, Charles had little concept of negotiation; he expected to be obeyed. Trouble started almost at once when Buckingham pushed his sister into the queen's carriage and tried to relegate her French attendants. In these small acts, political issues were at stake. The new queen's attendants were French Catholics, which would become a matter for dispute, but it was essentially an issue of protocol that might reflect on relations with Louis of France; for Buckingham it was a chance to promote his relatives.

The queen was a daughter of France, one of Europe's premier powers – the match was impeccable regarding status – but in England her religion was immediately a problem. In his religious practice, Charles was serious and genuine – as he often was not in politics. As a king, he would increasingly be thought insincere, but his Protestant faith was profound. In religion, Buckingham had less influence, whereas Henrietta-Maria knew that guarantees to English Catholics had been included with her marriage treaty and that she was their champion. Charles also had to contend with highly charged public opinion. The men who were elected to the Commons were not just Protestant, but often strongly Calvinist; to them, any tolerance of Catholicism risked backsliding to a state of political servitude and moral degeneracy. They believed the papacy was corrupt and infected with evil, that national self-determination went hand in hand with the moral urgency of the Reformed faith.

So Charles was caught in a bind. If he honoured his marriage treaty, his ministers and parliament would be implacably opposed. If he did as parliament demanded and penalised the Catholics, he would break his undertaking to the French king. His Scottish subjects were, if anything, more Calvinist than the English, but they at least were far away, whereas Londoners could see the priests who said Mass at court. His Irish subjects, however, were overwhelmingly Catholic – although implanted Protestants and packed parliaments curtailed their power. The tensions within his kingdoms were difficult enough, but meanwhile Charles had undertaken to involve himself in an escalating European war. To pick his way through this mesh of competing interests would take great skill. His father's ministers were experienced, but Buckingham, who had the king's ear, was young, inexperienced and very confident.

The queen was only fifteen but she was full of opinions and warm emotions which she was quick to express. 'The Queen,' a courtier commented, 'howsoever little of stature, is of spirit and vigour, and seems of more than ordinary resolution. With one frown, divers of us being at Whitehall to see her, being at dinner, and the room somewhat overheated with the fire and company, she drove us all out of the chamber. I suppose none but a Queen could have cast such a scowl.'[1]

Apart from his new consort, Charles had much to address. Henrietta-Maria arrived on 12 June, and on 18 June his first parliament met. Charles needed large sums of money for the war. James had tried to limit his involvement, hoping an alliance with Spain would reinstate Frederick, but eventually he agreed to fund an expedition under Mansfeld. After their journey to Madrid, Charles and Buckingham knew that Frederick could expect no help from Spain and their policy shifted to war. The English elite were keen to contest Spanish and Habsburg power and Charles was determined to support his sister's cause. However, war with Spain might endanger Ireland; his ministers in Dublin said they needed £3,000 a month to defend the island.[2] The costs would be high and would require strong parliamentary support.

Mansfeld's expedition quickly fell foul of inadequate funds and aims. As Charles came to power, the Bohemian crisis was escalating into a much wider conflict. King Christian of Denmark, Charles's cousin, had entered the war to reinstate Frederick in the Palatinate and Charles promised him a monthly sum in support. The Protestant states were alarmed by the growing power of the Habsburgs in Austria and Spain, with their restrictive Catholicism. France, too, might challenge Habsburg power yet Richelieu remained ambivalent. However, the Dutch policy was clear: having fought Spain for independence, they were now at war with them in Flanders and at sea. In June, the city of Breda fell. Tensions were rising. A general contest with Habsburg power was joined to the religious struggle.

When parliament assembled in London in June 1625, it was well attended. Members wanted to see and hear from the new king; they expected to be informed about the fleet which was being assembled in Plymouth and about military plans to retake the Palatinate. Charles spoke only briefly, but this was probably a relief to the members who remembered the long speeches of the late king. However, neither Charles nor his ministers made clear his actual war policy, nor what it might cost. If strategy was unclear in Charles's mind, the funds he had promised were known to his ministers but not made clear to parliament. For the members, this was an early glimpse of Charles's defects as a ruler. Either he saw no need to explain himself or was not capable of doing so, nor of persuading people to agree with his aims; he thought it was sufficient to merely state his requirements. So, when the Commons spent its time complaining about religious laxity, voted only a tiny subsidy in comparison to his financial needs and began to openly criticise Buckingham, Charles simply dissolved parliament.

Henrietta-Maria had brought with her an entourage of attendants including her priests. Charles's mother had been a practising Catholic in a modest way, but a French queen with priests saying Mass to a large French household at Whitehall produced a different spectacle to the worried courtiers. Other people began to attend – some were French visitors, but English Catholics also came to the queen's chapel in growing numbers. There was grave disquiet among the ministers and Charles was critical of his little queen, expecting her to practise her religion quietly and privately.

Increasingly they fought. Henrietta-Maria's dowry had brought useful cash but issues such as management of her dower lands and household, and the selection of her attendants and managers, led to acrimonious quarrels. Charles complained to Buckingham that he was not master in his own household, so the duke appointed himself as marriage councillor and advised, or sometimes threatened, the queen. She answered him pertly and said she was sure the king had nothing to complain of and that she and Buckingham might be friends, but she continually resisted having all his female relations in her apartments.

Meanwhile, the war in Europe was going badly. Mansfeld's troops, yet to be paid, became ill and began to desert. English people knew that their princess and her children were exiles in The Hague. Britain had troops overseas, but what was government policy?

Struggling for funds in England, Charles saw an opportunity to improve funding in Scotland. Up to the age of twenty-five, Scottish kings had a right to revoke gifts made during their minority. In October, Charles used his Scottish Privy Council to make an Act of Revocation. By bending the rules, Charles revoked all land grants made since 1540, which included all the church property granted away at the Reformation. It was an enormous amount of land and the owners were shocked. Charles probably meant to leave ownership intact while extracting money, but that was not made clear to the owners. Nor was a full parliament called, only a Convention of Estates. It was sufficiently docile to grant some tax but complained about government policy. A commission was set up and after several years an agreement was reached whereby owners paid to hold their land and tithes. The crown improved its funding, and the kirk received more revenue – although, to the disappointment of its members, not as much as promised. By clumsiness, Charles had alienated many of the nobility and landowners.

In Ireland, his government made promises which were never kept and which had much graver consequences. When war with Spain threatened, the Old English Catholics had been refused the right to form a defence militia as the New English did not trust them with arms. To protect from Spanish fleets, the Irish army would have to be expanded but that would mean greater English subventions. So, a deal was negotiated whereby the Irish would pay subsidies in return for 'matters of grace and bounty'. The most important of these were in religion and land rights – the right for Catholics to worship without penalties and to receive security of land titles; there would be no more 'discoveries' of defective title. A formal parliament was not called but property owners began to pay the subsidies in good faith, in return for these 'Graces'.[3] In fact, the Graces were never granted.

Charles was making enemies by poor handling of political processes, by breaking promises and by promising contradictory policies to opposing sides. He promised his English parliament that he would enforce the laws against Catholics, but he had sworn to Louis of France that he would remove them. He had raised a fleet and promised the Dutch and Danes funding and ships, but he had no money. His most galling and personal failure was with his wife, who was the least docile or obedient creature he had encountered.

In September 1625, the English fleet sailed out from Plymouth to attack Cadiz. Buckingham as Admiral of the Fleet had appointed the commanders but made bad choices. Lacking supplies and a clear strategy, the expedition failed in all its aims. Throughout the winter, its ships limped back to England in disarray.

Money was a pressing issue. Charles called a second parliament in 1626, but it was no more successful. In the first, members had been tentative about criticising a minister; in the second, the Commons directly challenged Buckingham, who was not only Charles's minister but his personal emissary and dearest friend. Once the attack began, all their latent resentment came out – at his freedom to advise the king, his swerves of policy and his enormous wealth. They voted to impeach Buckingham. When the trial opened, Charles stood beside his friend; but two days later he lost patience and had two of the duke's leading opponents arrested. The Commons began to draw up a general remonstrance, a form of complaint which was to become all too frequent in the coming years. Charles desperately needed subsidies, and he demanded them. But his authority was weakening, and to prevent the Commons pressing their charge against the duke, the king dissolved his second parliament.

Charles's relationship with his wife had not improved – if anything it was deteriorating – and he felt the only way to get control of the situation was to remove her extensive French entourage who supported all her wilful exploits, such as interrupting Anglican services, refusing to attend the coronation on religious grounds and visiting Tyburn to commemorate the Catholic martyrs whom the English regarded as dangerous rebels. Charles reckoned that once the French household had gone, Henrietta-Maria would be under different influences and would have to listen to him and to the ladies he chose to attend her.

So after dinner one evening in July 1626, he escorted his queen to her apartment, locked her in and told her that her French retinue would have to leave. Outside, according to his orders, his minister was sending the French entourage away. Charles had not bargained on the queen's reaction. She ran to the window, smashed the glass and shouted to her ladies below. Charles had to drag her away while she clung ferociously to the window bars, cutting her hands. The 'Messieurs' were eventually sent back to France, but a few ladies were allowed to remain with the furious young queen.

This in itself was not enough to alter the marriage. Rather it was the destiny of the Duke of Buckingham which caused a change. Buckingham was a self-confident man and, although his strategies generally resulted in failure, he was undeterred. Charles was not without capable ministers: Richard Weston, the Lord Treasurer; John Williams, Archbishop of York; Henry Cary, Lord Falkland, Lord Deputy in Ireland; and later John Stewart, Earl of Traquair, in Scotland. None were outstanding but all had abilities which Charles could and did use. But Buckingham could influence the king as no one else could and, as Admiral of the Fleet and a member of the council for foreign relations, he had gained control of the war.

None of Charles's kingdoms had sufficient funding for its own government, but the economy of all three countries was growing; with careful management, far more could be achieved. The Netherlands proved that – a smaller country with fewer resources developing quickly with a well-funded government. Inefficiency was obvious – much of Scotland's revenue was spent on pensions. In Ireland, the great Catholic landowners were increasingly alienated from the crown. In England, Charles was at odds with MPs, who represented the country's wealth. In order to prosper, it was essential that the crown establish good relations with the elites of all three kingdoms.

Charles, however, already had a funding crisis. His first parliament, ignoring convention, had only awarded tonnage and poundage for one year; when that was up his officers just continued to collect it. When he asked for subsidies, he was rebuffed by parliament. He had raised some money in the City of London but when he applied to the Corporation for a loan they refused him. Then he attempted to raise loans from taxpayers by compulsion. There was a precedent for this; forced loans had been raised before under privy seals, and Charles, who had made great promises to the King of Denmark and others, was swayed by his advisers into trying the same method. In fact, they went much further and attempted to collect the equivalent of five subsidies. Charles issued a letter to all the dioceses, explaining that he had followed the counsels of parliament by prosecuting the war against the Habsburgs and that he must meet his war commitments. He wrote that we 'cannot now be left in that business but with the sin and shame of all men'; it was his duty to defend the realm, but parliament had left him unable to do so.

The Forced Loan was collected successfully at first, but resistance grew. By the end of 1626 several people had been imprisoned for refusal to pay. Then the judges refused to sign papers which declared the loan legal. Early in 1627, men were sent out to the shire counties to collect the funds. Although most people paid, those who refused were often men of standing and their resistance could hardly be overlooked, as poorer men were starting to follow the example. At the same time, the problems of war were physically present as unpaid soldiers wandered the countryside, alarming the local people. There was resistance to impressment and men were threatened with hanging, although the threat was not carried out.

Resistance to the Forced Loan has often been cited as the beginning of real opposition to Charles's government. John Hampden distinguished himself by being imprisoned for his refusal to pay, as did Sir John Eliot and many others. Sir Thomas Wentworth of Yorkshire also refused and was imprisoned. However, most people did pay and a quarter of a million pounds was raised for the war effort. But the campaigns were badly executed and the aims were either unclear or considered ill-advised. Charles, who had determined to fight Spain, now became engaged in an escalating dispute with France. Yet, within England, resistance to crown policy grew.

Relations with France were breaking down over the Huguenots. The Protestants of La Rochelle had gained considerable autonomy but France had recently regained control of the area. Henri IV's policy, and subsequently that of Richelieu, was for toleration, but increasingly confrontation was brewing. In 1626, France offered England a treaty to aid the war against Germany, but Charles quibbled over the terms. Instead, he set himself up as guardian of the Huguenots and by 1627 England was at war with France, sending a fleet to La Rochelle. This time the Duke of Buckingham was not only commander but on board. The troops landed on the Isle de Re, but after besieging the main city, the English were beaten off with heavy casualties. The remains of the expedition retreated back to Plymouth and Portsmouth.

The demands of the war and Charles's resolution to carry on with it drove him back to parliament early in 1628. The men imprisoned for refusing to pay the Forced Loan were freed in early January, and parliament met on 17 March. By the time that this third parliament gathered, grievances had mounted. Apart from the conduct of the war and its funding, religion was a growing cause of complaint.

During the first two years of Charles's reign, there was a distinct change in religious policy. Because it emerged as a core grievance – Oliver Cromwell considered religion the underlying and most important issue – historians have given Charles's religious policy considerable attention. Single epithets like Puritan or Arminian were often used, and still are; they are useful but can be inaccurate or simply terms of abuse. Many Calvinists resented being called 'Puritan', whereas they denigrated others by calling them 'Arminian', suggesting they leaned towards Catholicism.

Several issues were bound into the struggle over religion: pure theology, the mores of society and the government's policies for church management. From his accession in 1625, Charles increasingly diverged from the way his father managed the church in each kingdom. It seems abstract now, but predestination was a core belief and a cause of conflict – the concept that an individual's fate was predestined at birth, either for redemption or damnation. True Calvinists believed in predestination but the theology was complex and there were schools of thought which parsed and multiplied an already difficult subject. King James thought it better not to discuss predestination and discouraged the subject. Milton, for example, who increasingly asserted his Calvinist vision, did not hold with the doctrine, but most Calvinists did and for them it was crucial – for only the 'elect' were predestined to be saved.

An individual could not strive for election – it was known only to God – but many Puritans experienced a spiritual crisis, during which they came close to God and recognised election in themselves. The elect distinguished themselves by the way they lived, constantly aware of God's presence, striving to know his will and to live in a godly state, but this took considerable spiritual drive. Conversion experiences were clearly intense and Puritan services used prayer and preaching to maintain a state of godly inspiration. Puritans relied on extempore preaching, something which James had permitted but which Charles, like Elizabeth before him, thought disruptive or even seditious.

Arminianism – the theology of Jacob Arminius of Leiden – did offer an antidote to the stricter ideas of Calvin and was therefore attractive to some English people who held milder religious views. There was naturally a spread of opinion, among both clergy and laity – theology was keenly debated.

Apart from theology, governance of the church raised other issues. The king was head of the churches of England and Ireland by statute, but in Scotland the Reformation had left an ambiguous concept of the 'Twa Kingdoms': church and state. James thought it essential to have authority over all three churches and prevented a separate Presbyterian hierarchy getting control in Scotland by inserting bishops who were answerable to him. Charles, too, was determined to set church policy but it quickly became clear that his methods and his taste in church government were different to those of his father.

The internal layout and furniture of the churches, as well as the services held within them, could hardly have been more emotive. This was the place where men and women entered a sacred space to join in prayer and strive to meet their god. The choice of clergy was crucial. James had grown up in Scotland and his essentially Calvinist views were reflected in his choice of bishops and archbishops. His policy had been inclusive – the acceptance of a preaching ministry left English Calvinists comfortable in the Jacobean church – but he moderated the Presbyterian system to keep control in Scotland. This alienated the most radical elements, and managed to create a broad and accommodating church.

Charles had a different upbringing and outlook. Like his father, he was a serious Protestant who saw his role as defending the reformed churches of the three kingdoms. Also like his father, he saw the Elizabethan church settlement as the right one, close to the purity of the early church but with forms which maintained 'holy order'. He listened attentively to sermons, was devout during prayers, and lived a seemly life in contrast with his father. Charles was influenced by Lancelot Andrewes, who was opposed to the Calvinists and took an earlier reading of predestination, derived from the church fathers, which emphasised God's foreknowledge of how humans would respond to the gift of faith but gave more hope of salvation. Charles thought Calvinists were troublemakers and against authority, while the Dutch Arminians seemed too popish to the king.[4] William Laud, who was a protégé of Buckingham and became Dean of the Chapel Royal in 1626, thought that predestination was a dangerous concept which undermined people's belief in salvation through Jesus. The recent Synod of Dort had settled Calvinist doctrine, but it seemed possible for Charles's clergy to uphold both Dort and the principles of the Church of England if they were careful. This, however, was not how Charles proceeded.

For Calvinists, individual salvation was not the only concern; there was also the redemption of the nation. Society as a whole must throw off its sin and become godly. At a time when the second coming was openly discussed, this became more urgent. For Puritans, the religious state of society posed both a practical threat, as Catholicism might creep back in, but also an urgent spiritual challenge as the nation's bond with Christ might be put in jeopardy.

In the physical forms of the church, the king created disquiet. Charles wanted order, obedience and seemliness in his church. He had a deep regard for the forms of the Elizabethan church with its altar, candles and surplices, but without ornamentation. Charles thought that an ordered service led to deeper religious experience. At Gloucester, Laud had moved the communion table to the east end and railed it in – an act considered far too ritualistic for Puritan taste. The king's position became clear from his appointments; the Calvinist clergy were overlooked for the senior positions and the stricter Protestants became alarmed. This move towards ritual and away from Calvinist doctrine alienated milder Puritans, chipping away at the broad support that James's church policies had enjoyed.

The first two parliaments of the reign complained of religious laxity, but the one that gathered in 1628 was more immediately concerned with law and the conduct of war. In it, Sir John Eliot of Cornwall, who had been an outspoken critic of crown policy in the previous sessions, complained that the king's methods were undermining the ancient laws and liberties of England. 'Upon this dispute not alone our lands and goods are engaged, but all that we call ours. These rights, these privileges, which made our fathers freemen, are in question.'[5] Eliot warned that the body of law so carefully built up in England over centuries was being put in jeopardy.

It was a stirring speech, but in this parliament Eliot was overshadowed by that hard-headed young Yorkshireman Sir Thomas Wentworth. It was the business of parliament, said Wentworth, to produce union between the king and his people. The illegal actions bemoaned by MPs were the result of bad counsel. Eliot wanted a full discussion of religion and the constitution, whereas Wentworth was concerned solely with bad governance and how it should be remedied.[6]

This parliament drew up a Bill of Rights which was mainly concerned with the war. It originated in a demand by Wentworth for an end to war-related abuses: illegal imprisonment, compulsory employment abroad, forced loans and billeting of soldiers on households without the assent of the householder. Since foreign policy and war were in the king's remit, attempts by parliament to control these issues were significant. Naturally Charles resisted. The issues recited in the Bill of Rights fell within his prerogative and were not the competence of the Commons, and Charles saw his prerogative as part of his inherited role, as gifted by God and not to be bargained away. Despite the Commons' offer of five subsidies, Charles continued to resist. Sir Edward Coke, who introduced the bill, held that the royal prerogative was granted by law and could be defined by law. Charles would not compromise and deadlock was looming, so Coke changed the form of the demand but not the substance. It became a Petition of Right to the king on behalf of all his subjects: against taxes and loans not agreed by parliament, against imprisonment without trial and against the compulsory billeting of troops. They also added a ban on martial law within the realm of England, but it had become a request rather than a bill. The Lords supported the Commons, giving the petition more force, but still Charles gave evasive answers. The Commons responded by drafting a Remonstrance. It complained of innovations in government and religion – such as Arminianism – and John Pym added the threat of the Irish, their Catholicism and their positions in the army, both as officers and troops.[7] Buckingham was severely criticised.

Charles could continue to resist, but the Commons would not vote him funds if he did. He decided to give way. His assent to the Petition of Right gave it the force of statute. There was rejoicing, church bells were rung in the City of London and crowds gathered around bonfires to celebrate. However, the king's agreement did not halt the Remonstrance, nor the complaints against Buckingham. In June 1628, Charles prorogued parliament.

Wentworth's impressive showing had been noted, and he was thereafter kept under consideration for government service. His challenges to the king had been limited to practical concerns, whereas many in the Commons such as Coke and Eliot had wider grievances about religion and the nature of the constitution.

As the Commons session ended, the career of William Laud took a great leap forward. Laud was an academic whose career until then had centered on Oxford. He was an energetic cleric with strong administrative abilities, but King James had considered him a 'restless spirit', and confined him to a Welsh bishopric, whereas Charles promoted him swiftly. Despite Laud's reputation as an Arminian, Charles had asked him to preach at the opening of parliament in 1626, which was provocative at a time when the Commons were constantly complaining about 'innovations' in religion. Now Laud was made Bishop of London.

In the Netherlands, Calvinists and Arminians were locked in a bitter struggle that was not only theological but reflected a deep political divide; the two sects took different sides over the conduct of the war. In England, Calvinists saw Arminian teaching as a slide towards the theology of Rome. Debate over the war was highly charged, for Elizabeth of Bohemia had shown her courage and was a Protestant figurehead; the failure to restore her and Frederick to the Palatinate was considered a national disgrace.

Charles, however, recognised that England's participation in the war would have to end. He had failed to supply King Christian of Denmark, who spoke bitterly about him. There was mutinous action among the fleet at Portsmouth and ill feeling in parliament. The subsidies that parliament had just granted would in no way meet the promises Charles had made to his allies.

Politically, it was a difficult time for the young king. In three years, the quarrel over the constitution had widened to become bitter and entrenched as it never had been in his father's lifetime. In government he was embattled, but a sudden tragedy transformed his personal life.

Charles and Henrietta-Maria had been living largely apart, although she appeared frequently at court and was learning English as fast as she could. The young couple had yet to come to an understanding. Then, one morning in August 1628, the Duke of Buckingham was attacked. He had been breakfasting at Captain Norton's house in Portsmouth and was coming downstairs with his attendants when he was set upon by an embittered sailor named Felton who stabbed him with a cheap knife. The duke bled profusely and died almost immediately. The assassin was arrested and the Privy Council tried to have him interrogated under torture, but the judges prevented that and Felton was promptly hanged. It was said that his motive was lack of promotion, but his action was widely celebrated nonetheless.

Charles was devastated and withdrew into his private chambers. When Henrietta-Maria heard the news she hurried to the king to comfort him and then to the duke's widow to console her. Henrietta-Maria was warm-hearted, responsive and affectionate. If Charles had previously suffered from her temper, he now responded to her sympathy. It was the moment at which the marriage changed from one of competitive misunderstanding to a deep and lasting bond. The queen was now seventeen and could speak her husband's language more fluently. Without the duke to dominate the king's attention and mould his attitudes, there was a space for Henrietta-Maria to come close. Charles mourned his friend, at first with withdrawal and self-control, then with frantic activity. In the country, there was popular rejoicing at Buckingham's death and this wounded the king deeply. He saw Buckingham as a national treasure, while the people blamed him for a series of humiliating military adventures. Charles was doubly grieved, but the natural warmth of the little French queen was comforting for the aloof and introverted king.

Henrietta-Maria's first child was born the following spring but was premature and did not survive. However, a year later, in May 1630, she gave birth to a baby boy. Prince Charles was the first heir to the throne born in England for almost a century and was a large, lusty child. Bells were rung and bonfires lit, while his father gave thanks at St Paul's Cathedral. But strict Protestants worried about the influence the queen might have on her son. After all, the king's sister, the highly popular Elizabeth of Bohemia, had many fine sons growing up as Protestants, albeit in exile in The Hague.

But Charles and Henrietta-Maria were more than man and wife; they were in love, and had great need of each other. She was in a foreign land and he was a solitary figure whose emotional life had been austere in childhood, odd in his father's day and then dominated by Buckingham. To discover marital rapport was a great blessing, and for a decade the king and queen enjoyed unusual happiness as Henrietta-Maria gave birth to a growing family of royal children.

The death of Buckingham left a vacuum in political life and many posts vacant. Treasurer Lord Weston was now able to extend his influence. It was Weston who persuaded the king to promote Sir Thomas Wentworth, who was made President of the Council of the North. No accord was reached with parliament, however. It was prorogued at the time of Buckingham's death, but when it reassembled in January 1629, despite the king's efforts at cooperation, the earlier disagreements resurfaced. High on the list of complaints was religion: toleration of papists and suspicion of Arminians.

The imprisonment of one member for non-payment of tax helped to inflame the debate on tonnage and poundage; members should enjoy freedom of debate and parliamentary privilege from prosecution. Charles adjourned the parliament, leaving members hanging about in London at their own expense, and when a further adjournment was announced this was seen as the last straw. Several members restrained the Speaker in his chair to prevent him ending the session, then locked the door and hid the key. That evening Charles had the leaders of the parliamentary opposition arrested, enforcing his reputation as a monarch who did not respect the rights and privileges of parliament. Charles thought the rancour and withholding of taxes the work of conspirators, and in the back of his mind he blamed them for the death of his beloved Buckingham. To regain order, Charles had nine members arrested, published a long explanation of his disagreement with the Commons and once more dissolved parliament.

The imprisonment and mistreatment of MPs was becoming a recurrent theme. When Sir John Eliot of Cornwall died in the Tower three years later, Charles prevented his body being taken home for burial in an act of spite whose corrosive effect he did not perceive. To Charles, people who blocked or disobeyed him were unsound in mind or illegal in intent. Three parliaments in four years had worn him out, so he found ways to do without them. He would not call another for twelve years.

Without that vital point of contact, Charles heard very little from his people. His ministers reported to him, but the shires and boroughs sent no representatives. English monarchs never went to Ireland, although Irish deputations occasionally came to court. However, the king did see that, as a Stuart, he must be crowned in Scotland.

9

The Political Nation

The members of parliament left London in 1629 in ill humour. Many had sat in all three parliaments of the reign but neither the king nor the Commons were satisfied with the results. The first meeting had been held in summer when gentlemen had much to attend to on their estates. Sessions has been adjourned and prorogued while members lingered in London, paying for lodgings and fearful of the plague, until they moved to Oxford with more fuss over rooms. The two parliaments which followed had been acrimonious. Now the Duke of Buckingham was dead, and England's part in the war was coming to a futile end. To the king and his ministers was left the dismal task of negotiating peace treaties with France and Spain. It was true that the Petition of Right had been accepted, but no agreement had been reached over tax or religion. Some members were satisfied, but many were aggrieved over religious policy. The new Bishop of London was William Laud, a man who belonged to the anti-Calvinist faction and who had earned the disapproval of George Abbot, Archbishop of York. At court, Laud had preached that the king's power came from God and the parliament's power from the king – views calculated to inflame MPs.[1] Laud was active in efforts to curb enclosure of land, railing against depopulation when villagers were forced to move as they lost access to land; this pressure also went down badly with the landowning House of Commons. Enclosure facilitated improved farming methods and was thought to increase national wealth, so in opposing it Laud seemed to be blocking progress.[2] In religion, too, the members thought he harked back to the Catholic past. There was divergence of religious views in the house but Puritan members were vocal and highly motivated. There was also a strong Presbyterian strain of thought. The gentlemen left London as spring came, but with no feeling of resolution.

Their journeys home were long, especially for men who came down from Northumberland or across from North Wales. Cornwall, as a mining county, had a large contingent who clattered down the long highway, although Sir John Eliot did not return to St Germans but died in the Tower. Members, keenly aware of their rights and now full of grievances, must have stopped at the inns and country houses on their way home and grumbled about proceedings in London.

These were men of property, sent to the Commons by elections which varied from one constituency to another. All the county seats were elected by 40-shilling freeholders, which included various forms of tenancy, but the elections for the borough seats were not standardised. In some the franchise was wide; in others the seat was controlled by one property owner or agreed between a few.[3] The members took their projects and grievances to London, which was an occasion to meet and exchange views, make purchases for their wives and daughters, or transact business.

There had been arguments over election results under Queen Elizabeth, but confrontations with the monarch had recently become more serious. Several members had been arrested, which was an abuse of their rights of free speech. Tax had been collected without the sanction of parliament ever since the young king's accession, and the Forced Loan three years earlier had led to serious conflict and several imprisonments. This was not the way of English liberties – by George it was not.

Some members had an easier journey home than others. John Hampden, MP for Buckinghamshire, could ride back to Great Hampden in a day. He was the eldest son of a gentry family whose fortunes had declined. A committed Calvinist, Hampden had already come into conflict with the crown when he, his uncle and friends had refused to pay the Forced Loan and been imprisoned for nearly one year.

John Hampden had many friends and colleagues in parliament, many of whom shared business interests. All of them came from the fertile lowlands surrounding London and shared a Puritan faith, looking for greater rigour in the church, usually on the Calvinist model.

The Reformation had been a massive struggle, like a butterfly wrestling its way out of a chrysalis. Its leaders, whether the king in England or theologians in Scotland, had faced down powerful forces while convincing their own populations. The change reached through law and landownership to parish ritual and down into the deep interiors of the self. Hopes for salvation, personal conscience, the nature of right and wrong, all were utterly changed. But habit did its work. The people of the West Country, for example, who had rebelled when Henry VIII changed church services, were now some of the most stalwart defenders of the Church of England. But those hoping for greater change and a stronger moral reawakening feared backsliding. They knew well enough how hearts and minds could slip. If the rigour of Calvinism was not pursued, how long before the common people were back tying ribbons on saints' toes and dropping fetishes in holy wells? Puritans abhorred such habits and strove for a conscious and thoughtful relationship with God. Already there were changes in church services – rather than greater purity the new king seemed to favour Arminianism, which Puritans saw as the top of a slippery slope back to cardinals' robes, blind obedience to the Pope and the end of mental effort.

Since the Act of Uniformity made it compulsory to attend services using the Book of Common Prayer and outlawed other forms of service, Puritans chafed under a religious observance which lacked the inspiration and immediacy they craved. For them, the rituals of the service were empty compared to the intense experience achieved by prayer groups, the sense of God's close presence which study and exhortation produced.

Over the next decade, many people observed the changes in the English church and made bold decisions. The *Mayflower* emigrants had left as religious dissidents during James's reign, but the 1630s saw an increase in America-bound emigrants who had previously been content in Church of England congregations. Under Charles, forms of service changed and preaching was repressed. The church seemed to be diverging from its spiritual beliefs and many sold their property to take ship for the New World. The voyage and the strange continent posed a challenge but also offered opportunity, both commercial and religious. Puritans combined moral rigour with hard work and enterprise; in many colonial ventures these motives were inextricably linked.

In American settlement projects, there were opportunities both for settlers and investors; indeed, some men with capital took shares or options without taking ship themselves. Some Puritan grandees had interests in several colonial ventures on the American seaboard or the Caribbean islands, where plantations were created. John Hampden was not an investor in the Providence Island Company but many of his relatives and associates were. On this island off the coast of Nicaragua, the company planned not only plantation but to build up a godly community and to harass the Spanish on the nearby shipping routes.[4] The group, which formed soon after parliament ended in 1629, included many disaffected Puritans from both the Commons and the Lords. Among the shareholders were Viscount Saye and Sele, the Earl of Warwick, Lord Brooke, Sir Thomas Barrington, John Pym and Oliver St John. Hampden was related to several of them through the Cromwells.

Hampden's father had married into the Cromwell family, as had Sir Thomas Barrington and the young lawyer Oliver St John. The Cromwells had been successful under the Tudors, and although Thomas was executed by Henry VIII his cousins continued to prosper. Sir Oliver Cromwell, who inherited Hinchinbrook House in Huntingdonshire, was a courtier and entertained King James lavishly there, allowing the king to hunt his land

William Fiennes, Viscount Saye and Sele.

Robert Rich, Earl of Warwick.

James Graham, 1st Marquess of Montrose.

in the freest possible way. When Sir Oliver went bankrupt, he hoped that King James would buy Hinchinbrook, but he was disappointed. Instead, the Montagu family purchased the property and gained the parliamentary patronage.[5] Sir Oliver's brother had died by then, but his nephew Oliver was farming in a small way in the area. The Cromwells were no longer ascendant, although all of them retained land and the status of gentlemen. Nephew Oliver had been given a seat in parliament by the Montagus and sat in the meeting of 1628–9; he made only one speech, and it was not well received.

Oliver Cromwell's father had died when he was eighteen, leaving him with a widowed mother and six sisters to support. He had married three years later, in 1620, to Elizabeth Bourchier, who probably brought a good dowry to the marriage as her family were well-off London merchants with property in Kent. Cromwell knew the Bourchiers through his relatives the Hampdens. He was a very physical young man who skipped lessons in Cambridge to play sport. He farmed his own land but his property was modest. During the parliament of 1628–9 he was suffering from melancholy, which was severe enough for him to consult a London doctor several times. In the following years, supporting himself as a farmer in Cambridgeshire, Cromwell had a Puritan conversion experience which set him on his course among the godly communities of East Anglia, and also seemed to alleviate his depression. As a new MP, Cromwell had been unremarkable but his in-laws, cousins and their circle had been some of the most robust opponents of the king during the parliament.

Cromwell did not invest in the Providence Island Company, but he was among the parliamentary group from which the investors were drawn. One of the most active shareholders was brought into the Providence Island venture by friends from Oxford University. John Pym, from Somerset, had already made his mark in the Commons.

The Providence Island company was short-lived. The owners allowed the settlers profits but no share in land, the island could not defend itself against the Spanish and despite the early introduction of African slaves, whose number swiftly grew, the only cash crop was tobacco, which was not sufficiently profitable. The goals of the shareholders were both religious and economic, an effort to save England through alternative expansion in the Caribbean; but the settlers were dissatisfied and the colony was overrun by Spain in 1641.[6]

Almost all the young men in this group had been to university and most had trained in the law, although their family backgrounds were mixed – some old gentry, some businessmen or lawyers. If the intelligentsia start revolutions, these were the sort of men to watch. The majority of Providence Island shareholders were Cambridge men, where the university was more infused with the new theology than was Oxford. East Anglia emerged as the most Puritan part of England, due to trade links with Scandinavia and the Low Countries, but both universities had updated their curriculum and their governance as first Renaissance ideas, then the Reformation, transformed learning.[7] As a result, monarchs kept a close eye on the universities and appointed chancellors who would conform to the crown's policies. When Charles made Buckingham Chancellor of Cambridge University in 1626 and then William Laud Chancellor of Oxford in 1630, he provoked a great outcry. Both men supressed predestinarian teaching. Academics resented the intrusion and felt Arminian ideas lacked rigour or harked back to outdated Catholic concepts.

Perhaps the Providence Island group represents the social mobility as well as the growth of education which had occurred since the Tudors took power. Despite England's system of ranks, men from modest backgrounds could rise to high office, make fortunes or move into the nobility. Landowners still dominated, but lawyers, merchants and other professionals became more prominent as the economy grew. Puritanism, so influential in growing towns and among the professions, was linked to their greater political assertiveness.

In parliament, men with a variety of interests came together to tackle the issues of the day, trying always to argue their way to consensus. When parliament was dissolved in 1629, connections had been made and business done. However, it would be more than a decade before parliament met again.

John Hampden went home to Buckinghamshire, John Pym went to the West Country, and the members of the wealthy and titled Rich family – also Providence Island shareholders – had their principal estates in Essex. Oliver Cromwell returned to his widowed mother, wife and children in Ely. Others delayed in London.

Viscount Wentworth set out on the long journey to his native Yorkshire. An intense and vigorous man, Wentworth was thirty-six and had sat in parliament since 1614. A man of 'piercing judgement into things and persons', according to Clarendon, he had been imprisoned for refusing to pay the Forced Loan and his complaints had initiated the Petition of Right.[8] But Wentworth was ambitious and practical, not a constitutional theorist but a man of independent ideas who wanted a job in government. He had sat on the Council of the North for over a decade but hoped for more and was now promoted. His speeches in the 1628 parliament had been noted, and in December he was made a viscount and Lord President of the Council of the North. Many said derisively that he had abandoned his opposition to the crown when offered promotion, but Wentworth was no ideologue.[9] He had often spoken of the need to find consensus, which parliament and the king had to some extent achieved in the Petition of Right.

Wentworth's first wife had died young, to his great grief, but when he remarried in the year of Charles's accession, it was with a depth of love that his contemporaries remarked on. By 1629 he had a young family whom he longed to be with, and he now returned to Wentworth Woodhouse, the family estate in Yorkshire which he had inherited from his father. The Council of the North, like that of the South West and of Wales, was designed to bring order to the more distant regions of the English state. There Wentworth honed the skills that he would soon take to Ireland.

The English parliament had dissolved, its members dispersed, but the two central issues of tax and religious policy had not been resolved. Parliament had left Charles without sufficient funding for government, had denied the customary grant of tonnage and poundage. He had added his own answers before publishing the Petition of Right, positions parliament had rejected, so he was criticised for false propaganda. Charles also continued to promote anti-Calvinists in the church. The English political elite dispersed, fuming with unresolved contentions.

Scotland was in a different position. Some of its leading figures served the king in both Scotland and England. John Stewart, for example, made much longer and more frequent journeys than any English parliamentarian.

The Scottish Privy Council had been reconstructed early in the reign, giving prominence to the docile Archbishop Spottiswoode but demoting the judges. From 1629 Stewart, soon to be Earl of Traquair, was steadily promoted as chief financial officer of Scotland. As his name suggests he too was a Stewart, of Anglo-Norman descent like the king, with a family seat in the Borders. He was clever with money and rushed up and down between the court and Edinburgh. He improved Scottish crown finances, but his style was abrasive.

The Scottish gentry were in ill humour with the king. When they last saw him, he was an infant with weak legs, but since then their church had been tampered with by his father, while Charles had begun his reign by contesting many of their land titles. The Revocation had led to a commission, hearings and arguments. Title deeds had been produced and pored over, lawyers hired, and at the end of it landowners had kept most of their property but had been forced to buy back some of their rights to it. It had been worrying and expensive.

Like England, Scotland was developing economically but from a much lower base and in different ways. In Scotland, education was a central concern. There were four universities in the northern kingdom to England's two and although students often had to take a final year in Europe to reach degree level, this was indicative of the nation's dedication to learning. After the Reformation, it was decided to create a school in every Scottish village; this failed through lack of funds, but the kirk was determined on a literate nation, godly and educated. Scottish universities produced lawyers and theologians who strengthened the kirk and gave Scottish cities a vocal group of professional men with sharp intellectual confidence.

Some Scottish nobles and courtiers had come to the English court with the Stuart kings. In 1629 the young Marquis of Hamilton was also on his way back to Scotland. He had a seat in the English House of Lords, but when parliament was dismissed he returned to Scotland, before leading the last effort by Charles's government to reinstate Frederick and Elizabeth in the Palatinate. Hamilton agreed with Gustavus Adolphus of Sweden to take a force of 6,000 men to fight in Germany, and Charles agreed to part-fund the expedition. It left in 1631 but was unsuccessful. Charles could not send extra funds and Hamilton returned to court in 1632, ending the last military effort by Charles on behalf of his sister.

Hamilton was close to the king – their fathers had been friends – but it was King James who had forced upon Hamilton a marriage that he considered greatly beneath him. After Buckingham was killed, Charles had given Hamilton the position of Master of Horse, but on condition that he consummate his marriage. A string of young Hamiltons were soon to be born.[10]

The old Earl of Montrose had chaired the Scottish Privy Council briefly but died in 1625. His eldest son and heir, James, became the 5th Earl and one of the leading nobles of Scotland but as yet, he was too young for politics – when the English parliament was dismissed, young James Graham was a student at St Andrews and about to marry. He had grown up on the family estates, one near Glasgow and the other at Old Montrose on the east coast. He spent his childhood in the fields and hills, fishing the cold rivers, learning to ride and hunt. He became skilful with a bow and deadly with a gun, hardened by wind and weather. At twelve he was sent to Glasgow for education and at university he read Sir Walter Raleigh's *History of the World* with great excitement. Now the 5th Earl and head of the Clan Graham, young Montrose would finish his education, marry and go abroad before he took up his role within Scotland's nobility. He had been brought up as a Presbyterian and would hold both to his faith and his native loyalties in a bold, clear-hearted way.

The Scottish political nation was in flux. When the monarch had resided in Scotland he held regular meetings of the Conventions of Estates followed by parliaments and legislation. He also sat with his Privy Council and, especially in the case of King James, gave his opinion freely to his ministers. He knew the nobles personally, a group he had greatly enlarged, and met the representatives of the shires and boroughs when they convened in Edinburgh. Since the king left, all was changed. Conventions met less frequently, parliaments seldom, although Scotland had far more meetings than either Dublin or London. But Edinburgh was a very altered city since the departure of the king. The royal court had acted as a focus of art and culture, social life and intrigue, as well as the centre of politics. Without that centre, the political concerns of the nation either simmered or found other forums for expression. The kirk – well-structured and assertive – became a natural place for opinions to coalesce. The houses of the nobility were clearly places where landowners grumbled and fumed over Revocation. The universities played a multiple role as educational establishments for young gentlemen, as religious foundations and as training colleges for the law. No wonder then that King James had exerted so much pressure on Andrew Melville, Rector of St Andrews, who had changed the curriculum and challenged the king but had subsequently been imprisoned and spent his remaining years abroad. Since then, Spottiswoode had been archbishop and rector, accommodating crown policy.

The religious culture of Scotland was very marked. Archibald Johnston of Wariston, for example, was at Glasgow University in the early years of Charles I's reign. He was the son of a wealthy Edinburgh merchant who was deeply religious and had a conversion experience then common among Puritans. In these transcendental crises, believers came to know their own grace and could be certain that they were predestined to be saved. Archibald's mother was a devout Presbyterian who fasted and prayed for ten hours for her son. Young people such as Johnston of Wariston lived in an atmosphere of constant religious inspiration. It was both severe and heady, working a kind of compressed passion into all their emotions and defining the way they spoke and thought. Young Wariston's social world was among the wealthy merchants and professional people of Edinburgh and he too would be a lawyer, but his inner world was already honed into a furnace of religious striving.

The earls of Argyll were powerful figures in Scotland, with their strategic territory in the west and sub-regalian powers there, but the 7th Earl had created a crisis for his son and heir, Lord Lorne. The earl had made his estates over to Lorne but retained all the income; he had married a Catholic second wife and left for Spain, so his title had been forfeit. Lorne faced losing his whole position. With the help of relatives and some softening by the crown, he retained his patrimony. In 1621, his father regained the title and eventually returned to live quietly in England, but he wounded Lorne again by leaving the valuable peninsula of Kintyre to his son by his second wife. Lorne had all the responsibilities, none of the income and was denounced as unfilial by his father. By 1629 however, Lorne had married and been appointed to the Scottish Privy Council, while his father was ageing and had become more docile.

The head of the Ulster McDonells was also a young man, and he had come to court in 1627 after two years finishing his education in Europe. He was 'bred the Highland way', wearing 'neither hat, cap, nor shoe, or stocking', as a child.[11] His father, who upheld traditional Gaelic culture and language, brought him up as a Catholic, but made clear his loyalty to the crown. The young heir, Randal, was described as 'a tall, clean-limbed, handsome man with red hair'; he had spent a decade at the court of King Charles and was popular among the courtiers.

The McDonells were the largest landowners in Ulster, with enormous influence, but they had only recently acquired their vast estates there. In comparison, the O'Neills were an ancient line, once kings of Ulster and, despite the Flight of the Earls, the family still had large landholdings and considerable influence there. By 1629, Sir Phelim O'Neill had come of age, gained control of his estates in County Tyrone and married a viscount's daughter. Like many young men of fortune, he was busy running wild and spending his inheritance.

The head of government in Ireland was Lord Falkland, who gave up his position as Lord Deputy in August 1629 and returned to England. A new deputy was not immediately appointed and authority was handed over to the Lords Justices, both of whom were New English or Elizabethan in origin. Richard Boyle was one; having acquired his Irish estates through sharp practice in the escheator's office, he had settled in Munster, raised a large family and bought the earldom of Cork from King James. The other was Adam Loftus, from a Yorkshire family promoted to a bishopric under Elizabeth. The Earl of Cork was an energetic entrepreneur who was developing his property and starting new enterprises, while Loftus was a lawyer. The two men led rival political factions and were bitterly opposed to each other. Power in Ireland was being wrenched from the grip of Catholics, whether Gaelic or Old English, and put into the outstretched hands of Protestant planters, of whom the Earl of Cork was the richest.

The 'Graces' that Charles had offered to the Catholics had been sent to England for agreement – Irish legislation was initiated by the English Privy Council – but the measures had not been given legal force. A few had been enacted, and when Catholics were freed from the oath of supremacy a golden opportunity arose for Catholic heirs to take possession of their estates; a rush ensued. The important issue of land titles had not been confirmed and among the old gentry of the Pale in particular there was continued disquiet.

The great Butler households in Kilkenny and Carrick-on-Suir were quiet, waiting for an Earl of Ormond to return and bring them to life. Walter, 11th Earl of Ormond had been released from prison but was still in London. His son had died, so the heir to the earldom was his grandson, the aforementioned Jemmy Butler of Kilcash. The crown had sent young James Butler to live with the Archbishop of Canterbury, where a strict Protestant education had done its work. He came to court in 1628, where he was able to meet and woo his cousin Elizabeth Preston, who now held the ancestral Butler lands. A girl of fourteen whose parents had both just died, she had been destined to marry a relative of Buckingham, but the duke was dead and his influence eclipsed. James Butler had his relatives' support and since he had grown up as a committed Protestant, no objection was raised to his marrying his cousin. On Christmas day 1629, with the consent of King Charles, the two heirs to the Ormond patrimony married and thereby rejoined the land to the title. The young Butlers swiftly returned to Ireland to take control of their estates and position. With Walter's death in 1633, James became the 12th Earl of Ormond and one of Ireland's premier aristocrats.

James Butler was heir to a great Anglo-Norman estate but Murrough O'Brien's lineage was quite different. He came from an ancient Gaelic Irish family and was descended from Brian Boru, the last High King of Ireland. The O'Briens had a position in Munster similar to the O'Neills in Ulster. Murrough's father died when he was young, so, like the Earl of Ormond, he was brought up in a Protestant household; he lived with Sir William St Leger, Lord President of Munster, whose daughter he married. O'Brien was a little younger than James Butler and both were Protestant aristocrats with Catholic relatives, but O'Brien's family were also Gaelic; as he matured, the difference came to matter. His loyalties would be severely tested.

The St Leger home was near the Blackwater River which flows east to the port of Youghal. Downriver from St Leger's estate was the Earl of Cork's residence at Lismore and at the mouth of the river was the walled town of Youghal, which Lord Cork controlled. The earl also had property and business interests in England, so often sailed to one of the Devon ports. These ports on the fringes of the Atlantic were the gateway to growing interests in the Americas. It was from Plymouth that the *Mayflower* had sailed, late in the reign of King James, and West Country families were prominent among those embarking for the New World. After several false starts in Elizabeth's reign, settlements were growing up, not only in the Caribbean but along the east coast of mainland North America. This small movement was about to escalate rapidly. Massachusetts received its charter in 1628 and settlement began with a few hundred people, but migration increased dramatically from this time. In the 1630s, around 50,000 people sailed from the three kingdoms to the east coast of North America, settling from Cape Cod to Virginia.[12]

Each colony, with its individual structure, had a charter from the crown, some granted to individuals and some to joint-stock companies which brought in settlers, motivated either by religion, commerce or both. Settlement was on a contractual basis, not unlike the way undertakers managed the plantations in Ireland and in the Scottish Highlands. The Virginia Company was promoted by West Country entrepreneurs including Sir Humphrey Gilbert, whose son was opening up Maine. Massachusetts was an early settlement of Puritans from Devon, Suffolk and the Netherlands. At first concerned with survival and their faith, the British settlers in the New World quickly began to create governmental structures and looked to England for their form. They developed rapidly, and as political divisions widened in England, Scotland and Ireland, so the plantations on the American coast and in the Caribbean became part of the political struggle.

With the end of parliament and the withdrawal of members to their constituencies, there remained in Whitehall the king's gentlemen of business, his ministers and the Privy Council. The life of the court continued, attended by the aristocracy and gentry – people whom the king came to know well and whose views he might consult. Some were hired for diplomatic service and others, like Wentworth, for domestic positions. His friends surrounded him, mainly English but also a few Irish aristocrats and the Scots who had come south with his father. Buckingham was gone but his wife Katherine was still at court, with her soft complexion and sweet nature. At court, politics was carried on and marriages were made, in the refined style on which Charles insisted.

But parliamentary politics had ended, and King Charles was in no hurry to call another meeting. The three he had held had been bruising experiences and brought little gain. Buckingham was gone, but in the place of that imposing presence stood the little queen, with her bright eyes and lively spirit. She had royal dignity but the warmth of a girl. A decade of marital happiness began for Charles and Henrietta-Maria, as children were born and the couple nurtured a mannerly and artistic court.

The king turned to his ministers for their advice and expertise on how to fund the state. After the three aggressive confrontations he had just experienced, he would not subject himself to another parliament if he could avoid it.

10

Without Parliament

By the time that King Charles dissolved his third parliament, the war within the Holy Roman Empire had run for a decade and the momentum was about to change. It had been precipitated by Charles's brother-in-law Frederick of the Palatinate, but already by 1629 England had lost the ability to fight. France too had an interest in confronting the Emperor; it had Habsburg rulers in an arc around it, in Spain, the Spanish Netherlands and in the Empire itself. But France, run by Richelieu, played a careful hand. To the north, the Scandinavians were motivated by religion, had growing trade interests in the Baltic and were assertive powers. Christian IV of Denmark entered the war early; Gustavus Adolphus of Sweden bided his time before pushing far into Germany as a conqueror.

England's role in the Thirty Years War ended early and had little influence on the outcome but it had a substantial backwash in both the islands ruled by the Stuarts. The financial demands of war and relations with Catholic Ireland both became critical during the short English war effort, but changes in foreign policy under Charles had long-lasting effects. After 1603, there had been a shift in policy from that of Elizabeth, who supported the Dutch Protestants and fought Spain, to that of James, who feared the sword and made peace. Chronically short of money, James used his position to avoid war and maintain the balance of power in Europe, but when his son-in-law caused an eruption in the Empire, that policy had to change. James gave modest financial support to Mansfeld to fight for Bohemia, but his principal effort was negotiation: with the French to support Frederick, but with the Spanish to exert influence on their cousins in Vienna and to get Frederick reinstated by diplomacy.[1]

It was a fruitless policy and James died before it was far advanced. Charles was by then under the influence of Buckingham. They attacked Cadiz and tried to relieve La Rochelle, but neither initiative was successful or even particularly purposeful. Over La Rochelle Charles displayed the inability to negotiate that would prove his greatest weakness. Richelieu was a skilled statesman who directed France throughout the reign of Henrietta-Maria's brother, Louis XIII; his offers to Charles I were met only by sulky refusals. In these early years of his reign, Charles still saw his job as giving orders; if they were refused, he pressed harder. He was far down the road to ruin before he showed any understanding of negotiation, and even then he never mastered it. He took the same tone with foreign powers. Unable to order them, he would become rigid. Blinkered in this way, he failed to spot the opportunities for cooperation offered by Richelieu.

To Christian of Denmark he made a large financial promise which he wholly failed to keep. Soon after his father's death, Charles had promised Christian £30,000 a month; he paid £46,000, but never made another payment. The following year Christian suffered two bitter defeats and cursed Charles roundly for his failure to pay. By 1629, Christian had made peace with the Emperor and it looked as though the House of Austria would be unopposed in central Europe. But meanwhile, Gustavus Adolphus of Sweden had enlarged his kingdom, developed his military skills and was poised to enter the war in league with the Protestant princes. As England's last commitment to the war broke down, the strongest Protestant ruler set forth on two years of blazing victories.

Conquest was the old way of asserting overlordship or suzerainty and it had profound implications. The Emperor had never conquered the patchwork of states over which he held sway, so its populace had far greater rights than conquered peoples had. Scotland had not been conquered by England and so retained all its rights to law and sovereignty. But Ireland had been conquered and, as would be asserted repeatedly, its people could not claim the rights of a free or sovereign people, nor the rights established in England, the state to which it was bound.[2]

For Charles I, the military adventures of his first three years as king were profoundly damaging. He came to a throne weighed down by debt, spent what he could raise on doomed expeditions, disappointed his Danish cousin and was then left with no strategy for helping his exiled sister. In the meantime he had pointlessly attacked Spain and played a weak hand with France. There were signs that he was asserting himself against Buckingham's dominance before the latter's death, but it was too late. Two expensive but pointless wars had been fought and the gulf between monarch and parliament widened dangerously. Once parliament was dissolved, the king had to raise funds without their sanction. He found funds for Hamilton in 1631–32, but essentially Charles was obliged to withdraw from the European conflict and as a result, the three kingdoms played no further part in the Thirty Years War. However, Charles made one last diplomatic effort for Elizabeth of Bohemia, which set foreign policy in a new direction. Making peace with Spain in 1630, the terms of the treaty were unremarkable, much the same as his father's in 1604. But in a further secret agreement, Charles undertook to join Spain in attacks on the Dutch Republic.[3] By this treaty, he pushed James's policy one stage further and into a reversal of that of Elizabeth. For her, the struggling Protestant states were religious liberationists. During James's reign there was a truce between Spain and the Dutch, but meanwhile the Netherlands had emerged as a major trading state rivalling London's position in banking and serving a similar market. From the new direction taken by Charles in 1630, the Dutch became rivals and enemies, creating a problem that dogged government for half a century, and which was eventually resolved with British dominance on the northern seas.

With Buckingham dead, the king's government reverted to a more normal shape. Perhaps the power Buckingham had exercised over James and subsequently Charles was more damaging than extravagance and commission-taking. Once the duke was gone, Charles had a range of advisors. His ministers gained influence and could carry their policies through. The Chancellor of the Exchequer, Sir Richard Weston, had opposed war with both France and Spain. Now promoted to Lord High Treasurer, he found ways to fund the crown and keep expenditure steady, and with time he improved the government's financial position. However, he had to do this by extra-parliamentary means.

Sir Francis Cottington had been Prince Charles's secretary and was an experienced diplomat. He took Weston's place as Chancellor and they became the key figures in government. William Laud became a Privy Councillor in 1627 as a protégé of Buckingham. There had been few changes to the Privy Council since James died; Lord Coventry, the earls of Arundel, Pembroke and Manchester, and Sir John Coke all had important offices and could press their opinions with the king. Within the Privy Council was a Committee for Ireland, which oversaw government in Dublin. Charles attended some Privy Council meetings and consulted with his councillors singly or in groups, but not every document signed by the king represented a decision taken by him; many were passed to him with cursory explanation. He was chief executive and set policy, but only certain areas held his close attention. Much government business was carried through by the ministers and secretaries.

The 1628 parliament had seemed at the time to be a critical meeting. Sir Benjamin Rudyerd, who worked for the Earl of Pembroke, had declared, 'This is the crisis of parliaments. We shall know by this if parliaments live or die.' When it voted subsidies, Charles was said to have been very moved and told his council, 'At the first I liked parliaments, but since (I know not how) I was grown to distaste of them. But I am now where I was. I love parliaments, I shall rejoice to meet with my people often.'[4]

This period of progress and cooperation had been followed by disagreement, suspicion and a bad-humoured dissolution. Yet Wentworth, having been a challenger of government, had been promoted and in 1629 he joined the Privy Council. It was Weston and probably Cottington who recommended him to the king. Once he became a councillor, Wentworth found a sympathetic ally in Laud, who, like him, looked for capable administration, strong central government and ministers whose primary aim was the king's business rather than their private interests. An unusual and ambitious man, Wentworth cared about the welfare of the people and government's role in promoting it, but he confidently challenged powerful men who stood in his way, and he was not shy about enriching himself.

The parliament had thrown up Wentworth and been dissolved with acrimony. It had created a firm resolve in the mind of Charles. Two years later, when Gustavus Adolphus was in a strong military position against the Habsburgs, Elizabeth of Bohemia begged her brother for financial help. It seemed the only chance of regaining the Palatinate. But not even this appeal would move Charles to call another parliament; he told his council that the constant talk of such meetings offended him and 'that he would never be urged by necessity or against his will to summon one'.[5] Instead his government struggled on Elizabeth's behalf – through diplomacy with Spain – while quasi-legal ways were found to raise money for government.

The king, of course, had his own estate which brought him an income. There were taxes he could collect without asking for parliament's consent and those for which he needed consent but was collecting anyway. Men had been imprisoned already for refusing to pay the Forced Loan and Charles, like his predecessors, used deeply unpopular measures derived from feudal rights, such as purveyance and the Court of Wards, to increase his income.

Despite the debt which his father left to him and his chronic shortage of money, for a decade Charles was at the centre of a charming court and was a patron of the arts. It was in the 1630s that Charles built up the exquisite picture collection which was one of his finest achievements. Probably from his mother, who had come from the Renaissance court of Denmark, Charles had developed a fine artistic sense. His first major purchase, the Gonzaga collection, laid the foundations and over the years he bought widely – wall panels for his palaces, individual masterpieces and exquisite drawings. He supported the tapestry workshop at Mortlake but much of the collection came from Europe.[6] Charles brought Van Dyck to England and commissioned portraits of himself, Henrietta-Maria and their children. As a result of the king's interest, other painters came from the Low Countries; Rubens, Honthorst, Mijtens and Van Mierevelt all painted the great figures of Charles's court, leaving a magnificent gallery but a certain poignancy, as we scan the faces of the men and women who would be protagonists in the conflict to come.

James's children had loathed their father's court with its swearing, drinking and louche behaviour. Charles was determined that his own would be elegant and fastidious. He liked hunting, where he could unleash some of the emotions which he normally held so carefully in check, but the tone of the court was disciplined. The king rose early and went to his prayers. The rooms were kept clean and smelling sweet.

Their court was mannerly and civilised. The king and queen hunted, enjoyed music and improved the buildings at their disposal. King James had planned to modernise the rambling mass of structures which made up Whitehall Palace but the Banqueting Hall, designed by Inigo Jones, was the only building completed. Charles commissioned Rubens to decorate the ceiling with paintings celebrating the achievements of his father. The plays and poetry then in fashion emphasised courtly love and platonic devotion. The royal couple enjoyed masques, and Henrietta-Maria even appeared in them, but nothing lewd or risqué was permitted.

All the same, the social standards did not please the Puritans. James I had issued the *Book of Sports* which permitted Sunday entertainments such as dancing. Charles's natural religious taste was in the centre ground, around the forms Elizabeth had given to her church. But the overt Catholicism of the queen, with her chapel, priests and Catholic friends, was an irritant to English Protestants. The perceived drift of Charles's church towards Arminianism and away from Calvinism displeased many. For the Puritans, the country was ungodly; they disliked theatre, deplored dancing on Sundays and thought the queen's chaplains creatures of the Devil.

The king's three principal churchmen had distinct views. James Ussher had become Archbishop of Armagh and head of the Protestant Irish church in the last months of King James's life; he was scholarly and Calvinist. Archbishop Spottiswoode in Scotland was also James's choice, a mild man with more Arminian views disliked by the Calvinists. Charles's own choice of churchman was an indicator both of his beliefs and his plans for the church. William Laud was a small man from a modest background, a capable administrator but not a man of vision or sensitivity. His views on the church suited Charles, who promoted him steadily, but Calvinists spoke of Laud as an Arminian and came to loathe him. His physical taste for the church, his emphasis on 'the beauty of holiness', which led to more decoration and formality, was deeply offensive to the Puritans.[7] When Laud was made Chancellor of the University of Oxford, both dons and gentlemen murmured and worried. But there was a wide diversity of belief within the three kingdoms, from Catholicism through to Puritanism, and among the Puritans there was constant Bible study, discussion and preaching that pushed ideas further from the established church. William Laud's beliefs were in roughly the median position, but that was useless when every man or woman had their passionate belief about salvation. It was not a matter of finding the centre ground when many imagined a life-or-death struggle for spiritual survival. Laud, like Wentworth, believed in a strong state, obedience to the ruler but also Christian sacrifice to the community, even by the rich and powerful: 'For whoever he may be, he must live in the body of the Commonwealth, and in the body of the Church.'[8] Laud hated economic individualism, but that was becoming one of the characteristics of seventeenth-century Protestants, along with enterprise and aspiration.

The universities had always been church institutions and their syllabus a mixture of law, theology and classical literature, but the arrival first of printing and then the Reformation, in a period of increasing wealth, had led to an explosion of printed books and authors. John Donne had gone to Oxford and subsequently transferred to Cambridge. John Milton was also sent to Cambridge by his father when he was fifteen, which was then the usual age of entry. Milton quickly showed his abilities with languages and his skill with poetic form. The plague was a scourge in London and Mr Milton senior moved his family to Hammersmith, 6 miles from Westminster, removing them from the narrow streets of the City of London where plague struck during the summers. Young John Milton was a studious boy who produced elegies in the accepted forms and who certainly was not radical in his youth. At Cambridge, he signed the three articles of religion as required by the university regulators. As society radicalised, however, the poet grew into a man of assertive and republican views. Contemporary society had tides which gathered strength and pulled with them the minds of individuals. Milton was an intellectual and took strong positions on the political and theological controversies of his time. In his youth he had some training in theatre – his father was a composer and the son acted and played music – while in 1634 he wrote a masque for the Earl of Bridgwater. This would not conform to the ideas of the stricter Puritans but it gave Milton a sense of dramatic scenes and a trained musical ear which prepared him for the poetic work of his maturity.

In this varied and intellectually vigorous society, the great forces of the universe were under constant discussion. Astronomy, natural science and mathematics were making substantial developments. The theology of the universe was in hot debate. Read about and preached about, the God who created our world, his benevolent son who taught love and forgiveness, as well as Satan, the fallen angel who tried to work destruction, all of them gradually took vivid dramatic form in the mind of the young poet Milton.

For most men, of a more martial or political temperament, caught up in debates about the boundaries of the common law and the shape of modern government, the rights and wrongs of society were not a matter of theology and poetry at all, but of legal struggle. England was a country of well-developed legal systems based on common law, with traditions of government and established rights. It was also the most dominant of the Stuarts' three kingdoms, because of its wealth and geographical position.

For the government, solvency and defence of the realm were always paramount. Defence rested on the navy and for England this was crucial. Scotland and Ireland both had important coasts, but were not in close proximity to the great powers of Europe as England was. Equally, trade was growing and merchants were ambitious. Shipping was vital for both defence and commerce. Every monarch had played their part in maintaining, building and enhancing the navy and Charles felt this duty keenly. There was an old precedent of ship money, but Charles collected the tax widely with controversial results. Since Plantagenet times, the crown had required the ports and coastal counties to provide ships or pay to build them. James had levied ship money in 1619 but now the government levied it on the whole country. That provoked a strong reaction and the government pulled back. In 1634 it was collected from the maritime counties and there was no protest. But this emboldened the government, and in 1635 new writs went out for larger sums and to all the English counties. Despite protest, most of the tax was collected and Charles sought to prove its legality by asking for learned opinion. Ten of the twelve judges consulted supported Charles, arguing that the king was empowered to judge on any danger facing the nation and provide for its defence.

Writs for ship money went out again the following year; it seemed to be an annual tax and resistance mounted. In 1637, Charles took a case against John Hampden for non-payment and won his case. The money was spent on the navy and a ship money fleet was built, so when France went to war with Spain in 1635 Charles was asked for a naval alliance. The queen naturally supported this request, but despite negotiations the fleet was not sent.

Yet, to the people of England it looked as though King Charles would follow the pattern of his French brother-in-law and this caused disquiet. In France, the government of Louis XIII was run by his Catholic cardinal without any public consultation. France and Spain might succumb to such a system, but in England the traditions of parliament and the common law were precious. The liberties of Englishmen had been struggled for and established; now it seemed they were being flouted. England had become a Protestant nation, but the French queen embodied other traditions. In London she was seen attending her chapel with French staff to hear Mass from Catholic priests, while in her native country government was run by a cardinal in the scarlet robes of Rome, which for Englishmen was inflammatory. France was the antithesis of the Republic of Geneva which Calvin had built, or the Netherlands with its elected ruler the Prince of Orange.

Calvin had clearly preferred a republican form of government. His theology emphasised the sovereignty of God, while also stressing obedience to rulers and the rule of law. But, according to Calvin, those who chose their own government were blessed: 'If we argue about human governments we can say that to be in a free state is much better than to be under a prince.'[9] The Church of England took a different view. In the prologue to the 1540 Bible, Cranmer wrote, 'Herin maye prynces learne howe to gouerne their subiectes: Subiectes obediece, loue and dreade to theyr prynces.'[10]

As Protestantism insisted that individuals command their own spiritual life, so congregations tended to become more assertive. There was public vigilance over the national church, and while Charles, like his father, seemed a committed Protestant, his wife was a French Catholic and the small Bishop Laud with his busy eyes was widely mistrusted.

Among the English there was deep unease about the Catholicism of Ireland and how it might affect allegiance to England. Few people knew much about Lord Wentworth, except in the north of England where he had ruled with vigour and determination. People in public life heard about his leadership style and wondered what was intended when, in 1633 and unexpectedly, Wentworth was promoted to be Lord Deputy of Ireland.

11

Charles, King of Scotland

As the triple crowns were not equal in power, coronation mirrored their status. Wales was part of the jurisdiction of England. The lordship of Ireland had become a kingdom under Henry VIII but was subordinate to England, and Richard II was the last reigning monarch to visit – none had been crowned there. However, the Stuarts had been kings of Scotland first and of England subsequently; Scotland was a sovereign kingdom. It was known generally that Charles would go to Edinburgh for his Scottish coronation; the question was when.

Now that the three crowns were united in one person, Scotland was not content with the way things had developed. The king was distant, and his role at the centre of Scottish political and elite life had collapsed. To actually proposition or influence him had become almost impossible even for the nobility – it was a long journey down, and life at the English court was expensive. Few Scots were now intimates of the king. At court the English laughed at their accents and behaviour. A few Scottish nobles and the king's ministers made a place for themselves, but if they lingered too long they became strangers in Scotland and lost touch with local issues.

There had been great changes in the three kingdoms because the economy of Europe was developing and men were less bound to land. For example, until 1587 Scottish titles were territorial, attached to the land and not the holder. The king created lands into an earldom and when the owner changed the title went to the new landowner.[1] Feudal tenure in England had been similar, but as feudalism died and new wealth rose, titles became personal awards, giving status and entry to parliament.

However, there was a great difference between the parliament of England and that of Scotland, where the single chamber gave Scottish nobles less legislative power. When King James was in Scotland this was balanced by those appointed king's lieutenant for their area. For those nobles who ran palatinates or tiny local statelets, or those who controlled clan land, James had reduced their power as he centralised his own, but many held official positions instead, meeting the king and influencing government. Now the king was English and absent.

The nobles had weighty responsibilities managing their own estates, but the sense of dwindling power and significance irked them. On top of that, the size of the nobility had grown enormously both in England and Scotland. In England, James had realised he could raise money by selling peerages and had gone busily about it through intermediaries. Baronetcies had been sold from the early years of James's reign but in 1616 he had started selling peerages. Buckingham had been his greatest broker and had effectively controlled the sale of Irish peerages, which were cheaper. By 1620, the whole order of precedence within the old nobility was under threat and many of the existing peers signed a petition in protest.[2]

Few Scottish peerages were sold but the nobility still doubled in size between 1603 and 1640, largely because men who acquired church lands had been awarded lordships with them. Other titles went to servants of the crown and to junior members of noble families. Among the new peers were the men who lost most by the Revocation; they kept their titles and were compensated for any land they lost to the crown, but many saw their estates traded for lesser ones and that was an insult they didn't forgive. The Revocation had improved the position of lesser lords and the clergy, and it also gave the crown a chance to stop some hereditary office-holding. These were all modernising policies, but Charles got little credit for them. It was typical of his rule that poor communication undermined what were often intelligent or efficient changes.[3]

By the early 1630s the Revocation had been worked through and the legal wrangling was largely over. Charles had talked about going to Scotland since the beginning of his reign but eight years went by before he returned to the land of his birth. He set off in May 1635 and made a long royal progress lasting a month until he entered Edinburgh on 15 June. He was accompanied by Laud, who was now Archbishop of Canterbury. Charles was crowned three days later in Holyrood Abbey, which had been ruined during the Reformation but was rebuilt for his coronation. Unfortunately, the service upset his Scottish subjects; it used the English prayer book along with Anglican clothes and ceremonies, which was normal for King Charles but far too elaborate and 'popish' for the plain tastes of kirk congregations.

Nor did Charles stay long in Scotland. A parliament was called to follow the coronation, which Charles attended, but that too caused discontent. Because the king could choose the Lords of the Articles, he was able to prevent grievances over the Articles of Perth and Revocation being aired. All the legislation was passed en bloc in one day with the king present so that he could see who might make a challenge. One hundred and sixty pieces of legislation were passed, including retrospective approval for the Act of Revocation and a substantial grant of taxation.

There were feasts at which loyal lords drank copious toasts to the monarch; these were precisely the sort of events that Charles hated, with wine splashing and glasses smashed. There was a short tour of the Lowlands, lasting less than two weeks, and then the king was riding away south. He was back in southern England by late July when Henrietta-Maria brought Prince Charles to meet his father just outside London.

The Scottish Privy Council had been running the northern kingdom under directions from the king, but without access to him nor much discussion about measures to be taken or explanations as to what was intended; the coronation visit had hardly given time to improve these relationships. James, Marquis of Hamilton represented Scottish interests at the English court, where he generally lived. He also had an English peerage, sat in the House of Lords there and knew the king well, as his father had known James. The Treasurer, the Earl of Traquair, also provided a link between Charles and Edinburgh. For the Scottish men of influence, however, the king's visit did not provide any real channels of communication. The Scottish people only caught a few glimpses of their monarch.

It may have been his visit to Scotland which brought the issue of Scottish religious habits to Charles's mind. When he saw the plain Scottish churches and had to sit through services without set forms but rich in extempore preaching, he was very displeased. Charles was well aware that his father had introduced the Five Articles in a General Assembly at Perth which had angered many Scots and that James had not been able to make himself head of the church in Scotland, nor to install a new prayer book there. Perth had been the limit of James's efforts.

Charles, however, having returned from Edinburgh, resurrected the prayer book project. Before he went to Scotland, he had sent for drafts of the book and now he pushed forward. Laud began to assert control over the Scottish bishops and they in turn were ordered to comment on the proposed prayer book. Having bishops at all was provocative to the Scots, but James had insisted. Soon, Laud sent canons to direct church behaviour in Scotland; these ignored the role of presbyteries and banned spontaneous preaching, which was common in Scotland. Work continued on the prayer book.

The kirk used the *Book of Common Order* for their services, brought by Knox from Geneva. The fervour which characterised the kirk had gone deep into Scottish society. In the sixteenth century, the Scottish people had bound themselves to uphold a pure faith and, in an echo of the Old Testament, had signed a covenant with God, a document which King James himself had signed. The forms of their faith were tenaciously held. Charles, however, wanted to bring the churches of his three kingdoms into conformity. He instructed Laud, who consulted the Scottish bishops and then prepared both the canons and new prayer book for Scotland. Late in 1636, Charles sent a proclamation to the Privy Council in Edinburgh ordering that the prayer book be bought by every parish – and used. Murmuring began before the book ever reached the printing press. It had been written by Englishmen in England, which was already greatly to its discredit. The king was impiously asserting himself as the head of their church, a position which only Christ could occupy.[4] By May 1637, the prayer book had been printed and the Scots could read it for themselves.

In theology it was not so far from the beliefs they held, but there were important differences. The very fact of change enforced by the king in London was provocative. The process by which it was foisted on them caused aggravation and affront. Their church was pure and national; the Scots were a covenanted people, sworn to live in God's ways. To insert a new liturgy into the kirk was a radical intrusion. Yet there is no indication that either Charles or Laud foresaw problems.

The book became available in May. Although it was disliked, people were cautious of speaking out. But there were meetings, and once word got out that it was to be used in Edinburgh, plans were made. There is little doubt that the subsequent protests were organised. Tensions were high. Nervously, church ministers decided to all start reading at the same time, to avoid being targeted. In St Giles Cathedral, the Privy Council were in attendance when the dean began to read from the book. At that, women in the congregation began to shout insults – 'traitors, belly-gods and deceivers' – then to throw their stools and finally to leave the kirk. Outside they continued to riot. When the bishop left St Giles, they threw stones at him. The dean hid in the church steeple.

The Edinburgh authorities forbade meetings, but the bishops could not force their clergy to use the book. When Charles heard of this, he was gripped by cold anger and ordered the Privy Council to arrest and punish the protesters, back the bishops and continue to carry out his instructions.

By September, much of Scotland was roused. A meeting to petition the king included ministers, lairds and nobles. Parishes, burghs and presbyteries had already sent up their petitions and all were handed in to the council. Demands were made to put bishops on trial for corruption of the true religion. Yet the more the council tried, tactfully or explicitly, to explain to the king that his policy had met implacable resistance, the more inflexible he became. He ignored their explanation of what was happening and ordered them to continue using the prayer book.

Charles had inflamed the one issue that united Scots of all classes. When council members and officials tried to restore order, they were roughly handled; by October, Charles had ordered his Privy Council to move out of the city. He also ordered all the petitioners to go home, but the nobles among them told the people to stay until a supplication was drawn up and delivered. By November, some members of the council had become disaffected from crown policy, while the petitioners had begun to organise. They chose commissioners to act for them, but as this became unwieldy committees were formed of nobles, gentry, ministers and burgesses. The committees came to be known as the Tables, and began to take on the nature of national leaders.

Early in the new year, Traquair was summoned to London to explain the situation to the king. He told Charles that to quell the disturbances he would need an army of 40,000 men, but Charles sent him back to Edinburgh with a stiff proclamation endorsing the prayer book, over which the king said he had taken 'great care and pains', and ordering the Scots to go home. If they disobeyed, they might be charged with treason.

This proclamation was read out in Stirling on 18 February 1638, and ten days later the Scots began to sign their National Covenant. The first covenant of 1557 had been followed in 1581 by the one signed by James VI, when Catholicism was resurgent; now a new document was composed. It emphasised the 'danger to the true reformed religion, the king's honour and the public peace of the kingdom by the manifold innovations and evils'. 'Before God,' signatories solemnly declared they would 'defend the aforesaid true religion' and to 'recover the purity and liberty of the Gospel, as it was established and professed before the foresaid novations'. They would 'stand to the defence of their dread Sovereign, the King's Majesty' in order to maintain 'the true religion and his Majesty's authority'.[5] The nobility signed first, then the lairds and gentry; before long, the Covenant had been taken out to the parish churches where the people of Scotland made their solemn bond.

To Charles, the Covenant was apparently not so much a declaration of religious belief as a sign of covert republicanism. In October 1637, he said to a friend that the Scots wanted to destroy 'the true state of monarchical government'.[6] His father's maxim had been 'no Bishop, no King', and Charles had learned it well. He knew he must assert his authority over both church and state, but if Scotland would not obey instructions then threats would have to be acted upon; authority must be backed up by force. He foresaw armed conflict, but had neither troops nor the funding he might need; nor was he sure which strategy to pursue. Charles procrastinated until June, when he sent his close friend and chief councillor James, Marquis of Hamilton to treat with the Scots.

Hamilton had known Charles since they were boys and he was familiar with the king's mind. A member of both English and Scottish privy councils, loyal to his monarch but Calvinist and on good terms with many in the Covenanting movement, Hamilton had some chance of success. He set off for Scotland to look for a compromise. By now, the king had realised the strength of feeling against his policies but to back off might show weakness and further undermine his authority, while to continue could only lead to conflict.

Rather than compromise, by June Charles was preparing for war. William Juxon, who was now Bishop of London and Treasurer of England, thought he could find £200,000, and Charles sent to the Low Countries for arms. The Covenanters were also sending overseas for military supplies. Rigid positions on both sides were leading to conflict. Hamilton had to tactfully suggest ways in which the king could meet the rebellious Scots halfway. The Covenanters wanted a General Assembly of the Kirk and a parliament. The king saw that he could not mount a military expedition that year; he needed more time. That gave Hamilton a small opportunity.

The king was receiving conflicting advice. From Ireland, Wentworth advised stern measures against the Covenanters. Archbishop Laud prevaricated. The English Privy Council was split: the queen and several Catholic noblemen were keen to challenge the Scots with military force, but many of the Scottish nobility were loyal to the Covenant. The young Earl of Montrose had signed it and gone to persuade the scholars at Aberdeen University, albeit without success. In this polarised situation, Hamilton conferred with Traquair and other ministers on ways to find common ground.

In September, crown policy was moderated. The prayer book and canons would not be enforced for now, and a different covenant – the King's Covenant – would be promoted so that Scots could confirm their loyalty. A General Assembly of the Kirk was to meet in Glasgow in November that year and a parliament would meet the following spring.

This was a substantial retreat on the part of Charles. His ministers hoped that the assembly and parliament would find a proper settlement. But the Covenanters felt their victory and knew that some in England sympathised with them, or had grievances of their own. Scottish opinion was torn between the king and the Covenanters, but Hamilton felt that sense would prevail if only Thomas Wentworth lost his influence on the king. His letters from Dublin gave quite opposite advice to that of Hamilton.

12

Thomas Wentworth in Ireland

Charles's coronation in Scotland coincided with the new administration in Ireland, as Wentworth waited until the king returned from Scotland before leaving for Dublin. Charles had delayed, so two years elapsed before Wentworth arrived to take up his appointment in Ireland. His reign there culminated in a drama linking all three kingdoms.

Wentworth was appointed in 1631 but that autumn his second wife died of a fall while pregnant and he was crushed by grief. Still President of the North, he had appointed a deputy but now had two appointments and a large workload. Tough as an official, his personal needs seem very different. He quickly remarried, to eighteen-year-old Elizabeth Rodes, the daughter of a Yorkshire gentleman, but then caused some scandal by waiting to acknowledge her. Wives were expected to be devoted and loving, but Wentworth also wrote of the equality between himself and his new wife. With each marriage he entered into a new intimacy with a single-minded devotion of his own. As an administrator he was stern, unafraid of challenging vested interests and poor at negotiation – but he was efficient. His close friendships were few, but strong and lasting.

In Dublin, he knew there would be many challenges. The outgoing Lord Deputy, Lord Falkland, had struggled, both against opposition in the Irish Privy Council and with the crown's stated policy. The Old English were pressing for the 'Graces' to be confirmed in law as they had been promised, but so far no statutes had been passed. Falkland, who was in contention with Vice Treasurer Mountnorris, went to England for consultation but did not return.

As often in the past, Irish government was left in the hands of the two Lords Justices: Richard Boyle, 1st Earl of Cork, and his rival Adam, 1st Viscount Loftus. They belonged to two rival factions in the Irish Privy Council, Cork to Falkland's. In fact, it seemed that Cork himself might become Lord

Deputy, but in 1631 the appointment went to Yorkshire's Thomas, Viscount Wentworth, which caused surprise in both London and Dublin.

The new Lord Deputy was thirty-eight years old. He had looked in vain for government jobs throughout his youth but had made himself conspicuous in the London parliament by leading the campaign for the Petition of Right and had been taken up by the council, then promoted to Lord President of the North where he had been a vigorous crown servant, confrontational but effective. However, he had no connection to Ireland. On the English Privy Council he had become close to William Laud, but Weston, the Lord Chancellor, was probably his sponsor. The king had agreed to his appointment, although he refused a request for an earldom; Charles thought Wentworth could wait.

The deputyship had often been a poisoned chalice and Wentworth's friends warned him that he might have been sent to Dublin out of spite, but the young baron saw it as a compliment. He was confident and energetic, so being offered one of the great offices of state was naturally enticing. He would be head of His Majesty's government in Ireland where his authority was only second to the king, but for all that, managing the factions and issues in Ireland had been more than many other politicians could achieve. Wentworth, however, was an able administrator and he now took stock as he prepared himself for the task. He said he would wait until His Majesty returned from Edinburgh, but the coronation was delayed several times.[1] That gave Wentworth time to prepare his ground.

The position was both prestigious and perilous. To rule on behalf of the king in Ireland meant navigating the factions in Dublin while mastering Irish issues and moulding them to crown policy. But the Lord Deputy was far from court, while rivals and malcontents were free to hurry to Whitehall and present their case behind his back. Wentworth carefully considered his strategy.

Thomas Wentworth attracted a great deal of attention, both from his contemporaries and from later historians, partly because his rule in Ireland culminated with disaster for him and with rebellion in the country he ruled, but also because his treatment by the Long Parliament was so radical and was a precursor of the great hatreds which subsequently broke into conflict. His part in precipitating the drama is still contested but there is no doubt that his nemesis was also the critical point in the king's own dilemma. Wentworth had an intense and charismatic personality, which for some time made him a very successful minister and then attracted the wrath of many parties. At first challenging royal policy, he swiftly became a crown servant and was criticised as a turncoat. Wentworth was ruthless and antagonised people but he had attractive qualities; his passion is so vivid, his devotion to each of his wives deep and his need for them profound. Once appointed, he was capable, energetic and effective in a role where many had failed. He was also ruthless and alienated powerful people whom he might have courted. Yet, for all his attempts at self-enrichment and self-aggrandisement, he was an enemy of corruption and a loyal servant of his king.

The byword for Wentworth was 'Thorough', and he certainly planned to be exactly that, but seventeenth-century government was a strange mixture of high-mindedness, sophistication and venality. Everyone who took up the crown's business enriched themselves from it; the important thing was how much of the crown's business they get done in the meantime. In the case of Wentworth, the answer is all of it – he pursued crown policy thoroughly and energetically until his last breath.

When he was appointed, it was clear what his aims and challenges would be. King Charles had dissolved his English parliament and hoped to avoid holding another, but crown finance was inadequate and crown debt a burden, and there was a great deal which the young king hoped to tackle. Ireland was a financial millstone and the man who could make it contribute to the king's exchequer would have an unusual achievement to his name.

As a Protestant and a close associate of Laud, Wentworth embraced the job of bringing the Irish church into line with the Church of England. Laud had managed church policy since early in the reign and became Archbishop of Canterbury in 1633, when George Abbot, who had been marginalised, finally died. Charles had picked Laud to run his English church and encouraged him to oversee the churches of Scotland and Ireland too. James Ussher, Archbishop of Armagh and Primate of All Ireland, was a learned man but his views were not those of Laud. As head of the Irish church, Charles planned to set its direction. Wentworth was to be the executor of that policy and Laud provided the new Lord Deputy with a chaplain, John Bramhall, who on arrival in Ireland was promoted to the bishopric of Derry and took on the job of reconfiguring the Irish church.[2]

Government over the whole island was not fully established. The Ulster plantations were recent and it was only since the Elizabethan conquest that Dublin had some hold over the Gaelic north and west, established with difficulty. Wentworth intended not only to make the king's writ run throughout the island but to run 'thoroughly'.

He prepared for the job by studying recent policy and by narrowing the lines of communication between Dublin and London. If he could control those he stood some chance. Wentworth asked the king for full control over appointments and to report to one of his officials, not to committees. A few letters would go directly to the king. Having agreed some policies with the king before he set off, and with a short chain of command between the deputy and the monarch, he had prepared well. Once in Dublin, he wrote frequently; as well as official reports he wrote often to Laud and also to other colleagues, keeping London informed and putting his activities in a positive light.[3] The king gave him support – not unquestioning or unconditional, but having chosen his deputy he stood behind him.

Waiting for him in Ireland were men with large vested interests, from whom he would have to extract taxes and whose cooperation had been so vital to previous deputies. Lord Cork was clearly the most significant. His landed wealth was enormous; he was a thriving entrepreneur but had trained in law, with which skill he had built his fortune. Cork was pragmatic and intelligent.

The immediate need of government was income. Before travelling, Wentworth prepared his ground. Cork wanted to use the recusancy laws to fine Catholics, but instead Wentworth once more offered the 'Graces'. The Old English responded by renewing the taxes and enough money came in to run the government for a year or so. Wentworth had breathing space. Lord Cork's policy had been brushed aside.[4]

With that agreed, Wentworth took ship for Ireland, bringing his young wife and the three children from his second marriage as well as his growing collection of papers. He meticulously kept copies of all his correspondence and his papers were carefully archived. The Wentworths arrived in Dublin in July 1633. The Lord Deputy had a residence in Dublin Castle, the old fortress near the River Liffey which for centuries had been the headquarters of government in Dublin. As Lord Deputy he had his own troop of soldiers and he rode out 'clad in black armour with a black horse and a black plume of feathers' to superintend their training. He had no practical experience of soldiering, and some mocked him, but Wentworth believed that as chief governor he should display the grandeur of his office.[5]

By challenging Cork, Wentworth appeared to be favouring the opposition, and for some time he did. Eventually he would challenge all parties. Government in Dublin was weak; individuals had siphoned off both power and property. Wentworth aimed to draw power away from the grandees and into his own hands as Lord Deputy. He was answerable to the monarch and all the king's subjects in Ireland answered to him; that was the theory and he intended to make it the practice.

Wentworth's motto, which he frequently quoted, was *stare super vias antiquas* – 'to stand over ancient ways'. How did he interpret this? Did it mean his rule rested on established law? That he stood firm on loyalty to the crown? Or did Wentworth see himself as upholder of English rights and liberties? Probably all of the above. Wentworth believed in the rule of law and often stressed the king's prerogative. The issue was locating the boundary between the two.

The society to which Wentworth belonged was highly legalistic, full of discussion about how law had developed and what it meant. The medieval period had created large quantities of legal records, deeds for land, judgements about inheritance, laws and charters. Storerooms and repositories were full of parchment rolls on which this mass of legal precedent was recorded. But there had been great changes in church and state; men disputed how the law stood and how it should develop. In Dublin the parchment rolls also recorded some very dubious transactions which had been fudged by smart fellows and powerful grandees – men like Lord Cork, who had acquired church lands by nifty use of legal devices, or the happy beneficiaries of King James's largesse when he gave away his lands in Ireland, which could only be made good by fudging leases. There was no doubt that both crown and church had lost their property in Ireland, reducing their income. If the crown was to become solvent or the church vigorous, lands must be returned. So of course there would be a contest.

It was primarily the New English Protestants who held church lands because they had taken advantage of the Reformation. Although Protestantism had made little progress in Ireland, the dismantling of monasteries and the confusion caused by the changes had allowed considerable pilfering of land. Wentworth planned to deal with the still strong Catholicism of Ireland by strengthening the official church. That meant getting land back, improving the ministry but also bringing more Protestants into Ireland by offering them land. In the absence of a rebellion which could be punished by confiscation, the way to get land for plantation was by investigating deeds and land titles. The Gaelic Irish who had never been part of the feudal system held their land by custom. The Old English had better land titles but they were mainly Catholics. Both groups now felt intensely insecure; in fact the 'Graces' on which they most pinned their hopes were what secured their ownership of land. Believing faithfully that these promises were to become statute law, they had paid subsidies without demur. When the new Lord Deputy called a parliament, their hopes seemed sure to be fulfilled.

The parliament of 1634 opened in Dublin in generous mood, and members agreed higher rates of tax than was usual. Convocation was called at the same time, and the bishops were urged to pass the Thirty-Nine Articles of faith on which the Church of England rested. This was out of step with the articles which Ussher had written for the Irish church in the reign of King James, and there was disquiet. After demur, the new canons were accepted but only to run alongside the Irish ones. Summer came, and parliament adjourned.

By the time it returned in November, Wentworth had carefully studied the clauses of the 'Graces'. He was forthright in stating that of the fifty clauses, only ten were to become law. Others might continue at the king's pleasure but the two precious items which guaranteed to the gentlemen their lands were not going to be confirmed. He told them this quite clearly on 27 November, and the following day there were storms in parliament. Government bills were voted down amid the general grievance. Moreover, church property was going to be returned and its current holders became quarrelsome. It took Wentworth some time before – using his allies and the pressure of his office – he once more got control of parliament.

If the law was to be the principal instrument of 'Thorough', Wentworth needed courts which would pass the necessary judgements. Four already existed and he beefed them up, especially the Court of Castle Chamber, which was an Irish version of the Star Chamber and under the control of the government. It could not pass a death sentence but it could inflict corporal punishment such as cropping of ears, boring through the tongue and branding – punishments which were also used in England. The court could punish a wide variety of crimes, which gave Wentworth latitude. After he attacked Mountnorris in 1635 and removed him as Vice Treasurer, Wentworth had complete control of the court and used it freely.[6]

It was here that Lord Cork had to explain his possession of church property, which led to a hefty fine. By steady effort, Wentworth's administration returned property to the church and increased its income, while making it conform to Laud's theology. This shift in belief and practice infuriated the Scots planters in Ulster, who had brought with them the Calvinism of the Scottish kirk.

At first it seemed that Wentworth would make an enemy of one of the leading noblemen of Ireland, but instead an understanding blossomed. Young Jemmy Butler of Kilcash had grown to be a man, married his cousin Elizabeth, who had inherited his ancestors' land, and together they were installed in the castle of Kilkenny. James Butler had become 12th Earl of Ormond in 1633, and when parliament opened the following year it was he who carried the sword at the head of the procession. Ormond challenged the Lord Deputy for referring to the Irish as a conquered nation, and there were other bristling encounters, but Ormond held one of the senior earldoms in the kingdom and the young man was trying to modernise his estate; he was someone to court not antagonise. Wentworth brought him into the council and they found a natural sympathy, both energetic and efficient with hopes for a better-governed Ireland.

However, Wentworth would only really prove his worth to the king and his London ministers when he made Ireland solvent. To do that meant getting parliament to grant taxes and improving the revenue from crown lands. Wentworth had a tool ready made for these tasks. In the days of King James, Sir John Davies had created a Commission for Defective Titles. As a lawyer and Attorney General for Ireland, Davies had a clear idea of how the constitution could be developed. First, based on the original invasion of Henry II, he proclaimed the feudal right of the king over the whole of Ireland, in superiority to any indigenous law. That put all the old Gaelic fiefdoms at risk and at the mercy of the commission; titles to land might be clarified and confirmed, or they might be challenged. If the latter, an owner could be made to pay greater dues to the crown, or the land could be confiscated. The way the commission was used depended on the landowner's identity.[7]

Wentworth got parliament to set the commission up again and it proved a powerful tool in his hands. The Old English could be made to pay more ground rent and many of them lost parts of their estate in a financial settlement with the crown. However, Connaught was far more vulnerable; it was largely Gaelic and, since all the owners were Catholic, Wentworth thought it ripe for plantation. In the east of the island, plantation was still being pursued, although the results were disappointing for the government. It had proved difficult to get planters. The Americas had opened up new opportunities and many men of Puritan spirit preferred the risks of the New World to Ireland, where the Lord Deputy's religious policies were antagonising the purer Protestants. Besides, plantation in Ireland was expensive and considered risky. The law was being used for a political project but potential investors were unsure it could succeed. These obstacles did not deter the Lord Deputy. Davies had made clever use of the law and Wentworth energetically carried the project forward; the law might be bent but it was not circumvented or ignored. However, its purpose was obvious to all: to dispossess the indigenous owners and the Catholic grandees in order to import English Protestants. A few Old English who had converted to the new religion supported plantation, hoping to profit from it, but the reaction of the Catholic Irish ranged from aggressively resistant to passively fearful. Wentworth argued that when modernising Britons tilled the land it would support more people. To indigenous peoples those arguments are simply the language of forced dispossession.[8]

Wentworth nonetheless pursued the policy energetically. The method used was to call a local grand jury who must find title for the king; then the process of reordering ownership could begin. But in Connaught he met resistance. The grand juries duly found the king's title for Roscommon, Mayo and Sligo, but Wentworth had decided to include County Galway in the scheme and it was here that conflict arose. Richard Burke, Earl of Clanricard was an Old English Catholic peer and a great landowner in Galway. He had supported Queen Elizabeth when O'Neill rose against her, had been a courtier in the days of King James, and now lived in England where he had an English peerage and estate. He had married the widowed Countess of Essex, and Robert, 3rd Earl of Essex had grown up in his household, where he had become very fond of his stepfather. With these connections, Clanricard could not be overruled lightly.[9] He would not tolerate an attack on his home county, where his own Irish estates lay, and with his position at court he could fight back. Agents for Galway set off for England to fight the plantation. Unfortunately, the old Earl of Clanricard died that winter and it was widely believed that Wentworth's attack on Galway landowners had hastened his end. His son Ulick took up the struggle and the Earl of Essex harboured a lasting animosity towards Wentworth for the attack on his stepfather. The Lord Deputy now had to battle against influences at court, the very thing he had positioned himself to avoid.

The difficulties of the Connaught project brought Wentworth back to England in 1636 when he spent six months at court agreeing his policies with the king and his government. Some thought he was losing his place, but in fact he was triumphant. The Galway delegates were sent back to Ireland and subsequently imprisoned until they gave in and found title for the king. Wentworth was pushing his policies through. He also began to acquire property of his own, in Wicklow and in Kildare, where he built himself a magnificent mansion called Jigginstown House. He had a share in the customs farm and the monopoly of tobacco. His income rose to £13,000 a year, although Lord Cork's was £20,000.[10]

Wentworth's attacks on the larger landowners were part of his goal of justice for 'the meaner sort' and support for more small farmers, whose industry he championed for the sake of Ireland's development, but the beneficiaries of his care were mainly those who started farming under the plantations rather than established Irish farmers. All the same, Wentworth was determined to challenge any abuse of power or contract, no matter how powerful the contractor. One of the most famous plantations in Ireland was actually reversed during Wentworth's rule, although against his advice. The Corporation of London had been strongly encouraged by James's government to take on the plantation of Derry but they were in breach of their terms; they had not brought in sufficient settlers, built fortresses or guarded the coast. The Privy Council in Whitehall found the London company in breach of contract; they were fined heavily, and after a long legal wrangle were forced to surrender the plantation. Wentworth's concern was the company's tenants, the farmers on the ground, and he tendered to take over the plantation himself, but in the end the crown retained it. This is one example where Wentworth was cautious about attacking a large vested interest, but it did him no good for the Londoners blamed him for their losses anyway.

Wentworth's policy of 'Thorough' was becoming a reality in Ireland. The exchequer had turned in a profit, Cork had lost the church lands he held, Mountnorris had been removed, the wealth of the church had been improved and Laud's doctrines imposed on its practice. Wentworth was beginning to impose a single system onto Ireland and to wrest public goods away from the grandees to return them to the public purse. He had laid the groundwork for the plantation of Connaught and was about to enact it.

There had been some troubling developments in England, which Wentworth heard about in ministers' letters. William Prynne, a Puritan lawyer, had written a tract on the immorality of theatre which criticised the queen for performing masques. He had been pilloried and had his ears cut off before imprisonment, but he had substantial public support. John

Hampden had refused to pay ship money, which precipitated a court case in November 1637, something the king hoped to avoid in case the whole procedure was judged to be illegal. Hampden lost the case but gained notoriety. The argument over the king's right to tax was reaching a wider and more excited audience.

By the time that Hampden's case came to court, Scotland was in a religious ferment. The riots in St Giles' Cathedral might have shown Charles just how strongly his Scottish subjects felt about their religion, but he had reacted as if the riots were simple acts of disobedience and only insisted that his policy be followed. When the Scottish kirk drew up the National Covenant in February 1638, Wentworth was well aware of what that would mean for his administration.

William Prynne.

Ulster had been of concern throughout his tenure in Ireland. The plantations had disrupted the whole shape of society in Ulster and the new settlers were only just getting their farms in hand. The debacle over Londonderry had reached confiscation the year before. As for the Gaelic Ulstermen, Wentworth was well aware of the antagonism they felt; he complained of the uncontrollable 'Os and Macs', but now he focussed on the Scottish Presbyterians whose religious practice he and Bramhall had struggled to alter.[11] The Ulster Scots had lived peaceably with the church of James Ussher, but as Bramhall had pushed through changes, Presbyterian ministers had refused to conform and been excluded from their parishes. Many had crossed to Scotland, for there was constant communication across the North Channel. Now, as the Scots rose in support of their religion, Ulster was of grave concern to Wentworth.[12]

With the Scots in a mood of religious revolt, Catholic aristocrats felt emboldened to offer their services to the king. Wentworth, meanwhile, who was quick to move on any issue, saw that the ferment in Scotland would likely lead to war, so when the Ulstermen also began signing the Covenant, the Lord Deputy hired more men to increase the government's army and sent to the Low Countries for arms. Soldiers were drilled and trained with new equipment; Wentworth was ready. His advice to the king was to be assertive. 'This is such insolency as is not to be borne by any rule of monarchy,' he wrote to Charles. All the same, he wrote, 'I must disadvise a rash and sudden declaring of a war...'[13]

The king listened to various noblemen who pressed forward with plans and suggestions. Hamilton was conciliatory as Wentworth was not, but there were other men at court whose suggestions the Lord Deputy found utterly deplorable. The most annoying, from Wentworth's point of view, was Randal, Earl of Antrim, who held a great estate in Ulster but had rivalries of his own to pursue.

13

The Great Men of the North Channel

Randal MacDonnell, Viscount Dunluce and son of the 1st Earl of Antrim, had arrived at court in 1627 when he was only twenty-two. He was tall and well-made with red-blond hair and was full of 'voluble charm'.[1] Like Montrose and many Highlanders, the young nobleman had been 'bred up the highland way', going without cap or shoes until he was seven, to toughen him up.[2]

The Earl of Antrim was a great landowner, based at the family fortress of Dunluce which was perched on a promontory on the north coast of Ulster, looking out across the North Channel to the Western Isles of Scotland where his kinsmen belonged. The young viscount spoke Gaelic as well as English and had been sent to Europe to acquire some polish. His father had enthusiastically supported plantation, even though he lost some land by it, because it brought in enterprising colonists who improved commerce and to whom he leased land.

Viscount Dunluce was an eligible young man but one excellent marriage fell through because his country seat was 'so remote'. When Randal did marry it caused a great stir and gossip because his bride was Katherine Villiers, widow of the Duke of Buckingham. She was seven years older than him and one of the wealthiest women in England. Their marriage in 1635 was of the couple's own making; his father at first was pleased, but the king and court frowned on it. Katherine was forced to give up control of her children's inheritance and her friends disapproved, while courtiers snubbed her.

However, the following year, the 1st Earl died and young Randal inherited the earldom. He was an exuberant Irishman with plenty to say for himself, while the king knew Katherine well and came round to her choice. So from being a minor courtier, the new Earl of Antrim became a close associate of the king and queen.

Katherine was a sweet-faced English rose who had played her part as devoted wife to the philandering duke but was said to have 'wit and spirit'.

The marriage to Antrim was her choice and was a social risk. Among the courtiers it caused a scandal which took some time to die down, but the couple lived in style, their liaison was gradually accepted and they became notable figures at court.

Along with his open manner, Antrim was open-handed or even reckless with money. Before long the wealthy couple had debts which grew alarmingly and became a problem. For this reason and because he was now lord of 340,000 acres, the Antrims moved to Ireland in 1638. Katherine left the court and the mansions she had known as a duchess to move to a stone fortress on a wild cliff in Ireland. Despite the luxurious furnishings which they installed, Dunluce was a clan stronghold, not a mansion in the English shires.

Ulster was already restive. The Covenant was being taken up all over Scotland and the Tables were becoming organised and assertive. There was sporadic disorder in Ulster and a Scottish minister brought over the Covenant so that Ulster Scots could sign. Charles's concern was not Ulster but Scotland; war was threatening and Antrim volunteered assistance to the king. He offered to bring together his clansmen and clients from both sides of the North Channel to form an army in Western Scotland. The idea was actually Hamilton's but Antrim saw an opportunity to both serve the king and attack the Campbells. So he put himself forward and began contacting the leading Scottish MacDonalds, warning them to be ready. Wentworth was appalled. Antrim was a grandson of Tyrone, the greatest Irish foe that England had fought. The idea of putting the crown's weapons into the hands of the Gaelic clansmen was too awful to consider. They were of uncertain loyalty, wild and changeable, and they were Catholic. Wentworth ignored Antrim's offer and delayed.

Charles was facing the consequence of his father's scruples. James had effectively demilitarised the crown and the excursions under Buckingham had shown how weak the government's forces had become.[3] Hamilton's idea might indeed provide troops but aligning himself with Catholic nobles was risky and would provoke further reaction. Wentworth had been strenuously promoting Protestant industry in Ireland and this would reverse the whole trend of his policy.

The king had responded to Antrim's offer and had gone further, promising the young earl that if he retook Kintyre he could keep it.[4] Antrim's ancestral passions were aroused. From Dunluce, Kintyre was visible on calm days. To win it back from the Campbells would be a glorious victory. The king's promise was delicious. But there were allies of the Covenanters at court, men like Sir John Clotworthy the Ulster planter from Devon who heard of Antrim's plan and suspected that the Catholic MacDonalds of the Western Isles might soon be mobilised and armed. So the information was passed back to Edinburgh where the Covenanting leaders were making their plans.[5]

Prominent among these leaders were the minister Alexander Henderson and the lawyer Archibald Johnston of Wariston; between them they had composed most of the documents pressing the Covenanters' demands. An enormous war of paper was breaking out. At the same time, the Covenanters put out feelers to Alexander Leslie, who had been a colonel in the army of the late Gustavus Adolphus and an intimate of the successful Swedish commander.

The year 1638 was critical for the leader of the Campbells. Archibald, Lord Lorne was running the great estates in Argyllshire and the Isles with all the political power that brought, but his father was still alive and in England, holder of the earldom and an enormous vexation to his son. Lorne was a strong Calvinist and ambitious for the great Campbell patrimony with himself at its head. The Campbells had not only territorial wealth and clan leadership but legal jurisdiction in Argyll and the Isles. The father had left Kintyre to the son of his second marriage but Lorne had managed to bring it back into the great Campbell patrimony of which he was the head.[6] He was a few years younger than Randal of Antrim and of the opposite faith, but both young men were energetically trying to improve management of their estates. Antrim was more commercially minded, whereas Lord Lorne was keen for public office.

Lorne was a significant figure on the Scottish Council because of his fiefdom and his ancestors' roles as government agents in the west. Before Charles even sent Hamilton to Scotland, he had called in Lord Lorne for consultation. The young peer was cautious but assisted Hamilton with his negotiations.

It was therefore all the more shocking for Lord Lorne when, during the summer as negotiations in Edinburgh progressed, he heard of the king's offer to Antrim. His Majesty had done the unthinkable – not only roused the Clan Donald and offered to arm them, but promised Kintyre as the spoils of war; Kintyre, which the Campbells had won from the MacDonalds at such cost, which the wayward father had gifted to the child of a Catholic marriage and which the son had used all his ingenuity to drag back. Yet still the young Campbell bit his tongue and kept quiet.

In the autumn, as the rowan trees on the hillsides held their clusters of red berries and their leaves began to flame, the king's offer was made public with all the concessions which Hamilton had devised. Both a parliament and a General Assembly of the Kirk were to be called. At the same time, the King's Covenant was promoted, and around 28,000 signed it – around half of them in the area of Aberdeen where the Gordons and the university were both influential. The Covenanters meanwhile were pressing ahead with preparations for the assembly on their own terms. In this uneasy interim, as snow lay on the tops of the hills, amid demands and threats, men began their journey to the Clyde for a great meeting of their church.

On the morning of 21 November 1638, the General Assembly of the Kirk met in Glasgow Cathedral. Crowds thronged outside, and inside the building was packed with people, including some gentlewomen. There were different strains of opinion within the Scottish church and in the past there had been contests over how assemblies should be run and who could participate. On this occasion, Hamilton had the authority of the king's seal to open proceedings and lead the discussions. It was a role he could not maintain.

Henderson, Wariston and their close associates were elected to the key positions, something Hamilton could not influence. He saw clearly what their agenda would be; his letter to the king was dismal in the extreme, telling him, 'I have missed my end, in not being able to make your Majesty so considerable a party as will be able to curb the insolency of this rebellious nation, without assistance from England, and greater charge to your Majesty, than this miserable country is worth.'[7] Hamilton thought Scotland needed a Lord Deputy to rule it, not the Privy Council, someone with executive power – like Wentworth in Ireland. He feared for his own safety and hoped his children would live and marry in England. Such was his depression over the tone of the assembly.

He tried to dissolve it but, now in session and with a taste of power, the Covenanters refused to go. The assembly met until Christmas, rejecting all the previous meetings held by King James, condemning the prayer book and canons as well as the Court of High Commission. Then they abolished bishops and rejected the Five Articles of Perth. In a month they refused the entire church policy of James and Charles until, just before Christmas, the assembly dissolved itself while Hamilton, leaving Traquair in charge, rode away south to report to the king. The leaders of the kirk dispersed but not all were content. Many preferred a more moderate approach – Hamilton had, after all, conceded so much – but the radicals now held sway. Having swept aside the religious wishes of the king, they had crossed a line. Now they wanted their decisions ratified.

While the assembly was in session, Lord Lorne's position had changed. His father, who had made his life so difficult for so long, died on 29 November – the day that Hamilton tried to dissolve the assembly. Lorne inherited the earldom of Argyll, and once it was his by right he felt secure in pursuing his own beliefs. He stayed at the assembly after Hamilton's dissolution and the following April he signed the Covenant.

This was not a total breach; many nobles had signed, including Montrose. However, the young 8th Earl of Argyll had ambitions and beliefs which began to push him along a path that was at first radical before twisting to reflect the odd shape of his personality.

By now, Alexander Leslie had been hired and was in Scotland with military supplies. In February 1639 he took command of the Covenanting army in Scotland. The first of the contesting armies had come into being. The

Covenanters set up shire commissioners to recruit men, but now resistance showed. In some places the Covenant was forced on local people, and when recruiting began the radicals found it hard to get sufficient troops.

The king was having his own problems raising an army. He had called up the militias in the north of England, and Hamilton was to lead a naval expedition to the Firth of Forth while Antrim's MacDonalds came in from the west. But the king was an inexperienced commander, funding was scarce and the militias were not fit for purpose. Wentworth had balked at arming MacDonalds of any stamp but in February the king ordered him to get on with it and to land troops of the regular Irish army at Carlisle by 1 April.

Early in March 1639, King Charles personally went to war, riding to York to join his army in the north. Troops had been mustered at Berwick and here the king camped. In the Borders, the Scots were massing.

Thirty-five years after the King of Scotland rode south to accept the throne of England, the two countries were at war.

14

The Bishops' Wars

King James had bragged that he ruled Scotland with his pen, but his son was learning differently. He had stirred the one issue which was central to Scottish identity and roused the nation against him. Initially, support for the king was in the north-east; Aberdeen and the Gordons under the Catholic Earl of Huntly held for the king, but most Scots nobles signed the Covenant. The Marquis of Hamilton's mother rode at the head of a troop of horse, armed with a pistol and silver bullets, setting off for Leith and saying she would shoot her son herself if he came ashore on the king's notorious business.[1]

Since attacking the king was treason and carried terrible penalties – always death and, save for the nobility, by hanging, drawing and quartering – rebellion was invariably directed against the king's 'wicked ministers'. In Scotland in 1638 the bishops were identified as prime culprits by the Covenanters, so the clerics fled the council and all but Spottiswoode disappeared from view.

Summer was the fighting season, and as the spring of 1639 advanced so did the king. Antrim's expedition was not ready; the MacDonalds had not gathered nor been armed. Charles had raised around 20,000 men from the trained bands and by calling on great landowners to bring out men, but to make up the numbers county authorities pressed men, many in poor health and with low morale.

Montrose, meanwhile, went north to secure Aberdeen for the Covenant; despite the presence of the Gordons, he was successful. Fife was in the hands of the Covenanters, as were Edinburgh Castle and almost all the Lowland castles including Dumbarton on the Clyde. There were no strongholds for the king, and, whatever his mother might have said, Hamilton could not land his troops on the east coast. He sailed into the Firth of Forth but warned the king he could only proceed by despoiling the coastal towns. Charles had offered that all issues would be resolved in a parliament if the Scots swore proper obedience to him, but Hamilton found it impossible to publish the king's proclamation. It was left to Charles's army at Berwick to overpower the Covenanters. Arundel was in command of the English forces with the Earl of Essex – an experienced soldier – as second-in-command. Unfortunately, at Henrietta-Maria's suggestion, he lost part of his command to the Earl of Holland. So the king's army began in a weak condition.

The Covenanters had to stretch their meagre resources to raise and equip their army, but they had enormous morale and a strong commander. Part of the Scottish forces remained in the north to oppose the royalists but Leslie led his main force to Kelsoe and positioned his men on the high ground. When Holland advanced with 3,000 men, he found the Scots just across the border and apparently in far greater numbers, so he withdrew. Leslie advanced – and then offered negotiations. Charles, aware that he lacked support in England and that his own councillors wanted him to call a parliament, knew he could not risk a military defeat. A treaty would buy him time while he explored other possibilities – overseas loans or new forms of funding.

On 11 June 1639, commissioners from both sides met; on the 19th they signed the Pacification of Berwick. Charles was one of the negotiators and showed some skill in debate, but also hauteur, vagueness and procrastination, something that would recur.[2] The Covenanters agreed to disband their forces and withdraw from the royal castles, and another General Assembly and the delayed parliament would be called; the kirk would decide matters ecclesiastical. Charles was planning to attend both those assemblies but further meetings with the Scots made him change his mind. He sent Traquair instead and rode away south. In his own mind, he seems already to have decided to fight again. He wrote to Wentworth in Dublin: 'Come when you will, ye shall be welcome to your assured friend, Charles R.'[3]

Wentworth arrived in London on 21 September 1639. His advice was to call an English parliament, echoing the opinion of almost all Charles's ministers. There was no other remedy. Council members offered loans for the war effort, Wentworth leading the way with £20,000. His strength of purpose was bracing for the king, who rewarded his Irish deputy with promotion to Lord Lieutenant, which carried more powers and a higher salary; Charles also made him Earl of Strafford and Lieutenant General of the forces for Scotland. In March, the Lord Lieutenant was back in Dublin briefly for the opening of parliament there, where he oversaw a vote of subsidies. Then, leaving his wife and children in Ireland, he returned to England and the king.

In Scotland, the General Assembly met at Edinburgh in August, where it reaffirmed everything decided in Glasgow and gave itself the right to meet annually. It closed and parliament met the following day, but Traquair could not control the members of the Articles. As a result, Covenanters got control of the legislative process and began passing legislation which radically altered the constitution of Scotland. Traquair desperately postponed it several times, and in June 1640 prorogued the session, but Wariston drafted a protestation denying the king's power to close the session without parliament's consent.

Despite this document, the parliamentarians did withdraw but they left behind a committee which was really a continuation of the Tables of the previous year. The Scots, without overtly breaking the law, had bent it until the Covenanters had control of the legislative process and were starting to form an executive.

In February, Traquair arrived in London with Scottish commissioners, of whom Charles had great doubts, suspecting them of complicity with English malcontents.

In April 1640, the English parliament met for the first time in eleven years. Elections were often uncontested but this time they aroused excitement and more were contested than usual.[4] The gentry who controlled rural elections and the urban householders who elected the borough members were all anxious to press their views; the country clearly wanted an agreement with the Scots. After eleven years, there were many new members but John Pym, who had been so dominant in the last meeting, now played a leading role once more. He came from a gentry background in Somerset but his father had died when he was a baby, obliging his family to purchase back his estates from the Court of Wards. Pym had spent much of the 1630s promoting the Providence Island venture but was now working in the Wiltshire Exchequer and had the patronage of the Earl of Bedford. Pym's commitment to purity of religion was strong, so changes in the church weighed heavily with him.

In the eleven years of Charles's personal rule, tax had been collected illegally and the Commons had many grievances. The king, however, saw the business of the meeting as raising money to fight the rebellious Scots. He came to the opening of parliament, but Lord Keeper Finch made the initial speech and asked for unconditional supply. If it was granted, parliament would meet again later in the year when grievances would be answered.[5] The king was anxious to prove that the Scots were the aggressors and had a supposedly treasonable letter from the Covenanters to the King of France, but the content was not damning and it failed to convince the members. It was used as a reason to arrest the Scottish commissioners, though. Ministers reiterated the treachery of the Covenanters and the extreme need of the country for funds with which to confound them.

Debates then began in both houses. Two key speeches were made in the Commons by the stepbrothers Francis Rous and John Pym. Both were West Country men, as Eliot of the last parliament had been, and both were Puritan. After his father's death, Pym's mother had married Sir Anthony Rous of Cornwall, so Pym had grown up with the Rous children – both he and his sister married into that family. Pym had studied at the Middle Temple and had a lawyer's mind. In the 1621 parliament, he had been the member for Calne in Wiltshire, but he shared religious views with Francis Russell, 4th Earl of Bedford and in each subsequent parliament Pym stood for Tavistock in Devon, as Bedford's nominee. Pym, who spoke well and served on several parliamentary committees, increasingly led debates and emerged as a parliamentarian of great stature.

John Pym.

The eleven years of Charles's personal rule had seen intense suspicion of the king's religious policies build up. Under her marriage contract, the queen had been permitted to practise her religion, with a chapel and chaplain, but naturally other Catholics joined her at the services and became known to her personally. When the Scots began recruiting men, the queen had turned to the Catholic peers she knew, innocently certain that they would support the king against such perverse Calvinists. To the Puritans of England, the whole direction of crown policy and allegiance seemed to be shifting towards the Catholics. The theology of the crown had been displayed by the books it published or condoned, as well as the ceremonies which Laud instigated – all anathema to Calvinists.[6]

So, when the session began both houses had heavy grievances. In the House of Lords, debate started while the bishops were absent in Convocation; Laud objected to this, but Lord Saye and Sele said they were unnecessary, which

Francis Russell, Earl of Bedford.

led to acrimonious exchanges. In the Commons, the religious policies of the king and the illegal collection of taxes were raised immediately by members. Pym spoke for two hours on these issues, asserting the rights of parliament in a carefully written speech intended for publication. Especially in the growing towns and cities of England, many inhabitants were literate, highly motivated about their religion and had the vote. Speeches were therefore written with publication in mind. Despite the crown's harsh censorship laws, pamphlets and handwritten texts tried to sway public opinion. The crown published its own proclamations and declarations as a struggle to influence the nation began.[7] In parlours and pubs, those who could not read heard others who could declaim the latest political literature; heated debate often followed.

The king was disadvantaged in parliament because his stammer made it hard for him to speak at length. On the advice of Wentworth, now Earl of Strafford, Charles went to meet his parliament and tried to influence the House of Lords. The peers decided that supply outweighed grievances and should come first but the Commons were only further incensed by this advice, since taxation was their special preserve. Strafford was now in the Lords and urged forward the king's business, but he was roundly criticised.

King James I of England VI of Scotland, Daniel Mytens. (© National Portrait Gallery, London)

Charles I with M. de St. Antoine (1633), Anthony van Dyck. (Courtesy of the Royal Collection Trust / © Her Majesty Queen Elizabeth II 2020)

Queen Henrietta-Maria, Anthony van Dyck (oil on canvas). (Courtesy of the Royal Collection Trust / © Her Majesty Queen Elizabeth II 2020)

Princess Elizabeth, Queen of Bohemia and Electress Palatine, studio of Michiel Jansz. Van Miereveldt. (© National Portrait Gallery, London)

Charles I, by Anthony van Dyck (black chalk on paper). (© The Rijksmuseum, Amsterdam)

George Villiers, 1st Duke of Buckingham, Pieter Paul Rubens. (© Gabinetto Fotografico delle Gallerie degli Uffizi)

Thomas Wentworth, 1st Earl of Strafford, studio of Sir Anthony Van Dyck.
(© National Portrait Gallery, London)

John Hampden, school of Godfrey Kneller. (By
kind permission of Banbury Town Council)

Randal MacDonnell, 1st Marquis of Antrim, John
Michael Wright. (By kind permission of Viscount
Dunluce)

James Butler, 1st Duke of Ormonde, Willem Wissing. (© National Portrait Gallery, London)

Robert Devereux, 3rd Earl of Essex, unknown artist. (Private collection; on loan to the National Portrait Gallery, London)

Prince Rupert, Count Palatine, Gerrit van Honthorst. (© National Portrait Gallery, London)

Edward Montagu, 2nd Earl of Manchester, Sir Peter Lely. (© National Portrait
Gallery, London)

Oliver Cromwell, after Sir Peter Lely. (© National Portrait Gallery, London)

Murrough O'Brien, 1st Earl of Inchiquin, John Michael Wright. (Image courtesy of Manchester Art Gallery)

James Graham, 1st Marquis of Montrose. (Photograph by Nick Birse via Wikimedia Commons)

Archibald Campbell, 1st Marquess of Argyll (portrait previously at Inveraray Castle, now lost).

John Milton (a young man thought to be the poet), by Peter Lely or his student Mary Beales. (By kind permission of the Master and Fellows of Christ's College Cambridge)

The Old Palace of Westminster, as it was in the reign of Henry VIII, H. J. Brewer (1884).

By early May, not only did the government lack subsidies but the Commons were about to debate a declaration sent down to them by the Scots. The Privy Council advised the king not to allow a worse situation to develop, so Charles went down to the House of Lords and dissolved parliament. The Short Parliament had sat for less than a month.

The king had command of the trained bands, but there were young people in London who could be roused in other ways. Placards began to appear calling on apprentices to join in hunting 'William the Fox' – William Laud – for bringing down the parliament. The archbishop had to leave Lambeth Palace but threats were also issued against Henrietta-Maria's mother, Marie de Medici, a tiresome old woman who had already caused conflict in France and had chosen to arrive in England at the worst possible moment and against Charles's wishes. Apart from her image as Catholic queen-dowager of France, an increasingly absolutist country, she arrived with an entourage and cost a great deal of money to keep. Placards also called for Henrietta-Maria's chapel to be torn down and rioters broke two of their imprisoned fellows out of gaol. Strafford urged the Privy Council to 'go on vigorously'; he believed 'the quiet of England will hold out long', and after these disturbances calm did return to London.[8]

The trained bands were being called up for war against the Scots, while the government tried to collect ship money and more obscure charges, such as coat-and-conduct money or billeting money, but it was increasingly difficult to even find collectors. The government's only other resource was loans, but both in London and overseas they failed to raise money. Now, even the Irish parliament became uncooperative. With the iron will of the Lord Lieutenant removed, his deputy failed to raise subsidies when the Irish Commons reassembled in June. However, the new army of 8,000 men which Strafford had created was still in readiness. At council deliberations in London, Strafford told the king, 'You have an army in Ireland that you may employ here to reduce this kingdom.' Whether he meant Scotland or England, his words were recorded by a fellow council member to be later used against him.[9]

In the shire counties, officials struggled to press men into the king's army. There were scarcely funds to pay or equip them. In Scotland, however, the Covenanting army had taken the north-east from the Gordons. Kirk leaders held another General Assembly in Aberdeen. The Earl of Argyll was emerging as a significant leader of the Covenanters and led an army of 4,000 men through the central Highlands to subdue any dissent. However, the Earl of Montrose, who had met Charles at Berwick, where some mutual sympathy had arisen, now began to doubt the cause which he had initially supported. As discontent grew, the aims and motives of those ranged against the king began to show more clearly – some more radical than others. Some who had joined in action against royal policy began to feel that confrontation was being taken too far, and perhaps had deeper aims.

The government in London resorted to desperate measures to raise funds, borrowing Spanish gold stored for minting in the Tower and impounding pepper belonging to the East India Company until the City of London protested so loudly that it was an honest trading city with a reputation to maintain that some seizures were reversed. Charles decided he would personally lead his forces. At last, an army was mustered at Selby and was marched to Newcastle under Conway, but the overall commander, Northumberland, became sick with fever and had to be replaced. Strafford, Lieutenant General and responsible for the Irish forces, despite his inexperience of war, was named as commander.

Strafford had been ill throughout the summer of 1640. Crippled by gout for some time, on arrival in England he collapsed with dysentery. Hardly recovered, he now took up a role for which he had no experience. In August, he set out north to his home county of Yorkshire. The king too went to join his army at York, while petitions were gathered for another parliament.

The Scots were already moving south. On 20 August they crossed the border into England. Conway moved part of his forces forward but the Scots were crossing the Tyne when the two armies met and fought at Newburn on the southern bank. It was a rout. Strafford had only just reached York when messengers galloped into the city to tell him of the defeat of his army. Three days later, the Scots marched into Newcastle.

A Great Council was called at York and the king was there on 24 September to open it. Covenanting forces had taken the principal Scottish castles; they had a strong hand. Against Strafford's wishes negotiations were opened with the Scots but the king had already announced that writs were going out for an English parliament; it would meet on 3 November. To his councillors, the king seemed confident, still believing that the aristocracy and gentry would support him and that he need not concede anything of substance to the Scots. But the Scottish army was camped in England; it held Durham and controlled Newcastle, which was the source of England's coal supply. Terms would have to be made and in October the king's commissioners agreed to pay the expenses of the Scottish army until parliament agreed a proper settlement.

At £850 a day, a bill was already being racked up. The king had no wish to meet another of his parliaments but with the cost of the Scottish soldiers mounting, the sooner he reached an agreement the better. So he returned to London, where the newly elected members were soon to come together in what would be a very long-lived assembly. It would outlive the king by many years and see its final days under his son, who in 1640 was a chubby toddler. King Charles returned to his family and to the spirited but very poor advice he often received from his pretty little Catholic queen.

The Scots settled down at English expense, while the Earl of Strafford withdrew the forces whose command had been foisted on him. For him, it would not be a very long parliament.

15

The Long Parliament Meets

The time available for elections was short but determination to sit in the coming parliament was strong and even more elections were contested than in the spring. The members came up to London as quickly as they could. Clarendon, in his famous history, says that when parliament met, 'as at first many members were absent, it had a sad and a melancholic aspect … which presaged some unusual and unnatural events. The king himself did not ride with his accustomed equipage nor in his usual majesty to Westminster, but went privately in his barge…'[1]

The members met within the old Palace of Westminster, a magnificent group of buildings on the banks of the river, set between the abbey and the Thames. At its heart was Westminster Hall with its great hammer-beam roof, but the Commons gathered in St Stephen's Chapel adjoining it and the Lords in their own chamber at the edge of the palace complex. Between the palaces of Westminster and Whitehall there were only gardens and yards, as the two palaces were adjacent and looked down to the Thames where several stone stairways gave access to the river. The king stepped lightly into his barge from the Privy Stairs of Whitehall and was rowed the short distance upriver to meet the members and open the session:

> And from thence, in great Solemnity, he came, accompanied with many of his Nobles, through Westminster Hall, and the Court of Requests, to the Abbey, where he heard a sermon preached by the Bishop of Bristol; and then came to the Lords House: Where his Majesty briefly, and the Lord Keeper more at large, delivered the causes of summoning this Parliament, such Members of the House of Commons as pleased, being there present.[2]

For Charles, it could only be a sad and difficult encounter. His kingdom had been invaded by his own subjects and he was being forced to pay them to withdraw. For a chief executive it was a humiliating failure of policy; for a war leader it was a capitulation.

The king had the right to propose the Speaker of the Commons but the City of London prevented the election of the man he wanted, so the king delayed while the election lists were pored over and another man chosen. His ministers decided on a barrister named William Lenthall who did not want the job but was prevailed upon.

The men who came together that November day could not know that their assembly would become a famous parliament, not only in Britain but in North America where its desperate constitutional wrestling would set the agenda for modern democracy. The members themselves were perhaps no more heroic or villainous than other public men but their times had reached a crisis – it was the ideas which the crisis squeezed out of them that proved vital as they struggled from one era of government into a new one.

Clarendon, who was there, and the great nineteenth-century historian Gardiner both emphasise the fact of the Scots army encamped at Newcastle and the English army in the north, both requiring payment. There was, of course, a third army and one which had been paid and armed: the new army of 8,000 men or more which Strafford had raised in Ireland. He was Lord Lieutenant still and his colleague, the Earl of Ormond, was the commander. The king had also put Strafford in command of the English army in the north. Two of the three armies were under his orders.

Strafford had retired to his family home at Wentworth Woodhouse. He knew well enough that if he left the old house and Yorkshire, where his army was encamped, he would be blamed for the current situation. Hamilton advised him to flee but that was not in Strafford's nature. The king sent for him and the queen entreated him to come. Strafford obeyed, although he told his friend, 'I am tomorrow to London, with more dangers beset, I believe, than ever any man went out of Yorkshire; yet my heart is good, and I find nothing cold in me. It is not to be believed how great the malice is, and how intent they are about it.'[3] So he set out for London on 6 November, riding slowly because he was still painfully unwell.

The parliamentary sessions began with a call for a fast, an explosion of grievances and the decision to put Irish affairs at the top of the agenda. The public fast was a sign both of Puritan culture in the Commons and the sense of crisis in the country. They needed the king's permission and asked for it, because the authorities occasionally called these days of prayer, Bible reading and sermons, with only a simple meal when the day ended, at times of national crisis. When Puritans called them without permission they were stamped on, but this time the king agreed – parliament and London would fast on 17 November and the whole country a month later.

Petitions arrived from counties and boroughs with a litany of complaints: about religious alterations, illegal taxation and imprisonment, as well as military annoyance and incompetence. People imprisoned under religious legislation had been kept in harsh conditions. Now that parliament had assembled, both Lords and Commons were tense with grievance and determined to take action. The general belief was that England was a mixed monarchy in which king and parliament had complementary roles. Charles himself admitted the right of parliament in making law and spoke of its role in the political life of England. The king's prerogative and the rights of parliament coexisted but parliament believed the boundary had been pushed far too far in favour of the king's powers and that the executive, having taken excessive power, had ruled incompetently.

To challenge the king, however, was dangerous – it could carry a charge of treason, so challenges were invariably made at 'evil ministers'. Clearly Strafford would be the prime target. He was the king's most forceful minister, uncompromising, effective and an experienced manager of parliaments. He was a member of the House of Lords, which meant he could only be tried by his peers, but the English House of Lords was now dominated by an energetic and reforming faction. They intended to redress the balance between parliament and king, between law and prerogative. They were acting perhaps not as radicals or revolutionaries, but rather as vigorous conservatives attempting to re-establish the system of the Tudors.

These parliamentarians, who formed the real opposition to the king, had been working on a political settlement to propose once parliament met. This was the first of many schemes whereby King Charles would be persuaded to accept changes of ministers and modifications to his powers in order to save his government from ruin. At bottom, Charles was motivated by his conscience and his sense of honour, but he often read political situations inaccurately. His friends and ministers understood his touchy self-image and advised him carefully, framing advice around these notions. His opponents read him differently. They found him hard to negotiate with, a man who made vague agreements which he subsequently did not keep. Charles felt keenly that he must defend the office of king and acted accordingly but his opponents saw only duplicity. From the beginning of the crisis, loss of trust and the rumours which grew from that played an enormous part in what followed.

In this first attempt to reach a settlement, parliament was led by the Earl of Bedford and a group of peers allied to him in the Lords – Robert Devereux, 3rd Earl of Essex; Robert Rich, 2nd Earl of Warwick; Edward Montagu, son of the Earl of Manchester; and William Fiennes, 1st Viscount Saye and Sele. Also closely aligned were Lords Brooke, Wharton, Paget and Howard. These men were middle-aged and some had sons in the Commons who supported their strategy, although Bedford's principal manager in the Commons was John Pym.

Pym had trained as a lawyer and was an able parliamentarian, skilled at pulling like-minded groups together and masterly at debate. This was important because although many members and much of the public were incensed at government activity, they were enraged for disparate reasons. Of these, religion was the most sensitive and inflammatory. The men who came together in 1640 to improve government did not, in fact, share religious views. Pym's chief associates in the Commons were John Hampden, Oliver St John, Denzil Holles, Nathaniel Fiennes and William Strode. The Commons had power over taxation and so an immediate hold on the king, but the peers had superiority in wealth and status, and controlled local patronage and the men on their estates. Peers were the heads of powerful families with long tentacles through society. Now, to manage this moment of crisis, it would take coordination of the two Houses, which was why the Bedford–Pym axis was so important.

Bedford was a moderate, respected by the reformers but known at court and by Charles, with a religious outlook compatible with that of the king. The Bedford–Pym group's plan was to gain control over ministerial appointments and reorganise crown finance so the government would become solvent. There was persistent talk of Bedford as Treasurer and Pym becoming Chancellor. Their bargaining chips were the presence of the Scots army, which made dissolution of parliament impossible; the dissatisfaction of the country, which could show itself in London mobs, especially if they were provoked by posters and speeches; and the financial weakness of the crown. Parliament was testing its ability to bring down Charles's ministers and to revoke unpopular legislation, but in doing so they were taking risks and in order to succeed they had to keep the support of several groups who might change allegiance or fracture. One problem was religion since the Scots were strongly anti-episcopalian, while the king was determined to retain bishops and parliament held a range of religious views.

The agenda of the English parliament was now bound to those of Scotland and Ireland. Charles could not dissolve the English parliament until he had paid the Scots, and the English needed evidence from Ireland in order to remove Strafford. The three political nations had become locked together. There was some Irish representation in London: Lord Cork had three family members in parliament and the Earl of Warwick found a seat for Clotworthy. Soon after parliament opened, Scottish commissioners arrived in London with eight key demands. While negotiating in the north, they had stipulated that any treaty needed consent from both Charles and the English parliament; in London the king was actually excluded from the negotiations, which were conducted by commissioners, although foreign policy and defence were clearly within the royal prerogative. To get evidence from Ireland, Pym announced freedom of travel between the two islands. Wandesford, who had been left in charge in Dublin, was losing control; a petition from the Irish parliament was read to the English Commons and Irish members prepared to go to London themselves to testify against the Lord Lieutenant.

The parliamentary leaders in London acted before the Irish delegation arrived. Strafford arrived in London on 10 November. English MPs had colluded with the Scots during the year and Strafford's advice to the king was to charge them with treason, but the Bedford–Pym group were preparing their own attack. Evidence was collected from Clotworthy, who recounted military plans made in Ireland, and from young Sir Henry Vane, who had gone into his father's study, read Sir Henry senior's official papers and copied out a damning quote made by Strafford in council.[4] The Bedford–Pym group expected more time to prepare their case but Strafford was in London meeting the king and might precipitate action against them. Pym took an official charge to the Lords, and when Strafford came in to take his seat he was made to kneel while the charge of treason was read against him. Then he was arrested.

With Strafford in the Tower, the Bedford–Pym group set about redressing the wrongs of the personal rule by taking many matters into their own hands. Commissioners for the Scots and English were working on a treaty, while the Irish delegation was helping to build the case against Strafford.

In Edinburgh, parliament had moved ahead of the English and had altered the constitution. It only sat on a semi-legal basis but throughout the summer of 1640, while its armies invaded England, it reorganised itself, legislated for a parliament every three years (the Triennial Act), took charge of the Lords of the Articles, removed the bishops from parliament, ratified all the Acts of the General Assembly and created a Committee of Estates to govern the kingdom. This had full executive powers, including tax-raising, which the Covenanters justified by the state of war and threat of invasion. Then, with great insouciance, they sent all these Acts to the king – not to ask consent but for his information.[5]

Argyll was not a member of the Committee of Estates, whereas Montrose was. In Scotland, the Covenanting armies aimed to get complete control of the country. Many royalists were attacked and the war began to show the old feuding tendencies of the Highlands. Robert Monro, son of a gentry family from Ross, had returned from the Swedish army to command the Covenanter troops in the north-east. Here, some royalists were taken prisoner and many had their property plundered or occupied. Argyll raised troops in his own territory which were under his command. His task was to guard the west coast should Strafford's army sail, but he also took the fight through the central Highlands, burning the Airlie House from which Lady Airlie fled in terror. It was being said – and sung – that the leader of the Campbells might become head of the nation before long and Montrose viewed with horror the rise of this secretive but ambitious man. In August 1640, Montrose made the Cumbernauld Bond with other moderate gentry to resist extremists and tacitly to resist the rise of Argyll. The Covenanters were beginning to split.

In Dublin, Christopher Wandesford had struggled as parliament became restive. Left in charge when Strafford sailed for England, he had great loyalty to his old friend but none of his commanding skills. The autumn session became unmanageable as charges against Strafford mounted, and to prevent more harm Wandesford prorogued parliament, but two agents had already left for London; once Pym announced free travel, the Lord Deputy's control slipped further. Wandesford fell ill and ran a high fever; by 3 December he was dead. A week later, the Committee of Thirteen left Dublin for London; their grievances were those of both Old English and planters.[6] There, allied with the New English in the Commons and with Pym's growing importance, they were able to influence any new appointments in Dublin. Instead of Strafford's colleagues, Charles appointed two neutral Lords Justices. Strafford's rule in Ireland was effectively over, and a warrant was sent for the arrest of his loyal secretary Mainwaring. When the Irish parliament reconvened in January 1641, it too set about drafting a list of grievances against the Lord Lieutenant, hoping to use these in the impeachment but also to strengthen the case for their own rights in Ireland.

In London, the House of Commons had set about undoing some of the king's most objectionable policies. The members pronounced ship money illegal, overturned Laud's recent Canons and started the process of impeaching both the Archbishop and Keeper Finch who fled abroad with another threatened minister. Laud was taken into custody. The Commons took great delight in freeing men imprisoned over church policy. A young MP spoke on behalf of John Lilburne, who had been flogged and imprisoned for publishing anti-episcopalian tracts. Lilburne was a firebrand and later became leader of the Levellers. The member who spoke for him was forty-one years old but only in his second parliament. Oliver Cromwell was described as poorly dressed, 'with a swollen and reddish countenance', and a sharp, 'untunable voice', by a Treasury secretary.[7] Cromwell was then a small landowner living in Ely but had been elected for Cambridge. In 1628 he had his seat from the Montagu family and had only spoken once but by 1640 he had been through a religious awakening and had asserted himself over local issues – the composition of his local council and the drainage of the Fens, over which he defended the rights of local commoners. When he entered parliament in 1640 he was involved with the group of Puritans to whom he was related and which included Hampden and St John. It was probably through the influence of the Earl of Warwick, one of their faction in the Lords, that Cromwell got the Cambridge seat, although a group of Aldermen there apparently liked the way he spoke at prayer meetings. In 1640 Cromwell was clearly acting as part of the Pym group in the Commons, where he spoke on their business and was put on significant committees.

With Strafford in the Tower, Finch out of the country and Laud in custody, Hamilton once more became principal adviser to the king. Charles was also

John Lilburne.

bombarded by the spirited ideas of Henrietta-Maria who conceived the dangerous idea of appealing to the Pope for help. However, Hamilton was a consensus-builder, always looking to find middle ground and stitch together compromises. His advice was to give a little and win back support. Early in the new year Charles began to do this, bringing some of the opposition into his Privy Council and agreeing to a Triennial Act, to great rejoicing. By compromising, he began to find support. There is no doubt that Charles's subjects were as angry and restive as his parliamentarians. The gentry had refused to pay the Forced Loan and ship money, some peers had refused to join the Great Council in York, seamen and apprentices attacked Lambeth Palace, and soldiers marching to fight the Scots had killed Catholics and torn down altar rails. The merchants of London had refused to lend money to the crown.

As Charles tried Hamilton's policy of concessions, he began to learn the art of politics. He still made enormous blunders, and before long he changed course, but whereas in the past he had seen his job as deciding policy and announcing it he now realised he had to sell his ideas and charm his people. At some of this he showed considerable promise. However, not all of the people ranged against him wanted to compromise; some would be happy enough if Charles remained obdurate. Events would show who belonged in that camp and where the various fault lines of opinion lay.

In January and February 1641, Charles followed this strategy. He would not yield over bishops, but if parliament accepted the structure of the church he would 'reduce all matters of religion and government to what they were in the purest times of Queen Elizabeth's day'.[8] He would give up any illegal forms of income and remove his wife's papal emissary. The Triennial Act was a popular concession and key parliamentarians – Bedford and Saye – became Privy Councillors. The king's position was strengthened by the Scots' uncompromising attitudes on religion; when they demanded that the English church conform to their model the Scots alienated part of the Bedford–Pym group on whom they relied.

On 22 March 1641, Strafford was impeached for treason. The trial was held in Westminster Hall where special seats and platforms had been built, since this was a great set piece and public spectacle. Impeachment was a medieval procedure which had been revived under James I and used unsuccessfully against Buckingham. For parliament its great advantage was that it did not require the king's consent, but in impeaching Strafford the members were taking a great risk because a charge of treason would be hard to prove against the Lord Lieutenant. Treason was a crime against the monarch and no one had been a more loyal servant to the king. Nor had Strafford worked in England; the charges against him all related to his career in Ireland, which was a separate jurisdiction. If the trial failed, its prosecutors would be dangerously weakened. They used Sir Henry Vane's evidence of Strafford telling the king that he had an army in Ireland which could be used 'to reduce this kingdom' as evidence of a threat against England, but it clearly referred to the Scots rebellion and the prosecution had little other hard evidence. Their strategy was to prove that the Lord Lieutenant had subverted the law and divided the king from his people. These charges were still weak but they hoped to show 'accumulative treason' by a series of the Lord Lieutenant's policies.[9]

The Earl of Strafford was not a well-loved man but he put up a clever and spirited defence. His courage and eloquence began to affect the onlookers and to win him sympathy, especially when the case against him seemed fabricated. The prosecutors feared the peers might acquit him.

Then, on 10 April, changing tack, Sir Arthur Hazelrig introduced a Bill of Attainder against Strafford. This would not require proof; it was an

Act of Parliament which would simply declare him guilty – but it would require the king's assent. The stakes were now higher. Notices began to go up around London naming those who might vote for Strafford's acquittal, until members of parliament became fearful and began to melt away. The Bedford–Pym group had become divided over the Bill of Attainder, and the king, who had watched the trial from a box behind the seats, saw his own decision coming closer. There had been time for compromise – Bedford could have wrung concessions from Charles in return for a deal over Strafford – but events were moving swiftly. The more radical MPs were determined on Strafford's death but Charles wrote to Strafford that 'upon the word of a king, you shall not suffer in life, honour or fortune'.[10]

Meanwhile, a marriage had been arranged between the nine-year-old Princess Mary and Prince William of Orange, aged twelve. The boy arrived in London and on 2 May the children were formally married at Whitehall with garlands and festivities.

The tide had turned against Strafford. In April, rumours reached London of a plot by the crown involving the northern army, which would march south, take the Tower and free Strafford – but the officers were against it. The Commons were informed and issued orders not to move the troops. Charles, however, continued with a scheme to take the Tower with a small force and free his minister. On 1 May, the king went to the House of Lords where he agreed not to employ Strafford again but said he could never assent to the Bill of Attainder. This had the negative effect of seeming to coerce the Lords. On 3 May, the plot to take the Tower was discovered; the following day, the Bill of Attainder was introduced in the Lords. Now the chance of acquittal became remote. In those early May days, the Commons frantically discussed the 'Army Plot', while mobs descended on Westminster and there were tumults around parliament and threats at Whitehall.

Strafford wrote the king a brave and subtle letter in which he absolved Charles of his promise. He wished to 'set your Majesty's conscience at liberty ... for the prevention of evils which may happen by your refusal to pass this Bill', as he hoped for 'that blessed agreement which God I trust shall ever establish between you and your subjects'. Strafford stated explicitly that Charles should not have intervened but left the peers to judge him. It was a courageous letter which gave Charles the right to sacrifice his minister. Used carefully, the letter might still have swung opinion, as a similar one from a priest had recently done.[11] The king did not try to use it. Peers were absenting themselves from the house and the bishops decided to refrain from voting. The chances of the bill failing were diminishing, soaking away. On 8 May, the Bill of Attainder had its third and final reading in the House of Lords. Out of one hundred and fifty peers, only forty-five actually voted; the bill was passed by seven votes. Now only the king's assent stood between Strafford and execution. The crowds stormed Whitehall, and the queen with her ladies hid in her apartments. The king was in agony. At last, fearful for his wife and children, he gave in and signed.

Strafford seemed shocked when he was informed, but he faced his death with dignity. He was executed on Tower Hill on 12 May, with a vast crowd to see the event. Charles could not forgive himself and swore he would never offer up a loyal servant again.

Bedford was already dead; he had succumbed to smallpox three days earlier. John Pym still led in the Commons – from the first meeting of the Long Parliament he dominated the chamber – but already his own group showed it was less compromising than him. Gradually, parliament agreed terms with the Scots and raised the money to pay them. Their presence was causing growing discontent in the north of England.

Concessions by the king continued but his attitude was changing once more. Compromise had brought a poor reward; Strafford was already dead. Nonetheless, he agreed not to collect tonnage and poundage without consent, while the courts of Star Chamber and High Commission were abolished. Parliament passed a bill banning its dissolution without its own consent. The king assented to this, giving the parliament unexpected longevity. He also disbanded his Irish army as he saw no way to pay for it.

Parliament had taken up the issue of bishops, in particular whether they should continue to sit in parliament. However, in May, Oliver Cromwell and Sir Henry Vane the younger introduced a more radical bill into the Commons which aimed to abolish episcopacy altogether. The Root and Branch bill followed a petition of the same name from the previous winter, which was originally the work of radical ministers but had gained momentum in London from the presence of the Scots, for whom episcopacy was anathema. But the bill was divisive, and presented Pym with a problem. It led to moderates leaving the party of reform and moving over to the king as the defender of the church. It showed Cromwell's motives more clearly; here he was not supporting the policies of his group, as he had done on committees or seconding bills, but acting on his personal beliefs.[12]

By June, parliament had agreed a peace treaty with Scotland, the Treaty of London, in which the recent Acts of the Scottish parliament were to be ratified, the 'incendiaries' of the recent troubles were to be tried and reparations paid to Scotland. Charles resisted the first and – mindful of Strafford – argued over the second until final judgement was left to him. On 10 August, the king ratified it and then, against the wishes of parliament, set off for Edinburgh. For some time he had been in correspondence with Montrose, and Charles now believed he had growing support in Scotland. The letters had been discovered and Montrose imprisoned, but certainly public opinion across Britain was shifting. If he built a party based on constitutional norms and he adhered to moderate policies, he could find support. Public opinion was becoming nervous of the changes underway and the evidence of radical aims emerging among some of the protagonists. If the king were reasonable and consistent, he had every chance of winning the support and respect of the majority. Sadly for Charles, he had neither the ability nor the patience to form such a party.

When the king arrived in Edinburgh, he was greeted warmly by the crowds. However, he found he had little control over legislation passed by the Scottish parliament, nor over the appointment of ministers and councillors. Newly assertive, the Covenanting movement was pressing its advantage. Through the autumn, Charles stayed on in Edinburgh trying to come to an agreement with the Scottish parliament over the fate of Traquair, who had been removed from office and against whom parliament was initiating proceedings as an incendiary, and over whom to appoint as ministers and councillors. The Scots wanted Argyll to become Chancellor but Charles held out against that. Another plot – to seize Argyll, Hamilton and Lanark – was named 'the Incident' when it burst into the autumn air, but Charles protested his innocence and allowed Hamilton to take the blame. Hamilton was being side-lined, both for policies which had failed but also for his closeness to Argyll. Charles kept up his strategy of compromise and reward; pensions were awarded and titles given out, with Argyll becoming a marquis and Leslie newly made Earl of Leven.

Charles was in Edinburgh when the final text of the Treaty of London arrived for his signature. It increased parliament's control over war between the kingdoms and promoted trade between them. Tax had been raised in England to pay the first tranche of the agreed costs and the Scottish army left Newcastle on 21 August; when it reached Leith, all but three regiments were disbanded.[13]

Back in London, parliament adjourned for the autumn. It had put through its most pressing legislation and had achieved many of the Pym group's aims, but both in Westminster and out in the country there was growing sympathy for the king. There was a dislike of the godly party and a feeling that the king had been pushed too far. On 21 October, MPs reassembled in Westminster and carried on with their programme, removing clergy from parliament and disbanding the army in the north. Pym planned to introduce a Grand Remonstrance detailing all that had gone wrong in the kingdom and stating parliament's plans for redress. But on 1 November, the day appointed for a major debate on the Grand Remonstrance, a group of Privy Councillors arrived breathlessly in the Commons 'and informed it of certain intelligences, that were lately come, of a great Treason, and general Rebellion, of the Irish Papists in Ireland; and a design of cutting off all the Protestants in Ireland; and seizing all the king's Forts there'.[14] There was alarm and consternation.

A committee was formed from the Commons and the Lords, to send men and ammunition to Ireland, to secure the Isle of Wight and to intern papists in England. Lists were to be drawn up of Catholics in the queen's household and all foreign papists were to be registered. All travel to Ireland was to be stopped. In high alarm, the Commons prepared to defend England and send troops to Ireland, but the king was still in Scotland.

Charles was playing golf at Leith when news of the Irish rebellion was brought to him. His initial reaction was that it might make the English rethink their recent 'follies', and this opinion, when reported in London, gave the Pym group a fillip: did the king not take rebellion seriously? The Commons had already drafted a list of their grievances in August; now they returned to the Grand Remonstrance and debated it more fervently.

By now, the king had left Edinburgh and was on his way south. He made a ceremonial entry into London on 25 November – he had realised that being a dignified king was not sufficient and that he needed public approval from all sections of society. This effort on his part was met by popular loyalty, but his opponents had already shown they could get people out on the streets too. The printing presses were busy throughout, with speeches, newsletters and pamphlets.

However, the documents causing the most alarm were the despatch sent by the Lords Justices in Dublin and the letters that followed. As autumn turned into winter, it became clear that the situation in Ireland was very serious indeed but in London, where the balance of power was still contested, it was difficult to coordinate a full government response. Strafford was dead and his army had been disbanded in the spring. Who was going to reinstate control? The Scots still had a functional military establishment and so they lost no time in sending an army to Ireland. Without sovereign status, and with a weaker political establishment, the Irish government could not resist this invasion by a foreign army, nor make an effective complaint. England had to act.

16

The Irish Rebellion of 1641

When the Ulster lords rose in rebellion in the autumn of 1641, their goals were limited and even those were not realised. However, the rising had far-reaching consequences, not only because of the event itself and its immediate repercussions, which were cataclysmic enough, but because reports written subsequently inflamed opinion and influenced graver decisions. The English and Scots already had a negative view of Irish Catholics, partly fuelled by fear, so when the brutal rebellion was reported with blood-curdling detail but then elaborated on and subsequently exaggerated, the response from the English government was severe.

The rebellion was a violent and radical event. Like most rebellions, it had long-term causes and a recent trigger. The conspirators were aggrieved over religion, angry about plantation and alarmed over land security; they had been let down over the Graces. Charles had offered much and given little but, for Irish Catholics, the two parliaments in Britain were far more malevolent than the king. The Irish also watched as the Scots invaded England only to receive influence and money as a result; this was a strategy they could copy. A plot germinated and was activated; it did not achieve its aims but it did unleash a groundswell of resentment, rage and lust for redress among the Catholic Irish, especially those in Ulster where plantation had been most recent and most comprehensive.

The resentment was long-term but the plot was a response to events in Britain. Irish Catholics were increasingly alarmed as the king lost power to parliaments in Edinburgh and London, which were in ever-closer cooperation. In December 1640, Charles had agreed to the 'Graces' in return for funding for his Irish army, but the Irish Council had prevented the legislation. The English parliament then demanded control over Irish legislation and Charles, under pressure, had agreed. For the Catholic Irish, the English Privy Council had been repressive enough – the English parliament would be far worse. The Root and Branch Bill showed the temper of the London Commons: strongly Calvinist, anti-Episcopalian and backed by Scottish Presbyterians. The Treaty of London had created a real transfer of power – it gave parliament management over the cessation of war. The Irish had experienced Strafford's ruthless policies but when he was tried and executed it was by Westminster, not under Irish justice. For Irish Catholics, the alignment of rigid Calvinists in England and Scotland, both with growing political power, was an existential threat. Plantation had already been extensive. The Old English of the Pale still held their lands and substantial wealth, but if the Puritan element got control, how long would that last?

The uneasy constitutional arrangements of the three kingdoms had only been held together by the king. Now, the Scots invasion had made radical changes and two assertive parliaments were gaining power. The two islands had become more closely linked. Clearly the conflicts in Britain would spill over into Ireland, where tensions were already so high.

Ireland was not homogenous. Ulster was different to the southern provinces of Ireland, with a smaller Old English presence; it had remained a Gaelic society until Tyrone's rebellion, after which the plantations had transformed it, creating simmering resentment.[1] From early in 1641, a group of Gaelic nobles led by Rory O'More and Conor Lord Maguire began to plan resistance. Once the 'Graces' were refused again, they resolved to act. The support of the O'Neills was essential; the Earl of Tyrone had fled but the name and the still large landholdings of the O'Neills were highly significant. The plotters contacted Sir Phelim, the family head in Ulster, and sent messages to Owen Roe O'Neill who was still in military service in Flanders.

The conspirators saw themselves as loyal subjects of the king, who was their only hope in the face of the Covenanters, the English Puritans and thrusting New English planters in Ireland. What they sought were the same liberties that English subjects enjoyed and to be ruled as a separate kingdom with its own parliament and judiciary, free from control by English councillors or MPs. They believed their Catholicism was compatible with loyalty to the crown. But to get a stronger negotiating position they would have to use force – the Scots had shown that. As reward for their rebellion, the Scots had been awarded concessions and compensation. As the Earl of Castlehaven explained, the Irish leaders 'saw the Scots by pretending grievances, and taking up Arms to get them Redressed, had not only gained divers Priviledges and Immunities, but got 300000L for their visit, besides 850L a day for several Months together. And this Precedent encouraged the Irish so much … that they offered it … as their chief motive of Rising then in Rebellion.'[2]

A coup against the weak Dublin government and seizure of some key forts would surely deliver to the Irish the same bargaining power.[3] There would be a rising in Ulster, while other groups seized Dublin Castle with its plentiful supply of arms.

The rebellion did not go as planned, mainly because it was leaked to government. In Ulster it was remarkably successful. Sir Phelim launched his enterprise on Friday 22 October, 'the last day of the moon' when the night was dark. He took Dungannon Fort and a string of other strongholds in central Ulster so that by Sunday he controlled the heart of Ulster. But in Dublin the rising failed. Not all the contingents turned up, but moreover, and fatally for the conspirators, an informer warned the Lords Justices. Forces were mustered and the government held Dublin Castle. Two leaders, MacMahon and Maguire, were captured.

On Sunday, Sir Phelim issued a statement saying they were not in arms against the king but only in defence of their liberties. No injury was intended to any of the king's subjects and any such injury would be remedied – everyone in arms should go home to avoid trouble.[4]

However the rising had already unleashed forces which would prove beyond the control of Sir Phelim O'Neill and his colleagues. In Ireland over a longer period, but in Ulster in a decade or so and intensively, foreign settlers had taken the best land, increased their political power and instigated a foreign culture. Over the last century, that culture was not only English but Protestant, a religion installed by conquerors, which removed absolution, the Virgin Mary and the Pope, replacing them with alien rituals. Loss of land, culture and religion had created fear and rage, not just among the gentry who lost power and estates but among the small farmers and rural folk who had been infiltrated. Now the rising unleashed this bitter resentment and violence broke out, often savagely. Protestant settlers were turned out of their homes, some were murdered and there were atrocities – people were herded into a building which was set on fire, others were deliberately drowned. Protestant settlers from Britain began to flee Ireland and some died on the journey. As Ulster erupted, so the rising spread south into the Pale and beyond. The leaders tried to regain control and instil discipline but the early atrocities were savage and the fleeing settlers who arrived in Britain with tales of horror had done their work.[5]

In the Commons in London, the initial reaction was to raise troops to be sent to Ireland and to defend England against papists, which included those in the queen's retinue. Increasingly Henrietta-Maria was under suspicion because of her religion and she in turn, although alarmed, took a line of robust indignation, urging the king at every turn to fight back rather than make concessions. For support, the queen turned to her natural allies, the royal family of France and the Pope, never thinking that support from Rome aroused visceral horror among MPs and provoked strong reactions in the English. Papist attack was their worst nightmare.

In the last year, Irish government had weakened. Strafford had certainly made enemies of every section of Irish society but he had made Ireland solvent, had given it firm government and reversed the pillaging of state assets by the grandees. He had raised and paid for an Irish army, but the Commons demanded it be disbanded after his execution. Since his death, the situation had unravelled; funds were now scarce and the Lords Justices weak. Part of the army had been sent overseas to fight for Spain.[6] Charles had appointed Lord Leicester as Lord Lieutenant but ordered him not to go to Dublin without his express command, so he was still in England. The administration in Dublin therefore had few resources: 2,000 or so long-term troops who secured Dublin Castle but insufficient funds or organisation to take on a national rising. Their first military expedition was defeated.

Charles was still in Scotland; he did not get back to London until 25 November. The king was unquestionably at the head of any national army – this was so ancient a concept that no one questioned it – but MPs did begin the long and painful process of pressuring Charles to assign that seminal power to parliament. There was no suggestion that the king's ministers should gain greater responsibility, firstly because the Commons was eager to control the appointment of minsters itself and secondly because ministers were beginning to turn over with alarming speed, requiring replacements. Strafford was dead, Laud in the Tower, and Finch and Windebank had fled. Even Cottington had given up one job and would retire as Chancellor in January next year.

While the king delayed in Edinburgh, a great deal happened in Ireland. On 4 November, Sir Phelim and Rory Maguire, brother of the captured Lord Maguire, issued a proclamation. It wished to all Catholics, both English and Irish, 'freedom of conscience and victory over the English heretics who for a long time have tyrannised over our bodies and usurped by extortion our estates'.[7] They declared that they had a commission from the king which complained of the usurpation of his power by the English parliament, authorised the holders of the commission to meet together and to possess the forts and castles of Ireland. This commission had a royal seal attached to it – which was in fact the great seal of Scotland and had been taken from another document. It authorised the Irish to seize the goods and property of English Protestants but not those of the Scots.[8] The commission had been forged – that much historians agree on – but to the Irish in 1641, it probably seemed genuine.[9] The commission spoke of the 'vehemence of the Protestant party' in Ireland and the danger to royal power.

In England, the king was suspected, although Pym never accused him of plotting with the Ulster rebels. This was not where their main suspicions lay. It was the king's use of an Irish army that alarmed them. Public opinion in England, however, was that Irish Catholics had plotted a general extermination of Protestants in Ireland.

The insurgents hoped to make common cause with the Ulster Scots, hence Sir Phelim's prohibition on seizing property from the Scots. This never had a hope of succeeding, as the Scottish settlers in Ulster immediately took up arms against the rebels. Instead of gaining concessions as the Scottish Covenanters had, the Irish rebels brought down vengeance on themselves. There was no sympathy for Irish political grievances in England; the country was seldom visited and poorly understood, but the principal reason was their religion, which was seen as degenerate and a threat. It was feared that European powers might take up the cause of Catholic Ireland as they had before and use Ireland as a springboard for an invasion of Britain. Charles was thought to lean towards Catholicism, so although he was not accused of giving Sir Phelim the forged commission, all his dealings with Irish Catholics were under scrutiny and often considered suspect.

Before we go any further it is important to note the growing role of rumour, plot and wild suspicion which had already reached a dangerous level. The king was the link between the governments of three dissimilar and restive kingdoms. Under attack, his grip was weakening. In response, instability and alarm grew. The centre could not hold, while factions were forming which tried to take his powers and award them to other institutions. Loss of trust became a crucial factor – trust in the king, but also between factions. There certainly were attempts to make side deals and use military force – both by the king and by others. But the suspicions between factions were almost as damaging for any negotiated settlement as the poor policy choices which were made. Throughout his reign, Charles had been suspicious of moves against monarchy, especially by the Puritans. The three kingdoms were fighting each other – the Scots had resorted to arms very quickly, while the principal charge against Strafford was use of the Irish army against England – but there was also allegiance between sects. The Covenanters had allied themselves both to the London radicals led by Pym and to the New English planters in Ireland, men like Clotworthy and Lord Cork. Charles in turn seemed to lean towards Catholics; he had tried to win over the Old English with the 'Graces'. Plots to take the Tower, to arrest radical leaders and to use existing troops were all in existence, but they were misreported and exaggerated alongside wilder rumours – that the king was being deposed, that the queen was a prisoner, that the king was complicit in the Irish rebellion or that the Irish planned to murder all Protestants.[10] The width of the Irish Sea and the deep religious distrust throughout both islands amplified and distorted even news based on reality. Later, when men tried to save themselves or write their memoirs, they frequently added new material to perplex historians. So plots and rumours will, from now on, be part of the climate of both islands.

In London, political allegiance had altered. John Pym had emerged as the leader of the Commons and the radical party, while a more coherent royalist party was forming around Hyde, Falkland and Culpepper. Pym still had considerable support in the Lords; despite the death of Bedford, the earls of Essex and Warwick with their friends were still of Pym's party. However, the House of Lords generally supported the king, while efforts by the Commons to remove bishops and Catholic lords from the upper house failed. The king had increased his support there by creating new lords and by bringing in the sons of others by writ. The Commons therefore, blocked upwards by the peers, turned to the people.[11]

The Grand Remonstrance had been drafted during the summer – principally by Pym and Denzil Holles – but it was read in the Commons on 8 November while the news from Ireland poured in and London was astir with tales of Catholic plots. The Grand Remonstrance was a long list of grievances, followed by a resumé of the parliament's achievements and then a set of policies which the Commons planned and which they demanded of the king. The final debate was on 22 November, as the king rode south from Scotland. It was a long and bitter discussion; the Grand Remonstrance was finally carried by only eleven votes. On 1 December it was presented to the king but Charles would not accept its prescriptions. He and Edward Hyde – later the Earl of Clarendon and author of the seminal history of the war – wrote a considered answer. Charles refused to remove bishops and although he said he opposed Roman Catholicism, he also intended to protect the church from 'schismatics and separatists'.[12] He rebutted charges against his ministers and deferred decisions on Ireland until the rebellion had been brought to an end. The Grand Remonstrance was never sent to the House of Lords – it was a challenge to the king, not projected legislation. During December, it was published in full and helped to fuel the tumults and turbulence in London which flared all through that month. The radicals were very effective at getting their people out on the streets.

While sustaining the pressure on Charles, the Commons was taking an active role in dealing with the Irish rebellion. The moment they heard the news, they ordered the raising of troops. However, the situation in Ireland was fluid. Parliament reassembled in Dublin on 16 November, now with the Old English in a majority. They sent Lord Dillon with a petition to the king, begging him not to send English and Scottish troops but to grant the 'Graces' and put Ormond at the head of the Irish government. If the Old English got security of their lands and freedom to practise their religion, the king would have their support. They had asked the Lords Justices for arms to defend themselves but without success. The Old English were the key group; the direction they took was crucial. The problem for Charles was that he was barely in control of his English administration and that to give concessions to Irish Catholics at such a moment would unleash on him the raw vengeance of the Puritans in parliament, as well as the London mobs who were furiously demonstrating against bishops and demanding changes in the government of the City. During the recent debates, Pym had told the Commons that all plots and designs leading to their current crisis were rooted in popery. In such a climate, to give Irish Catholics tolerance would be utterly self-destructive for the king.

The reports coming from Ireland were horrifying. Stories were told of settlers stripped naked and bound, left to die. The number of reported deaths grew – early in December it was said to be 30,000. Clotworthy told the Commons of gruesome atrocities in which women and children were victims, eyes were plucked out, genitals cut off, pregnant women slashed open. Woodcut block prints illustrated pamphlets and newsletters to drive home to the English public the savagery of the Irish.

The Irish rising of 1641 is a dramatic example of newspapers not just reporting but creating events. The aftermath of the rising was violent enough but the exaggerations of the pamphleteers and news writers helped to fuel panic in England, where reconquest and reprisals were urgently called for. Over the next few years, evidence was collected in Dublin; much of it was hearsay, but it gave credibility to the wilder reports. We still live with the consequences, so the pamphlet writers of 1641–6 have much to answer for. They culminated in Sir John Temple's account published in 1646.[13]

By spring 1642, it was reported that 154,000 Protestants had been killed and by 1646 when Temple wrote his account, that had risen to 300,000. Historians believe there were only around 100,000 Protestants in Ireland all told and the killings had all occurred in the first few months. Modern historians have worked hard on this rebellion and calculate real casualties of around 4,000. More may have died from illness or exposure while fleeing, as many had their clothes stolen.[14]

In reality, the rebel leaders in Ulster were an association of monarchists pressing for rights. Loyalty to the crown was probably not their gut feeling, but it was their only realistic aim. They formalised this position in mid-November when all those who had joined the insurgents took an oath of association, professing loyalty to the king and defence of the Catholic religion. However, the popular revolt was spreading. The Lords Justices refused to arm the Lords of the Pale. Sir Charles Coote, a New English settler with land in Connaught, took troops to recover Wicklow but his brutal efficiency and his attacks on Catholic gentry helped to polarise the Old English. Where was their greatest safety? Which side was their best choice? The king seemed unable to offer them anything, parliaments in London and Edinburgh were violently anti-Catholic with no respect for their property rights but only talking of further confiscation. The popular rising was violent; increasingly the leaders' own families and property were at risk. The situation was spiralling out of control. The Lords of the Pale had to make a choice.

In December 1641, the Ulster leaders invited the Palesmen to a meeting at Tara and then on the Hill of Crofty in Meath to make an agreement. In the face of a common enemy, the old rivalry between the Gaelic Irish and Old English tipped over into an alliance. Different by origin, they shared a religion. Landowners in other regions of Ireland, either sympathetic to the cause or fearful of anarchy, began to join the rebellion in order to lead and control it. In March 1642, the clergy proclaimed that Catholics were engaged in a just war for their rights and called for a meeting with the nobility and gentry. In June, a group met at Kilkenny calling themselves the lords and gentry of the Confederate Catholics. This was the first meeting of a body which effectively ruled Ireland for eight years. Proclaiming its loyalty to the king, claiming rights for the Irish parliament, it asserted a national and Catholic government for Ireland.

While this body was gradually coming together, Protestant planters hurried to defend themselves. The Dublin government rallied but needed increased forces. While still in Edinburgh, Charles had appointed Ormond as commander of the Irish army and ordered him to enlist men to put down the rebellion.[15] Many planters fled the island or rushed to walled towns for safety. The vulnerable might leave for England, but the men joined the crown forces centred on Dublin and Cork to crush the rebellion, regain control of Ireland and take back their land.

Events had moved swiftly in Ulster. The new Scottish settlers formed an army, taking their instructions from the Lords Justices in Dublin. This Laggan army proved to be a considerable fighting force, inflicting serious damage on the insurgents. Meanwhile, the Covenanters in Edinburgh were galvanised by the peril to their fellow Scots in Ulster. They wanted to support the Ulster planters but also prevent contagion into Scotland. The Highlands and Islands were populated by Gaels, who spoke the same language as the Irish and many of whom were Catholic – the rebellion might easily spread across the North Channel.

It was in Ulster that Randal MacDonnell, Earl of Antrim had his ancestral estates greatly increased by plantation. When the rebellion broke out, he was in Dublin with Katherine, his countess. Antrim was an extroverted and loquacious man – some found him charming and sympathetic, others thought him preposterous and unreliable. Strafford had had little time for the earl but his description of the man in 1639 captures the dilemma of this McDonell leader: 'His lordship was in [as] differing tempers as ever I saw him: sometimes the grand-child of great Tyrone ... and sometimes again he descended ... to make himself like one of ourselves.'[16] A Gaelic chieftain or an English lord – which was he to be?

The Earl of Antrim was the natural head of Clan Donald on both sides of the North Channel. During the Bishops' Wars, he had offered to bring out the MacDonalds to support the king, although the plan had failed. He had a seat in the Irish House of Lords and the Dublin parliament had been exceedingly active recently, so Antrim and his countess were in Dublin when the rebellion erupted in Ulster. Antrim was certainly a courtier but he was Catholic and Gaelic, his loyalty both confused and suspected. His estates were threatened and although his factor organised to defend them, he could not hold out for long.

Before the rising, the earl had apparently been plotting to reassemble Strafford's army and use it against Pym and parliament, should Charles and circumstances require it. This 'Antrim Plot', so damaging to the reputation of Charles, was disclosed by Antrim himself in 1650 when he was trying to ingratiate himself with the English republicans – later again he denied it. It seems unlikely to have validity but was part of the undercurrent of fear and suspicion – of the Irish army with its Catholic soldiers, of the way that Charles might use it, and of the earl with his mixed loyalties.[17]

The Irish army was certainly contentious. Under Strafford, there had been plans to use it against the Covenanters, although it had never embarked. Since his death, some troops had gone abroad; most had been disbanded and paying for those still in arms was a problem for the Lords Justices. However, Charles had given Ormond command of the crown forces, Protestant planters had joined them and other troops began to arrive in Ireland.

Both the king and his English parliament wanted to crush the Irish rebellion, but Pym and his colleagues were determined that any army raised should not be under the king's command. It would take time to hire troops, provide equipment and transport, and to secure sufficient funds to put it in the field, so when the new year of 1642 began, orders had been given but few men had embarked.

Although all three of his kingdoms were in political uproar, in many ways Charles had strengthened his position. He had learned to court public opinion and explain himself. He had built a royalist party in the English parliament and won back the support of part of the Scottish political class. In Ireland, the insurgents proclaimed allegiance to him, although to his enemies this made him look complicit. All the same, he had considerable support. The problem was how to use it.

Henrietta-Maria, however, was in a vulnerable position and she had the king's ear. It was part of Charles's self-image as king that he took his own decisions and listened to a range of advice, but the excited urgency of his wife was certainly influential. Her instinct was to fight back against every challenge and this affected the king, especially as he was so concerned to protect her and their children. This helps to explain why he pursued several strategies at once and changed strategy before an effective one had done its work. We cannot always know what caused the change of course: a significant event; a mixture of impatience, fear and uncertainty; his wife's strident suggestions. To re-establish his authority he would have to achieve some compromises, but his skills were poor in this regard and in each of his kingdoms the political nation was fracturing. How could consensus be reached when each of his parliaments had factions which were growing far apart? Scottish and Irish armies had already taken action.

In January 1642, the king took a dramatic step which backfired on him disastrously. Fearful for his queen, Charles decided to impeach five members of the Commons: Pym, Hampden, Holles, Strode and Hazelrig. The Attorney General laid the articles of impeachment against them in the House of Lords, which was not only provocative but irregular – impeachment was for parliament to use, not the king, while the members were protected by privileged rights. The Lords did not act on the articles, so the king assembled 400 soldiers to go to parliament and arrest the members. Pym and his colleagues had been warned, so they left the chamber and went by barge to the City of London which gave them support. In fact, the Common Council of the City created the Committee of Safety, which determined to take charge of London's militia, the trained bands.

The king had overplayed his hand and London was becoming a dangerous place for him. On 10 January 1642, he left Whitehall for Hampton Court and then Windsor. It was a more complete departure than he could have known – when he saw his capital again he would be a prisoner. Meanwhile in the Commons, Oliver Cromwell moved for a defence committee. When this was formed, it took a decision which parliament had proposed but rejected more than once: it decided to take control of the country's armed forces. Of all steps, this was seminal in leading to conflict since command of the country's armed forces was without doubt the king's sole prerogative. The committee decided that each county militia should be put under a lord lieutenant chosen by parliament. The Militia Ordinance passed both houses of parliament in mid-February, and with it parliament wrested control of the local armed forces from the monarch.

The queen was now going abroad. Her daughter Mary was already married to the son of the Prince of Orange and the boy's family had asked for her to come to Holland. Parliament, which had prevented the queen leaving the country the year before, now agreed, perhaps hoping her absence would make agreement easier. Charles and Henrietta-Maria travelled together to Dover, where they parted with clinging embraces and affectionate murmurings. When the ship began to move out to sea, Charles rode down the coast to keep sight of it.

Henrietta-Maria and her daughter arrived in Holland via the estuary of the Maas and when they came ashore they were met by Charles's sister Elizabeth, the exiled Queen of Bohemia, who had brought her daughter Sophie with her. The two girls were a similar age. Henrietta-Maria and Elizabeth had never met before and as they rode to The Hague together they had plenty of time to talk. It was a poignant carriage ride; Elizabeth had been driven from her kingdom and bore her exile stoically, while Henrietta-Maria had all but fled from hers. They did not share a religion and Elizabeth disapproved of her sister-in-law's attitude, which was to make war on parliament rather than come to an agreement.

Henrietta-Maria's presence in The Hague was a slight embarrassment for the Prince of Orange, whose countrymen were strongly Calvinist and largely republican. But the queen had escaped safely and brought jewels in her luggage, so she settled into the apartments provided for her and wrote to her husband who had set off for York.[18] There Charles hoped to work up support among the northern gentry. In London, parliament sent the Militia Ordinance to the king for his assent, along with a request that he return to his capital – but Charles refused both. Instead he rode to Hull, ostensibly to 'inspect the magazine' which he hoped to secure for his own forces since Hull was a principal arms store for the crown; but Sir John Hotham, acting on orders from parliament, would not admit him. It was a humiliating moment for the king and a serious blow to his military aspirations.

Spring was coming, which meant that armies could soon be on the move. In Ireland, Ormond led the Irish army against the rebels and retook parts of the Pale. In February 1642, Charles proclaimed all those in arms as traitors and English crown troops under Monck landed at Dublin to reinforce the Irish army. In March, Ormond drove the insurgents back from Drogheda, an important port north of Dublin. In April, Scottish forces disembarked at Carrickfergus in Ulster under the command of Robert Monro, a seasoned officer from the Swedish army. As Ulster towns which the rebels had taken fell to the combined strength of Monro and the Laggan army, the position of the Ulster rebels weakened. The king's proclamation of February had destroyed their claim that they were fighting for him. Nonetheless, when the Confederacy was formed in June, it proclaimed its devotion to the monarchy.

In London, the fate of Ireland was being decided by legislation. The parliament in Westminster had decided to finance the suppression of the rebellion by raising £1 million against the surety of Irish land, which would be confiscated once the rebellion was crushed. Exact rates were stipulated and there were plenty of subscribers. It was widely believed that the Irish rebels had conspired to extirpate all the Protestants in that country and the lurid news reports had created rage and revulsion. Besides, it might turn into a handsome investment; there was known to be good farmland in Ireland. Oliver Cromwell was one of the Adventurers, with a stake of £600, which was a great deal of money for a man of limited fortune.[19] The Adventurers' Act was passed in March 1642 and sent to the king for his assent. He complained that it took from him the power of mercy and clemency but, fearful of seeming soft on the rebels, signed it.

This further weakened the Irish rebels' position and the Scots were inflicting heavy losses on them in Ulster. However, by spring the insurgency had spread all over Ireland – deep into Leinster and Munster where most of

County Cork had been lost to government. Local leaders had great influence; Galway stayed largely loyal to the government due to the influence of Lord Clanricard, whereas in Munster, where the rule of St Leger was heavy-handed, he and his son-in-law Lord Inchiquin lost control of much of the province when the Catholic gentry of the south came out for the rebels.

To the Irish, the Adventurers' Act clearly showed the intentions of Westminster and highlighted how strongly the constitution was set against them. Their own parliament was powerless against London and the king had given his assent to the bill. For over a century, Irish parliaments had struggled against the English Privy Council, but now the English parliament was asserting its supremacy over Ireland; the position became more threatening.

It was at this point that the meetings were held – first at Kells and then in Kilkenny – at which the Irish insurgents began to organise themselves. On 7 June, an oath of association defined the Confederate Catholics of Ireland.

In Ulster, the Scottish army was taking its toll on the insurgents, who were on the point of fleeing when they heard that Owen Roe O'Neill had landed on the coast of Donegal with arms and men. More troops were on their way from Flanders. In September, Thomas Preston landed in Wexford. He and O'Neill were both Catholics from Irish gentry families. They were in their late fifties, experienced and battle-hardened, having spent all their adult lives in military service under Spain, the champion of Catholic Europe.

All the leaders of the contest which would follow were now in the Irish theatre of war. The summer campaign of 1642 had already staked out much of the ground. The Irish government held the cities of Dublin and Cork, with their hinterland, and had retaken some key fortresses in Ulster. The Confederates held much of the centre of the island of Ireland and were creating institutions from their headquarters in Kilkenny.

The Scots had resorted to arms four years earlier. The English, however, with their massive parliamentary traditions and devotion to legalistic procedure, were still engaged in an intense battle of wills at Westminster. It took them longer to reach the point of conflict and, of course, to fight the king was treason. But in August, Charles would raise his standard at Nottingham and ask his countrymen to join him. As the harvest was brought in, England too went to war.

17

Taking Positions

The king's relationship with London had deteriorated sharply before he left the city in January 1642. Having attacked the rights of parliament by trying to arrest five members, Charles precipitated their flight to the City of London, which declared the king's actions illegal. That night rumours that Charles was sending in horsemen caused a panic and without the mayor's orders the trained bands turned out fully armed. These artisans and traders, like the apprentices earlier in the year, now identified the king as enemy or potential aggressor. The mayor and council resolved to appoint their own officers for the bands but it was parliament who chose Captain Skippon to command them. The London institutions were closing ranks against the king.

He had lost control of his capital and when he left London, Charles was only acknowledging that loss. The Commons, including the five members, returned to Westminster and 'King Pym' reigned there. Parliament was unconstrained as it had never been before, but how would it tackle the enormous problems still before it: its alliance with the Scots, the religious passions of England or the demands for liberty and rights by the rebellious Irish? How would it manage the factions fighting in Ulster or raise funds to prosecute the wider Irish war? What form of religious settlement did it envisage? So far, parliament had inched forwards with Pym consulting the law at every turn – sometimes stretching but always resting on it. For that was parliament's cause – the common law and the rights of parliament. They had charged Strafford with subverting the law, then the king himself with contempt of parliament – the law was precious. But now there were two governments in England. Up to now, king and parliament had struggled over where the boundary lay between their powers, but with no compromise achieved the two branches of government had broken apart. Charles might have left his capital but the king was still head of state with considerable prerogative powers. In London, parliament began to rule by committee, statute and ordinance although, as Charles pointed out, without his consent such orders had no legal force. Parliament argued that, according to fundamental law, it had a duty to maintain security – but it was a thin argument.

Scotland presented a greatly changed political system to challenge Charles. Parliament there had taken control of legislation, removed bishops, created executive committees and ensured that every three years a new parliament would be called. Having modernised and empowered Scotland's legislature, the Covenanters planned more thorough religious change but the Privy Council was still in office in Edinburgh and it was the king who appointed ministers, over which there was a sustained wrangle.

For the Scots, there were military bills to face. Although England had paid part of the agreed compensation bill, most of the 'Brotherly Assistance' remained outstanding. To fund Monro's army in Ulster, the Scottish Privy Council took out a loan but, before long, the Edinburgh parliament turned against the Privy Council and began to sidestep them, ruling through committees.

Churchmen were not to sit in the Scottish parliament – Argyll was adamant about that – but the General Assembly of the Kirk was also meeting regularly and was intent on making religious practice throughout Scotland uniform on its terms. To oversee this, the assembly set up a permanent Commission of the Kirk which turned into a powerful body, watching every church and presbytery with searching eyes.

Government by parliament meant a plethora of committees and many commissioners – because as the old structures were challenged and superseded, new bodies were formed to rule. Having agreed the Treaty of London, negotiations continued between London and Edinburgh, with a brief to maintain the peace, get the armies paid and to agree terms for free trade, something on which Scotland was especially keen. However, the Scots were insisting on uniform religious practice throughout Britain and on their terms. Their English friends, most of whom were not Presbyterians, were worried.

In Ireland, like England, there were now dual structures. The king's government held Dublin, while the Confederate Catholics set up headquarters at Kilkenny around 80 miles south-east of the capital. By the end of 1642, the Confederates held most of the country. In Ulster, the Scottish army had taken the east coast counties of Down and Antrim with the town of Newry and the castle of Carrickfergus. To the south of them, Ormond's troops had regained control of the Pale for the king. Cork city, with its vital harbour and the hinterland to its north and east, was also held for the king by St Leger and, after his death early in 1642, by his son-in-law Murrough O'Brien, Lord Inchiquin. In August, Inchiquin won a significant victory at Liscarroll in north Cork, greatly extending the area controlled by crown forces in Munster. Galway was not in Confederate hands and their hold on Connaught generally was less sure. All the same, by the time that Owen Roe O'Neill and then Preston arrived in Ireland in 1642, the Confederates had a groundswell of support throughout the island.

Once the Confederacy was set up, it became far more than a military command and assumed the government of the country. Order had broken down swiftly as rebellion spread and the nobles, gentry and clergy who met at Kilkenny sought to replicate the king's government. Provincial and county councils took over the role of JPs and a Confederate bureaucracy grew up, keeping records and levying tax. However, their main job was to hold the country by military strength, so four armies were created, one for each province, commanded by Owen Roe in Ulster, Preston in Leinster and Garrett Barry in Munster, with less regular forces in Connaught. They could raise manpower but lacked guns and cavalry. Gradually, however, they acquired a navy and before long they also opened diplomatic negotiations with European courts. In this they had the advantage of men trained in religious houses in Europe with a command of European languages, as well as Catholic noblemen who could represent them.

In England, the summer of 1642 was a mixture of megaphone negotiation and preparation for war. The king issued declarations emphasising the concessions he had made, his natural position in the constitution and his role as guarantor of law and justice. He affirmed his commitment to the Church of England and his condemnation of the Irish rebellion (which was spoken of by some as the queen's rebellion). Parliament claimed to be protecting the 'Protestant religion, laws, liberties and Peace of the Kingdom' and they condemned the delinquents who fought for the king, whom they announced must bear the cost of the war.[1]

Parliament's agreement with the Scots to hold a religious convention seems to have caused disquiet as English people feared their church practices would be eradicated; many Anglicans had deplored Laud but feared Puritanism far more. Around London and in East Anglia pure Calvinism was strong but elsewhere in England, people were apparently suspicious of alterations to their church and upset by events in the capital. Extra tax had been raised to pay the Scots, but surely now that fight was over. Why could king and parliament not agree? What was the problem?

Once the king left London, parliament could instigate more of its own programme. In February, a day of fasting and humiliation was created, to be held on the last Wednesday of every month. The Puritans believed that England's troubles could only end when God had been propriated and his providence won, which meant English people humbling themselves before him and acknowledging their sinfulness. They should spend the fast day at church, praying and listening to preachers.[2] In September, parliament ordered the closure of the theatres. For decades, the city authorities had been concerned about theft and raucous behaviour occurring around playhouses but the court supported theatrical activity, which had helped it to survive. Now Charles had left London, parliament – nervous of drama stirring up debate, and disapproving of godless behaviour – shut the theatres down.[3]

The king had infuriated many people, but parliament had alarmed them. Rather than backing off, members published a statement of intentions which went even further. The *Nineteen Propositions* was the next marker, a list of demands for constitutional change which parliament proposed to the king. Its aim was to subject the monarch, his ministers and the judiciary to parliament itself. The privy council's size and decisions would be controlled. The education and marriages of the royal children would require parliament's consent. Catholic children must be educated by Protestants.[4]

Parliament thought the king's position weak but the *Nineteen Propositions* were a fundamental change in the constitution of England which would give power to a parliament which many people felt was alien to them. It helped to propel moderate Englishmen towards York where the king was based. *The King's Answer* was duly composed and then a pamphlet war broke out, with the lawyer Henry Parker making the most influential argument for parliament and asserting that 'power is originally inherent in the people'.[5] While fighting men sharpened their pike heads and cleaned their muskets, academics honed their arguments.

There was also a contest over the loyalty of the fleet, which the king lost. In July, the admirals accepted the Earl of Warwick as Lord Admiral and, with him, the navy chose to support parliament. The struggle for the county militias was more closely contested. Charles tried to get around the Militia Ordinance by using the older Commission of Array and succeeded in mustering men in eleven counties. They were untrained and unfit but each county had weapons which both sides wanted to control. However, militias existed to protect their own counties and the men would prove stubbornly unwilling to go elsewhere.

Parliament had more success with recruiting foot soldiers than the king. In the Midlands, significant numbers of men came to their musters voluntarily, whereas the king's recruiting drives produced poor results. He got more support from the gentry who could provide horses and form cavalry regiments. However, the split between king and parliament ran through all classes. Overall, recruiting on both sides was slow and public reaction seems mainly concerned to prevent or avoid war. English men and women were resistant to fighting and perhaps unsure why the conflict had erupted, but all the same they were reading pamphlets, discussing issues and gradually forming opinions about where their loyalties lay. As more men congregated, bringing their arms, clashes inevitably occurred and those small conflicts caused alarm and raised tension.

Charles was in York with his ministers when he was joined by his nephew Prince Rupert, the second son of Elizabeth of Bohemia. Elector Frederick had died in 1632 and since his death their eldest son, Charles Louis, was Elector Palatinate in name but had yet to recover his inheritance. He had been in England for some time but his allegiance was uncertain. The king feared that radical Protestants might prefer his nephew, while Charles Louis thought parliament more likely to give him military support. His brothers Rupert and Maurice, however, stayed with their uncle throughout the war and Rupert was made general of horse in the summer of 1642.

Having published the *Nineteen Propositions*, the main aim of parliament was raising its army. MPs promised funds and the Earl of Essex was appointed general. Parliament's legal position was that the king had taken up arms against his own people and they named their army's governing body the Committee of Safety, to protect the country in this emergency. Formed in July 1642, it had members from both Lords and Commons, among whom were the Earl of Essex, Lord Saye, Pym, Hampden and Holles. The Committee of Safety grew into a form of governing executive. Gradually two governments were taking shape in England, both with armies.

The king chose a ceremonial call to arms in Nottingham on 22 August. He raised his standard and summoned his people to help him suppress the rebellion led by the Earl of Essex. This had resonance because the earl's father had rebelled against Queen Elizabeth and been executed. The current earl had a chequered past. His first wife had left him for Robert Carr, the favourite of King James, and in the ensuing divorce his ex-wife declared the earl impotent, causing scandal and humiliation. Worse followed when his estranged wife was found guilty of poisoning her secretary. Essex's second marriage had also failed but he had made a successful career as a soldier and then as a politician. The marital disaster had estranged Essex from James and he had suffered military humiliation under Buckingham, so although he had been a lieutenant general in the king's service, he was no friend of Charles.[6]

As the protagonists collected their forces, parliament had the advantage because the City of London supported them, with its considerable wealth from trade and banking. The Earl of Essex was popular and a leading peer, so he could raise troops in London and the home counties, especially since parliament could pay the soldiers. Loyalty to the king was sometimes traditional, a matter of honour or a fear of his enemies. Catholics in particular were generous, alarmed by the Puritan tone of parliament. By giving commissions to noblemen and landowners who could raise their own regiments and choose officers, gradually Charles assembled a royalist army.

The opening clash was at Powick Bridge, which briefly gave Essex control of Worcester. Some of his dragoons ran into Rupert's rear-guard protecting a supply train making for the king at Shrewsbury. Curiously, it was in this district that the war would finally end a decade later. Two thousand cavalry were involved and the king's had the better of it. It was barely more than a skirmish but gave Rupert and his cavalry confidence. When the king took his army out of Shrewsbury making for London, Essex also moved his troops. The two armies marched east, towards the road from the Midlands down to London. On 23 October the first pitched battle of the Civil War was fought at Edgehill near Banbury. The king, who in many ways was an uncertain man fearful of his dignity and honour, had from the first been willing and even eager to fight and now remained with his army, sleeping close to his men when the day ended. The battle was inconclusive but Charles had retained the open road to London, whereas Essex remained to his north-west. Charles used this advantage to take Banbury and occupy Oxford, which became his headquarters.

Some peace feelers were offered by parliament but Charles would not recognise their emissary. Instead he set off towards Reading and ordered Rupert to attack Brentford. Meanwhile, Essex went down Watling Street and got between the king and London but his forces were routed at Brentford, which Rupert allowed his men to sack. The king's army was now within 10 miles of London. But the City trained bands and many new volunteers formed up under Essex at Turnham Green, making a total of around 24,000 men. The king's army attacked on 13 November but could not break through this determined force, despite the latter's lack of training. Charles's army took Kingston but could not clear the road into London and so the king returned to Oxford for the winter.

Summer was the fighting season but in the winter it was hard to find quarters and provisions for large numbers of fighting men. King Charles lived in Christ Church College, where he could look out on the meadows and walk by the Thames. It was congenial enough for a man at war. Essex meanwhile had returned to London. In Ireland, the commanders spent the winter in their fortresses: Monro held Carrickfergus Castle, Ormond held Dublin with its castle, and the walled city of Cork was headquarters for Murrough O'Brien, Lord Inchiquin.

The young warrior Alasdair MacColla MacDonald had seen some action in Ulster. A cousin of the Earl of Antrim, with similar loyalties, he had initially joined the forces raised to protect the McDonell estates from the rebels. However, when Monro landed in Ulster the following April, the position changed. To Alasdair, the Scots seemed a greater threat than the rebels and he harried Monro's forces, although without success. The Scots quickly took Dunluce Castle and swept across the Earl of Antrim's lands. Forced to retreat, Alasdair MacColla slipped away across the River Bann with his troops, changed allegiance and fought alongside the Confederates, where he was seriously injured. Negotiations with the Scots led only to treachery and Alasdair spent the winter of 1642/3 hiding in Confederate territory, where conditions were rough and his position vulnerable after his several changes of allegiance.[7] He would not resurface until late in 1643 when new plans were being made.

The Earl of Antrim had been imprisoned in Carrickfergus Castle after Monro seized his lands in May 1642. However, he escaped in the autumn and hurried over to England. His ultimate aim was to get leverage in any peace negotiations but as long as the war was on, he was determined to capture Kintyre from the Earl of Argyll. This objective chimed exactly with that of Alasdair MacColla, whose native island of Colonsay had been taken by the Campbells and whose father and two brothers were still imprisoned in the Campbell's fortress of Inveraray Castle. A big war acts as cover for smaller wars and the antagonism between king and parliament was hardly more bitter than the seething rivalries between Clan Campbell and their Gaelic enemies Clan Donald.

Would 1643 give them a chance to attack Campbell territory? Antrim, accompanied by his countess, travelled to York where the earl once more offered the royalists support in Scotland – hoping to further his own plans. As head of the MacDonalds, he had aims on both sides of the North Channel: to liberate his own estates in Ulster and to retake the MacDonald territories in Scotland.

Henrietta-Maria was still abroad, but she too was busy plotting and planning. As the year turned and the spring flowers began to show, all these plans began to blossom into action and once more men buckled metal to leather, there was the ring of blades against stone and of horses' hooves on cobbles. As warmth came into the sun, and the fighting season began once more.

18

Civil War in England – Royalists Ascendant

As 1643 began, there were opposing forces in all three kingdoms, all with different aims but partially allied to each other. The Covenanters and the Westminster parliament were negotiating an alliance but disagreed over church policy. In Ireland, both Monro and Ormond were ranged against the Confederates, but Monro was hired by Edinburgh, whereas Ormond was the king's commander – and the Confederates too proclaimed loyalty to the king. The English parliament loathed the Confederates but viewed Ormond with suspicion.

As conflict started, many peers and royalists left the English parliament to join the king but even among those who remained there was a broad range of opinion, which widened as the war progressed. When government collapses, many forces swing around that empty centre, fighting for power but also struggling to re-establish control and prevent chaos. In this whirlwind, alliances were formed and broken across the three kingdoms, which give the appearance of disloyalty and apostasy, but few people were genuine turncoats – rather the political landscape was shifting and they lodged on it precariously, slipping, looking for handholds. So, the years from 1643 onwards were a period of armies fighting in pitched battles and at fortified buildings, but among changing alliances and political formations. Loyalties were sorely tested.

During the winter of 1642/3 there was a significant peace party at Westminster. Londoners, nervous of the king's army and now being taxed by parliament, demonstrated against the war. Among both Lords and Commons, enough members pressed for a deal to oblige Pym to negotiate. A new set of terms were taken to the king by commissioners, but although the *Treaty of Oxford* was less draconian for the king than the *Nineteen Propositions*, Charles was unmoved. He would not hand over 'delinquents' – that is his Scottish ministers – to their enemies and would not abolish bishops, nor would he give parliament control of the church or the armed forces.

Henrietta-Maria was still in the Netherlands trying to get support for Charles. Frederick Henry, Prince of Orange was in a difficult position. He was delighted that his teenage son had married Princess Mary but had not bargained on her mother also coming to live in The Hague, especially as a political fugitive. The Princes of Orange had status and power in the United Provinces but they were not sovereigns; power technically lay with the Estates General which were more sympathetic to the English parliament than to King Charles. Nonetheless, the prince allowed several royalist refugees to join the queen, a few of his own officers were permitted to join Charles in England, he guaranteed some loans and permitted shipments of arms. Princes Rupert and Maurice of the Palatinate had left The Hague to join Charles in August 1642 and the queen had managed to send a shipment of arms with them. Other cargoes got through but some were intercepted. Henrietta-Maria tried to raise money, negotiate with merchants and was in contact with other European princes. She worked hard on her husband's behalf. Further loans from Dutch merchants were possible but she wrote to her husband, 'This country is too trying to the patience of persons who, like me, have scarcely any.'[1] She was against Charles negotiating with his enemies and was considered by many as a goad who drove him to fight, although she wrote to him in October 1642, 'I am thought to be against an accommodation. I confess that I am against a dishonourable one, such as they would wish to make you enter into.'[2] She was not timorous but had been threatened repeatedly by both parliament and the London mobs. The royal family of France had invited her to join them but she protested to Charles that she wanted not to go to Paris, but return to him, 'for, were it not for you alone, I swear that I would not live an hour in this world'. She had not been safe in London and Charles, who cherished his wife and children, felt angrily the need to get control of his country and provide for the safety of his family. Charles anyway was minded to fight and willing to do so; in fact, he proved himself a daring and resourceful commander now that he had forces to lead. The peace party pressed on but by April it was clear that the military contest would continue.

At last the queen's attempts to raise money and find shipping were successful, and in February 1643 Henrietta-Maria set off to rejoin her husband. She had pawned her jewels and extracted loans, and she then suffered tempestuous storms at sea. But the queen was as determined as she was impatient and courageous, with a belief in God as her guide and safeguard. Although her small fleet was forced back to port in Holland and then ran an uncertain course past parliamentary vessels whose orders were to open fire if they saw her, the queen was in haste to help arm her husband and be once more beside him. She finally disembarked at Bridlington in Yorkshire with money, weapons and ammunition. At Bridlington, her party found shelter in houses on the quayside, but had to quit them at 4 a.m. when

England, Wales, Scotland and Ireland in Sept 1643

— England - Scotland border

---- Highland Line

— — Boundary between Confederate Catholics and Protestant forces

England - Royalist territory

England - Parliament territory

✕ battlefield

The Scots army had been disbanded in 1641 and Scottish forces were not in action 1641-3. The Covenanters controlled the Lowlands and believed, mistakenly, that they had the allegiance of many Highland clans.

Inverness

Aberdeen

North Sea

HIGHLANDS

Perth
Dundee

Stirling

Glasgow
Edinburgh
Berwick

ATLANTIC OCEAN

Newburn ✕ Newcastle

Coleraine
Londonderry
LAGGAN ARMY

SCOTS

Carrickfergus
Belfast
Dungannon

Lough Neagh

ROYALIST

ROYALIST

Irish Sea

York
Bridlington
✕ *Adwalton Moor*
Hull

Galway

Dublin

Chester
Newark
✕ *Winceby*

Nottingham
Shrewsbury

Kilkenny
Limerick

Liscarrol
✕
ROYALIST

Waterford
Lismore
Wexford

Gloucester

Edgehill
✕

London
✕
Turnham Green

Cork
Youghal
Kinsale

ROYALIST

Oxford
Bristol
Newbury ✕

ATLANTIC OCEAN

Exeter

Plymouth

English Channel

|—— 100 miles ——|

Territory controlled by contending parties in September 1643.

parliamentary ships fired briskly at the harbour where the ammunition boats still lay. Henrietta-Maria wrote to Charles, 'the balls were singing round us in fine style', but a daughter of France and of Henri IV was not to be quelled by such a bombardment.[3] She was escorted safely to York, which was a stoutly walled city held for the king.

While negotiations continued, parliament organised its forces. They created regional armies to control their key territory: the Midlands Association and the more famous Eastern Association. The Eastern Association held East Anglia and Hertfordshire, an area where Puritanism was strong. The Earl of Warwick had estates in Essex where he was a powerful influence. The city of Cambridge and the surrounding market towns were Puritan but the villages far less so.[4] With the support of Puritan gentry in the area, parliament could collect tax and enforce their oath, confiscating horses and arms from those who would not swear it. Edward Montagu, who was a leading radical and married to Warwick's daughter, succeeded his father as Earl of Manchester that winter and in July 1643 took command of the Eastern Association. So, parliament began in traditional fashion, with noblemen in command of their armies.

In similar fashion in Scotland, the Earl of Leven commanded for the Covenant in the Borders while the Marquis of Argyll was lieutenant in the west. In Ireland, the commanders were also nobility, whether Irish like Inchiquin or Old English like Ormond.

The armies were created to press political positions but those aims became defined by religion. As Oliver Cromwell said later, 'Religion was not the thing at first contested for; but God brought it to that issue at last ... at last it proved that which was most dear to us.'[5] He was talking about parliament's forces where the conflict had begun over the constitution – yet their constant refrain was the king's religious policies. In Scotland and Ireland, religion was also central to the conflict, although in both countries the constitutional rights of the nation were being pressed. In Scotland, the Covenanters wanted greater say over the formation of governments and greater power for the kirk. Having created new parliamentary structures, they were defending them. In Ireland, the Confederate leaders demanded greater rights: in religion, in security of property and in legislative autonomy from English politicians.

In England, the religious question was causing increasing disquiet. The moving spirits in parliament, who had pressed the king so forcefully until military conflict erupted, were all of the godly party. Their devotion to the Bible and demand for pure living, their Calvinist theology and intensive preaching, their attacks on bishops and church ritual; all these made the plain people of England anxious. In June, parliament ordered nothing to be printed without the approval of the Stationers' Company, giving them the control over publishing which the king had previously enforced. The *Book of Sports*, which under James and Charles had permitted and encouraged sports and pastimes on Sundays and holidays, was banned.

Support for the two sides was largely geographical. In the south-east of England there was more support for Puritan aims but in Wales, the south-west and northern England loyalty to the monarch was strong. Armed forces were gradually drawn from these areas to form Charles's three principal armies. Sir Ralph Hopton MP commanded in the south-west, the Earl of Newcastle in the north, while the king himself led the forces based at Oxford. Prince Rupert, as general of horse, led a cavalry unit of 3,000 men. With the return of the queen, her especial friends were promoted, which caused rivalry but did not bring military success.

The campaigning season began in spring but peace negotiations spluttered on into April. Although the king was strongest in the west and north of England, parliament had forces in both Devon and Yorkshire. The king hoped that Scotland might stay out of the action and some Scots join his cause – he left Hamilton to parley with the Covenanters. Charles tried to win over Monro and offered to support his army in Ulster, even though he had never authorised it, but Monro remained loyal to the Edinburgh government, which paid him by forced loans. That government was now an uncomfortable mixture of the Privy Council and the new Covenanter-dominated committees.

Charles saw that Ireland offered him opportunities and throughout the winter of 1642–3 he pursued them. In October, Westminster had tried to bring the Dublin Privy Council round to their side but both council and parliament stayed loyal to the king and expelled the English delegates. As Charles needed Irish troops, he ordered Ormond to negotiate with the Confederates who responded that if their rights were granted, 'we will convert our forces upon any design your majesty may appoint'.[6] Charles was not worried about enlisting Catholic soldiers under his standard but he was alarmed lest the Scots should hear of it and be roused once more. Ormond nonetheless obeyed, setting stiff conditions but opening talks with the Confederates in March, even while still fighting their forces in Wexford. It was the beginning of a slow process which ended hostilities but solved neither side's problems.

Meanwhile, the wily Earl of Antrim was trying to advance his scheme. Edward Hyde thought Antrim 'a man of excessive pride and vanity, and of a marvellous weak and narrow understanding' and it was certainly true that Antrim plotted much but delivered little, although for a man so active in the war he survived it remarkably well.[7] Antrim was in York where he put his proposal to the Earl of Newcastle. As always, the thrust of it would be his MacDonald Ulstermen attacking the Campbells in Kintyre. It was wrapped up inside a wider strategy against the Covenanters, which meant overcoming Monro, crossing to Scotland and joining the Scottish royalists in arms.

Antrim certainly worked hard to fight for his king but he never forgot his main aim, which was to wreak havoc on the Argyll dominions and take back his ancestral Scottish land. In March, Henrietta-Maria arrived in York where Antrim unfolded his plan to her. To forward this, by April he had hurried back to Ireland but in May his plan was scuppered when he was captured at sea and once more made prisoner at Carrickfergus. Letters were found and Monro made it known that the papist Earl of Antrim was plotting against Scotland under the direction of the queen.

Despite plots and machinations, the fighting season got underway. The war was a mixture of sieges, skirmishes and pitched battles.[8] Large houses, castles and walled towns acted as garrisons, while ports were vital. The contenders tried to expand their territory, hold roads and bridges, and, during battle, reduce the enemy's army while trying to capture their valuable military supplies. The year 1643 saw the king's greatest military successes. Hopton had a notable victory at Stratton in Cornwall and, with Prince Maurice, went on to take Taunton and rout Waller near Devizes in Wiltshire. Prince Rupert took Bristol and Prince Maurice took Exeter. In the south-west, Plymouth was the only major town still in the hands of parliament when 1643 drew to a close.

In the Midlands and the Thames valley, Essex proved a lacklustre commander, but Lord Brooke was more effective until killed at Litchfield by a bullet in the eye. The royalists were trying to clear a corridor for Henrietta-Maria to bring her troops and munitions to Oxford but it was June before fierce fighting made it safe for her to lead her troop of 4,500 horse and foot from York to Newark in Nottinghamshire. Some stayed there but after two weeks the queen set out for Oxford, having written to Charles, 'I carry with me three thousand foot, thirty companies of horse and dragoons, six pieces of cannon and two mortars.' She enjoyed being at the head of an army, picnicking in the sun with her men and riding on horseback at their head without concessions to feminine delicacy. She told Charles she felt like Alexander the Great.[9]

Essex's army had been immobilised at Reading by typhus but was moving north when Rupert led one of his daring cavalry attacks at Chalgrove, in which John Hampden was fatally wounded; he died six days later. Essex's forces were scattered, allowing Rupert to meet the queen at Stratford and escort her towards Banbury, where Charles came out to meet her with their two sons Charles and James. The boys were thirteen and ten, living with their father in Oxford. The younger children, Elizabeth and Henry, had been detained by parliament and put under the guardianship of the Earl of Northumberland at Syon House, west of London, causing their mother constant sorrow and concern. But now she was back with her husband and elder boys. Reunited, Charles and his queen returned to Oxford the following day, amid ringing church bells and cheering.

In Yorkshire, the Fairfaxes – father and son – were parliament's commanders, but the Earl of Newcastle defeated them in battle at Adwalton Moor near Bradford. The royalists had another victory at Roundway Down, north of Devizes in Wiltshire. But consolidation in the north and west had brought the king no closer to dislodging the Puritans' power in East Anglia and the lower Thames. In turning back from an assault on London the previous winter, Charles had lost his chance of taking his capital city. He and his advisers knew how perilous such a fight would have been, but the chance would be slow to come again.

Even as his armies took their victories, the forces arrayed against him were coming together. In July, the Westminster Assembly met to settle the shape of the English church. The eight Scotsmen who joined the English clergy and MPs had a crucial influence. If the Scots and English could reach a religious agreement, the greatest impediment to military alliance would be removed. The Westminster parliament had become more Puritan since the royalists left to join the king, but among the Puritans there were great differences. Presbyterians wanted a single national church without bishops and free from royal control; for Independents, freedom to worship according to their own understanding of God's word was essential. However, an alliance with Scotland was essential too and only a Presbyterian church would satisfy the Scots, which is what the Westminster Assembly chose. Soon a delegation left London for talks in Edinburgh and in September the Solemn League and Covenant was signed, by which the Scots brought the English into their movement. The new pact pledged a common religion throughout both islands, preserving that of Scotland while reforming those of Ireland and England. It was hard to define that reform to the satisfaction of both Scots and English but Sir Henry Vane the younger – who was emerging as a parliamentarian leader and a skilful drafter of texts – found a subtle phrase. Reform would be 'according to the word of God, and the example of the best reformed churches', which gave the English leeway to avoid the strict Scottish church form.[10] All the MPs still in Westminster signed the new Covenant. With this sacred bond in place, the Scottish army would mobilise and pincer Charles from the north.

So, the royalists urgently needed more support. Hamilton was working on the Scottish nobles but Ireland was crucial. Just as the Westminster parliament signed up with the Scots, Ormond finalised a truce with the Confederates of Kilkenny. This peace, called the Cessation of Arms, was good news for Charles and Ormond was promoted to Lord Lieutenant. Still aged only thirty-three, he was growing into the role of premier statesman of Ireland but he had lost control of his own estates at Kilkenny. Autumn was closing in as these pacts were made, but the Cessation alleviated Ormond's need for troops and in November 1643 part of his army arrived in Cheshire to beef up the royalists in the north-west.

The Cessation gave the Irish commanders breathing space. Inchiquin was commander of the crown forces in Munster but also hoped to become Lord President of the province, a role he had fulfilled since the death of his father-in-law St Leger, but without royal appointment. Despite being starved of money for his army, before the Cessation Inchiquin had delivered a decisive victory for the king at Liscarroll and had proved his worth. He had also sent troops to his majesty in England. So in January 1644, he made his way to the court in Oxford, expecting the king to confirm this rank and reward him with the presidency of Munster. Instead, Charles had already given it to one of his courtiers, Lord Portland, an Englishman who had no plans to set foot in Ireland. Inchiquin was incandescent. Charles was about to lose one of his ablest commanders.

From Europe, Charles received some modest support from his Danish cousin but the French delayed.[11] Louis XIII had died, the new king Louis XIV was a child and Mazarin, who had succeeded Richelieu as chief minister, bided his time.

The Solemn League and Covenant signalled the failure of Hamilton's policy – the Scots were neutral no longer. In fact, Hamilton and his friends were likely to lose their estates if they did not sign the new bond. The Scottish armies were gathering. Argyll had been given a military commission for the Highlands, while Leven already had troops massed in the Borders. So Charles turned from negotiation with the Scots to plans for war – which the Earl of Montrose had been offering for some time. He had been kept at a distance but now Charles gave the head of the Grahams a commission as his lieutenant in Scotland. If the Highlands were to be awakened then so must the Western Isles, and therefore the North Channel was again a crucial issue. Luckily for the king, Antrim had once more escaped from Carrickfergus and this time the Cessation allowed him to plot with the rebels as well as the king. Antrim hurried to a Confederate meeting in Waterford, talked up his wife's royal connections and got himself appointed lieutenant general of Confederate forces. From here, Antrim made haste to Oxford where he stressed his commanding role with the Confederate Catholics and proposed a new plan for the king. It was much the same plan as before, except that this time he could offer Charles Confederate troops and could ally his forces with Montrose.[12] At last Antrim's scheme came to fruition, launching the most extraordinary campaign of the war.

On 1 January 1644, Leven marched the army of the Solemn League and Covenant across the Tweed into England. It was a force of 21,000 men, each regiment formed into kirk sessions with ministers and elders. It marched slowly south, plundering and antagonising the Northumbrians until Leven attacked Newcastle on 3 February and settled to a siege.

To bolster his credentials as a constitutional king, Charles took Hyde's advice and called a parliament in Oxford. Hyde was against dissolving the one at Westminster; Charles, he felt, must stand by the laws he had agreed to and make no precipitous moves.[13] The council was with the king at Oxford, the parliament there could sanction taxes and county authorities in royalist territory still answered to Charles. Through them, he could maintain legitimate civil government and raise vital funds.

Paying for the armies became a matter of controlling territory. The king's legal claims were stronger than parliament's, but the MPs controlled richer territory. Both sides levied taxes which became increasingly heavy. In the areas they controlled, parliament set up County Committees, removed any royalist gentry from county administration and put in their own men whose job it was to make monthly assessments, collect tax and confiscate royalist property. In 1642, they had set up a Committee for the Advance of Money which forced loans but paid them back annually with interest. The Committee for Compounding of 1643 took control of royalists' estates and levied fines for their return. This both raised money and aimed to weaken support for the king. Parliament also introduced the hated excise which was levied on beer, tobacco and luxuries, so tax was being paid lower down the social scale and working men began to complain.

The Westminster parliament lost its guiding spirit in December 1643 when John Pym died of cancer. Those members of the Commons who had originally challenged the king were thinning out; some felt parliament was pressing the king too hard and had joined him, and some had died. Initially, parliament had created the Committee of Safety to prosecute the war but with the Scots alliance, a single war council was created for the whole island called the Committee of Both Kingdoms. Young Sir Henry Vane suggested it and his close ally Oliver St John nursed it through parliament. Vane's father had been a diplomat and Vane was a clever man, a religious idealist and a subtle operator in parliament. With the death of Pym, these two were emerging as leaders in the Commons – Charles referred to Vane as leader of a party in the house.[14] The Committee of Both Kingdoms was formed in February 1644 and signalled a new direction. Holles and his associates were excluded from it – the English contingent was made up of Vane's associates, including Oliver Cromwell, William Waller and Arthur Hazelrig, and the radical peers. The committee, which met at Derby House, gave the Puritans an executive body for the whole island to prosecute the war.

The royalists would have to move swiftly. The troops from Dublin joined the North Wales royalists but were swiftly overcome at Nantwich by Sir Thomas Fairfax who was proving a formidable commander. So was Colonel of Horse John Lambert, a Yorkshire associate of Fairfax, who now took the woollen towns of the North Riding of Yorkshire. The king's territory in northern England was being squeezed.

Parliament reorganised its forces and focussed its strategy. By taking troops from the Earl of Essex, it strengthened the Eastern Association under Manchester. Oliver Cromwell had become a central figure among the radicals in the Commons and was now commissioned as Lieutenant General of Horse and second-in-command to Manchester. As spring advanced, the Committee of Both Kingdoms was massing its forces to attack the two royalist cities. Essex was to move on Oxford, while Fairfax was advancing on York with the Earl of Manchester diverted to join him. Prince Rupert was making great advances through the north-west with his cavalry but he had to choose between turning south to defend Oxford or north to defend York. Essex was closing in on Charles, but before Rupert could turn south the king made a daring feint and escaped from Oxford.

The queen had already left. She had been ill with rheumatic pain during the winter and was pregnant again. Oxford was crowded with councillors and soldiers, under military threat and rife with disease. The king had ridden out with his troops to the siege of Gloucester the previous year and was now planning another sortie. Essex was coming closer. Henrietta-Maria lost her bold intransigence and became fretful, fearful. If she was captured, Charles would be hopelessly weakened. In April 1644, she left Oxford via Abingdon to Bath and from there south to Exeter, leaving her sons with Charles in Oxford. She was in Exeter when her last child was born in June, a girl named Henriette Anne.

With the queen safely out of Oxford but Essex based nearby at Islip with troops along the east bank of the Thames, the royalists tried a mixture of false intelligence and military surprise. They put out reports that Charles was coming to London to make peace while the king led his forces out of Oxford on a fake attack on Abingdon which drew parliament's troops in pursuit. Slipping between the two armies, Charles made off west along the Cotswolds, and now Essex made a mistake. He and Waller were not far behind the king, but he decided to go south to relieve Lyme Regis while Waller never closed with Charles, who rode safely into Worcester. Rupert was free to defend York. Only the queen was still in danger, as Essex came nearer Exeter. Leaving her baby with friends there, she was carried by litter into Cornwall. A royalist who saw her in Exeter described her as 'the woefullest spectacle my eyes ever yet beheld'.[15] She had partial paralysis, constriction of the heart and had lost the sight of one eye. Avoiding bands of rebel soldiers, Henrietta arrived at Falmouth where a Flemish fleet took her on board and carried her out into the Channel with parliamentary ships in pursuit.

Mazarin had mixed feelings about receiving her, but Henrietta-Maria's nephew was King of France. As they neared the Channel Islands, French ships appeared, at which the parliamentary pursuers turned back. The little queen came ashore in Brittany, to the astonishment of the local fishermen. She was moved to a spa in the Loire Valley to recuperate, but when her brother Gaston, Duc d'Orleans arrived some weeks later she could still barely walk. Her journey to Paris was slow, but three months after fleeing from Cornwall she came to the outskirts of Paris, where the queen mother and six-year-old king came out to greet her. The French royal family welcomed back the sister who had left twenty years before to become Queen of England.

Charles had become a daring commander. Through the summer he and his forces began to threaten the territory of the Eastern Association, while Rupert collected forces for the relief of York. The city was under siege from the Scots under Leven, Fairfax with his northern army and Manchester with his Eastern Association. Its defence was crucial to the royalists. The approach of Rupert precipitated a climactic battle 7 miles from York.

As Rupert closed with the northern forces at Marston Moor, Alasdair MacColla was crossing the Irish Sea. Having raised 2,000 men, Antrim enlisted his cousin Alasdair, the young warrior from Colonsay, to lead them. He had received little support from the Confederates, but Ormond had provided ships and supplies. Alasdair MacColla and his men sailed from Wexford, which meant a long journey north through the Irish Sea avoiding enemy ships, and disembarked at Ardnamurchan in Argyllshire on 4 July. Here Alasdair had two setbacks: he learned of the death of his local ally and his transport ships were captured. Cut off from retreat and lacking reinforcements, he had no option but to fight his way inland and try to enlist support.

19

The Emergence of Oliver Cromwell

The reorganisation of the parliamentary forces in the summer of 1643 strengthened the Eastern Association and brought Oliver Cromwell into a prominent military command. The original arrangement had been unsatisfactory; Essex was not linked to the regional associations and seemed unwilling to prosecute the war fully. With separate armies hiring troops, the men had proved fickle, moving from one to another if the conditions seemed better or melting away after engagements. Nor were the regional armies coordinated with each other. Parliament saw that changes were essential.

More men were recruited, a new army created to defend London, and Grey was replaced by Manchester in command of the enlarged Eastern Association. His second-in-command was Lieutenant General Oliver Cromwell, with whom he and his family had been associated for some time. Manchester confessed himself 'no experienced souldier, therefore he would rather be guided, than guide'.[1] He was the head of the Montagu family, his cousins had bought Hinchinbrook from the Cromwells and Oliver had become an MP as a client of the family,[2] but Manchester was a political leader, while Cromwell had become a highly effective soldier.

Oliver Cromwell had made little impression when he entered parliament in 1628 but was more confident when he sat as member for Cambridge in both the short and long parliaments. He belonged to the minor gentry of East Anglia but his father's death when he was eighteen had left him to support his mother and six sisters on a modest inheritance. He married three years later and began a family, so his responsibilities began early. A decade later, he sold the property he had inherited and talked of emigrating to America, but made no moves to go.

His wife, Elizabeth Bouchier, came from a well-off merchant family, with business in London and a property in Kent, whom Cromwell knew through his relatives the Hampdens. Elizabeth probably brought a good dowry to the marriage, although records are scarce and in the early 1630s Oliver was living as a tenant farmer at St Ives near Cambridge, a member of the minor gentry but in modest circumstances. It was at the time of the move to St Ives that he experienced an intense spiritual awakening or 'conversion', which set his mind into the shape it retained for the rest of his adult life.

His fortunes changed when he inherited much of his uncle Thomas Steward's estate in 1636. The year before, an inquiry had been launched into Steward's mental health and hostile biographers accuse Oliver Cromwell of instigating this as a device to get control of his uncle's property in advance. The evidence is not conclusive but should not be dismissed.[3] This unseemly episode may partly explain Cromwell's intense self-accusation in his letter to his cousin in 1638 when he wrote, 'You know what my manner of life hath been. Oh, I lived in and loved darkness, and hated the light; I was a chief, the chief of sinners.'[4] But Cromwell was also said to have been a rake in his youth and may have had other reasons for shame.

So, his early manhood was a mixture of limited resources, family responsibility and physical vigour which crystallised into a mature man who felt himself in close and constant proximity to God. The inheritance did eventually come to him from his uncle, despite the court case and family tensions. It included the patronage of several church livings and a house in Ely to which the Cromwells moved. From his late thirties, the society of his Puritan in-laws and their circle set the shape of his career. Once he entered parliament, he naturally worked within this group: Hampden, St John and the radical peers. He made a strong stand over rights for local people when the Fens were drained but it was the outbreak of war which made his career.

The rising in Ireland in October 1641 and the king's attempt to arrest four members soon after Christmas galvanised Cromwell. He invested £600 in the Adventurers' scheme to retake Ireland, which was a large sum for him. The Commons was in an agitated state early in 1642 and Cromwell was notable for pressing drastic measures. He moved that a committee consider military measures against a feared Catholic threat, and when the committee was set up, although not a member, he urged it to take decisive military action.[5] Cromwell sat on the Council for Irish Affairs in April and was clearly greatly alarmed by the threat he perceived from Irish or foreign Catholics.

It was the risks he took that summer which suggest both his fears and his motives. His demands that supplies be prevented from reaching the king in York and that ships should guard the mouth of the River Tyne to prevent foreign aid being sent to the king were just words spoken in parliament – although definite enough. But in August he took action when he hurried to Cambridge, for which he was then member, to organise resistance to the king. He seized arms and ammunition in Cambridge Castle and, using a small band of soldiers, he intercepted money and plate leaving the university bound for the king. Charles had not yet raised his standard, and the war had not officially begun; had events turned out differently, Cromwell could have been charged with robbery or much worse. But he had set his course.[6]

As soon as the war began, Cromwell raised a troop of eighty horsemen, and taking Desborough his brother-in-law with him, rode off to join Essex and the main parliamentary army which fought at Edgehill that October. He showed no doubts and from the first he risked being charged as a rebel, which was treasonable, but for him the urgency of parliament's cause and the fear of Catholicism were overriding motives.

The army of the Eastern Association was formed the following spring. At that stage, the royalists were ascendant through most of the north-east, with a strong garrison at Newark in Nottinghamshire. A Midlands Association was already being formed when an ordinance was passed to set up the Eastern Association, which was to defend Hertfordshire, Essex, Suffolk, Norfolk and Cambridgeshire with the Isle of Ely.[7] Under the leadership of Major General Lord Grey of Warke, Cromwell was promoted from captain to colonel and was immensely active in recruiting and training troops. When Grey was sent to reinforce Essex's army, Cromwell was left to guard the Eastern Association's frontier with the royalists in Lincolnshire.

Cromwell was forty-four and had no professional military training. He later told the Swedish ambassador that he had followed the campaigns of Gustavus Adolphus avidly and thanked God for his victories.[8] The campaigns were reported in detail in *The Swedish Intelligencer* and other pamphlets, so even non-combatants had detailed knowledge of the Swedish strategy and tactics. With family duties, Cromwell had not been free to go abroad but he was naturally athletic. Growing up in Huntingdon, as a boy he could ride and hunt over his uncle Sir Oliver's fine estate at Hinchinbrook. At Cambridge his tutors complained that he was too often out doing sports when he should have been studying, so he was already the tough physical man who became such a notable cavalry officer. The only way he could have gained military experience was in the militias. During the reign of King James, militia training was almost discontinued, but his uncle Sir Oliver had been captain of the Huntingdon militia in the days of Elizabeth and as a county leader and JP would still have been responsible for training when Oliver was young.

Oliver Cromwell was a fine horseman, loved hawking and had great physical stamina, which later events proved. Nonetheless he had no experience of battle until he took up arms for parliament in 1642. He brought to soldiering his practical intelligence, which was strong, his endurance and determination, but he was ruled by his political and religious convictions which were welded together. He recruited quickly but the men who joined him came because of the standards he set and the commitment that he showed. Cromwell said that he sought 'to stand with them for the liberty of the gospel and the laws of the land'. Richard Baxter, the Presbyterian author, wrote, 'These men were of greater understanding than common soldiers, and therefore were more apprehensive of the importance and consequence of the war.' Because they joined Cromwell's regiment for a cause they understood, rather than a soldier's pay, they fought more valiantly and were less likely to flee.[9]

Cromwell had a clear idea of who to recruit and how to train them. He wanted men of honesty and conscience, but he was unconcerned about the sects to which they belonged. Since he himself had a powerful religious understanding and vivid sense of God's presence, he was keen to recruit men of a similar type. Some belonged to the new sects that were springing up as the war began, and Cromwell was criticised for this, but their very religion gave them fighting spirit and looking for stout fighters with true religion in their hearts gave Cromwell a tolerance of their beliefs. He was criticised by his fellow gentry for his selection of officers but he said, 'I had rather have a plain russet-coated captain that knows what he fights for, and loves what he knows, than that which you call a gentleman and is nothing else. I honour a gentleman that is so indeed.'[10] Many of his officers were his relatives; almost all his troops were led by members of his family while his troopers were recruited among the yeoman farmers and artisans of East Anglia, people among whom he had lived and with a cast of mind he knew.

Cromwell's regiment was governed by strict discipline; there was no swearing or name-calling, and men found drunk were put in the stocks. If they stole or plundered they were punished; if they deserted they were flogged then dismissed. There were constant drills and exercises until they moved as one. Even beaten and routed in battle, they would rally and regroup to await orders. Cromwell learned his art alongside his men until they earned themselves the name Ironsides. They were spoken of with awe by the royalists and by their fellow parliamentarians; in the counties where they came to fight there was some acceptance because they tolerated no violence to civilians nor looting of towns.

Practical, capable and resolute, Cromwell was a natural for his new career. His troops were well fed and properly clothed, although not even he could get them paid on time. Their weapons were swords and pistols. Cromwell saw that they had good horses, buying them himself at fairs and markets, but when he failed to get what he needed he would commandeer them from country people.

His passionate commitment to the cause was evident from the start. He had taken control of Cambridge before war even began. Early in 1643 he arrested the sheriff of Hertfordshire for proclaiming the king's commission of array and sent him as prisoner to London. He fortified Cambridge without respect for the buildings or colleges, pulling down structures and placing fortifications among the college gardens. When Lord Grey left to join Essex not long after the Eastern Association was formed, Cromwell had responsibility but also a free hand. He swept through the eastern counties intimidating and arresting as royalist and papist anyone who did not commit themselves to parliament.[11] Throughout 1643 he held the northern frontier of the Eastern Association territory and had some success in skirmishes and smaller battles by which he held the Earl of Newcastle at bay. These engagements were not as important as the quality of his regiment and his close relationship with his men, however. From the first, he saw any victory as an act of God, but there were many failures in 1643 which he tended to blame on his fellow commanders' unreliability.

Before his spiritual awakening, Oliver Cromwell had recurrent health problems: melancholia, depression and hypochondria. His 'conversion' apparently resolved whatever internal dilemmas underlay those conditions. The war showed Cromwell as a confident man; the anguish of his youth had left him. Instead he had become a natural leader, impatient and critical in times of failure, passionate and certain when driving forward his chosen cause. That certainty and discipline made him a very inspiring leader for fighting men.

In July that year, at Gainsborough, he met Henry Ireton, who was of a like mind. Ireton came from a godly family of minor gentry and had trained as a lawyer. He shared a deep Puritan commitment with Cromwell, who made him deputy governor of the Isle of Ely, where he alarmed religious conservatives. Their careers became linked.

Manchester's appointment as commander of the Eastern Association in August 1643 was the beginning of a more assertive role for those forces. Manchester, like Cromwell, tried to recruit godly officers; the two men had much in common and had belonged to the same group at Westminster which had done so much to press the rights of parliament; Ireton served under them. In the autumn of 1643, they reinforced Hull, when Fairfax broke the siege and then advanced against the royalists in Lincolnshire who checked their advance south. Westminster was pressing the Eastern Association to actively take the fight to the royalists in the north, but the local authorities in the eastern counties saw it as a defensive union. Militias in other areas took the same line and when marched up to county boundaries refused to cross them and turned away home. If parliament was to win the war, this reluctance had to be overcome. During the summer of 1644, however, the tides of war changed – in Ireland, in Scotland and also in England, where Cromwell's career went from a minor and local role to that of a national commander.

The Cessation in Ireland, agreed in the autumn of 1643, had allowed crown forces to cross the Irish Sea and aid the king, but it caused problems of allegiance. For both Puritans and the papacy, this truce was suspicious or even abhorrent – crown forces being mainly Protestant and the Confederacy Catholic. It caused some shifts of allegiance, which altered the balance of forces. For the Adventurers, waiting in England for their allotment of land, the Cessation was infuriating. They had subscribed money to beat the Irish rebels but had got little action for their investment – war in England had seen to that. Now the effort to crush the rebellion had been deliberately halted. Many landowners in Ireland, whose property had been overrun by the rebels, had lost their income and control of their estates. The Earl of Cork had thought Ireland settled and developing on the English system; the rebellion was a terrible shock to him and he died soon afterwards, but his son Roger Boyle, Viscount Broghill, stepped into his father's role as a leader of the planter interest and took up a military command in Munster.

As commander of the crown forces in Munster, Inchiquin was effective and became a key figure in the Irish war but his background was very different to the Boyle family. Inchiquin was a Gaelic nobleman and related to many of the Catholic nobility but he had been brought up a Protestant and was fighting to protect their interests. The decisions he took in 1644 changed the balance of power in Ireland. There was intense rivalry between him and Broghill, who viewed Inchiquin's Catholic connections as suspicious and used them to blacken his name. They were both ambitious young men, Inchiquin the finer soldier but Broghill the more able politician, but it was the king who swung the pendulum and lost Inchiquin's support by giving the Munster presidency to an English courtier. When Inchiquin discovered this in Oxford, he left in a towering rage. Once back in Cork he let it be known that he was changing his allegiance. He could get no supplies from Charles in any case, and his men were Protestant; some were uncomfortable with the Cessation, although the truce was patchy, with local skirmishes still occurring. Following a suspected plot to take the ports, Inchiquin expelled the Irish inhabitants of Cork, Youghal and Kinsale. Shortly afterwards, in July 1644, Inchiquin declared for parliament and abrogated the Cessation. Six months later, parliament appointed him their Lord President of Munster, although they were no more forward in providing money or military supplies. Broghill, too, declared for parliament and commanded the port of Youghal.

As long as Inchiquin fought for parliament, the king had lost Cork and much of Munster to parliament. As it turned out, the new Lord President would still have to negotiate with both Ormond and the Confederates to keep his men supplied. Broghill, however, with sterner religious views and an English background, was far more fearful of the Catholics and disapproving of the Cessation. Both men aimed to protect the Munster Protestants but had dissimilar views about how to do that. In any case, they were swept apart again by changes in the political position in Westminster.

When the war began, parliament had been split between radicals and royalists but the latter had left to join the king; now a new split was opening up within parliament which would define the war. After Bedford's death, and more particularly since Pym's, the party had splintered. The two factions were known as Independents and Presbyterians because of their religious aims, but more importantly they differed over their goal and strategy for the war. The Presbyterians wanted a single national church to which everyone in the country belonged and they looked for a settlement which included all three kingdoms. Uncomfortable with a single form of worship, the English Independents were concerned with religious liberty, and many of their adherents belonged to the 'gathered churches' – local groups which came together to worship according to their conscience. This religious behaviour was taken up by the American colonists in New England and it gave each congregation an intense group mentality. Critics thought it radical and destined to lead to schism. The Independents were more tolerant of the radical sects which were starting to appear as the central government collapsed – the Baptists and Seekers for example. This was anathema to the Presbyterians, for whom unity was essential and who, in Scotland at least, had brought their church into Covenant with God.

As regards the war, the Presbyterians had developed as the peace party, looking for a negotiated settlement with the king, whereas the Independents planned to pursue the war to final victory. They too would negotiate with Charles, but only after they had beaten him and cut off all his options. The attitudes of the Independents also showed in recruiting. Cromwell was now a key member of the Independent war party and had recruited for his cavalry on the basis of belief. Many came from among the godly people of East Anglia, but more cautious MPs worried that his men were religious radicals with motives of their own.

In Ireland, this split was acting on the allegiances of the Protestant forces. Inchiquin was linked to members of the Presbyterian party who hoped to include Ormond and the Scots in a settlement. Broghill was involved with the Independents whose attitude was more uncompromising. When the Committee of Both Kingdoms was formed, it stipulated that all troops should take the Solemn League and Covenant; Broghill took it and enforced it, while Inchiquin did not.[12]

While the balance of forces in Ireland remained confused, with a truce dampening the fighting, the conflict in both Scotland and England dramatically altered. Alasdair MacColla came ashore in Scotland just as the Eastern Association linked up with the Scots in northern England. As the king's position in Yorkshire plummeted, so his star rose in Scotland due to the valour of Montrose.

20

Cromwell and Montrose
Win Victories

Alasdair MacColla sailed from Wexford with his Irish troops on 27 June 1644. The plan was for him to meet Montrose in Scotland and try to raise the Highlands to fight for the king. The plan went horribly wrong but the two commanders did meet and won a series of extraordinary victories.

While Alasdair was making his perilous way through the Irish Sea to Scotland, parliament's forces were closing in on York. The Scots Covenanters had crossed the border in January and settled into a siege of Newcastle for two months, until Leven moved his troops south to join the Fairfaxes – father and son – and laid siege to York. In May, Manchester was ordered north to join them. In southern England that summer, both sides had mixed fortunes but it was Essex's decision to go south to Lyme which allowed the king to leave Oxford and move around the west Midlands. Prince Rupert was unsure whether Oxford and the king were in danger and whether he should return there, but Charles ordered him to relieve York where the Marquis of Newcastle had already taken most of his forces. Rupert obeyed, reaching the city and conferring with Newcastle on 1 July. It was the prince's decision, against the advice of Newcastle and his junior officer, to give battle on the following day.

The allied generals – the Scots, with Manchester and the Fairfaxes – were moving south the next day to block Rupert's river crossing when they realised that the royalist cavalry was drawn up on Marston Moor, a few miles from York city. Among them were Goring, Byron and Langdale, all of them commanders of note with experienced troops numbering around 18,000. The parliamentarians and Scots combined outnumbered the royalists with around 28,000 men, of whom 20,000 were infantry, but the allied troops were very mixed and Rupert had made a calculated judgement that he could successfully oppose them.

It was thundery on 2 July and the royalist soldiers waited all day in their battle formations as the Puritan forces moved into their positions. It was nearing seven o'clock and Rupert had told his men to eat when the Puritans attacked. They had the benefit of surprise, but Rupert was a successful cavalry officer who had learned his trade fighting for his father in Germany; he was quick and versatile on the field and experienced in strategy. He massed his men and the cavalry charged, which broke Cromwell's lines. It was Leslie and the Scots who attacked Rupert's flanks and gave Cromwell a chance to regroup. This turned the tide of battle; in fact, Rupert barely escaped capture. The fighting raged on as Goring attacked on the other wing, routing Fairfax's cavalry, although Lambert regrouped his troops with Cromwell's. Fairfax and Leven both left the field of battle but Cromwell rallied his men and fell on the now disordered royalist cavalry and routed them swiftly. Only the Whitecoats, who were Newcastle's infantrymen and armed with pikes, fought to the bitter end.

Manchester was on the field of battle at Marston Moor. He congratulated his men as he rode round the field as the day ended when many other commanders had fled, but Cromwell led his men personally as they leapt forward for the fight. His relationship with them was of another order.

For the parliamentarians, it was a triumphant victory. They took 1,500 prisoners including many of high status, as well as royalist guns and colours. Some 4,000 men were buried after Marston Moor, many of them from the north country fighting under Newcastle, and this huge death toll effectively lost the north of England for the king. Two weeks later, York – the royalist capital of the north – surrendered to Fairfax.

In light of this, there was no excuse for Essex and Manchester when Marston Moor was only followed by losses. Essex had turned south in June, into Devon and Cornwall, where he was chased by the king before he fled from Lostwithiel by boat, leaving 6,000 men to treat for surrender.

Nor did Manchester or Leslie press home the advantage which the victory at Marston Moor had given. There was no excuse except the one which Manchester gave, that 'this war would not be ended by the sword'.[1] Unlike his general of horse, Manchester was not a natural soldier and was horrified by Marston Moor and the sufferings of York. There was also ill feeling among the Scots, who contested Cromwell's version of events and felt that Marston Moor was as much their victory as his.

Cromwell wrote of Marston Moor: 'Truly England and the Church of God hath had a great favour from the Lord, in this great victory given unto us.' He went on, 'The left wing, which I commanded, being our own horse, saving a few Scots in our rear, beat all the Prince's horse. God made them as stubble to our swords.' He was actually writing to tell Colonel Walton that his eldest son had suffered a broken leg due to cannon fire but that the young man had died when they tried to amputate. Cromwell went on to praise the young soldier and to remind Colonel Walton of the boy's place in Heaven, and that Christ's strength would bring comfort to the father's sorrow.[2]

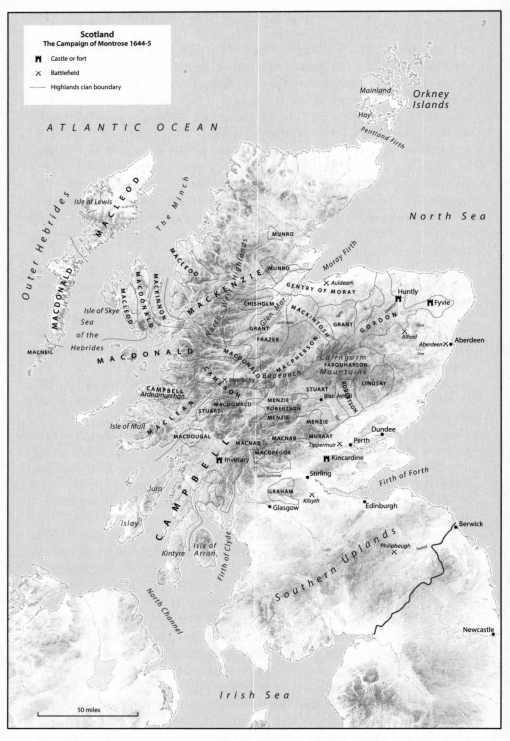

Scotland – the Campaign of Montrose 1644-45. Covenanter clans: Campbell, Murray, Grant, Frazer, Mackenzie, Lindsay and the gentry of Moray. Royalists: MacDonald, Maclean, Stuart of Atholl and Appin, Cameron, Menzies, Robertson, Farquharson, Macpherson, Mackintosh, MacGregor, MacNab, Gordon of Huntly.

His analysis of the battle, however, clearly showed his cast of mind. Cromwell was now a fully battle-hardened cavalry officer, confident of his abilities. He made clear that his wing had beaten Rupert but their prowess was also ascribed to God's favour. The victory was a mark of God's providence, a message of his blessing which heartened both commander and troops as they moved on to their next encounter.

Cromwell's exasperation with Manchester, with Essex and with the wider conduct of the war displayed the drive of a successful commander who was being held back by the incompetence of politicians and non-combatants. He had become a professional soldier and he demanded a single professional army with which to fight. Manchester now became Cromwell's main object of attack. The two men became bitterly opposed and they spent the winter in London pressing a case against each other in parliament.

While the parliamentarians were struggling with each other over strategy and leadership, the king's two great champions had arrived in Scotland to launch the royalist campaign. Alasdair MacColla and his men made their hazardous sea journey in June and disembarked at Ardnamurchan in Argyllshire on 4 July. When he found no allies waiting for him and his ships lost, Alasdair had no choice but to cut his way through Argyll territory to join other royalists.

It was dangerous for him to be in Campbell country, but Alasdair had the advantage of surprise. His men advanced by sudden attack – burning, killing and stealing cattle as the villagers fled into the hills. They blazed their way along the shores of Loch Awe but Campbell strongholds were being alerted and forces gathering. Alasdair made for Skye but found little support; he was Irish and alien.

In the north-west of Scotland, the Gordons strongly supported the king but had made little impact on his enemies. They were supposed to rise in arms to coordinate with the Ulstermen's advance but in fact they had tried to rise in the spring and been savagely crushed by Argyll. This had left the Highland leaders uncertain and unwilling. Alasdair led his men with their baggage and camp-followers across the central Highlands but the expected Highland reinforcements never appeared. By the time they reached Badenoch they were in alien territory, exhausted and with little ammunition. Alasdair sent a message to Montrose in Carlisle but believed that now only divine intervention could save him and his 'Irishes'.[3]

Montrose had left Oxford with the king's commission in March, planning to raise an army and cut his way through the Scottish Lowlands to meet Antrim's expedition. But in Cumbria, Montrose raised only 800 men who left him at the border; in Dumfries he failed to raise troops and so he returned to Carlisle. From there, he joined Rupert for part of the summer campaign – but his business was in Scotland. After Marston Moor, his cavaliers rode south to rejoin Rupert, believing any further royalist action in Scotland was now impossible. Not Montrose. He rode south with them for some time but he and his two friends dropped behind and, when the column was out of sight, they turned their horses' heads about and rode for Scotland. Dressed as Covenanters, with Montrose as a groom, they crossed the border country and reached Stirling in four days but pressed on to Perthshire, where they sheltered with Graham of Inchbrakie, a relative and ally of Montrose. The news was all of royalist defeat. Argyll had ravaged the Gordons, the Campbells were in arms and Aberdeen was taken for the Covenant. Even with Graham at Tullibelton, Montrose was not safe in the house but had to hide in the woods and sleep in hunters' bothies. It was late in August and the colours of the hills were beginning to change.

It was a poor position for the king's lieutenant to be in, yet Alasdair MacColla's urgent message reached him. The messenger asked directions from Inchbrakie and so it came to the hands of Montrose, who sent a reply telling Alasdair to meet him at Blair. This was not easy country for the Catholic Irish but Alasdair obeyed, marched his men into the braes of Atholl and took Blair Castle. Alasdair was on the moors, forming up his troops against local levies, when he saw two figures walking over the hills towards them. The Atholl men knew who this was and shouts rang out. Alasdair was expecting royalist cavalry; instead he met a slim young man in his early thirties with grey eyes searching his own, with no troops but a great name and the king's commission.

Now recruits came in, drawn to Montrose and the royal standard, but Lord Elcho was at Perth with a Covenanting army; time was short. Three days later Montrose, Alasdair MacColla and 2,700 men met an army of 7,000 infantry and 700 horse at Tippermuir outside Perth.[4] The royalists had an extraordinary victory. Montrose drew up his men only three deep instead of six, otherwise they would be outflanked. Using tactics learned from the campaigns of Gustavus Adolphus, all ranks fired at once. Elcho's men were levies, Montrose's volunteers, while Alasdair's had old rivalries and terrifying methods. Their equipment was poor; some had only stones. But at Tippermuir, Elcho felt the full force of the Highland charge. It was a maelstrom in which the Ulstermen with their Badenoch allies hurled themselves with pike, claymore and axe in an attack of implacable ferocity. The Lowlanders crumpled and fled. Tippermuir was the first battle of an astonishing campaign. The Highlands had created a new fighting force on behalf of the king.

Montrose and Alasdair MacColla won a string of extraordinary victories. Using the skills of the MacDonald clansmen, adapting to wild terrain, with experience from the European wars, Montrose fought a war of movement as he brought his men through the hill country until he saw his advantage. Argyll, not a natural soldier, was beaten by Montrose in the north-east and even fled from his own castle of Inveraray as the Clanranald men, from Ulster and the Isles, rose and came burning through the Campbell lands. Montrose and Alasdair's six great victories, at Tippermuir, Aberdeen, Inverlochy, Auldearn, Alford and Kilsyth, gave the royalists a temporary dominance in Scotland.

Montrose had seen his advantage when the Covenanters had sent their armies out of Scotland – first into Ireland and then into England – but it took great daring to rouse the Highlands as he did. His campaign prevented the Covenanters sending further troops into England and made Leven loiter in the north of England to prevent English royalist troops getting through to aid Montrose. His campaign could not secure victory for Charles but it tipped the balance and delayed defeat. It also encouraged Antrim to try again later.

Montrose had believed he could take Scotland for the king, and his courage in that ancient service made him legendary, but on the ground his alliance with Catholic Irishmen created suspicion. His drummer boy went into Aberdeen as messenger and was shot leaving, enraging Montrose; after their victory, he allowed the troops to ravage the city and its people, which gave both him and his Irish fighters a reputation as savage and wild.[5]

While the parliamentarians failed to take advantage of their first great victory, the king's two champions in Scotland took the war into the heart of Campbell country. After the victory at Aberdeen, Alasdair MacColla went west to support Irish troops holding the castle of Mingary. His arrival led to the Campbell troops' withdrawal, and, encouraged by this show of strength, other MacDonalds began to join MacColla's forces. Montrose for his part remained in the east, trying to get support from the Gordons and then penetrating into Morayshire where he was surprised by the advancing armies of the Covenant led by none other than the Earl of Argyll himself. Montrose held the massive fortress of Fyvie Castle as the Campbell advanced swiftly on him, but his forces were smaller and he had very few cavalry. Montrose, as always, used geographical advantage and the ferocity of his troops to their utmost. Lowland troops were disciplined, but the Irish and the Highlanders were able to withstand the weather and long marches in the hills as the Lowlanders could not; in battle the Gaels had a ferocity which was unmatched. Montrose held Argyll at bay through two days of fighting at Fyvie, before slipping away with his troops into the hills. He sent his cavalry to winter quarters and the campaign should rightfully have ended for the year but that was not Alasdair MacColla's intention. He still had to win the freedom of his father and brothers, and he still intended to destroy as thoroughly as possible the power of the mighty MacCailein Mór in the old MacDonald lands. He rejoined Montrose and proposed a winter raid into Argyllshire.

Montrose was horrified. His plan was to seek shelter and food in the Lowlands. Winter in the Highlands was tough enough without going out on campaign with all the demands of feeding men and trudging them over wet bitter hillsides, but worse again was the idea of entering the Campbell territory and rousing the clansmen in their own well-known lairs. The passes were steep, the coast serrated and hard to march across. But Alasdair MacColla insisted that the power of the Marquis of Argyll must be broken. When it was put to a Council of War they supported him. There would be an attack on the Campbell lands.

They left their headquarters at Blair Atholl on 11 December, making their way along the shore of Loch Tay heading west. As they came into Campbell country, the army split into three, each travelling like purging wrath down the glens, burning houses, killing men and driving away the cattle. Colonel James McDonnell reported to Dublin how 'throughout all Argyle, we left neither house nor hold unburned, nor corn nor cattle, that belonged to the whole name of Campbell'. Montrose too reported how they 'laid waste the whole country of Argyle'.[6] Over 800 men were killed as the royalists came slaughtering down the glens. Only a few small groups already known to be loyal to MacDonald were completely spared.

This was a different form of warfare, with another purpose to the power struggles which were taking place in the lowlands of England. Alasdair MacColla's enemy was the Campbells as a clan, and his purpose was to free his family from their dungeons while eliminating them from land once peopled by MacDonalds. To do that, the slaughter of Campbell men and the destruction of the crofts and villages of Argyllshire was seen as necessary and crucial. Wars had been fought this way in the Gaelic lands in the past and, in fact, Elizabeth's armies had practised total war in Ireland within living memory, leaving whole counties bereft of people and food. Similar tactics were being used there now, by both sides.[7] Montrose and Alasdair MacColla went through Argyllshire with fire and the sword. There is no record that Montrose demurred while the Gael slaughtered; it was a common war policy.

The Marquis of Argyll had returned to his castle at Inveraray, sure that no enemy could enter the Argyll territory, but Alasdair MacColla and the Highlanders knew those hills and the passes through them. As he heard of the approaching war bands and his men reported seeing the smoke of the burning houses, the marquis ordered his galleon and escaped down the loch, leaving the little town of Inveraray to be burned by the royalists. From Inveraray, Montrose withdrew northwards to regroup and some of the Highland chiefs came in to join him. The Marquis of Argyll had been humiliated. But he had all the more motive to retaliate. He gathered Covenanter reinforcements, together with Campbell relatives and their men, before taking his army north to confront Montrose when the royalists were forced south for supplies.

At the end of January, in the worst of Scotland's winter, the royalist army inflicted its most daring defeat on the Campbell commander who was camped across their path at the mouth of the Great Glen. At the northern end was another Covenanter army; Montrose could well be trapped. By a two-day march over the shoulder of Ben Nevis in cruel weather and with meagre supplies, the royalists surprised the Campbell army at Inverlochy and inflicted a shock defeat. Once more the marquis boarded his galley and left his men to withstand the raw strength of the Irish and Highland troops. To thwart Alasdair, he had his father and brothers sent to Dumbarton and then Edinburgh Castle. However, Montrose and Alasdair now had a good catch of Campbell prisoners who could be held for exchange.[8]

The poets who followed the Gaelic armies were delirious with war-song for the great victory of Clan Donald. It had begun on the feast of St Brigid: the priests had blessed the men, and among them the victory was seen as a Catholic victory over the heretic.[9] It was part of the fierce Gaelic civil war between the old Lords of the Isles and the Campbell interlopers; a more passionate affair than any matter between the king and some kirkmen in Edinburgh.

However, the winter campaign of Montrose and Alasdair MacColla had a national effect. It destroyed the invincible reputation of the Campbells and stole from the marquis his pride of place as leader of the Covenanting forces. It also made the leaders in Edinburgh withdraw both commanders and men from England to strengthen their army in the Highlands. After Inverlochy, the men of the kirk searched in their hearts for the meaning of these losses and concluded that God had used their enemies, many of whom were papists and Irish, to chastise the kirkmen for their sins. Also, Inverlochy brought the Gordons out to support Montrose at last, despite their smarting from his early attacks on them under the Covenanting banner. MacColla still hungered for his father's freedom but Montrose believed his mission was to destroy the king's enemies in Scotland and draw the Scottish armies out of England.

The courage, endurance and ferocity of the Highland royalists had won victories and renown. Montrose wrote to the king believing his victories would rekindle royalist fire in the south. Gaelic poets composed verse in praise of the great triumphs over the Campbell forces. But in England the royalist cause was in trouble. True, the parliamentarian victory at Marston Moor and the subsequent fall of York had been followed by weak military leadership and scandalous defeats. But Montrose now heard that the king was negotiating with the Covenanters.

It was true. The Scots commissioners in London were the chief instigators of a new overture to the king. The *Uxbridge Proposals* were offered as a form of treaty to the king in November 1644. Negotiations followed throughout the winter but as parliament was still demanding control over the army and church, there was no chance that the king would agree. The more decisive debate took place among the parliamentarians themselves that winter. It was a long and often bitter deliberation, but decisions were taken and when spring came a new military force was already being drilled and equipped, ready to take the field that fighting season.

21

The Creation of the New Model Army

England had been at war for two years when parliament had its victory at Marston Moor. The battle confirmed Oliver Cromwell as one of the most effective commanders in parliament's army, a reputation that had grown steadily since war had begun in 1642. Marston Moor and the fall of York should have led to a wider victory but Essex had gone to Cornwall and been beaten by the king there while Manchester had not pursued the advantage. Leven, meanwhile, seemed most concerned about keeping his army intact.

For those prosecuting the war, another growing problem was local resistance to any form of war at all. In March 1645, Prince Rupert had to fall back when Clubmen threatened his troops, showing the strength of resistance. These were groups formed from local people in England who, exasperated by contending armies and plundering soldiers, arming themselves mainly with farm implements, attacked soldiers and demanded their removal. With public discontent rising, the war party had to press swiftly on to victory if its aims were to be achieved.

However, the Presbyterian party in parliament increasingly urged a negotiated peace with the king. The rift between them and the Independents was becoming acrimonious and Cromwell attracted especial antagonism. He had claimed the main credit for Marston Moor, which the Scots felt was at least partly theirs, but the main problem was adherence to the Solemn League and Covenant. For the Scots this was fundamental – to their alliance with the English, to their joint plans for the future and for the respect they required for their religion. Cromwell and St John were pressing for liberty for 'tender consciences', which would allow the radicals and sectaries among the English troops freedom of religious practice. The Scots already thought the Lieutenant General antagonistic to them, and this breach of the Covenant enraged them.[1]

After Marston Moor, disagreements developed between Manchester and Cromwell. Late in 1644, Cromwell and Waller reported to the Commons on the recent campaign. What had gone wrong, why had the victory at Marston Moor not led to wider successes? Cromwell and Waller both blamed Manchester, who clearly did not believe the differences between king and people would be solved by military victory; Ireton provided evidence. By criticising an earl who was his commanding officer, Cromwell was taking a risk. When Manchester replied, he accused Cromwell of wanting the end of all nobility and of fierce antagonism to the Scots. These jibes were only partly true; Cromwell believed in, even relied upon, social hierarchy, but he was becoming antagonistic to the Scots, who discussed impeaching him with Holles and friends but were told it would not stick. The lawyer Bulstrode Whitelocke told them the Independents were now too strong in the Commons. Indeed, as the Independent party strengthened, so the Scots began to lose their hold on London.[2]

However, the period of Scottish influence had spelt the end for Archbishop Laud. He was still in the Tower, but during 1644 the Scots demanded his impeachment. Laud's former victim William Prynne, who had been mutilated and branded for seditious publishing, was given the satisfaction of managing the charges but, despite tampering with evidence, the case was too weak. Alongside treason and the advancement of popery, one of the other charges against Laud was his opposition to enclosure. Parliament disliked his efforts to curtail their property rights.[3] The impeachment, like Strafford's, limped along and seemed unlikely to lead to conviction, so the Commons introduced an ordinance of attainder and the London mobs once more set up their cry – against 'William the Fox'. Despite this, the Lords were slow to assent. In January 1645, they gave in and, since parliament no longer sought the king's consent, Laud was executed on 10 January.

Organising the war effort had absorbed parliament's energies in the beginning, but now, as members became irate over the conduct of the war, so the ultimate aim came into question and on this a fundamental rift emerged. The evidence suggests that at this stage all the parliamentary leaders expected to restore the king; the question was on what terms. Debate raged around how to bring him to terms. What was the endgame? What strategy should the commanders follow?

In England, the war was a set of skirmishes and sieges with occasional pitched battles. It was a war with expected behaviours and rules, both informal and military. When a civil war ends, the protagonists will have to be reconciled, so the leaders tried to avoid extreme methods. As Christians, there were expected standards of conduct and there were laws of war which were customary throughout Europe. Military law was distinct and codified, to be enforced by commanders and court martials. In England, the war leaders made strenuous efforts to enforce these rules; it was well known how savage the war in Germany had become. Leaders also feared the rabble; war might lead to a general breakdown of law and order. So, the laws of war were read to the troops, and commanders gave orders about conduct and punished offenders – plunderers, for instance, might be hanged. But control of the troops became increasingly difficult and commanders varied; Sir Richard Grenville was notorious as a 'bloody and violent' commander. Nor were the laws of war benign; they depended on the situation. A city that was besieged but refused to surrender was not owed quarter, and Rupert's troops wreaked vengeance on Leicester when it fell.[4] Each side told of the atrocities of the others, which rivalled the stories of horror told about the Irish rebellion, but local people already knew how the various armies had behaved. Town dwellers suffered the terrors of siege, destruction and plunder; women and children could be vulnerable. Rural people lost crops and livestock. For the civilian population, war was impoverishing and unpredictable – often terrifying. Commanders, including the king, struggled to control their troops, especially when paying them was so difficult.

The point of warfare was to test the strength of the opponent. In victory, the winner came to peace negotiations with the upper hand. If the king was defeated it would prove that he did not have absolute power, but neither Essex nor Manchester wanted to push Charles that far. Increasingly, they held back as the war party urged a tougher fight. The war party thirsted for a final victory and full capitulation by the king, after which parliament could dictate terms. So, as the year turned and 1645 began, the struggle to control parliament's army intensified.

The conduct of the war did not satisfy any of the parliamentary factions. Manchester did not disguise his distaste for a policy of total victory. The carnage of the war in the north and at the siege of York had horrified him. Besides, parliamentarians were taking the ultimate risk, as he pointed out: 'If we beat the king ninety-nine times he would be king still, and his posterity; and we subjects still. But if he beat us once we should be hanged and our posterity undone.'[5]

The war party did not answer this directly but pressed for a swift victory. Parliament had support from part of the population but risked losing it and was suspected by many. In the December debate, Cromwell summed up his position: 'For what do the enemy say? Nay, what do many say that were friends at the beginning of the parliament? Even this, that the members of both Houses have got great places and commands, and ... will perpetually continue themselves in grandeur, and not permit the war speedily to end, lest their own powers should determine with it... If I may speak my conscience without reflection upon any, I do conceive if the army be not put into another method, and the war more vigorously prosecuted, the people can bear the war no longer, and will enforce you to a dishonourable peace.'[6] Cromwell and Waller both emphasised that parliament could not afford three armies, none of which was at full strength. They, and Massey, insisted that a single professional fighting force was essential. The war party agreed and many MPs

England and Ireland: Battle sites, 1644–49.

England and Ireland 1644-49
Battle Sites

× Site of battle

North Sea

Irish Sea

Celtic Sea

English Channel

Berwick

Newcastle

Hull

York ×

Marston Moor × *2 July 1644*

× Preston *17 Aug 1648*

× Winwick *19 Aug 1648*

Rowton Moor

Chester × *24 Sept 1645*

× Nantwich *25 Jan 1644*

Newark × *5 May 1646*

Nottingham

Shrewsbury

× Montgomery *7 Sept 1644*

× Naseby *14 June 1645*

× Cropredy Bridge *29 June 1644*

London

Oxford

Gloucester

Bristol

St Fagan's × *8 May 1648*

× Langport *10 July 1645*

Exeter

× Torrington *16 Feb 1646*

Plymouth

Lostwithiel ×
21 July–3 Aug 1644

Belfast

× Benburb *5 June 1646*

Dublin
Rathmines ×
Aug 1649

Dungan's Hill × *Aug 1647*

Wexford

Waterford

Kilkenny

Limerick

× Liscarroll *July 1642*

Lismore

Knocknanuss × *13 Nov 1647*

Cork

Galway

50 miles

thought this obvious, although the peace party suspected that Independents would command the new army but they were now the minority.

Who should command? Picking over the record of their commanders would be contentious and unproductive, so they chose a simple course and excluded all members of parliament. No members of either house should hold a military command or any civil office conferred by parliament. The army must be entirely reorganised, while all members should relinquish their military commands.

It took considerable political skill to manoeuvre the twin ordinances through both houses of parliament but Cromwell spent three months in London that winter where his political skills showed signs of maturing alongside his military ones. He and Vane guided the legislation through. Despite much reduced attendance in the Lords, many remaining peers resisted the Self-Denying Ordinance. It was far more revolutionary than it seemed. Throughout the feudal period, the nobility had been war leaders – that was their core function in the hierarchy of the state. Even in an army of rebellion, they were shocked at losing their military role.

The Self-Denying and New Model Ordinances began in the Commons late in 1644 but it was February of the new year before both had been passed by the Lords. They would transform the conduct of the war.

While the Lords delayed, the Commons began building their new army as a parallel force and allowed the other armies to wither. By cutting off funding to Essex, they starved his army of troops and supplies, while they awarded funding to the new. The Commons held the purse strings, which was their hold on the Lords as it had been on the king. To conform with the Self-Denying Ordinance, they chose as commander-in-chief of the new army a man with radical views but no seat in parliament. Sir Thomas Fairfax had fought alongside his father Lord Fairfax and was inspiring in the field. But the terms of his commission disturbed the Lords deeply. Essex had been required to protect the person of the king, since the official reason for the war was that it was a struggle against the king's evil counsellors, against Irishmen and papists, not against the monarch himself. This time that clause was deleted. Perhaps by now the prosecutors of the war had gone too far to uphold this fiction, but the Fairfax commission put into writing what before had been only tacit: the war was moving from resistance towards outright revolution.[7]

By the spring of 1645, the old armies were atrophying from lack of men, money and officers. Fairfax chose his own officers from the previous army, picking the best but temporarily leaving Lambert in command of the northern army. Fairfax also hired troops from the regional forces, so the other parliamentary armies were hollowed out. Oliver Cromwell was due to lay down his commission under the Self-Denying Ordinance in April 1645 but he was fighting under Waller in the west when the time came and could

Sir Thomas Fairfax.

not be spared. Even when Waller stood down, Cromwell was still mustering troops in the Midlands and fighting around Oxford.[8] Early in June, Fairfax and his war council asked parliament to appoint Cromwell as Lieutenant General of Cavalry in the New Model Army. The Lords never answered this request but the Commons agreed. Six days later, the New Model Army was on the field of battle at Naseby.

The Eastern Association continued to exist but lost its central treasury and supply system.[9] It became an administrative body concerned with the defence of its own counties and their local militias. The real fighting force, with its steely commanders, emerged elsewhere. Cromwell took to the New Model Army the standards he had set for his own troops and God's blessed victories kept rolling in.

22

Naseby and Philiphaugh – Royalist Collapse

The Cessation of Arms in Ireland in 1643 freed up royalist troops to strengthen the king's armies in Britain, but those troops proved of little benefit. The only real support that Charles received from Ireland was the expedition of Alasdair MacColla, whose Irish troops formed the core of Montrose's campaign and whose ferocity was unstoppable.

So, Lord Castlehaven's hope that the Irish could benefit from rebellion, as the Scots had, was unfounded. He mentioned that the Irish hated the Scots beyond all nations and felt that the Irish had far greater grievances. The Scots had been 'suffered to introduce a New Religion' so why should the Irish be punished 'in the Exercise of their old, which they glory never to have altered'?[1] In temporal matters, the Irish had been subject to plantation, challenges to their land titles, new taxes and removal from public office in favour of planters. Castlehaven carefully distinguished between the initial and bloody rising, which was of the 'rude rabble', and the creation of the Confederacy by which the Irish pressed their grievances and tried to defend themselves. In 1645, the Protestant forces still held the principal ports – Monro in Ulster, Ormond at Dublin and Inchiquin at Cork – but the Confederates controlled most of the island as well as Waterford and the Wessex coast, so territorially their position was strong. What they lacked was military hardware.

Throughout 1644 and 1645 the Confederates were in negotiation with both Charles and Ormond for better long-term conditions for the Irish: repeal of the Penal Laws and a reversal of Strafford's plantations. Charles listened to both Catholic and Protestant delegations of Irishmen at his court in Oxford and offered the Graces once more. What he actually wanted was Irish troops, but the regiments sent to Wales soon crumpled and many soldiers signed up with parliament where pay was more secure.

There was still fighting in Ireland. In Ulster, neither Monro nor the Laggan army answered to Ormond, so neither were part of the Cessation.

The defection of Inchiquin in Munster and Coote in Connacht, both to parliament, revived the war in the far south and west, but 1645 in Ireland was a year of only local struggle on the periphery, with an area of truce at the centre of the country but little momentum towards a resolution.

In Britain, however, 1645 was a momentous year. The Committee of Both Kingdoms attempted to direct the war and interfered with its new commander, Sir Thomas Fairfax, but once the New Model Army was formed and trained, its very size made it formidable.[2] However, spring was well advanced before the political and practical difficulties were solved.

Within parliament, there was a struggle for control of both civilian government and the army. Having evolved from great councils which aimed to find consensus and had long-established traditions, parliament hung on tenaciously to its procedures. The role and rights of parliament were paramount; they were the thing for which they fought, the cause itself. But the system was fraying. Under the constitution, loyalty to the monarch was paramount and the king should assent to all statutes, yet parliament was making great changes by order and ordinance, and by one such ordinance royalists were obliged to take the negative oath: 'I will not directly or indirectly assist the king in this war.'[3] Those who had supported the king had their estates confiscated. Until they compounded – paid heavy fines – the estates were let and the income taken by parliament. With the king absent, parliament used its own authority to dismantle the feudal instruments of which it had complained so bitterly; the hated Court of Wards was abolished by order, along with land tenure by homage or knights service.[4]

Most of all, parliament had to fund the war. The assessment, the new property tax first instigated under Pym in 1642 and first collected in London, had been extended to all counties controlled by parliament. The overall rates were twice those paid when subsidy was collected by Charles I's government. County committees had grown up haphazardly as local officials were replaced by men who were sympathetic to parliament and it was they who set the assessment quotas. Being on good terms with the county committee could greatly reduce a landowner's tax. Throughout the war, London was the principal funding source for parliament, which had taken out large loans from the Common Council of the City of London and did so again in 1645 to fund the New Model Army. The creation of the excise, levied from 1643 on luxury items of consumption like ale, was especially effective in London, which was a centre of consumption and an easy place to collect the tax. Since it brought in substantial funds, parliament could also borrow against future excise receipts. A new funding source for government had been created but the people's pleasures had become more expensive. The county committees and the heavy burden of taxation became an increasing source of grievance.[5]

Despite having funding, parliament found it difficult to recruit the New Model Army. Fairfax presented his choice of officers to parliament, later adding others such as Ireton. Cavalry was brought over smoothly enough from the other armies but infantry was scarce and poor people were targeted for impressment. They were very resistant and had to be guarded until they were marched off to Reading where the army was assembled.[6] Once there, they still posed problems, robbing when they could and deserting after payment or battle. However, large numbers were conscripted; there were around 24,000 men by June 1645. Of those, 7,000 were under Cromwell who had recruited them – half of them infantry. The religious beliefs of the men were very mixed. Cromwell's troops shared his beliefs and set the tone for the army, but in the drive to build a large force quickly an assortment of men was brought in, including royalists, tramps and desperados, while many had no religious conviction and some had very disputatious ideas. The delay in forming up this new army gave the royalists an advantage, mainly in the west.[7]

The spring campaign in Scotland was triumphant for the royalists. They funded themselves as they could, by plundering or extracting money from the Covenanters, moving through the hills until they could manoeuvre the enemy into battle in a place and time of their choosing. Success breeds success; the battle of Inverlochy impressed the Highlanders and this brought in more support. Montrose had a setback at Dundee but on 4 May, at Auldearn near Inverness, the royalists had a famous victory over the Covenanting army under Hurry, half of whose army were killed. This was the high point of Alasdair MacColla's career as a swordsman. 'Health and joy to the valiant Alasdair who won the battle of Auldearn with his army,' the Gaelic poet declaimed. 'Helmeted men with pikes in their hands were attacking you with all their might until you were relieved by Montrose.' For the bards, pride of place went to the Gael.[8]

Two days after the battle at Auldearn, Alasdair MacColla learned that his father and brothers had been released in a prisoner exchange. Their great foe had given up the MacDonalds of Colonsay at last.

The Montrose–MacDonald campaign was a series of marches and skirmishes; they were always on the move until the enemy was brought to battle. While Montrose manoeuvred, Alasdair went raiding, taking some of his Irish troops to create diversions, plundering and extracting goods from the enemy, but always aiming to destroy Campbells. The war in the Highlands was of a different type to that in the Lowlands, for clansmen were the enemy whether in arms or not, and Alasdair MacColla's only way of taking Kintyre permanently was to destroy or drive out all the Campbells on the peninsula.[9]

In the spring, the king had several successes in the south and west of England but his position looked increasingly vulnerable. So, he made a new arrangement for his eldest son, sending Prince Charles to Bristol with a council of his own, ostensibly to manage the war in the West Country but principally to divide father and son in case the king was captured.[10]

Summer was coming. The king called a general rendezvous of his forces at Stow-on-the-Wold in the Cotswolds. After disagreements, the English royalists

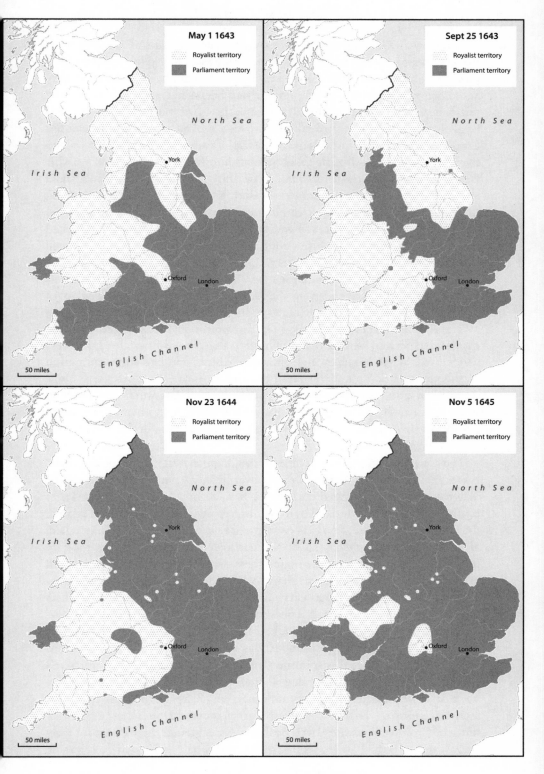

Territory held by the king and parliament, May 1643 – November 1645.

split into two – Goring took his forces west to check Fairfax at Taunton while Rupert pressed for the main army to move north to first relieve Chester and then attack the Scots under Leven. Leven was alarmed by Montrose's victory at Auldearn, where 2,000 Covenanters had been slain, and he was moving north in case Montrose came down into the Lowlands to join the king's English forces. The main royalist army also moved north and east under Charles's command. Fairfax's army was split and not at full strength when the Committee of Both Kingdoms ordered him to Oxford to lay siege. This would threaten the royalist capital, so to draw Fairfax off, Rupert attacked and took Leicester. The Committee of Both Kingdoms wisely responded by turning decisions over to their commander-in-chief, and Fairfax also moved north to meet the king's forces. It was at this crucial moment that he requested parliament's permission to hire Cromwell as Lieutenant General. Cromwell was still an MP, so this meant overruling the Self-Denying Ordinance. The Lords demurred but the Commons assented and the crucial decision was taken. When Cromwell rode into the New Model lines at Kislingbury on 13 June 1645, he was greeted with a mighty shout: 'Ironsides is come.'[11]

The royalist leaders had attempted to bring their forces together in the Midlands and had waited near Daventry, unaware of how close the New Model was. When Rupert realised their proximity and had some intimation of their numbers, he and the king decided to move north towards their stronghold of Newark. As they travelled, the royalists were shadowed by some regiments of Cromwell's troops who were moving towards the south. Parallel to the royalists and not far away, the whole mass of the New Model was on the march.

The royalists reached Market Harborough in Leicestershire, and at nearby Naseby Rupert posted guards who were surprised by parliamentarian scouts. When a few guards escaped back to the royalist lines, the king realised that battle with the New Model would be hard to avoid. Rupert argued against the fight, but if they went on to Newark their rear would be savagely attacked, along with the baggage train. Charles was for giving battle, so they took up the best positions they could, ranging their cavalry across a low ridge of hill at Naseby. The New Model cavalry took positions across a second ridge to the south with around 1,000 yards of open ground between. The royalists were numerically disadvantaged, less so in horse but gravely in foot soldiers.

On 14 June, the royalists attacked first and the New Model buckled; Skippon, a senior roundhead officer, was wounded. But Cromwell's troops had both numbers and discipline. Ireton led a charge against Rupert's cavalry but he too was wounded. Rupert's troops became distracted and went off in chase after fleeing roundheads, which weakened the royalists at a crucial moment. The king was only just prevented from leading a charge himself. Cromwell's cavalry, well positioned, decimated the royalist foot. By early afternoon the battle was lost and Charles had fled towards Leicester.

Many of his staunchest infantry were Welshmen, and as the defeat became total as many as 4,500 prisoners were marched away south. Their women, perhaps because they were taken for Irish, were slaughtered or had their faces mutilated to mark them as whores. The king lost his wagons and guns, but perhaps worse was the loss of his personal papers which laid bare all his negotiations, including those with the Irish for troops.[12]

In July, the royalist commander Goring lost a major battle at Langport in Dorset where his forces were decimated; Cromwell believed that 2,000 men were killed or captured. The New Model began its penetration of the West Country.

Montrose, however, was still ascendant. In August he won another great victory at Kilsyth near Glasgow and marched into the city triumphant. Montrose's letter to the king announced that he had Scotland at his feet but in reality he could not take his troops into Edinburgh where the Covenanters were still firmly lodged. Once in Glasgow his troops began looting, and to curb this Montrose withdrew to Bothwell where he camped. Here he knighted Alasdair, who went on a brief campaign in Ayrshire. But when he returned, he found many of his troops had left, discontented at their loss of plunder in Glasgow. Also, as Lowlanders joined, the Highlanders and the MacDonalds felt disadvantaged. Alasdair went to round up his men but did not return; many argued later about his intentions. The Highlanders dispersed while Alasdair and his clansmen, temptingly close to Argyll and the enemy, moved away west to pursue further revenge against the Campbells.[13]

This left Montrose weakened, and Huntly of Gordon also marched his men away home. The king's commander now had only 1,000 men and moved off into the Borders where he lingered. David Leslie was moving north with a Scottish force of 6,000 men who refused to stay in England with Scotland undefended. Montrose seems to have lingered partly out of loyalty to his king and partly hoping for support among the Border lords, but at Philiphaugh his tiny army was attacked by Leslie. It was a rout – Montrose himself had to flee, but the Irishmen who had been the core and driving force of his victorious army were surrounded and slaughtered.

Alasdair and Montrose never fought together again. Through the winter of 1645/6, Montrose tried to recruit but many of his associates were executed by the Covenanters and Huntly would not coordinate with him. In July 1646, on the king's orders, Montrose abandoned the campaign, made terms with Middleton and left Scotland to find a command overseas. Alasdair MacColla, however, spent the winter in Argyll, attacking and mauling the Campbell territory. By the beginning of 1646 he had control of Kintyre but not the Campbell fortresses. Here he found himself a bride, a MacAllister girl who came from Kintyre and who bore him two sons. He was the darling of the Gaels and many girls surely envied her.

These were days of satisfaction for Alasdair, but for Montrose and the king they were times of loss. After Naseby, Charles clearly knew that fate was turning against him. He began to prepare his son. The Prince of Wales was fifteen, a tall, strong boy like his French grandfather. He had his own council in Bristol where he was nominally in command, although when he asserted himself he was overruled by his father or advised differently by his ministers. Prince Charles was still in Bristol when the king wrote to him privately after Naseby:

> if I should at any time be taken prisoner by the rebels, I command you (upon my blessing) never to yield to any conditions that are dishonourable, unsafe to your person, or derogatory to royal authority, upon any considerations whatsoever, though it were for the saving of my life...[14]

In August 1645, Prince Charles and his council moved to Exeter to oversee the royalist forces in the West Country but he did not stay long. James, Duke of York remained in Oxford.

In September, under intense pressure, Rupert surrendered Bristol, which so angered the king that he withdrew the prince's command. Soon afterward, Charles heard that Montrose had been defeated at Philiphaugh and had lost his army. Fairfax was pushing on through Hampshire and Wiltshire, while Prince Charles moved further west to Launceston in Cornwall.

The king was on the move, trying to connect the pieces of his armies without success and retreating to one of his strongholds at Newark in Nottinghamshire. Here Rupert struggled to see his uncle, desperate to be cleared of disloyalty in losing Bristol. Since the early death of his father Frederick, Rupert had looked to Charles as a father figure and now he was distraught at being thought cowardly and unworthy. The king would not see him but his council heard Rupert's case and cleared him. Relationships within the royalist councils had become strained and full of rivalry. Charles's experienced councillors Hyde and Digby had long since gone west with Prince Charles and would soon leave England altogether.

Charles and his queen were both negotiating – Charles with the Irish, the queen with the Pope. But neither was successful and both were accused of double-dealing. Besides, the Pope had sent his nuncio Rinuccini to Ireland with a mission to harden the stance of the Confederates. England had been lost to the Reformation under the Tudors, but Ireland had kept the faith. The Vatican's policy was to never compromise with schismatics, nor to make truces with a Protestant king but to hold Ireland fast in her loyalty to Rome, so Rinuccini, brought into the council of the Confederates, argued against the negotiations with Charles. The nuncio was not entirely successful but he had considerable influence. As a result, Ormond, who was trying to use the Cessation as a basis for a full royalist alliance in Ireland, found his task considerably harder.

For the king, options were narrowing. Sometimes he seemed confused, occasionally almost despairing, but he had a personal certainty which overrode defeat. In August 1645 he told his army, 'I resolve, by the Grace of

God, never to yield up the church to this government of Papists, Presbyterians or Independents, nor to injure my successors by lessening the crown of that ecclesiastical or military power which my predecessors left me.' The crown was a sacred trust from his ancestors which he meant to hand on intact to his son.[15]

Increasingly, the Celtic countries seemed to offer Charles more hope than England could. Early in 1646 he was negotiating with the Scottish government through an agent named Montreuil, appointed by Mazarin. Perhaps if he accepted the kirk's cherished forms in Scotland they would drop their demands on the English church and agreement could be reached. He had little time; in February, Fairfax successfully stormed Torrington in North Devon and it became clear that the West Country was falling to parliament. Charles wrote urgently to his eldest son.

On 2 March 1646, the Prince of Wales, with his council and followers, sailed from Pendennis in the Fal estuary in Cornwall and landed in the Scilly Isles. Before the end of March, the king's army in the west had capitulated. His troops were defeated in the Cotswolds, and early in April Exeter surrendered. Prince Charles was almost captured by parliament's fleet, which surrounded St Mary's, the island where he sheltered, but a storm scattered them and the prince's party escaped to Jersey, which was fortified, held by the royalist Carteret and close to France. Here Prince Charles stayed, learning to sail and charming the people until in June the queen demanded his presence in France. By then, Henrietta-Maria, her eldest son and Mary, Princess of Orange were the only members of the royal family who were free.

Late in April, Fairfax prepared to storm Oxford where the king was based. Charles disguised himself as a servant and slipped out of the old city in the small hours with two companions. He seems to have been unsure where he would go, at first travelling towards London but at Harrow turning north towards Norfolk, perhaps making for the coast. On 5 May the king, accepting the small assurances which the Scots had offered through Montreuil, rode into their camp at Southwell from where they were besieging Newark. From here he ordered Newark to surrender and the capitulation of Oxford followed. The royal children were taken into the custody of parliament; James, Elizabeth, Henry and the baby Henriette were all brought to London.

The king had lost his power and was a captive. Others might rule the three kingdoms, but on what basis? Parliament had challenged the king and raised an army to defend the laws and liberties of England. On what legal basis could they rule without the monarch? More to the point, what intentions did the Scots have, either for the king or for their armies in England and Ireland? The Westminster parliament had defeated Charles in England but they had only one commander in the Irish theatre, Lord Inchiquin, who struggled even to hold the harbours of Cork and Youghal. Each kingdom had a rebel government and men in arms. The legal ruler, the king, was a prisoner of the Scots. Clearly, negotiations must begin once more.

23

The War of Ideas

When King Charles surrendered to the Scots in May 1646, he had lost the war but he still hoped to win the peace. He had support in all three kingdoms, there was a great yearning for peace and besides, his enemies were split. By careful negotiation, he might build a royalist party, agree terms with the Presbyterians and so outmanoeuvre the most radical forces ranged against him. However, the radicals had the New Model Army, the most powerful fighting force within the two islands. The complexity of the situation would plague even a skilled negotiator, whereas Charles was not highly skilled and was now isolated from his advisers. The Scots prevented almost all contact with the king, while the servants who waited on him were chosen by his captors. Once Charles ordered Newark to surrender, the Scots moved north where negotiations began. In Newcastle the king was subjected to lengthy debates and then sermons from Alexander Henderson on the true form of the church. When he was able to correspond with his wife, Charles told Henrietta-Maria, 'I never knew what it was to be barbarously baited before,' but the Scots began to see that on religion the king was as inflexible as themselves.[1]

Charles was a highly controlled and mannerly person who negotiated by prevarication and multiple messages, but now that he was a captive and the debates were in earnest, the stubbornness which underlay his prevarication began to show. His motives were still not obvious and his attitude to religion vexed the Scots as much as their sermons tormented him. The Scots longed for England to embrace their form of church government and worked hard to achieve it, but parliament had other concerns, demanding custody of the king and sending proposals for a new constitutional settlement. The king debated and prevaricated. While political leaders wrestled, the three kingdoms had changed and were changing still. Public debate was lively and contentious.

Censorship had broken down and newsbooks had broken out. From the calling of the Long Parliament, the crown lost its control of printing. The

Commons freed the most famous publishing prisoners: Leighton, Burton, Bastwick and Prynne. Writers, printers and publishers burst into action. In November 1641 the first newsbook had appeared in London, *The Heads of Severall Proceedings in this present Parliament*,[2] which gave news of 'these kingdoms' during that momentous time. Pamphlets were single publications but the newsbooks developed as weekly productions in a numbered series, giving domestic reports which previously it had been illegal to print. They proliferated quickly as conflict spread, for the issues were enormous and the nation hungry for news. Generally published in London, the newsbooks relied on the postal service, both for reports coming in and for circulation out to county towns. The political news was generated and reported in London by both king and parliament, but after Charles created his court and military headquarters at Oxford a royalist press became very active there. News of conflict was taken from wherever trouble had flared, and if the postal service was inadequate then carriers brought reports to the presses. Although that first publication in November 1641 carried parliamentary reports, news was already coming of the Irish rebellion and the newsbook contained letters from Ireland 'shewing what distresse and misery they are in'.[3]

The printing press therefore became a tool of the conflict. There were presses in all three kingdoms; pamphlets, books, proclamations and orders, even petitions were produced in capital cities and county towns. But the newsbooks were produced weekly and sold for 1 penny. It seems only London had the commercial vigour to make this a going concern. Also, London was the hub of all the postal routes: to the West Country, to the Channel ports, to East Anglia, to the north of England and Scotland, to Holyhead and the Irish Sea where packet boats crossed to Dublin. As a result, the newsbook sprang up in London and it was a decade before attempts were made to publish them elsewhere. They reported the news but some were also lively efforts at persuasion and propaganda, since the battle for hearts and minds was strongly engaged.

Censorship had been practised by the crown since printing began. It was a reciprocal arrangement whereby the Stationers' Company had a monopoly on the print trade, licensed texts for publication and kept a register of them. Authors could protect their copyright by submitting a manuscript, publishers protect their profits by lodging a printed copy, and the crown had a single agency through which to enforce censorship. Under Elizabeth a Treason Statute covered publishing misdemeanours, enforced by the Court of High Commission. There had been unlicensed printing – some domestic, some smuggled in from abroad – but penalties could be severe: under Elizabeth, John Stubbes and his printer had their right hands cut off, while under Charles, William Prynne lost his ears and was branded, put in the pillory and imprisoned. Even in the stocks he continued to publicise his views until he was gagged. Pamphlets which Prynne composed in prison were published anonymously abroad and smuggled back. The book for which he was mutilated and jailed was *Histrio-Matrix*, an attack on stage plays. As Henrietta-Maria had just taken part in a play at court the book was seen as an attack on the king and queen. Prynne was fiercely critical of cross-dressing and the effeminacy of theatre, which he linked to popery and sodomy. But the urge to publish was powerful, and one of the Long Parliament's first actions was to free Prynne and his fellows.[4]

The debate was on and scribblers of every persuasion were rushing into print. Censorship had suppressed the publishing of ideas just when those ideas were most vigorous and demanding. The printing press was already two hundred years old but the Reformation had provided a galvanising effect which was still building up to a crescendo. Printers made a good living out of Bibles, prayer books and religious tracts. By the reign of Charles I, between a third and a half of all males could write, with numbers for women a bit lower. Schools had become more widespread, giving many poor children a start in reading. The greatest change over the previous century was in secondary and university education. The state was growing and employing more civil servants, while the demand for lawyers increased, so not only the gentry and clergy sent their sons to university but increasingly merchants, artisans and tradesmen too.[5]

In growing towns, an educated population had emerged with material and intellectual aspirations. Their reading centred on the Bible, but at grammar school they learned Latin and at university they read classical authors. Latin gave access to the ideas of ancient Rome and the intellectual publications of Europe, but most importantly it was the language in which the law was recorded. Young scholars might also learn science: Elizabeth's sailors had studied astronomy, navigation and cartography; Copernicus's work had been published in 1534; and in England William Harvey's observations on the circulation of blood were in print in 1628. Both of these were in Latin but a growing number of natural science books were published in English.

The concentration on Bible reading had a powerful effect but texts were available about law, governance and constitutional concepts. Classical authors wrote of Rome's transition from a republic to a caesarate, which offered inflammatory comparisons. Among recent thinkers Machiavelli was influential, as were continental scholars such as Bodin. Writers like Moore were still read but now England began to spawn more urgent works of political philosophy.

Scotland had great educational aspirations but fewer resources. Ever since the Reformation, the Scots had aimed for a school in every parish and now the Covenanters legislated for it. Scotland had four universities to England's two, funded by confiscated episcopal lands. Poverty wore down the desire for education in much of Scotlandm, but in the Lowlands learning flourished and printing presses were active. When the Covenant was first signed, so many 'rebellious pamphlets' were published that Charles had issued a proclamation commanding his subjects not to receive the seditious publications issuing from Scotland.[6]

Ireland was in a different situation. Before the rebellion there was only one printing press in Dublin, controlled by the government. Books and pamphlets were imported but only the gentry had the means to get them. Printing in Gaelic was uncommon and continental works scarce. As conflict increased, the Dublin press expanded its production. After the Confederation set up its headquarters at Kilkenny, they got hold of a press to promote their cause and to print proclamations as well as previously suppressed Catholic works. This was set up in Waterford and by 1646 they had a second one in Kilkenny. By 1648 there was also a press in Cork. The power of printing was important to the war and several of these machines were later seized.

In Britain the shape of the Reformed church was in contention, but in Ireland the issues were quite different. Catholics were fighting for the right to practise their religion and the constitutional debate in Ireland had a quite different shape. Those issues were seldom heard or considered within Britain.

Overall, Ireland got a very bad press on the sister island. The war had created many factions across both islands, with interrelated issues, but one central aim of the Westminster parliament was to prevent any reversal towards Roman Catholicism. Newsbooks had developed from continental *corantos* which reported on the war in the Holy Roman Empire, where a Catholic Habsburg regime was challenged by Protestants. Across Europe, the Reformed churches were struggling for survival and Puritan leaders in Britain felt themselves part of that struggle, a seminal battle against papacy. For them, Ireland was always the weak link which might drag them back to the old ways. They had escaped from a system they thought corrupt and full of darkness into the light of the Gospel – they were not going back.

So, the English presses seldom discussed the aims and needs of Irish people of any rank but only spoke of the plight of Protestants in Ireland, or in vitriolic terms of the 'Irish papists' or the 'Irish rebels'. Any concessions to them were vilified. In 1643, when Ormond concluded the Cessation with the Confederacy on behalf of the king, the *Perfect Diurnal* reported how incensed the Scots were, 'terming it the most damnable designe ever yet set of foot for the extirpation of Protestants and ... the setting up of Popery in all three kingdoms'. The queen was Catholic and the king suspect; when Charles showed sympathy for Ireland's complaints or supported the 1643 truce between crown forces and the Irish Confederacy, MPs were enraged, considering it an alliance with rebellious papists. It made many of them cold with fury.[7]

A pamphlet of 1644, printed in Bristol, offered to 'enlighten you more in Irish affaires' and put forward the case for the Cessation, which it considered a 'true Act of State' which had now become 'the discourse of every common subject of all the three kingdoms over'. The author said that the Irish were fearful of an increasingly powerful Scotland and pointed out that 'the example of Scotland, wrought wonderfully upon the imagination of the Irish, and filled them with thoughts of emulation'. When the Irish saw the animosity towards English Catholics by the current parliament, fearing what might happen to them, they planned 'some meanes of timely prevention ... which pusht on the Irish to take up Armes'. It was Charles who saw how 'an inhumane designe between [the parliamentary commissioners] and the Scot, in lieu of suppressing an insurrection' seemed likely to 'eradicat and extinguish a whole Nation to make booty of their lands'.[8] To preserve the kingdom of Ireland, Charles was moved to call a Cessation, especially since the men and money which parliament had raised to suppress the Irish rising had been used for other purposes – for fighting against the king himself.

What the reading public of England thought of this production it is impossible to say, but it remains among a bound collection of pamphlets which one reader found important and preserved.[9] The writers had an audience, and although some newsbooks sprang up only to fold again after a few months, the most successful ran for years and provided a good living for their publishers and writers.

The king's cause was put forward by *Mercurius Aulicus*, which John Birkenhead published in Oxford to promote the king's cause. But as royalist defeats cut off parts of the country and news became harder to collect, issues were delayed and in 1645 *Aulicus* ceased to be published.

The most brilliant of the newsbook writers was a man from Burford in Oxfordshire named Marchamont Nedham – to rhyme with freedom. He had studied at university, gone on to be a clerk at Gray's Inn but then studied medicine. In the summer of 1643, Nedham became the controlling voice of *Mercurius Britanicus*, a parliamentarian weekly set up to combat the propaganda influence of *Aulicus*. Nedham was a natural journalist who worked swiftly and had a sharp turn of phrase:

If it be thus dangerous to speak towards the king, what will become of the ... ministers in this cause, that have preached so plainly in your pulpits? What will become of the famous and godly Master Prynne, that called even the king himself *Popish Royall Favourite* in his book? ... If it be unlawful to speak plainly to the king in his ways, what is it to go out to battle, to shoot at that army where his person is engaged? Pure Oxford doctrine as ever was taught... This is only to make our weapon fall out of our hands, this is water sprinkled upon us, to cool us in this cause, now we are pursuing it so hotly.[10]

[W]ere there any hope of accommodation, or the least proffer of but one hopeful treaty, I would lay out all my ink to woo the people on both sides to a general acclamation of peace, but I despair of this so great happiness:

our adversaries are both untractable, and implacable, they never make overtures of peace, but for some by-ends… Oh that I had a voice of thunder to awaken and undeceive the deluded people all over the kingdom.[11]

Living in London, Nedham seems to have been adept at catching not just news flowing in from the provinces but also the talk of the town.

He was a controversial man, sporting an earring and a wig which gave him a sharp style among the Puritans in their sombre colours – tall black hats and white lawn collars. The court style was ornate – silk and satin decorated with lace and gold thread, while men wore their hair long and even the Puritan leaders were seen with shoulder-length hair and silver buttons. But Nedham seems ahead of fashion with his wig, which only became popular in the 1650s.

Nedham was well read in both political theory and history. He knew Machiavelli and English literature, and as the debate over the constitution heated up he absorbed new ideas and arguments such as the programme of the Levellers.[12] But Nedham was a pen for hire. In 1643 his *Britanicus* was a parliament-sponsored publication but by 1647 Nedham was writing for the king. Many thought him an intellectual mercenary – which he was – but circumstances had also changed. He was also passionately anti-Presbyterian, for the Scots had shown how an autonomous church could accrue power and enforce its will on lay government.

The issues at stake were enormous: the struggle to define the state and the nature of government. What is power? Who should exercise it and by what right? Who should decide the religion of the kingdom – the king, parliament or every individual for themselves? Should there be a single structure for the church and should that be dictated by the king, by parliament or by the church as a separate and autonomous body? If the church was separate would it behave as the Roman church had done, as a state within the state? Who should control the armed forces? What is the proper relationship between the government and the representatives of the people?

The right to publish freely was also under discussion. In 1641, parliament had closed the courts of High Commission and Star Chamber which had given king and council powerful controls. The Earl of Clarendon recorded that from the early days of the Long Parliament 'preaching and printing increased to that degree that all pulpits were freely delivered to the schismatical and silenced preachers, who till then had lurked in corners or lived in New England; and the presses [were] at liberty for the publishing the most invective, seditious, and scurrilous pamphlets that their wit and malice could invent'.[13] Godly reformers who had opposed Laud's controls had not foreseen a wholly unbridled press and complaints increased, not least from the Stationers' Company, which had lost its monopoly. Parliament freed William Prynne and his fellow prisoners to overturn the king's censorship but then found they wanted to impose some controls of their own. Parliament first ordered the stationers to control titles printed, but when that proved ineffective they got up a committee for printing.

It was hard for either side to control what was printed in a divided country; when one printer was summoned to appear before the parliamentary committee, he fled to the king at York, taking his printing press with him. Several orders were issued by parliament regarding printing but it was June 1643 when an ordinance for licensing was issued, and even that could be eluded.[14]

Unbridled printing had increased the book and pamphlet trade enormously, although blatant anti-monarchical works were avoided or censured by parliament – the king was still the king. But books were contentious and public book burnings became more frequent. The Earl of Strafford's name sold publications swiftly; over a hundred publications dwelled on his case.

John Milton published a tract on a free press in 1644. Milton had developed from a precocious scholar and poet to an opinionated author through the awkward interlude of a collapsed marriage. In 1640, he was living in lodgings in Aldersgate and working as a schoolmaster, but his political and religious views were hardening. As publication broke loose he engaged in a pamphlet war by attacking episcopacy. In Oxfordshire on an errand for his father, Milton met and married a seventeen-year-old girl whom he took to London, but after a few weeks she deserted him and returned to her parents. Milton, furious and humiliated, launched a publishing campaign in favour of divorce, but in 1643 other issues were paramount and his work was ignored, then put on parliament's list of books to be suppressed. His bride's family, fearful that divorce might succeed, persuaded Mary Milton to return to her husband and by 1646 a daughter had been born. In the midst of his marital problems Milton published *Areopagiticus*, which argued for the right to publish without prior censorship, but not for a totally free press. Milton was strongly opposed to Roman Catholics being able to publish or promote their religion, but he also contested the work of the Westminster Assembly, writing that 'New Presbyter is but old Priest writ large'.[15] He was becoming more strident and more Independent.

He also wrote about how poets were protected by Alexander the Great – Milton was fearful of the king's army marching into London. Alexander had spared the house of Pindar during his invasion of Thebes and Milton likened this to his own plight in 1642 after Edgehill when the road into London was open and many expected Charles to march his army into the city. As a classicist, Milton was well aware of how victorious armies behaved in large cities. 'Lift not thy spear against the Muses' Bowre,' Milton's sonnet implored – as if a poem could restrain an army. In fact, the king had not marched in at all.[16]

Milton was finding his political voice while a much younger poet, skilful but not yet published, was overseas throughout this period. Andrew Marvell had been at university in Cambridge when his father drowned in the River Humber in 1641. With a small inheritance, he left England in 1642 and worked as a tutor to gentlemen's sons in Holland, France, Italy and Spain throughout the First English Civil War, not returning to England until late in 1647. By then, Marchamont Nedham's career had taken some dramatic turns. After the king's letters were seized at Naseby, Nedham had published them in *Britanicus* but when he mocked the king's speech impediment he was reprimanded by the House of Lords.[17] In 1646, during negotiations between the English and the Scots, Nedham described Charles as a tyrant, for which he was fined and imprisoned. After that his publications were anonymous and he took up his other profession as a physician. Yet in 1647, he met the king while he was a captive at Hampton Court, was forgiven by his sovereign and became the editor and chief author of *Mercurius Pragmaticus*, a royalist production which pulled no punches. If this behaviour seems mercurial, by 1647 much had changed and power was shifting, like heavy cargo in the hold of a ship.

Nedham's changes of side allowed him to argue many different aspects of contentious issues from a variety of angles, as if he was having a raucous conversation, not just with his fellow countrymen but with himself. Writers were the voice of the people in conflict and the English in particular were not just at war, or negotiating a peace, but wrestling with ideas and attitudes on how government should be constructed.

Surely the most influential pamphleteer, John Lilburne had become a significant figure by 1645. He had been a pupil of Bastwick, but had turned against him, got into a furious contention with the Presbyterians and was developing radical ideas which brought him into conflict with both houses of parliament. Lilburne had experienced a godly conversion as a young man, and had been an anti-episcopalian tract writer, for which he was flogged and imprisoned, but when the Long Parliament released him he developed first as an Independent in loud and angry conflict with Prynne and Bastwick, whom he had followed into prison, then – becoming louder and more contentious – he started to publish pamphlets promoting a far more radical change in the structure of the state. Walwyn and Overton, to whom Lilburne grew politically close, held similar but less strident views. The core of Lilburne's philosophy was the natural equality of all men, and that government should be by consent:

> God, the absolute sovereign lord and king of all things in heaven and earth, the original fountain and cause of all causes; ... who made the world and all things therein for his own glory; and who by His own will and pleasure, gave him, His mere creature, the sovereignty over all the rest of His creatures... The first of which was Adam, a male, or man ...; out of whose side was taken a rib, which by the sovereign and absolute

mighty creating power of God was made a female or woman called Eve: which two are the earthly ... begetters ... of all and every ... man and woman that ever breathed in the world since; who are, and were by nature all equal and alike in power, dignity, authority, and majesty.[18]

Lilburne's analysis of history was clear and stark:

The history of our forefathers since they were conquered by the Normans does manifest that this nation has been held in bondage all along ever since by the policies and force of the officers of trust in the commonwealth, amongst whom we always esteemed kings the chiefest.[19]

Walwyn and Overton were more concerned to defend religious nonconformity than Lilburne was. Walwyn held a position based on natural law; he and Lilburne had both studied the jurist Cooke, who had been so influential in the days of James I. Ideas on law, politics and religion overlapped and were being promoted in churches or published in an urgent public debate. By 1647, the arguments and conflicts were shifting. After the defeat of the king, Presbyterians became more ascendant in parliament and were strongly linked to the Scottish regime controlled by the Covenanting movement. All those strains in English public opinion which saw Presbyterianism as a new form of oppression were coming together but also developing new arguments.

In London in particular, Independent congregations were becoming established which developed into new sects. The Family of Love had existed in Elizabeth's England, the Seekers were less well defined, while the Baptists and Anabaptists both dated from the previous century; both rejected infant baptism but disagreed with each other.

As the likelihood arose of a new settlement for church and state, so the argument about the shape it should take became louder and more desperate. Nedham – whose *Mercurius Pragmaticus* stated that its aim was to 'write the king back into his throne'[20] – thought that all public actions were the result of personal interest and loudly dismissed any claim by one faction or party to speak for 'the people' as though they were a single coherent group. Nedham was more concerned about the rule of law and the survival of existing institutions than more abstract political notions which would not lead to political settlement.

Meanwhile, Walwyn, Overton and Lilburne began to develop a practical programme based on the demands of the common people and the soldiers, whose views they canvassed. As they promoted this programme, the army officers gave them the name Levellers – men who would level all property rights and status. The influence of the Levellers within the regiments stirred up the soldiers to make new demands and led to a crisis in the New Model Army.

Yet while this printing war and impassioned debate continued, the theatres were dark and silent. Charles and Henrietta-Maria had enjoyed theatre; masques combined many art forms and were performed at court. Milton had written masques as a young author but Puritan diehards like Prynne had risked a great deal to attack theatre. For some time, London magistrates had viewed theatrical events with disapproval, believing they encouraged brawling, pickpockets and promiscuity. The theatres were generally on the south bank of the Thames, which put them outside the mayor's jurisdiction, while the king's patronage had protected the dramatic arts. Once Charles left London, parliament had control. In September 1642 it ordered all playhouses to close. Theatres could create disturbances as crowds were swayed by strong emotions. Parliament was taking no chances with an art form which incorporated group emotion and political innuendo. Some productions continued in an irregular fashion until 1648, when the ban became far more stringent.[21]

The public life of England was going through a strange metamorphosis. People debated the rights and wrongs of war, intellectuals put forward vigorous arguments over the constitution, theologians wrestled over the shape of the church, Independents thirsted for national salvation, but the performing arts were muffled in the capital of England by a cautious and godly elite. Drama was no longer available either for entertainment or as a form of persuasion. Charles, the great patron of painting, was in captivity; but the importance of the written word, the vital significance of texts, was never so high.

Yet all this discussion was at the periphery while the central debate was between commissioners – for Scotland and parliament – and the king. Texts were written as blueprints for a settlement and argued over. Meanwhile the New Model Army was dormant, in garrisons and temporary quarters, stationed in many counties but with its headquarters in East Anglia, where it soon had a testing discussion of its own.

24

Negotiations and the Sale of the King

The king found he had been greatly mistaken about the Scots. He thought Montreuil had made an agreement with them on his behalf but wherever the misconceptions arose, the Scots denied any such agreement. Charles could not get messages to his wife for three weeks after he left Oxford and when he did write in May, sending his letters with Ashburnham, who was a trusted attendant, and with Montreuil himself, he wanted Henrietta-Maria to understand 'the base usage that I have had since I came to this army'. He admitted that 'to deal freely with thee, my condition is such, that I expect never to see thee, except, by the queen's sending to me persons of secrecy and dexterity, I find means to quit for a time this retched country. Wherefore I earnestly desire thee to think of this seriously and speedily, for, upon my word, it will not admit of long delay.'[1]

Henrietta-Maria was intensely active on her husband's behalf but limited by the situation in France. Her brother Louis XIII had died early in the war, leaving a child heir, Louis XIV, born in 1638. Since then the government of France had been in the hands of Henrietta-Maria's sister-in-law Anne of Austria – 'the queen' in Charles's letter – and Cardinal Mazarin. Both had sympathy for a fallen monarch whose wife was a princess of France, but neither would hazard France's position for Charles's cause – they questioned his judgement, and besides, parliament and the army held the English capital and all the major ports, leaving few military options.

Henrietta-Maria, who had already raised one army and taken it to England, was now intriguing with the Pope and the Irish. She was a force to be reckoned with and was now demanding that Prince Charles leave Jersey and join her. She greatly complicated Ormond's position in Dublin, where Charles still had some loyal forces, but Charles too had undermined Ormond by sending the Earl of Glamorgan to make terms with the Confederates. Glamorgan agreed generous terms to the Catholics regarding their religion but the terms were discovered and published in London, further blackening the king's name with the Puritans. Ormond arrested Glamorgan and Charles disowned the treaty which the earl had agreed. These intrigues failed to provide extra troops for the king but further undermined his reputation. In reality, the king was a captive and would have to negotiate – initially with the Scots, although there were many interested parties making substantial demands.

This did not deter Randal MacDonnell, who had been elevated to marquis in 1645 as thanks for launching the Montrose and MacColla campaign. Eager to regain his lands in Ulster and Kintyre, and to crush the Campbell power while supporting Ireland and the Catholic religion, the Marquis of Antrim now launched another campaign. In possession of frigates and having also promised military aid to Spanish Flanders – for Spain was seen as a friend of Ireland – the marquis also set out for Scotland on the king's business. Despite promises, the Confederates provided almost no support and, at the last minute, tried to block the expedition but Antrim got away with his frigates and around 700 men, arriving at Campbeltown in Kintyre at the beginning of June 1646. Alasdair MacColla was still there with his men, terrorising the Campbell settlements and largely dominating the peninsula.

Antrim had great ambitions and planned to raise the king's friends in the Highlands to provide a force of 30,000 men and take control of Scotland. He did raise a force – perhaps as large as 12,000 men – but the king was now a prisoner of the Scots and Antrim was not powerful enough to free him from captivity in Newcastle. His expedition was alarming the Covenanters but also the royalists by confusing the king's negotiating stance. Undeterred, Antrim sent messages to Paris asking the Stuart royal family for their blessing.[2]

During that summer, the queen was reunited with two of her children. Prince Charles left Jersey in June and joined her in Paris. In August, the baby Henriette Anne was smuggled from Oatlands Palace by her governess and also brought to France. However, three royal children and the king remained captives in England. To the sixteen-year-old Prince Charles, Antrim's efforts in Scotland looked promising and he sent messages of encouragement.

The king, however, was in a difficult position. Since he was held by their army, Charles had to negotiate with the Scots but they had different aims to their allies in the London parliament. Since the collapse of the king's government, power had not been firmly grasped anywhere; all the parties possessed fragments of it and jostled for more. The constitution still held; it gave the king and the various parliaments some legitimacy, but each kingdom had new institutions with command over armies.

The new committees – of Both Kingdoms, of Safety, of Estates – had taken on executive power in England and Scotland and had men in arms. Of the old structures, the Scottish Privy Council had lost power and the parliaments meeting in Edinburgh had not been called by the king. The king's council had dispersed and his English armies had been decimated. In Ireland, Ormond was the legal head of government and had troops but the Confederates had created a General Assembly to replicate parliament, which elected a council to run civil government and manage their army. Of the other Protestant forces, Inchiquin held Cork and Monro was still in command of Carrickfergus Castle in Ulster, but Monck had been imprisoned in England by parliament.

Further splits had recently arisen in Ireland. The papal nuncio Rinuccini's arrival with £12,000 and armaments had first galvanised and then divided the Confederate Catholics.[3] His uncompromising position was splitting the uneasy alliance of Old English and Old Irish within the Confederacy. The nuncio approved of Irish intervention in Scotland but refused to give Antrim supplies. However, the Confederate victory at Benburb in Ulster, soon after the king's surrender, strengthened the nuncio's faction and convinced him that Ireland could hold out against British forces and should not make terms with Charles. Soon after Benburb, and on the king's orders, Ormond cemented a peace treaty with the Confederates but this only split the Confederates further, as the Old English supported it but the nuncio denounced any pact with Protestants and subsequently declared excommunication on those who followed it. This greatly undermined any benefit that Charles might have received from Ormond's peace. The crown had also lost the support of Inchiquin, the Protestant commander in Munster who declared for parliament, and Broghill, who followed suit at Youghal.

So, the power that Charles might rely on from armies was very slight in that summer of 1646. The Marquis of Antrim was still at large with active forces in Kintyre, but that undermined the good faith of the king's undertakings. He was under pressure to stand all his military men down and negotiate a lasting agreement. Physically, Charles was in a weak position.

However, he had the natural strength of his position; the people of England were exhausted and impoverished by war, they longed for an end to conflict and a return to normality, of which the king was guarantor and symbol. Nor were Charles's enemies united; far from it. Even the Scottish-parliamentary alliance was fraying. The Westminster Assembly was laboriously finding some common religious ground but the Scots wanted an entirely autonomous church while the London Presbyterians wanted one under the control of parliament. Charles was adamantly opposed to either, as the Scots soon discovered. The Independents did not want a national church at all.

During the summer, as Charles was exchanging religious papers with the Scottish divines and being tormented by sermons, the Scots did everything they could to get him to sign the Covenant and agree to impose their system on all three kingdoms. It took time for them to understand that he would not. Worried that Charles might make a deal with the Independents in London and that the English army might block their return home, the Scots tried to find agreement with the Presbyterian faction in the Commons, to speed up an agreement with the king. It was not easy to coordinate the Scottish delegates – the Edinburgh parliament, their army in Newcastle and their commissioners in London – even though they were of one mind. The Committee of Estates, for example, knew the terms which Montreuil had offered Charles but the Scots parliament did not and the Scots army denied them.[4] To clarify their joint position, Argyll went to Westminster and discussed terms in person with the Scottish commissioners. On this basis, they delivered blunt proposals to the king but offered no negotiations – Charles said they may as well have sent a trumpeter to announce them. The Scots also sent their terms to France, so that Henrietta-Maria could persuade her husband, if necessary, with Queen Anne and Mazarin to back her up. But the terms, known as the Newcastle Propositions, were unacceptable to everyone. Under them, royalists were to forfeit land, Presbyterianism was to be installed in all three kingdoms, Catholics were to be penalised and parliament was to take control of the armed forces and appoint officers of state and judges.

Henrietta-Maria advised Charles to agree about religion. He refused, and they began to squabble, but when he seemed willing to concede some control of the militia she was horrified – what sort of king was it who did not command his own armies? 'Keep the militia and never give up, and by that everything will return,' she wrote, 'and God will send us the means of replacing ourselves.'[5] In the winter, when the negotiations had been dragging on for months and Charles seemed to be swayed, the queen became shriller: 'And with the granting the militia, you have cut your own throat, for having given them this power, you can no longer refuse them anything, not even my life, if they demand it from you; but I shall not place myself in their hands. I would venture to say, that if you had followed our advice, your affairs would be in a different state from what they are.'[6]

The French government made it clear to his captors that Charles must come to no harm, but they would not intervene on his behalf. Their agent advised Charles to give in over church government but Charles would not. He had learned his theology and statecraft from his father and had taken James's maxim 'no bishops, no king' to heart. To Charles, Presbyterian church government would remove religion from control by the crown. 'Moreover,' Charles wrote to his wife, 'they will introduce that doctrine which teaches rebellion to be lawful and that the supreme power is in the people, to whom kings (as they say) ought to give account, and be corrected when they do amiss.'[7]

Apart from the loss of power, Charles believed that to disband bishops or alter the church would break his coronation oath and would be contrary to Anglican teaching, both of which he took very seriously. He felt he had already erred and he was contrite, would not go further into transgression. 'I made that base sinful concession concerning the Earl of Strafford for which – and also that great injustice to the church in taking away the bishops votes in parliament – though I have been most justly punished, yet I hope that God will so accept of my hearty (however weak) repentance and my constant adhering to my conscience that at last his mercy will take place of his justice.' He was sure that any further relapse 'will procure God's further wrath upon me, as also make me inconstant in all my other grounds'.[8]

Henrietta-Maria had no patience with her husband's religious scruples which, being part of Protestant theology, hardly concerned her. But Charles was determined and when she badgered him, he was only hurt. 'Whatsoever chiding my wilfulness ... may deserve, for God's sake leave off threatening me with thy desire to meddle no more with business;' he wrote; 'as thou lovest me give me so much comfort (and God knows I have but little, and that little must come from thee)', and he begged her not to forsake him and his concerns.[9] A Scotsman, Will Murray, was sent to help him and he persuaded the king that a short compliance with Scottish demands might not offend his conscience. The two sides were far apart but the king sent two answers to parliament and although they refused them, the negotiations continued.

Charles was confined in the mayor's house in Newcastle but in the wider world, all the contesting forces were still active. Help was sent by his daughter, Princess Mary of Orange, in the form of a Dutch ship which lingered in Newcastle harbour, ostensibly having its hull cleaned but waiting, should he try to escape. At Christmas he made a half-hearted attempt, was brought back and guarded more closely. However, support for the king was growing. The armies were unpaid and mutinies had occurred in many counties. The civilian population had paid high taxes, had soldiers quartered in their homes and had had horses, grain and livestock requisitioned. They were impoverished and exhausted, wanting only a return to normal life.

Meanwhile, Antrim and Alasdair MacColla were still in Kintyre and the nuncio now seemed keen to provide men for Antrim's projected army. For Charles, these manoeuvres only undermined the chances of a deal and the king saw he must act. In October, he was able to send an envoy to Kintyre where Antrim was assured that as soon as 'the marquis of Argyl is forfeited', Kintyre would be given to Antrim. This was an extraordinary promise and Antrim at last complied, sending home the troops from the other clans, although he and MacColla remained in the Western Isles, taking forts and harassing fishermen.

Back in Ireland, the Confederates failed to capitalise on Benburb. Rinuccini denounced the peace with Ormond but his threat of excommunication to those who supported it only led to unrest. In response, Owen Roe's troops marched on Kilkenny and installed Rinuccini as leader there, ousting the Old English who had made the peace with Ormond. The nuncio, now ascendant, ordered an attack on Dublin. O'Neill and Preston stayed loyal to the nuncio and, following his orders, marched on Dublin but winter conditions and a growing animosity between the two commanders made them withdraw. With Confederate attention diverted, Inchiquin advanced in Munster. Ormond had few resources and his monarch was in captivity but the withdrawal of O'Neill from Dublin gave him time to plan. As a Protestant and a loyal servant of the government, he now turned, as Inchiquin had before, to the London parliament for military support.

Antrim's efforts had not been very productive but were praised among his associates in panegyric speeches – the 'true nobleness inbred in their [Clan Donald's] bloud, is the true cause that thou art truly good and goodness causeth you to undertake heroic labours for king and countrey's sake'[10] – but in January 1647, the Confederates called a General Assembly to try to breach their divisions, and at last Antrim left Scotland to attend, leaving MacColla in Kintyre.

The Scottish army was deeply unpopular in northern England and its men wanted to withdraw but they had not been paid. Unable to get from Charles the one thing they really cherished – their own church system – they did see some progress in parliament, which had slowly passed legislation to disband the Anglican church system and replace it with one agreed by the Westminster Assembly. For the Scots, this was not perfect but it was far nearer their ideal than anything that Charles would accept. So they began to press for payment and to talk of handing over the king. Hamilton wanted Charles brought to Edinburgh where he thought he could rally support, but Argyll and the kirk were against it and they were the stronger party.

The debts accrued by the London parliament during the war were far beyond their ability to pay. However, the abolition of bishops gave parliament control of valuable episcopal lands which could be sold or rented out. This would not pay the English armies but it would partly pay for the Scottish forces. A sum of £400,000 was agreed, of which parliament could raise £200,000 straight away; this was paid to the Scots. So it was, early in 1647, that parliamentary commissioners met Leven and took custody of the king. On 30 January, the Scottish army packed its kit, turned its back on England and marched away north to the border. Newcastle fishwives yelled 'Judas' at them as they left. The legend that they sold their king for pieces of silver was strengthened by Charles himself, who said they sold him 'at too cheap a rate'.[11]

The king was taken south by parliamentarians to Northamptonshire. Crowds gathered on the route, cheering him on his way, and when he arrived at Holmby – one of England's great houses – he lived with regal style, a full household staff and banquets of many courses. The local gentry came to pay their respects and he was able to visit nearby country houses, frequently going to Althorp, which was just across the valley, where he played bowls.

Charles was better placed now and could get wider advice than he had in Newcastle. His personal support was growing but his military position was in collapse. Ormond, the last of his commanders with a viable army, believed he had insufficient strength to hold Dublin if attacked, so in the month that Charles arrived at Holmby, Ormond opened negotiations with parliament. The king might be living in something like his accustomed style but he had no armies, only his position and his wits.

Parliament, on the other hand, was now so confident of its victory that it began debating which of its regiments to disband. They still had the task of retaking Ireland, which was now top of their military agenda and becoming urgent; they had raised money from the Adventurers five years earlier but little had been done. However, the re-conquest of Ireland would not require all the men still in arms; some of the troops could go home. Parliament planned to disband part of the New Model Army and send part to Ireland but they wanted to reorganise the regiments under different commanders. Since the Presbyterian party had become ascendant in parliament they were determined to get control of the army, which was full of men whose ideas and allegiance were Independent. With strong godly beliefs and fond of extempore preaching, the soldiers of the New Model would resist any state regulation of their religious life, and aside from that the Presbyterians suspected that political radicals were also active among the troops. Cromwell, so noted a cavalry commander and second-in-command of the army, was particularly suspected by Presbyterian members because he opposed the religious settlement they had agreed with the Scots.

In this volatile political landscape, and due to frequent by-elections, the character of the Commons had altered. Seats had been vacated either by deaths or by the exclusion of royalists and as a result two hundred and seventy new members had come in during the war, among them many Independents and radicals, such as Fleetwood, Ireton and Ludlow – all army officers – and Thomas Harrison, also an officer but more noted for his millenarian beliefs. So, the Commons in the spring of 1647 was a very different body to the one which had met in the winter of 1640; the centre ground had shifted and compromise was increasingly difficult as the house was split over contentious issues.

When Oliver Cromwell wrote to his commander, Sir Thomas Fairfax, on 11 March 1647, concerning quarters for his troops, he remarked bitterly on attitudes to the army: 'There want not, in all places, men who have so much malice against the army as besots them; ... Never were the spirits of men more embittered than now. Surely the Devil hath but a short time. Sir, it's good the heart be fixed against all this. The naked simplicity of Christ, with that wisdom he please to give, and patience, will overcome all this.'[12]

Parliament had other armies in England, but after a struggle among members in the winter of 1646/7, Massey's Western Brigade had been disbanded. The Earl of Essex had died and been given an extravagant funeral, while his army was no longer intact, but Poyntz's Northern Association army remained viable.[13]

Civilian command of the armies also changed when the Scots left; the Committee of Both Kingdoms had been formed when the Scots–English alliance was made and was now wound up. Instead, a new committee was created to manage the re-conquest of Ireland. The English members from 'Both Kingdoms' were joined by Holles, Clotworthy and five others. Their meetings – like those of 'Both Kingdoms' – were at Derby House on the Strand and they were known as the Derby House Committee. This group played a crucial role in the crisis brewing in the army, and later, when the membership of the committee had greatly altered, they managed London's policy towards Ireland. The work of the Derby House Committee would have radical and long-lasting effects.

If the English armies were restive but not in action, in Scotland and Ireland there was still fighting. Monro's troops refused to leave Ulster or disband until they were paid, leaving Owen Roe's with no fortress; roving armies displaced local people who in turn became a hazard.

Leven's army had been partly paid by London and returned to Scotland. Some were disbanded but a third of the troops were retained to chase out the remaining royalists. They first went north against Huntly, who retired into the hills, then – fleeing the plague – the Covenanter army marched swiftly west where, on behalf of the Campbells, it took revenge on the MacDonalds.

Alasdair MacColla was still in Kintyre, where he had wintered with his men, but he no longer had the military strength to withstand the Covenanters. Argyll returned with the Covenanting army, eager to see his hated enemies punished, captured or driven out. As regards Alasdair himself, Argyll only pondered 'whether they should make him shorter or longer' – hang him or behead him.[14] As Leven and Argyll advanced the MacDonalds withdrew to Islay, but by the time that the Covenanters came ashore there Alasdair had pulled his forces back to Ireland. Only his old father was left; released from Argyll's prison, he remained stubbornly within his promontory fortress of Dunyveg. In the face of the Campbell forces, he came out twice, once to parley and a second time to get whiskey, but when he appeared again he was taken prisoner. Argyll made sure he was hanged. Meanwhile, his warrior son had rejoined the Confederates in Ireland.[15]

With no royalists still in the field in England, parliament had at last sent money and arms to Ireland, not generously but enough to allow Lord Inchiquin, a vigorous and uncompromising soldier, to fight his way out of Cork city and take increasing territory throughout southern Ireland. Ormond, in command at Dublin Castle but with barely the strength to hold it, had to choose. He was a Protestant royalist but, with the king disabled, Ormond saw parliament as the legal government. However, by the time that parliament's commander, Michael Jones, arrived in Dublin with 2,000 troops in the summer of 1647, a radical change had occurred in England.

The New Model Army, whose collective temper had smouldered as the first orders for disbanding were received, had defied parliament and made an audacious move of its own. Above all things, an army must obey commands, but a strong army is also a creature in its own right, a large animal held together by powerful bonds. The New Model would resist dismemberment. If Ormond had known in June 1647 what was going on in East Anglia, would he still have given Dublin to Colonel Jones? His alternatives were poor; he had made peace with the Confederates, but since Benburb the nuncio's faction was in power, undermining its effect. Jones, on the other hand, represented the Westminster parliament, and Ormond's career had been defined by loyalty to the legal government. But as Jones arrived at Dublin, the New Model Army was testing that concept of loyalty and legality to the limit.

In the summer of 1647, a meeting of the full army was called which drew up political documents of its own. Then it made an audacious move to challenge parliament. By the time that Ormond handed over Dublin Castle to Colonel Michael Jones at the end of July and sailed for England, there was uproar in London and the army was just outside the city.

In the play for power, the army had made its move.

25

The Army Makes Its Move

With the clash of arms falling silent and troops quartered around the countryside, ideas and emotions became audible as men discussed their aims and whether they were being achieved. Some had fought for a wage, many had been conscripted, but the men of the New Model and especially those in Oliver Cromwell's regiment had joined for a cause. They now expected to be paid for their labours and to see that cause triumph.

Parliament had problems: it was split and had massive bills to pay. The latter concerned not only the soldiers and the armaments supplied by private companies but also claims for requisitioned goods and for damages.

Many of these bills would never be met but even the core costs were estimated at £3 million.[1] The City of London had been generous, indeed responsible, for parliament's success but there were limits to its funds and the City was mainly Presbyterian, which influenced their relationship with Westminster.

Meanwhile, the Adventurers were clamouring for action. They had put up over £300,000 to subjugate Ireland, which was to be repaid in confiscated land, but very little had been done. Inchiquin held Cork for parliament and came to London in May 1647 to consult. He had the staunch loyalty of his troops and, having prised some funds out of parliament, that summer he took back much of the south of Ireland, fighting his way up through Tipperary and Waterford until he controlled Munster. However, Confederate forces were entrenched throughout the centre of the island and still threatened Dublin. If the Adventurers were to be satisfied – indeed if England was to reassert its sovereignty over Ireland at all – a major military campaign would have to be launched.

So the Derby House Committee made plans, and in doing so the committee and parliament enraged the New Model Army, upsetting a precarious balance of power which precipitated a new contest, this time between parliament and its army. When government collapses, it is very often the army which takes power, but England in the 1640s had strong institutions – the war had been fought to maintain parliament. Unlike Scotland and Ireland, England had fought for established laws and rights. Now that the clash of metal had ceased, though, the discussion of rights erupted among the winning side.

The parties in parliament, known as Independents and Presbyterians, had been divided over the conduct of the war and disagreed over church government, the Presbyterians wanting a state church under the control of parliament while Independents demanded freedom of worship. Now the war was over, the very real question arose of which group would retain power. Led by Holles and Stapleton, the Presbyterians in the Commons were more united and coherent than the Independent members who, despite their majority, did not act as one. There was hostility to the New Model in the City of London and some Independents also felt that the army had served its function and should be disbanded. Unlike the Committee of Both Kingdoms, Derby House had a Presbyterian majority and as they were in charge of the re-conquest of Ireland, they could determine the shape of the army to be sent there. Once a settlement with the king was reached, those who achieved it expected promotion to government, but the Presbyterians saw the New Model as an obstacle to that settlement. They wanted it disbanded, and the Derby House Committee was the body to put that into effect.

While terms were being agreed with the Scots, parliament remained fairly united, but once the Scottish army marched north these divisions swiftly opened up. The Presbyterians dominated: in the City, in the Derby House Committee and in the Commons itself. A new church system was being legislated for on their terms, and under their direction the armed forces were to be drastically reduced. Part of the New Model would be sent to retake Ireland, but it would be under new leaders and must conform to the new church rules; it must not include MPs. That ruled out Cromwell, Ireton and their close associates. Ireton had married Bridget, Oliver's second daughter, in June 1646 and the two men were close. Cromwell was ill early in 1647 but when he returned to the Commons he raised no objections. It was the troops who reacted angrily to the proposals.

The New Model was a cohesive army with high morale which had won parliament's victories; these were battle-hardened men belonging to tight fighting units. They had endured much for their cause. Their regiments, their commanders and their allegiances were one powerful focus of emotion. To break up regiments and send men abroad without pay was scandalous; a petition began to circulate among the regiments in Norfolk during March 1647 which turned into a campaign of documents. From soldiers' demands, through the first statements of political aspiration, a new movement grew.

At first their demands were solely for pay and conditions – they wanted their arrears, indemnity for acts of war and no compulsory service outside

England. However, parliament saw the petition and panicked. Another document was circulating from a very different source, but the two together gave the Commons real alarm. The second was overtly political, got-up by John Lilburne and his colleagues. Lilburne, Walwyn, Wildman and Overton had been publishing pamphlets since 1645 and were now a cohesive pressure group, although Lilburne and Overton were back in prison for attacking the peerage. The Leveller leaders were London-based and writing for a civilian audience, but during the spring of 1647 their ideas began to infiltrate the army. Their petition spoke of the Commons as 'the supreme authority', a concept which challenged the constitutional role of the king and Lords. It called for freedom of religion, law reform and an end to tithes. Parliament had already seen this document when it got sight of the army's. It seemed as though the army and radicals were challenging normal authority. Denzil Holles, leader of the Presbyterians in the Commons, claimed that, although the war was over, the New Model was still recruiting and increasing its strength.[2] He saw it as a threatening force and he hurriedly wrote the *Declaration of Dislike*, which criticised the army's petition and warned that those who promoted it were 'enemies of the state and disturbers of the public peace'.

Enemies of the state! The New Model Army, men who had fought and whose comrades had died to protect the state and its institutions – to be described in such a way was intolerable. The army never recovered from this insult and spent the rest of the summer trying to remove its authors from the Commons. At first their methods were measured and new documents were drafted, but the powerful group psyche of the army had been roused. Cromwell was in London to attend Commons sittings, but Fairfax was with the army. Obedient to the Commons, he suppressed the petitions and read out the *Declaration of Dislike* to each regiment as parliament commanded. The army went ominously quiet while Derby House finalised its plans.

Parliament had the good of the country to consider. The cost of maintaining the army fell on local people through the county committees which raised the assessment money, while many troops were billeted on households. The burden could not be borne much longer in a country depleted by years of war. But the army feared that an early disbandment might allow further eruptions of discontent. Nothing had been settled for the king and kingdom. The army felt that its demands were so clearly just that they repeated them in various ways throughout the spring. But many in parliament feared the New Model: its Independency in religion, its military strength and the cast of mind of its officers, especially Cromwell. Fairfax alarmed them less; they felt that he was a man of honour, appointed by parliament and faithful to that command. His wife was a Presbyterian, which influenced his position. Cromwell, however, was an Independent, a powerful and revered cavalry commander who, for all his clarity in words, was opaque in many ways. His motives seemed unclear and there was suspicion of him, which Cromwell felt: 'It is a miserable thing to serve a parliament, to which, let a man be never so faithful, if one pragmatical fellow amongst them rise and asperse him, he shall never wipe it off.'[3]

As discontent rumbled through the army, parliamentary commissioners came to meet the officers and discuss their plans. The chain of obedience which binds soldiers into a viable army was being tested. Those basic allegiances – of Fairfax to parliament, the officers to Fairfax and the men to their officers – were being stretched. Which of those bonds would hold?

In other parts of the two islands, armies were still active. In Scotland, Leven's army had been partially disbanded but, with Argyll at its head, the remaining core was tearing its way through the lands of the MacDonalds and their allies in the west. Inchiquin's army, on behalf of parliament, was successfully taking territory in southern Ireland which it could then put under contributions and so pay for itself.[4] Ormond, contained in Dublin, spent the spring of 1647 negotiating with the London parliament, while they in turn negotiated with the king. In this uneasy lull, the New Model became restive.

Lilburne's pressure group had become significant. It was Cromwell and his son-in-law Ireton who gave Lilburne and his friends the name 'Levellers'. In earlier conflicts over enclosures protesters had levelled fences, but the men whom Ireton called Levellers were pressing for social levelling of a wider kind. When they talked of the Commons as the highest authority in the kingdom, they were contradicting the ancient constitution in which the monarch and both houses of parliament held sovereignty. As the Westminster parliament, the Scots and most of the Irish wanted Charles to regain his three crowns, this was provocative. The victors of the war wanted the constitution adjusted but the question was on what terms. The Levellers wanted an entirely new basis for the constitution.

During that spring of 1647, Charles lived in the style of a king at Holmby, but commissioners from parliament oversaw his conditions and prevented contact with his chaplains or Anglican services. The garrison that guarded him was under Colonel Graves. From his arrival in February and until April, Charles could not communicate with his wife. On his behalf, Henrietta-Maria made sporadic attempts to negotiate with Scotland and Ireland although her position was weak. In May she wrote to Mazarin of 'the proposition of reconciling the Scotch and the Irish together; you will find it important enough for the welfare of the kingdom of Ireland, and the affairs of the King, my lord',[5] but France would not take risks for either Charles or Ireland. It was in south-east England that the power players struggled.

Early in April, Derby House finalised its plans for Ireland which parliament then approved. Fairfax and Cromwell, with three other regiments, were to constitute the standing army in England. The rest of the New Model would either be disbanded or could take service in Ireland. When the Commons commissioners arrived at army headquarters in Saffron Walden, Fairfax convened 200 officers to meet them. Colonel Lambert put questions to them but the answers were unsatisfactory. Men who enlisted for service in Ireland would not serve under their old commanders; in particular instead of Fairfax and Cromwell, Massey and Skippon had been named as commanders of the expedition. Nor were there guarantees on pay in Ireland or the arrears of pay already owing. The commissioners wanted the officers to promote enlistment for Ireland, which Fairfax scrupulously performed, although within the army those who signed up were reviled.

Enlistment for Ireland became contentious and parliament, to show that further service in England was not an alternative for any but the designated regiments, tried to hurry disbandment. The army was under threat, splitting over enlistment for Ireland while threatened by the Presbyterians who would dismember it. But the soldiers had a strong sense of solidarity. This was a great and victorious fighting force with tremendous morale. Many officers felt as their men did and it was they who composed *A Vindication of the Officers of the Army*, stating their intention to stand with their men regarding their grievances and asserting that the people had the right to petition.[6] They were still smarting over the *Declaration of Dislike*.

Not long afterwards Fairfax fell ill and retired to London for a month, but the troops produced *The Apology of the Common Soldiers of Sir Thomas Fairfax's Army* and showed it to their general before it was published.[7] This was a more concerted attack on the Commons for 'having lately tasted of sovereignty and being lifted beyond their ordinary sphere of servants, seek to become masters and degenerate into tyrants'. This idea – that an elected parliament can itself become a tyrant – would be asserted loudly over the coming years. By now, parliament had sat for six years and could not be dissolved without its own consent. People were beginning to feel that the Commons was all-powerful and entrenched. But the king was a prisoner; where else could authority reside?

The *Apology* incensed Westminster. They had received two scurrilous petitions and now a highly offensive document from the common soldiers. They saw Leveller influence at work; the army had become 'one Lilburne throughout'.[8] Parliament sent four officer-MPs to investigate: Skippon, Cromwell, Ireton and Fleetwood.

Parliament was right that, by the end of April, Leveller influence in the New Model Army was growing. The regiments had appointed agents or Agitators to take soundings but also to spread ideas. They met in a central committee and through this network the political ideas of Lilburne and his colleagues were seeping through the army. Afraid that parliament would make some Presbyterian deal with the king, many in the army hoped for an agreement of their own with King Charles.

Their priority, however, was their demands as soldiers – their pay and conditions. They held consultations and by mid-May were gathered at Saffron Walden where several officers collected their men's views to write a single document for presentation to parliament. Cromwell read it to the Commons himself. It was about employment terms, and not incendiary, but Cromwell warned the Commons that officers were losing control of their men.

Fairfax ordered the men not to act without their officers and to stop attending the Agitators' meetings, but he was not obeyed. Parliament began to look for other military support: the London militia, other regiments from the war and possibly the Scots might be able to stand up to the New Model.

Charles was still at Holmby House. He had parliamentary commissioners and a small garrison to guard him but he lived in royal style and seemed well on his way to being reinstated. In mid-May he sent an offer to parliament of three years of Presbyterianism and ten years of control of the militia. The Commons majority and their Scottish colleagues accepted this offer and the Earl of Lauderdale went to Holmby, giving Charles direct contact with Edinburgh. The Presbyterians planned to bring the king to Oatlands, his palace on the Thames near London, to make a full agreement. Charles was very keen to get to London, where he believed he would be welcomed as a returning monarch. To forestall trouble from the New Model, the Commons hurried on with disbandment. For the Agitators, therefore, time was of the essence, for a settlement was about to be made in which their aims would not even be heard. Some of the Agitators began to plan an audacious move. The men of Rainsborough's regiment and Cornet Joyce from Fairfax's were the main actors in the plan. By their action they precipitated the army into making its move.

On 29 May, Fairfax held a Council of War with his officers. The men and most of the officers demanded a general rendezvous of the New Model Army. Fairfax had either to abandon his army or agree to the meeting; they would hold it come what may. He decided to hold the meeting and told parliament so, 'to keep the army from disorder'.[9] The rendezvous was called for 4 and 5 June at Kentford Heath near Newmarket. The whole army would muster and decide its strategy. That meant the radicals had little time. Fairfax was respected but the Agitators were now directing men against the orders of their officers. Parliament wanted swift disbandment and control of weapons; it ordered that the artillery train, stored at Oxford since the war ended, be taken down to London. These arms were guarded by Colonel Rich's men but they refused either to obey the orders or to disband. As directed by the Agitators, Rainsborough's men supported them. The men also seized the disbandment pay. Also by command of the Agitators, Cornet Joyce was given command of 500 cavalrymen detached from three regiments, who hurried to support the action at Oxford just as the rest of the army was moving up to Newmarket. Having secured the artillery train, they prepared to go north for another special mission. This last was a truly grave matter, and Cornet Joyce first galloped to London to consult his senior officer.[10]

Cromwell was in his lodgings in Drury Lane, London, at the end of May. Known to be sympathetic to the radicals' concerns, it was to Cromwell that Cornet Joyce turned to clarify his mission. On 31 May he arrived at Drury Lane and spent some time with Cromwell discussing possible contingencies.[11]

Two days later, Joyce galloped up the drive at Holmby with a mission to secure the king. Charles had gone to Althorp to play bowls and Joyce's troopers did not arrive for two more hours, so Joyce had a nervous wait. This was followed by a night of inaction. During it, Graves, the commander of the garrison at Holmby, galloped away and Joyce suspected that Graves would raise the alarm. However, in the morning, Cornet Joyce took control of the house and informed the commissioners that his orders were to prevent Charles being taken to London. The garrison raised no difficulties as they were greatly outnumbered by Joyce's men. Joyce wrote to Cromwell for instructions the next morning, but during the day he and his troopers grew more disturbed by the thought of Graves returning with larger forces. That evening Joyce demanded to see the king. Eventually, the commissioners allowed him into the king's bedchamber; Charles was already asleep.

The king was roused and Joyce, in his most civil fashion, warned the king that he would have to move the following day. The king asked for assurances that he would be well treated, would not be forced to betray his conscience and could take his servants with him. The following morning, the king stepped out of the house where the troopers were drawn up in formation. Joyce was in command. 'Where is your commission?' Charles asked the young officer. Joyce made a few inconsequential replies, but when the king pressed him Joyce pointed to his troops and said, 'Here is my commission.' Charles, with his quizzical wit, said, 'It is as fair a commission and as well written as I have seen a commission written in my life,' or so Joyce later told Rushworth, the secretary to the army.[12] They set off, but Joyce was unsure where to take the king. He and Cromwell had discussed securing the monarch and preventing the Presbyterians taking him to London; Cromwell was a skilled dissimulator and later fell out with Joyce, so what he really told the young man on 31 May is not certain, but while he certainly agreed to Joyce securing the king, he might not have ordered his abduction. Joyce wanted to take Charles to Oxford, but the king refused. After discussion, it was apparently Charles himself who chose Newmarket.

The king thought he might get better terms from the army than from parliament, and he always thought he could play his enemies off against each other, so reaching the heart of the army offered new possibilities. Besides, he had no choice. While he and his escort set off for East Anglia, Oliver Cromwell was riding out from London to the same destination. Charles slept the night at Hinchinbrook House, the mansion where Oliver's uncle once entertained King James. Here, Joyce wrote to one of his accomplices in the army, urging him to bring as many men as possible to the rendezvous, for he was afraid of a severe penalty from Fairfax and wanted support. He enclosed a note which stated that 'my best old friend had consented hereunto' and that he was obeying orders of some sort. This and Joyce's later testimony suggests that Cromwell himself had agreed to the abduction of the king, something which Cromwell constantly denied. He had confirmed Joyce's mission to secure the king, but Joyce and Cromwell disagreed bitterly over whether a more drastic contingency was discussed – and perhaps the instructions were simply unclear.[13]

The next day, the king set out again with Joyce and his escort. Charles was in high spirits as local people spread green boughs on the road before him, and bonfires were lit for him in Cambridge, although he was prevented from entering the city. Fairfax was fully engaged in managing the rendezvous when he heard that the king had been abducted and was approaching. He wanted Charles immediately returned to Holmby, but on 5 June the king arrived at Childerley Hall. This was near Newmarket, where the army was on the second day of its meeting.

Fairfax, Cromwell, Ireton and other officers rode over to Childerley to meet Charles. Possession of the king was now added to Fairfax's problems and he wanted Joyce court-martialled, but Charles seemed keen to reach the army rendezvous. He had warmed to young Cornet Joyce, who was courteous and spoke confidently. The commissioners were still with the king, and wanted to prevent his meeting the army, but Charles managed their confusion subtly and got his own way; he was to proceed to his own hunting lodge at Newmarket. The parliamentary commissioners said their authority had been terminated at Holmby so, like it or not, the army had now secured their monarch. He had been held by the Scots and by parliament, so here was his third chance. He was taken to his hunting lodge, where he spent two weeks living with greater freedom than at Holmby.

The army rendezvous had already created a significant document. *The Solemn Engagement of the Army* was a form of army covenant in which the men bound themselves together, agreeing to disband only when their demands were satisfied and also demanding – in the name of 'the freeborn people of England' – that their enemies in parliament be purged. To make sure these demands were met, the creation of a new body was announced: the General Council of the Army. Each regiment would send two officers and two elected soldiers to join the Council of War which was composed only of officers. The General Council proved a formidable body and, once elected, the Agitators got a formal role in the army structure. Having covenanted itself to hold together, the army began to advance towards London, for nothing is so convincing as thousands of fighting men on the move. The march gave the officers time to visit King Charles and confer with him; he remained in the army's possession but agreed to stay on at his hunting lodge. Leaving him there, on 12 June the army marched south. Throughout the following month, the great mass of the New Model was on the move to London in a show of strength.

At Newmarket, the king also received a visit from Lord Lauderdale, who arrived on 20 June with a pass authorised by parliament, which put the king back in touch with his Scottish allies.

In London, there was disturbance and alarm. The New Model was approaching and Presbyterians looked about for military support – from the City or from their allies in Scotland. Other discontented soldiers, the Reformadoes, who had already been disbanded without pay, began to besiege parliament, causing further uproar. General Massey, a parliamentarian officer and Presbyterian, rode through London warning people to arm and Presbyterians – both English and Scots – even sent a message to Henrietta-Maria urging her to send Prince Charles to Scotland to head an army of invasion.[14] In theory, parliament still had armed forces, but not massed and ready. There was the army gathered at Worcester to go to Ireland, the Northern Army at York under Poyntz and the City's trained bands. Parliament also had forces in Ireland: the 2,000 men under Colonel Michael Jones who arrived in Dublin Bay just as the New Model set off south, and Inchiquin's in Cork. But strengthening their position in Ireland would not save London if Fairfax meant to take it. The New Model was moving steadily south and by 12 June was at St Albans, where it stopped to prepare new demands.

The Declaration from Sir Thomas Fairfax and the Army was the first overtly political document which the soldiers produced. It justified its speaking for English people and on political issues because it was not 'a mere mercenary army, hired to serve any arbitrary power of a state, but called forth and conjured by the several declarations of Parliament to the defence of their own and the people's just rights and liberties'. It insisted that MPs who had abused their powers, defamed the army or been unduly elected should be removed, and only morally sound men should be appointed. Parliaments might err or prove unsatisfactory, so they should not sit for too long. The current Commons should fix a date for its own dissolution and future parliaments should sit for fixed periods to prevent them sitting indefinitely when no other power could dissolve them. Seats should be reapportioned to make parliament more representative. The right to petition was to be acknowledged, the powers of the county committees restricted and the accounts of the nation published.[15]

Several historians believe the author of this document was Ireton, Cromwell's son-in-law and an MP, who showed a clear mind and an aptitude for constitutional theory. Now they were venturing into politics, the army leaders drew on their recent experience as well as theoretical debates in books and pamphlets, but also as members of independent congregations which ran themselves democratically.

The animosity between the Presbyterian leaders in the Commons and the army was now intense. Holles is said to have pulled Ireton's nose in an altercation, but it was deeper than personal insult; there was a profound disagreement between the groups.[16] As the king's authority collapsed, parliament found itself holding power it had not sought and it had to improvise systems. The army was fearful of disbandment; who would pay them or protect them from prosecution? But their hopes for society grew from their churches: the Presbyterians for a national church structure; the Independents wanting liberty to build congregations as they pleased. The army had fostered personal self-respect in the soldiers and a brotherhood of shared ideals. Would they give that up lightly because MPs ordered it? They would not. They had more respect for Charles, who had led his army personally and seemed to relish military life.

The army's next salvo, *Heads of a Charge*, was delivered to the Commons two days later, demanding the impeachment of the eleven MPs including Holles and Stapleton, who had insulted the army and were obstructing liberty. Parliament delayed considering this document but continued recruiting for Ireland and told the army to send in proof if it wanted the impeachment considered. The army officers replied that they had proof enough and that parliament had impeached Strafford, Laud and Finch on the basis of accusation only. Meanwhile, the City of London was organising its defences as best it could, calling in the trained bands and getting permission from parliament to raise cavalry. The army accused parliament of trying to throw the kingdom back into war, of rousing the militia and intriguing with the Scots.

At the time, the Scottish army was in Kintyre and crossed to Islay where it discovered that Alasdair MacColla had left for Ireland with his men. They had to content themselves with hanging his aged father. Nor were the Scots united; both Hamilton and the kirk wanted the king reinstated – but Hamilton by peace, while the kirk was now willing to fight. With the MacDonalds subjugated, the Scottish army was free to come south.

In England, the army demanded answers from parliament. It issued another *Remonstrance* before marching to Uxbridge on 25 June from where Fairfax placed his regiments in an arc from Watford to Staines. The City of London had made efforts to form up the trained bands but it also put out feelers to Fairfax to improve relations. To keep up the pressure, some radical regiments moved closer to the capital but were recalled. Parliamentary commissioners came out to negotiate with Fairfax. As tensions rose, the eleven members withdrew for their own safety, Holles included.

The king was carefully kept within the army's area of control. Parliament wanted him taken to Richmond but the army decided on Hampton Court, via a series of country houses. As the army marched to Uxbridge, Charles moved to Hatfield House. The officers were keen to conciliate and make terms with Charles, allowing his friends to visit him, and Fairfax permitted the king both his chaplains and a service using the Book of Common Prayer, which was precious to the king. 'This army speak to me very fair which makes me hope well,' he told a friend.[17] Parliament objected but, overall, MPs were becoming more conciliatory and Fairfax withdrew a little, reaching new headquarters at Reading on 3 July. Charles moved too, to Lord Craven's house at Caversham. Here he could communicate freely with his wife and 'anybody else whom I please' and his children James and Elizabeth were brought to visit him, 'to his infinite content and joy'.[18]

At Caversham, the army leaders came to negotiate with the king. Fairfax let his lieutenant general take the lead and Cromwell had an interview with Charles on 4 July which seemed to satisfy both of them. The army was keen to reach a settlement and thought the Scots and parliamentarians had used the wrong methods. They were about to discover that Charles was a very awkward negotiating partner, but at this stage they were keen to earn his goodwill, hence their allowing him access to his chaplains and children.

With every move, it became clear how much loyalty and affection the king still commanded. When the royal children came to see their father, well-wishers littered their way with flowers and boughs, as they had for the king in East Anglia. The army leaders saw their captive as a strong bargaining chip through whom they could dominate parliament and with whom they would make a deal. So a three-way negotiation developed, with the Scots as fourth. The king, the army, parliament and the Scots were all sending documents and intermediaries. Parliament wanted the king returned to their control, but now that he was embedded in the army they made stipulations that neither should approach London. The eleven members had withdrawn from the Commons but the army had wider aims and many grievances. So for two months the army approached, withdrew and circled London while attempts at a settlement were made. All three had power – king, parliament and army – but none were able to use it decisively. Instead they struggled with the intellectual core of the revolution they had unleashed, looking for a new balance of power. As they did so, fears and grievances broke loose in the heat of the London summer.

There were already suspicions about Cromwell but it is difficult to quantify them as most appeared in documents written later, when he had assumed power. He was certainly closer to the radicals than Fairfax and he had certainly connived in Joyce's expedition to secure – if not to abduct – the king, but Cromwell was respectful to Charles and was seen with tears in his eyes when the royal children were reunited with their father. Like Fairfax, his primary aim was to keep control of the army and to prevent further war. Unlike Fairfax, he was an Independent. Cromwell told Sir John Berkeley, who had been sent by Henrietta-Maria to assist the king, that the army wished for no more 'than to have leave to live as subjects ought to do and to preserve their consciences' and 'that they thought no man could enjoy their estates quietly without the king had his rights'.[19] If the king failed, the system would fail and no landowners wanted that. Cromwell also told Bellièvre, whom Mazarin had sent to assist the king, 'No one rises so high as he who knows not whither he is going.'[20] Many historians have interpreted this as Cromwell speculating on his own assent. The remark is typical of Cromwell, who could be blunt and clear or tantalisingly obscure. In action he was similarly divided – the decisive cavalry officer and administrator would sometimes be a subtle operator who deliberately delayed or veiled his motives, possibly even to himself. Cromwell was loyal to his social group; many of the New Model's officers came from minor gentry families or those with property who were wary of profound social disruption. As power shifted in the following two years, Cromwell can be seen defending the interests of this group, but he also became silent or physically absent at key moments, leaving a shadow over his motives.

Charles's motives were not in doubt but his methods were. He would negotiate with one group but when another made an offer he would switch to them, leaving both expecting some settlement. He saw the proliferation of factions only as an opportunity for his reinstatement, probably with his powers unchanged, and he spun out negotiations until another faction made its move, to the great perplexity of both his friends and his challengers. For all this, he was never able to use the rivalries of his enemies to advance himself. Ireton, trying to show Charles that his power was limited, told him, 'Sir, you have an intention to be the Arbitrator between the Parliament and us, and we mean to be it between your Majesty and the Parliament.'[21] Charles's method frustrated everyone, both his contemporaries and historians, but in a curious way he was right. They could prevent the exercise of his power but they were discovering how difficult it was to prise that power off him.

One source of satisfaction for the king was the escape of his eldest son from Jersey to France. Henrietta-Maria had become ever more insistent, fearing he would be captured too, but the prince had a council of his own, which the king had set up when his son left Oxford. His councillors were divided, but the prince obeyed his mother and left for France, joining her at Saint-Germain where he caused problems of protocol and later international relations. But the king felt a little lighter, knowing that if he were forced into concessions his heir was outside the reach of parliament and might in time repudiate those terms. The king apparently saw his role as a sacred trust bequeathed to him by his ancestors and had little intention of signing away any part of his powers, believing that to do so would 'be disastrous to the well-being of the country'.[22] He knew the views of the 'rebels' were not those of the majority of his people and that strengthened his resolve to thwart them.

Parliament still had troops in York commanded by Poyntz but they too began to listen to Agitators sent from the New Model and by now were becoming mutinous. Early in July, Poyntz was taken captive by his men and taken to Reading where he was liberated by Fairfax but no longer had men to command.[23] The Presbyterian majority in the Commons was losing its commanding position. Acknowledging this, on 19 July they gave Fairfax command of all the forces in England and Wales. The eleven members, seeing their position weaken, obtained permission to go abroad and left the country.[24]

Now drawn up at Reading, the army took stock. It was Ireton who presented the army's first constitutional document, the *Heads of Proposals*. On 16 July, the General Council of the Army was called into session at Reading, where the Agitators pressed for a renewed march on London. Cromwell spoke against such a naked use of force. Ireton said that before they embarked on such a scandalous course they should consider 'what it is that we intend to doe with that power when we have it'.[25] The Agitators wanted only to take it from their enemies, who had insulted them and refused to pay them, but Cromwell asked them to be careful. They had already made demands which Fairfax had pressed with parliament; if the soldiers were to achieve their aims, they must prepare their ground, read over the documents they had already published and be consistent. Their position must be clear.

We know what was said at the Great Council of the Army, both at Reading and elsewhere, because William Clarke, one of the secretaries to the New Model Army, understood the recently developed shorthand system and recorded verbatim the debates of the Army Council. His papers survived and were deposited in Worcester College, Oxford, where the historian Sir Charles Firth found and edited them for publication in 1891. As a result, we hear the voices of the army throughout their year of transition and debate. At Reading, Mr Allen, the most vociferous of the Agitators, was all for marching swiftly on London, for he said, 'I think very few of us [believe] that they are at the present gainers, or likely to be gainers.'[26] But the arguments of Fairfax, Cromwell and others swayed him, for next day after Ireton spoke, Allen told the meeting, 'I thinke that the thinges in hand hee names are things of great weight, having relation to the settling of a kingdome, which is a great worke; truly the worke we all expect to have a share in, and desire that others may alsoe. I suppose itt is nott unknowne to you that we are most of us butt young Statesmen, and nott well able to judge how longe such thinges which wee heare now read to us may bee to the ends for which they are presented, and for us out of judgement to give our assents to itt must take uppe some time that we may deliberate upon itt.'[27] As novice statesmen, they needed time to think things through.

That same day, the army debated the *Heads of Proposals*. Evidence suggests that Ireton was advised by the Independent peers Saye and Wharton when he composed the text. *Heads of Proposals* was less punitive for the king than the *Propositions of Newcastle* but less advantageous than the Presbyterian proposals of spring 1647. *Heads* offered the greater religious freedom, but it weakened the power of bishops and left royalists open to heavy penalties – both red lines for Charles. Under it, parliament would control the army and also appoint the chief officers of state for a period of ten years, something which Charles had previously seemed to accept. The privy council was to be replaced by a council of state, of 'persons now to be agreed upon', and this body would control the trained bands. Royalists could not hold office for five years or sit in parliament for ten; they would have to compound for their estates depending on their involvement in the war. In religion, the army made more concessions to the opinions of the king than parliament had offered. The Book of Common Prayer would be permitted but neither it nor attendance at the parish church would be compulsory. Bishops could continue but would lose much of their power.

Heads of Proposals was sent to parliament for consideration and peace looked likely. Parliament was keen to placate the army and stood down its own forces. Fairfax had full command and the eleven members were going overseas. The Presbyterians had capitulated. In response, the army withdrew northwards to Bedfordshire, taking Charles with them and depositing him at Woburn Abbey. As they moved, the officers came for interviews with the monarch, but as they tried to close a deal new eruptions broke out in London.

The army might have been aggrieved but so were many others. The Reformadoes were unpaid and aggressive, while apprentices were easily stirred up by Presbyterian leaders in either the City or Westminster who accused the army of heresy and of keeping the king from a settlement. Although partially paid, the army was still a great financial drain on the whole country. The citizens of London were roused and mobs began to descend on Westminster on 20 July 'in a clamorous and tumultuous way'. On the 21st, these crowds signed their own *Solemn Engagement* pledging to bring the king to Westminster for a personal treaty between him and his parliament.

It was while London was in ferment that *Heads of Proposals* was offered to the king. Charles was at Woburn and open to negotiations, so Ireton with three other officers visited him for four hours of discussion. Charles now thought he might play off the army against the Presbyterians and hoped he could push the officers for better terms. 'You cannot be without me,' he told them, 'you will fall to ruin if I do not sustain you.'[28] In order to justify their actions, the army leaders urgently needed to make a deal with the king and restore him to his throne; but now they began to experience the quirks of Charles's nature as other had before. Berkeley, who had been sent by the queen to advise the king and was on good terms with the army officers, thought never had a kingdom been offered back so cheaply, but Charles would not accept the *Heads of Proposals*. The army was left in limbo, asserting its position but without an agreement with Charles on which a final settlement could be based.

Meanwhile, parliament voted the Londoners' *Solemn Engagement* treasonable and tried to take control of the City's trained bands, with the result that the mobs turned on parliament and on 26 July invaded the Palace of Westminster and broke into the Commons chamber, where they abused and attacked members until they voted to bring back the king. 'Vote, vote,' they shouted at the members. Parliament then adjourned for three days but when they reassembled, Speaker Lenthall, Manchester, the Speaker of the Lords, and fifty-seven members of the Commons were all missing; the leading Independents had left parliament and joined the army. The Commons elected a new Speaker but as parliament can only sit when the Speaker is present, this was highly contentious. London itself was now divided, for although they feared the army, the City was in contention with the Commons over the trained bands.

In a curious echo of that fateful day when Charles took soldiers to parliament, now the City Council and mob were invading parliament. The army too threatened force if the Commons did not obey. As London roared and trembled, across the Irish Sea Ormond finally gave up Dublin Castle to Colonel Michael Jones and sailed for England. The following day, Fairfax – carrying the king, the Speaker and the Independent MPs with him – began marching to London. During this progress, the negotiations with Charles continued, for the army longed passionately to have an agreement signed before they arrived in the capital so they could reinstate not only the Speaker and MPs but the king himself. Charles, however, had become obstinate, even quite surly. He was now in regular contact with his Scottish supporters and began to think they would prove more satisfactory than the army. Berkeley questioned whether parliament would ever ratify the *Proposals*, even if the king did accept them. The officers said mildly that they would ask the Commons to confirm them and Colonel Rainsborough blurted out that the New Model would make them.[29] Talk of purging parliament was already in the air.

So the army set off for London while still in discussion, the men intent on getting their rights, the king intent on regaining his, and the army leaders caught between many volatile forces. Fairfax, who believed strongly in the rights of parliament but had an army to control that carried displaced members in its midst, rode steadily down to the capital. Southwark wanted to defend itself rather than accept the City militia, but in any case the army had the upper hand; four regiments and two guns convinced Southwark to open its gates. The City followed by yielding its forts to the army, even agreeing to hand over the Tower of London. Fairfax brought his men through London – laurels in their hats to signify victory – and saw the members reinstated to their rightful place in the Commons. The Lords had few members now, as only the leading Independent peers still attended.

The king was duly taken to Hampton Court, while the army camped at Kingston on the river. Parliament revised its *Propositions* and sent them to Charles, who now had two offers. That was dangerous, as he would hope for rivalry and contention, ultimately closing a deal with neither. On his journey south he had also seen Lauderdale again, who undermined Berkeley's advice by making suggestions of his own. Meanwhile, Ormond arrived from Ireland to confer with the king.

Despite its show of force, the army had only got a fraction of its demands. On 27 August, Fairfax moved his army headquarters to Putney, on the River Thames south-west of London, and here much of the army stayed until 17 November, obliging London to provide them with supplies. The heath and woods of Putney gave the troops space to camp, and in the parish church the soldiers could hold their meetings as well as address themselves to God. So, on the south bank of the Thames, a short ride from the Palace of Westminster where the Long Parliament was still in session, the now rebellious army spent many weeks debating the future of the kingdom.

26

The Putney Debates

Among the blizzard of pamphlets published in the 1640s, those of Lilburne and his associates stand out. Under the 'ancient constitution', sovereignty lay with king, lords and commons; now parliament wanted some of the monarch's prerogative powers. Lilburne, however, argued for a new constitutional basis and government by consent, suggesting sovereignty lay with the people who awarded it to their ruler. Henry Parker had published this view in 1642 and behind it lay a rich literature of theories of government which stretched back to Roman authors. In recent European thought Bodin, Grotius and Machiavelli were widely studied. Hobbes was out of England in the 1640s and only published *Leviathan* in 1651, in which he argued for a strong sovereign power to which people permanently transfer their natural rights – ideas which led to social contract theory. Sovereignty by the consent of the people did not originate with Lilburne but he was a gifted synthesiser and avid reader, and adept at influencing ordinary people. He was no Locke or Montesquieu, but more of a Thomas Paine.

John Lilburne had been to grammar school but not to university or the Inns of Court, yet his knowledge was prodigious and self-taught. He had enormous mental energy, absorbing complex ideas and using them to press for radical policies. At the age of twenty-three he had been convicted of importing illegal books, whipped, pilloried and imprisoned in irons, where he believed he had been left to die. This harsh sentence may have created his lifelong rage and sense of grievance but more probably he was a confrontational man who got into trouble early. It was Henry Marten, lawyer, republican and a friend of Lilburne, who said, 'If the World was emptied of all but John Lilburne, Lilburne would quarrel with John and John with Lilburne.'[1] Having been punished over Presbyterian tracts, Lilburne attacked the Presbyterians and took an Independent position. He fought bravely during the war, including at Marston Moor, but he criticised Manchester and was imprisoned by parliament in 1645 and again in 1646 for libel, scandal and illegal printing. During his imprisonment he abandoned Independency while building his own party, the Levellers, which had become influential among the army Agitators. By then Lilburne was well known in London, where several thousand citizens signed a petition on behalf of 'Free-Born John'.

Lilburne talked and wrote repeatedly of the rights of 'Free-Born Englishmen'. It was a clever contraction of several emotive ideas. Freeborn status and servitude harked back to feudalism, and, although there were no longer villeins, land was still held on terms derived from feudalism while the 'Norman yoke' was scorned as crushing those natural rights which men had held in Saxon times. That Englishmen had rights was at the core of the parliamentary cause; 'the liberties of the subject' were guaranteed by law and Magna Carta. By switching the phrase around, Lilburne deleted 'subject', inserted patriotism and opened the door to Englishmen as citizens rather than as subjects.[2]

The political theories of the period are complex; the ideas of major writers both overlap and disagree in subtle ways. For Lilburne and his colleagues, asserting their political programme was the pressing issue. Lilburne, Overton, Wildman and Walwyn did not hold the same political or religious views but they developed a joint manifesto which was first circulated in London and was then energetically promoted in the army. For Lilburne, the law was paramount, 'the only known and declared rule, the laying aside whereof brings in nothing but Will and Power, lust and strength'.[3] Although Leveller demands varied a little over time, they all envisaged a reform of church and state requiring a new constitution. Lilburne's key demand was law reform; the law was generally carried out in Latin, probate was managed by the church, the court system was often controlled by the monarch and the nobility had privileges. Lilburne passionately wanted equality before the law.[4] Other Leveller demands included freedom of religion, the abolition of tithes and monopolies and the satisfaction of the soldiers' demands. The Levellers appealed to natural law; for example, Overton wrote, 'To every individual in nature is given an individual property by nature not to be invaded or usurped by any.'[5] For Overton this came from God via nature, for Lilburne directly from God. This was at odds with the view of society which prevailed in the seventeenth century, whereby God created humans in dominion over animals and stratified them into orders, creating a hierarchical society which its promoters considered balanced and stable.

When the Levellers had petitioned parliament, their petition had been burned. But when the army asserted its claims, it became a new power in the land which the Levellers hoped might push for greater changes. The army – especially its officers – was bound by its allegiance to parliament, and even Lilburne saw that to change the law by force of arms was self-contradictory. But the army had shown its hand and come down to the capital to assert its rights; it was an opportunity the Levellers could not afford to miss, especially since the army had not made a treaty with the king but was camped uneasily beside the Thames trying to decide its strategy.

Charles was at Hampton Court in what turned out to be halcyon days. He had his chaplains, his children came to visit and the gentry collected about him as if his court was performing normally. Ormond was able to consult with him there when he arrived from Dublin. But Charles had no executive power and was still negotiating to get it back. In September he turned down parliament's proposals and said he thought the *Heads of Proposals* more likely to bring peace, but still he made few concessions and seemed far from agreement. The army was stuck, which gave the Agitators time to stir up the troops.

The emergence of the army as a political player in its own right and one with radical aims made many people reassess their position. Sir Edward Nicholas summed up the position: 'As the king at first called a parliament he could not rule, and afterwards the Parliament raised an army it could not rule, so the army have agitators they cannot rule. What the end will be, God only knows.'[6]

Marchamont Nedham shifted position completely. He had spent a year practising medicine but he managed to get an audience with the king and went on bended knee to beg forgiveness. Then he took up his pen for the royalist newspaper *Mercurius Pragmaticus*, the aim of which was 'to write his majesty back into his throne'.[7] *Pragmaticus* spoke respectfully of Fairfax but was sour and disparaging about Cromwell and constantly complained about the cost of the army. People would not trust parliament again, the paper said, and 'will not beare the blood-letting of their Purses any longer'.[8] Debts were growing by £100,000 a month but the army had been paid only a fraction of what it was owed.

The army headquarters at Putney were only a ferry ride from Fulham and a short way from Westminster. The Agitators were all lodged together nearby and in September Fairfax instigated weekly meetings of the General Council of the Army to be held in Putney church. Lilburne, who despite the army's presence in London was still in the Tower and furious, considered the General Council as the new command structure of the army, on the grounds that the *Solemn Engagement* had made the army a free association rather than employees of the state.[9] The commanders, of course, did not see it that way. Cromwell knew Lilburne, who had served in his regiment, and he visited him in the Tower but did not hasten his release. Nedham too was sympathetic to 'my friend Lilburne' and published his advice to the soldiers, but he was taking a different direction.

The first General Council meeting at Putney was held on 9 September. The Agitators criticised Cromwell and Ireton for being too close to the king, but the Agitators themselves were being criticised by the Levellers who thought the soldiers too concerned about their pay and too unconcerned about the constitution. The Levellers had managed to insert new agents into five regiments, including those of Cromwell and Ireton, which had always been radical in religion and politics.

The meetings began with prayer before discussion started and most of September was taken up with the *Heads of Proposals* – for example whether parliament should be biennial or triennial and how long it should sit – and their own pay, as they complained bitterly that London was evading tax and not paying its assessment to parliament. Responding to army pressure, parliament did earmark new funds for the army, so the soldiers felt they were making their case.

Parliament, however, had some satisfactions of its own. In Ireland, having taken command of Dublin from Ormond, Colonel Jones had engaged Preston's Leinster army and beaten it decisively at Dungan's Hill in August. In September, Inchiquin moved up through the valleys of Tipperary to take the ancient fortress of Cashel where his ancestors had once ruled. Here he set

Commissary General Henry Ireton.

fire to the cathedral, killing soldiers, priests and civilians and thereby earning the name *Murchadh n dTóiteán* – Murrough the Burner. Inchiquin now controlled the southern half of Ireland for parliament and was closing in on Kilkenny. Monck had also given allegiance to parliament, been released from the Tower and given control of parliament's forces in Ulster; early in October he joined with Jones to push back Owen Roe O'Neill. So parliament was gradually taking territory from the Confederates, as it had contracted to do with the Adventurers over five years earlier. But Inchiquin too had heard of the New Model's demands and was troubled by them. So were the Confederates. As the New Model became a separate political force, so the factions in Ireland reassessed their positions.

Leveller pressure was creating a new situation in Putney. On 18 October the new agents presented a radical document to Fairfax called *The Case of the Army Truly Stated*. He was both alarmed and displeased; the army's actions were attracting strong criticism and *The Case of the Army* had already been printed, causing more controversy. It was a hybrid document, part Leveller theory and part practical demands; for example, it stated the sovereignty of the people but also demanded an end to excise on beer, fabric and clothes.

The document complained that the demands of the army and of the freeborn people of England had not been met: 'We not only apprehend nothing to have been done effectually, either for the Army or the poore oppressed people of the nation, but we also conceive, that there is little probabilitie of any good, without some more speedy and vigorous actings.'[10] The authors wanted the current parliament to be dissolved within the year and the vote given to all males over the age of twenty-one. Before the king regained his rights, the people must have theirs, of which many were listed. This was far beyond any programme put forward so far.

When he had the document, Fairfax called a General Council to discuss it. Henry Ireton had married Cromwell's daughter Bridget; he and his father-in-law were the principal officers facing down the demands of the men. They condemned *The Case of the Army* and indeed, many resented the criticisms of the army which it contained. A committee was chosen to scrutinize it, composed of both officers and Agitators, three of whom were known radicals including Sexby. The aim was to answer the criticisms but mainly to discover the authors. When the next General Council met on 28 October, several new agents had arrived, bringing with them two civilian Levellers, Wildman and Petty. The army leaders expected a discussion of *The Case of the Army*, but instead they were presented with yet another document which was a short and succinct Leveller manifesto entitled *The Agreement of the People*. Fairfax was ill and at Turnham Green, so Cromwell was chairing the meeting. It was harder for him and Ireton to deal with *The Agreement of the People* than *The Case of the Army Truly Stated* because it was not a complaint about the army but a constitutional proposal of a radical kind. It again declared the sovereignty of parliament, but demanded it be elected by all adult males and that *The Agreement* itself should be unalterable. Petty promoted it and hoped the army would adopt it, after which it was read out.

Cromwell took his time to react to this. 'Truly this paper does contain in itt very great alterations of the very Government of the Kingedome ... and what the consequences of such an alteration as this would be ... wise men and godly men ought to consider.' He agreed that 'the expressions in itt are very plausible', but asked, 'How doe wee know if whilest wee are disputing these thinges another companie of men shall gather together, and they shall putt out a paper as plausible perhaps as this?' Even if they decided that it should be put into practice, would people accept it?[11]

Ireton insisted that the army had already put out papers and made engagements; it could not contradict those with a whole new scheme. Lt-Col Goffe had other worries; he moved that 'there might bee a seeking of God in the thinges that now lie before us'. He felt that 'wee have in some thinges wandred from God'. Cromwell reacted immediately to this; he thought 'itt be requisite that we doe itt speedily, and doe itt the first thinge, and that wee doe itt as unitedly as wee can'. For Ireton, 'That which Lieut Col. Goffe offer'd hath [made] a very great impression upon mee; and indeed I must acknowledge to God through him, that, as hee hath severall times spoke in this place, and elsewhere to this purpose, hee hath never spoke butt he hath touched my heart.'[12]

So it was agreed that half of the following day would be given over to prayer, but Wildman and Petty were concerned about *The Agreement* and pushed the discussion on. Colonel Rainsborough spoke clearly and simply: 'For my parte itt may bee thought that I am against the kinge, I am against him or any power that destroy God's people,' and he said, 'That which is deare unto mee is my freedome. Itt is that I would enjoy, and I will enjoy if I can.'[13] Cromwell warned that so radical a change in the constitution could only be instituted through violence, but he hoped that a prayer meeting would bring them to one mind before God.

So on 29 October, half the day was put aside for seeking God – 'let us but search our owne spirits with patience, and looke by the light of God within us'; for reason must be subservient to the spirit of God, not vice versa, said Capt. Clarke.[14] Goffe was concerned as to where the Antichrist was at work. It was foretold in the Gospels that in the last days, Jesus Christ would have a company of saints to bring in his kingdom. The soldiers had engaged to do Christ's work, and some supposed that the last days were upon them as they struggled to create a godly kingdom. But suppose they were setting up those whom God wished to cast down; suppose they were preventing the emergence of the saints. Cromwell was still prevaricating. There was much good in *The Agreement*, but it might break their former engagements and then they were not free to act.

Petty pressed the soldiers to go through their engagements and show what points were at issue. Cromwell said the most important thing was that God should remain with them: 'If God saw it to destroy, nott only kinge and Lords, but all distinctions of degrees – nay if itt goe further, to destroy all property, ... if I see the hand of God in itt I hope I shall with quietnesse acquiesce.'[15] Now that a more profound revolution was envisaged, which might overturn property rights and status, Cromwell was careful. He would always search for God's will, but equally he belonged to the gentry and had property.

So, *The Agreement* was again read out and Ireton led the discussion. He disagreed with full adult male franchise. Mr Petty countered that 'we judge that all inhabitants that have nott lost their birthright should have an equall voice in Elections', and Rainsborough agreed, 'for really I thinke that the poorest hee that is in England hath a life to live as the greatest hee'. All those who lived under a government should give their consent to it. Ireton demurred, saying that only those with 'a permanent fixed interest' in the kingdom should vote, not foreigners. Everyone could drink water, breathe air and walk the highways, but choosing the government was different. Parliament made laws and people who owned land or maintained trade should choose the representatives; that was the fundamental constitution of the kingdom. He might have a small share – 40 shillings worth of property a year – but such a voter was equal to a knight of the shire. If you change that, he argued, you do away with property altogether. Rainsborough argued it out. Why did some men have property and others not? What had the army fought for if people were bound by laws in which they had no voice at all?[16]

Petty hoped that the king and the Lords would be thrown down but property preserved. Cromwell thought that wishful thinking. The franchise could be enlarged but to admit everyone would surely destroy property. Slowly the meeting identified people who would be omitted as voters. Ireton answered Rainsborough's question: 'I tell you what the souldier of the kingedome hath fought for. First, the danger that wee stood was, that one man's will must bee a law.'[17] They had fought for the rights of parliament, not to overturn the constitution. Nor did he believe that people lived by the right of nature, for if they did there would be no property.

Cromwell then criticised Sexby for being divisive. In any case, he thought they were wasting time. Everyone at the meeting wanted the 'Representative' – that is the parliament – mended, but to go as far as the Levellers wanted meant Cromwell might have to withdraw. Sexby was stung and was 'sorry that the Lord hath darkened some soe much as nott to see itt'.[18] Petty reminded them that 'you would use all your indeavours for the liberties of the people'; if the constitution prevented that liberty, then the constitution should be annulled. So here was the nub, said Cromwell. Is the Leveller constitution better than the one we have? Waller said if they did not hurry up and decide, they would be 'kick'd and spurn'd of all the world'.

Ireton thought they might alter the constitution 'from a better to a worse'.[19] So exclusions to the franchise were agreed; servants, those who received alms, apprentices – these were not to vote.

Then the radicals challenged Ireton's *Heads of Proposals*. Under it the king and the Lords could veto legislation, but the radicals thought this a form of tyranny and demanded that these 'negative voices' must be removed. Wildman made a strong case for *The Agreement* but Ireton thought the peace of the kingdom was paramount; there was no security or authority in *The Agreement*, either for the soldiers' rights or for the good of the nation. For Wildman, the restoration of the king would certainly give him back his veto over law and over their own indemnity – they would all end up in court.

On the third day of debate, the officers and the agents met once more and found some common ground. Parliament should be dissolved on 1 September 1648 and then meet biennially from April to September. When it adjourned it should appoint a Council of State to continue its work. The council could call an extraordinary parliament but the king could not. Constituencies would be reorganised into equal sizes. The current Commons should decide on the franchise but enlarge it as much as possible based on the current constitution. Certainly everyone who had fought for parliament should be able to vote, as they had won the war.

The debates continued into November as a split developed regarding the king. Wildman was strongly against a monarch, Lilburne mildly for. Several soldiers talked of the king as 'guilty of all the bloodshed' or 'that man of Blood'.[20] The officers were losing control of the debate and Fairfax's return on 5 November did not restore their command. Rainsborough sent a letter to the Speaker rejecting a letter of Cromwell and Ireton's and this infuriated the latter who stormed out of the meeting. By 8 November, the Leveller agents were pressing for another general rendezvous, but Fairfax and Cromwell used this proposed meeting as an excuse to send the Agitators back to their regiments. They had listened to the men's ideas; now they were moving to regain control. By pressing the Commons for swift payment of arrears, the commanders won over many of the men and when Fairfax called the rendezvous he spread it over three days and held it in three places – the whole army was not to come together. The Levellers protested but the regiments were widely dispersed and Fairfax wanted to speak to each individually.

While they had been debating the future of the kingdom, others had drawn their own conclusions. Nedham had followed all the news coming out of Putney and made some sharp comments. In *Mercurius Pragmaticus* for 19–26 October 1647 he wrote,

> Mr. Cromwell hath [parliament] in a Mill, and grind they must, seeing they are at his Beck, who holds a whip and a Bell over their guilty Heads, and hath a trick or two in his head, to maintain them a Parliament, or

no parliament, when he pleases: So that when he hath used them long enough under the name of a Parliament, then (perhaps) they shall be disbanded several waies, that the Sword-men may stand forever...

For 26 October–2 November:

They are resolved to make us all Princes, in cutting asunder the very sinewes of all government whatsoever by these following positions: as that all Power is originally and essentially in the body of the People.

And for 2 November–9 November 1647:

I perceive they meane to bring his Majesty to the Stake with all speed.
... soveraigne Oliver is content that poor Charles should live still at Hampton, on condition he will be quiet, that is never seeke to be restored again.
It is like to prove true what I told you, that we are not to have much use of kings any longer, because the Saints being made of finer metal, may bruise them in pieces like a potters vessel.

Nedham claimed to have his news from the 'Adjutators' of sixteen regiments but the interpretation was his own.

At Hampton Court, the king had drawn his own conclusions. He had promised not to escape but on 30 October he rescinded his promise. He feared being poisoned and talked to his attendants, Ashburnham and Berkeley, of escape, but his dilemma was acute. If he fled the country he was abandoning his principal kingdom and might never regain any of the three. Nor was there an obvious place to go – foreign princes had not agreed on asylum for him. So he made a muddled escape, leaving Hampton Court at dusk, crossing the Thames by boat and galloping away with Berkeley and Ashburnham. Charles thought ships were ready on the coast but they were not. So he went to the Earl of Southampton's house just outside that city while Berkeley and Ashburnham sounded out Colonel Robert Hammond, the Governor of Carisbrooke Castle on the Isle of Wight. Hammond was a parliamentary commander who had become disturbed by army radicalism and managed to transfer to Carisbrooke where he was removed from the turmoil. His uncle was one of the king's chaplains and at a meeting he had seemed sympathetic to the king. However, giving Charles sanctuary was too bold a step. 'Oh gentlemen,' he told the two royal emissaries when they explained their mission, 'you have undone me.'[21] Instead of abandoning the plan, Berkeley and Ashburnham took Hammond to Charles and thereby compromised both of them. So the king went with Hammond to

Carisbrooke and reopened correspondence with parliament. The members had tired of the king's negotiations; they answered only with an ultimatum.

The Four Bills, presented to Charles on 26 December, would give parliament command of all sea and land forces for twenty years and annul any oaths or declarations made against parliament, among other demands. Parliament refused to negotiate with the king any further until he agreed these terms, but the king had other offers.

Even at Carisbrooke Charles could receive visitors, and the Scottish commissioners soon arrived. The Scots were now offering better terms and would not insist on Charles signing the Covenant. On 26 December, the king signed an agreement with them. In the *Engagement* he did at last come to terms with one faction among his troubled kingdoms, because the Scots were offering an army. In retaliation, parliament passed a Vote of No Addresses, cutting off negotiations.

While the king was making his plans at Carisbrooke, the army leaders were taking back control of their troops. The Levellers too were active; on 9 November, they presented *The Agreement* to parliament, which roundly condemned it. So the Levellers published a letter inciting the soldiers to mutiny, but part of the army was turning towards Fairfax who was offering pay and indemnity if order was restored.

The first rendezvous was held at Corkbush Field, near Ware in Hertfordshire. Fairfax and Cromwell were concerned in case orders had been disobeyed, but in fact only two regiments had discarded their officers and come to Ware without orders. They were strongly Leveller and had copies of *The Agreement* stuck in their hats. Fairfax spoke to each regiment in turn but with the radicals there was no more compromise. Cromwell rode among them himself, plucking *The Agreement* out of their hats. An inquiry was held as to why they were there without orders and eight men were court-martialled, of whom three were sentenced to death but only Richard Arnold shot. The Levellers made a martyr of Arnold, but the second and third rendezvous went off without further disobedience or mutiny.

In Ireland that November, parliament's army fought a major battle at Knocknanuss, near Mallow in north Cork. Inchiquin was victorious over Taafe's army, effectively destroying the Confederate army of Munster. During the battle, Alasdair MacColla was stabbed in the back and with his death the fighting force of the MacDonalds was finally extinguished. Inchiquin, however, was now in a powerful position in the south of Ireland.

Fairfax had regained control of his army. Although the General Council met several more times, the fire had gone out of it. The Levellers were still active but they had failed to take over the army's agenda. Regarding a settlement, momentum seemed to have swung back to parliament, but that was deceptive. While the aims of the New Model Army had been so uncertain, a new royalist party had been forming. There would be war once more.

27

The Second Civil War

The First Civil War had been an attempt to curtail the powers of the king but the second was an attempt to restore him. The Scots provided the main army but much of the second war in Britain was the result of spontaneous uprisings by exasperated people who wanted to be rid of the army and have the king back, along with normal life.

On 19 July 1647, parliament had appointed Fairfax as commander-in-chief of all the forces in England and Wales, including those being mustered to reconquer Ireland and those who would soon be disbanded. John Lambert was to command the northern forces. He had served under Fairfax from the outbreak of war, had fought in the north and south-west for parliament and was prominent in the revolt of the army during 1647. He was a rising star and close to both Fairfax and Cromwell. The standing army was gradually being reduced and paid, which brought down the unbearable costs to government and allowed Fairfax to assert control over the core of the army which remained, for the New Model was still largely intact.

However, none of this could placate the plain people of England, many of whom had seen no reason for the first war and had formed up into Clubmen groups to keep all armies out of their local areas. The monthly assessment was bleeding people dry while royalists had seen their property confiscated and had to compound to get it back; many were insolvent and some lost their property altogether.[1] Disruption to trade had affected merchants and artisans. When the Puritan parliament began clamping down on English people's leisure and pleasure, they hit a nerve.

In 1642, theatres had been closed and a monthly day of fasting and humiliation ordered. Since then, the parliamentary regime had banned maypoles and forbidden dancing, sports or pastimes on the Lord's Day. The Directory for Public Worship had reduced baptism, weddings and funerals to spare events without ritual or festivity. In June 1647, the feasts

Major General John Lambert.

of Christmas, Easter, Whitsun and holy days were abolished. Instead, the second Tuesday of every month was a new secular holiday. In February 1648, the theatre closure became permanent and actors flouting it were to be whipped. The Blasphemy Ordinance had a different aim; under it those denying God, the divinity of Jesus or that the Bible is the word of God were to be imprisoned. If they failed to recant, they were subject to the death penalty. This was an attempt to crush the heterodox ideas which had exploded since the Church of England had collapsed.[2] A Puritan lifestyle and heavy taxation led to revolt against the new regime by the wider populace.

The plain people of Scotland held mixed views. In the Lowlands, where Calvinism was strongly held, the radicalism of the war years had enjoyed support. But here too war had cost money and lives; when Hamilton levied troops in the spring of 1648 there was resistance. The Highlands had been another country throughout, more royalist, partly Catholic and coming out to fight when local loyalties demanded it, not for national issues. Scotland was owed money for the war by England but payment was slow to come in, leaving Scotland's own resources very overstretched.

Ireland had not just been taxed and fought over but starved. Some say the conduct of war in Ireland was influenced by the increasingly ruthless war methods seen in Europe during the Thirty Years War, which was now ending; some argue that Ireland's unsettled political culture meant that conventions of warfare had not been established. But whatever the reason, the war in Ireland was hard on the general population in ways not seen in Britain.[3] Livestock were stolen in their thousands and crops were burned. Alasdair MacColla had burned his way down the glens of Argyll slaughtering Campbell villagers – was this the normal form of warfare among the Gaelic clans? Scorched earth tactics had been used during the Irish Wars under Elizabeth.[4] Whatever caused it, both Inchiquin and his Confederate opponents set fire to harvests and emptied whole baronies of cattle until Ireland began to depopulate swiftly.

So the plain people of the three kingdoms had suffered enough from warfare and most wanted peace, but the New Model, now the army of England, was still 24,000 strong with a political will of its own.[5] If an army is ruling you, and you want to be rid of it, how could you achieve this except with another army?

This is how it seemed to the Scots and Irish, as well as many English people, who made their move in the spring of 1648. The *Engagement* of the Scots was no secret; as soon as Lauderdale and his colleagues returned to Edinburgh after their agreement with Charles and reported to the Committee of Estates, the news was out. The *Engagement* split the committee, with a majority in favour of Hamilton, Lauderdale and support for the king, but Argyll and the kirk party opposed. When parliament met in Edinburgh, with royalist members now returned, it too supported the *Engagement*. Bitterness grew between the factions and several duels occurred.[6]

In retaliation, parliament in London immediately dissolved the Committee of Both Kingdoms and closed down their joint endeavours, but Hamilton and his party were now ascendant in Edinburgh. This time the leaders had switched round; Hamilton the compromiser now led the war party, while Argyll and the kirk opposed.

Ormond had been forbidden further access to the king and left for France. Charles had asked him to consult the queen and Prince Charles, but Ormond also sent his man Barry back to Ireland to sound out Inchiquin. The position in Ireland had altered and Ormond believed the time was right to build a grand alliance for the king. Rinuccini's inflexible policy had split the Catholic party. The nuncio's purpose was to fully reinstate Catholicism in Ireland, even if that meant the island came under French or Spanish rule. After the Confederate victory at Benburb the nuncio had thought they could defeat the Protestants unaided, but late in 1647, while the New Model were debating in Putney, Rinuccini's policy met disaster.

The Earl of Antrim was at the heart of the Confederacy by now, and since the nuncio favoured further war against Scotland Antrim tended to his party. When Alasdair MacColla had returned from Scotland, it was to Antrim at Confederate headquarters that he had made his way, asking to join their Ulster army, but instead he was sent to Munster to fight under Taafe. As a result, he had been in the conflict at Knocknanuss when Taafe unwisely brought Inchiquin to battle, leaving his army decimated and Alasdair MacColla among the dead. Inchiquin's victory in Munster undermined the nuncio's hopes of a full Catholic victory.

The Confederates saw they needed help. They decided to send envoys to the queen, as well as to Spain and the papacy. Antrim was among those chosen to go to Paris; he knew the queen through his wife Katherine who was now in Waterford. Antrim had played many parts during the war, from privateer with rented ships to ally of Strafford and then Ormond, then instigator of Alasdair MacColla's expedition with Montrose. Now he was envoy of the ultra-Catholic party. Antrim was considered ambitious and people believed that he hoped to replace Ormond as Lord Lieutenant, although he had none of Ormond's skills. Nonetheless, Antrim set off with the Confederate emissaries for France.

In Paris, Henrietta-Maria had been given authority by Charles to act for him but the key person was Mazarin. He had already met Ormond, the king's Lord Lieutenant, whom he thought capable and loyal. Henrietta-Maria too took Ormond's advice. She received Antrim and the Confederate envoys graciously but was non-committal. If the king's case was to be saved, troops in Ireland and Scotland were essential and Ormond suggested a strategy to raise them.

Ormond stressed the importance of winning over Inchiquin for the king. The Munster commander was known to be unhappy with the Independents and the recent moves by the English army were disturbing him. As an O'Brien, from a Gaelic Catholic family, the Independents scorned him and preferred his rival Lord Broghill. Westminster had never supplied the forces in Cork properly and now the ascendancy of the Independents and their army was making Inchiquin uncomfortable.

Before the grandees in Paris and Edinburgh could make a move, trouble erupted in South Wales where troops resisting disbandment were supported by their officers and began to demand the restoration of the king and the Book of Common Prayer. They already held Pembroke Castle and now they occupied Tenby. Fairfax sent one of his officers but it was April before he reached West Wales to find that disaffection had grown and South Wales was in revolt against the Puritan regime. Cromwell was ordered down there with five regiments.

It was spring and the fighting season; trouble began to break out across southern England. In March, bonfires were lit in London on the anniversary of the king's accession and passing coaches were stopped, obliging passengers to drink his health. Charles had made an escape attempt but was now a closer prisoner at Carisbrooke Castle, on the Isle of Wight. In April, London's trained bands interfered with boys playing tip-cat in Moorfields. Apprentices took offence at this and attacked the city forces until a mob began shouting for King Charles. Around this time, the fifteen-year-old James, Duke of York escaped from St James's Palace and was spirited away to Gravesend and the Netherlands. His sister, Princess Elizabeth, and the nine-year-old Henry, Duke of Gloucester were left behind as captives.

Inchiquin declared for the king on 3 April 1648 and by late May had signed a truce with the Confederates. Rinuccini was outraged that his Catholic Confederates could ally with the man who burned Cashel and killed priests, but by excommunicating all those who supported the truce he caused a painful split in the Confederacy.

Meanwhile, a riot broke out in Norwich; then 2,000 people from Essex brought a petition demanding the restoration of the king and the disbanding of the army. On 12 May, a riot broke out at Bury St Edmunds over a maypole and shortly afterwards a procession with a petition in Surrey was met by troops, leading to casualties. It was followed by a popular rising in Kent and defection of part of the fleet to the king, under cover of which royalists took several coastal castles.

Cromwell was on the Welsh Borders, marching towards Pembroke, while Fairfax, who had been ordered north by parliament to meet the Scots, instead marched to Kent and dispersed a royalist army. The mood in London was uncertain. The Derby House Committee shifted their forces, and there was fighting at Kingston. By early June there were royalist risings in Cornwall, north Wales, Northamptonshire and Lincolnshire. Pontefract Castle had been taken for the king, and East Anglia, which had been the heartland of parliament's cause, was now marked by sporadic royalist risings. By then, Fairfax had sent Waller to Cornwall and Lambert to the north, while he turned to Colchester in Essex. Then nine more ships joined the royalists. The Puritan grip was weakening.

Royalists had gathered in Colchester, which they could strongly defend; their numbers were growing and the naval revolt threatened the Puritans' supremacy in the south-east. Half the New Model was with Cromwell in Wales, yet London was in turmoil. Fairfax could not leave the south-east, since London itself was vulnerable. Instead he settled down to a long siege of Colchester.

On 8 July, the Duke of Hamilton entered England at the head of a Scottish army of 10,500 men. He was not a natural soldier but Montrose was in Brussels and Hamilton had to make good on the *Engagement* for his king and had pulled together a royalist army. The General Assembly of the kirk thundered but Hamilton made his way slowly south. English royalists had already come north and managed to take the fortresses of Berwick and Carlisle, which controlled the border.

Prince Charles was now eighteen, a well-made young man who was taller and sturdier than his diminutive parents. As war broke out again, he set off hastily to the Netherlands where the ships now loyal to his father collected him and sailed into the mouth of the Thames, blocking trading vessels and aggravating the great men of the City who now hardly knew whose enemy they were, between royalists, the New Model and the vexations with parliament over London's defences.

At the end of July, parliament agreed to send commissioners to Newport on the Isle of Wight to negotiate a treaty with the king. Unrest in England had not created a royalist army which could rival Fairfax's forces, but trouble was widely spread and the New Model menaced by threats – in Portsmouth, Oxford, Devon and Cornwall. Cromwell was still in Wales as his siege train had sunk in the mouth of the Severn, delaying his attack on Pembroke Castle.

Cromwell had become a focus of suspicion for all those who feared the Independents. It was apparently to aggravate Cromwell that the Houses of Parliament voted to free John Lilburne. *Mercurius Pragmaticus* praised Lilburne's 'late moderation' which had impressed the moderates in parliament so much that 'they all joined together against Cromwell's faction'. Nedham expected that 'it will not be long ere Mr Speaker and Noll Cromwell be both brought to the stake' now that Lilburne was loose 'to have a bout with them'.[7] Nedham was over-optimistic.

Hamilton was moving slowly, waiting for artillery and for part of Monro's forces from Ulster which were coming over to join him. Hamilton had stayed to the west of the Pennines to make this rendezvous but also to join Langdale with his 4,000 men and hoping to meet Byron who was in north Wales. At Kendal, Hamilton lingered until George Monro caught up with him.

Pembroke Castle surrendered on 11 July, leaving Cromwell free to go north to confront the Scots. He marched first to Leicester to pick up artillery, before moving further north to join Lambert at the siege of Pontefract in Yorkshire. Lambert had bolstered his few regiments by recruiting, but all he could do against the Scots was to block the passes which they might use if they tried to cross into Yorkshire. Meanwhile Cromwell brought his troops up the eastern side of the Pennines. They were tired and ragged, marching steadily but without haste, stopping at Leicester to recruit. At Nottingham they got new shoes and stockings, so they pushed on to Doncaster where they waited three days to pick up the artillery train from Hull. It had been a long march from south-west Wales but they moved north again to Knaresborough, where they met Lambert and learned a little of the enemy's dispositions.

Hamilton had far greater numbers than Cromwell. Monro joined him at Kendal and, with Langdale's troops, Hamilton commanded over 20,000 men and hoped that when he reached the Midlands he would pick up a surge of royalism. Cromwell had around 8,600 men and no precise information about the Scots army, but his urgent aim was to break Hamilton's forces before they got further south. By a swift movement across the Pennines, Cromwell achieved one of his most daring and significant victories.[8]

The Scots, unaware of how close Cromwell was, were moving south through Lancashire. The River Ribble runs south-west from the Pennines to the coast and Preston lies a little north of the riverbank. The road ran through Preston to a bridge just south of the town. On the evening of 17 August, the duke was still north of the river at Preston, while part of his army, including most of the horse, had crossed the Ribble and was strung out along the road to the south. Monro was slightly further north than Hamilton. Langdale was to the east, upriver and higher in the hills to act as a protecting flank. New Model scouts had spied him, and in response Cromwell urged his men up over the hills in a fast two-day crossing. Always swift to size up his best chance, Cromwell's next move was crucial to his victory. He decided to not only make Hamilton fight but also to cut off his retreat to the north where Monro might reinforce him. By risky but decisive action, he could break the Scottish forces into two.

On the morning of the 17th, Hamilton sent most of his forces across the river to join the vanguard, leaving two infantry brigades and around 1,500 horse with the duke at Preston. Monro was still to his north. The Scottish infantry under Baillie were crossing the Ribble as, upriver in the hills, Cromwell attacked the flanking royalists. Langdale was a tough and experienced soldier; his forces stood their ground for four hours, but eventually they could not hold the roundheads off any longer and were driven back. Cromwell had the benefit of surprise – Hamilton thought him 200 miles away and even when news of the attack reached him at Preston he at first assumed it was a minor parliamentarian leader.

Cromwell swept down the valley into Preston, routed the troops left in the town and fought for control of the bridge over the Ribble. Hamilton led the cavalry but Cromwell gained the bridge. Hamilton rejoined his army by swimming the river. He still had the numbers but now he was divided from Monro and his retreat north was blocked. By then Cromwell already had 4,000 prisoners, a significant diminution of the Scots forces. Unable to muster his troops, Hamilton retreated south with Cromwell following him. Despite attacks from the Scottish rearguard cavalry, Cromwell caught up with Hamilton at Winwick, near Warrington, where the Scots stood their ground bravely, but they had lost their ammunition train and after several hours they broke ranks, with 3,000 men dead or captured. Hamilton's men were inexperienced, with low morale, while Cromwell's troops were

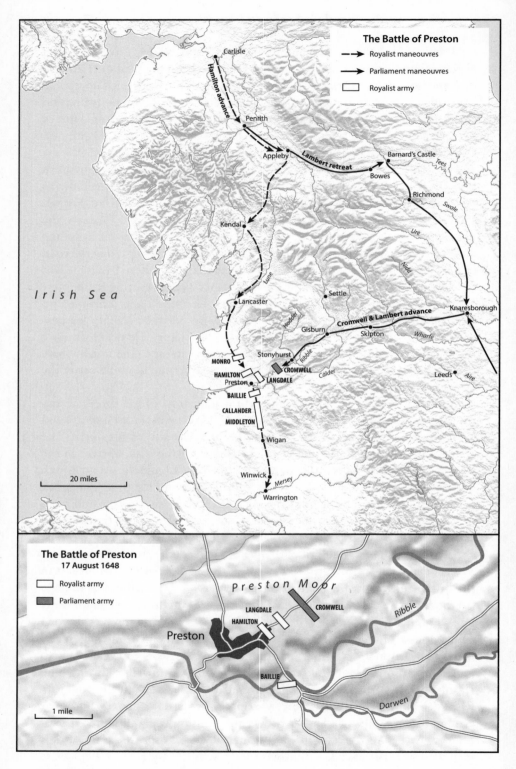

The Battle of Preston, 1648.

some of the toughest fighters in Europe. Another 4,000 Scots under Baillie surrendered. Cromwell had become known as Ironsides but after Preston the name was given to his fighting force as well.

On 20 August, Cromwell wrote to Speaker Lenthall: 'Sir, I have sent up this gentleman to give you an account of the great and good hand of God towards you, in the late victory obtained against the enemy in these parts.'[9] From Warrington, Cromwell was writing a long, detailed account of his actions since meeting Lambert at Knaresborough. Despite the swift movements and heavy fighting, Cromwell's reports after battle always have a sharp brilliance that the adrenalin of victory gave. He was a man of fifty now, tough and increasingly confident, sure of his excellence as a war leader and tactician but also inspired by the marks of God's favour which he saw in every victory. His enemy was now split. Cromwell would go north after Monro, while Lambert closed with Hamilton.

'The Duke is marching with his remaining Horse, which are three thousand towards Namptwich,' he told Lenthall. The local people, including the gentry, were against the Scots, taking them prisoner or killing them. 'Most of the nobility of Scotland are with the Duke,' Cromwell wrote. 'If I had a thousand horse that could but trot thirty miles, I should not doubt but to give a very good account of them, but truly we are so harassed and haggled out in this business, that we are not able to do more than walk at an easy pace after them.'[10]

Monro retreated across the border into Scotland but Hamilton's soldiers mutinied at Uttoxeter and the duke surrendered to Lambert on condition of their lives. For a man of compromise, he had proved himself brave in the field but he had neither good troops nor military skills. In December, Hamilton was sent as prisoner to Windsor Castle where he briefly saw the king, but he did not long outlive him.[11]

The great fortresses of England were crucial to the ultimate victors of the war. Pontefract Castle in Yorkshire held out against the roundheads, as did Colchester in Essex, but the royalist insurgency no longer had any hope of success. Conditions in Colchester were hard and in late August terms of surrender were agreed; the leaders, however, were shot. There was talk of Prince Charles sailing to Scotland, but no agreement was reached as he would have to take the Covenant and the prince returned to the Netherlands. In the south-west of Scotland, where Presbyterianism was at its most stern and unbending, the people of Dumfries and Galloway gathered in a fury against the summer campaign. Why they were the most obdurate Calvinists is not clear. Some historians say it was local leadership, but the proximity of Ulster seems to be the reason. There was considerable migration in both directions; it was here that Catholicism and Calvinism met face to face, both in armies, in landownership and in culture.[12] Here and in Ulster, religious feeling was utterly polarised.

Enraged at Hamilton's campaign, the people of south-west Scotland gathered to march on Edinburgh. They were of all classes, and half were on horseback. Known as the Whiggamore Raid, it soon became a serious threat. Once Argyll and his troops joined the marchers, the Whiggamores became a powerful and vengeful force. With the help of the Covenanting generals they swept into Edinburgh and took the castle. The Committee of Estates no longer had authority and withdrew to Stirling. Their only remaining troops were those under George Monro, but their morale was low after their retreat; they had little support and were not strong enough to fight. The Engagers had had their moment and lost; they resigned their authority over government in Scotland. The Whiggamore Raid showed the Scottish tide turning once more towards the kirk party. Monro's troops aimed to return to Ulster but Monck moved swiftly to take the great fortresses there, blocking their retreat across the North Channel. Drifting in the Lowlands, Monro's men were cut up by the Whiggamores.

By late September, Cromwell was at the Scottish border. Scotland had invaded and England would respond. How would Argyll react now that English forces were moving north? He engineered the surrender of the fortresses of Berwick and Carlisle to the English but this was not enough for Cromwell, who judged the situation in Scotland still a threat. There were Engagers in arms, royalists arming in the Highlands, and the Whiggamores – as Covenanters – were sworn to uphold the king.

Cromwell believed that Scotland was unstable and a threat to England. He sent Lambert on ahead with several regiments while he waited for the consent of parliament to proceed. Then he marched north. Argyll met him at the border and tried to prevent him entering Scotland, but Cromwell reached the Scottish capital without resistance. By 4 October, the New Model leaders were in Edinburgh, where Cromwell supped with Argyll and came to an accommodation. Both countries had invaded the other and victory for one could mean vassalage for the loser. Sovereignty was at stake. The Covenanters might control governance in Edinburgh, but Argyll and the kirk did not have full control of their country; Scotland was not homogenous and was swithering back and forth in its loyalties. Between Argyll and Cromwell there was no common religious bond but the marquis saw he needed the support of the New Model army to maintain order and he asked Cromwell to leave some troops behind when he left. So, the two leaders made an uneasy accord; there was little sympathy between the Scottish Presbyterian and the English Independent but to their enemies they were both Puritans.

Cromwell left Lambert to enforce discipline in the Scottish Lowlands while he rode south to stamp out royalism in the north of England and to force the surrender of Pontefract. There he lingered as irrevocable decisions were taken further south.

While Cromwell was asserting control in Edinburgh, Irish factions made common cause. Ormond returned to Ireland, landing in Cork on 30 September to ally with Inchiquin and to pursue negotiations with the Confederates. As the king's party in Britain collapsed, Irish people of almost all factions saw how vulnerable they had become to the Puritans who now held power in England. Against a far more formidable enemy than the one they had first risen against, they started to pull together. However, Protestant officers were unhappy about an alliance with Catholics, which delayed agreement. The Old English still pressed for religious concessions but tended towards allegiance to the king. Ulstermen like O'Neill held out for the nuncio but most of the Confederacy was shifting. At the penultimate moment, Ireland was coming together against a common and formidable enemy.

In London, parliament wanted an immediate settlement with the king. Havering and negotiating had been going on for over two years and all it had brought was a resurgence of war. For Charles, the defeat at Preston was the end of a cherished hope – that Scotland would regain for him his three crowns. When commissioners arrived at Newport in the Isle of Wight for new negotiations, they had an easier time than the various groups who had wrangled with Charles over the previous years. He still insisted on consulting lawyers, but by mid-November he had made large concessions – far larger than before. On key points he made counter-proposals, but Newport offered a real chance of reinstatement, albeit with greatly reduced powers.

Some of Charles's antagonists believed that negotiations were pointless. Once restored, what guarantee was there that he would keep to the terms of any treaty? The Levellers watched as all their cherished hopes drifted away – Newport would bring none of their aims. Nor did the army see its goals being met.

The Levellers were holding regular meetings at the Nag's Head tavern in London. Lilburne had been let out of prison and was playing a leading role in discussions. The Levellers saw the proposed Newport Treaty as a dangerous waste. Now was the crucial moment, the time when a genuine parliament on a wide franchise could be set up; now was their chance to get an *Agreement of the People* on the form of government.

The army was more concerned about the power of the king. If he was restored, they would be dangerously exposed. They had taken up arms against him, many of them early in the conflict, and unlike the earls of Essex and Manchester they had fought to the finish. If Charles was restored, given his popularity and the deep resentment against the army, his position would be strong and theirs very weak. They had fought to curb his power and make sure that England's limited monarchy was not turned into an absolute one, by Charles or any other monarch. It must be proved now, once and for all, that no king was above the law, or they would end up like the French under Henrietta-Maria's nephew, with no representation at all.

Fairfax was in the south-east all through the autumn and Henry Ireton, Commissary General of Horse, was with him on the campaign. After the fall of Colchester, Fairfax moved his headquarters back to St Albans. It was harvest time. Fairfax spent the early autumn trying to get his men paid but he would not intervene in parliament's negotiations. Cromwell was still in the north. So as the army became once more drawn into politics and into discussions with the Levellers, it was Ireton who led the talks on behalf of the army.

Henry Ireton came from a similar background and region to Cromwell. His family were strongly Puritan, which, combined with his training as a lawyer, austere personality and unbending will, gave him a clear purpose. He also had intellectual powers well suited to framing a new constitution. Ireton had met Cromwell early in the war and in 1643 he became deputy governor of Ely under Cromwell where he tried to shape the isle into a godly commonwealth. He fought at Marston Moor and Naseby. His marriage to Oliver's daughter Bridget Cromwell occurred at the height of the Puritans' triumph after the fall of Oxford in 1646. In his views and aims, Ireton was more speculative than his father-in-law and cast about looking for new solutions to Britain's constitutional struggle; but now, in the tense and charged autumn of 1648, Ireton lacked the personal support of Cromwell and ran into opposition from Fairfax. Ireton wanted to prevent the Newport Treaty and he was not alone in that. Pamphlets and petitions were printed which objected both to the restoration of Charles and to the current constitution, however much power was transferred to parliament. There was a tide of opinion which demanded justice, that the author of the nations' misfortunes should be held accountable and that a new direction should be taken.[13]

The Levellers were petitioning parliament in favour of a new constitutional arrangement, but they got no response. Edmund Ludlow, who had fought in the war before becoming an MP and was an uncompromising Independent, was determined that the Newport deal should not go through and warned Fairfax against it. Frustrated, he turned to Ireton, who also spoke to Fairfax and begged him to purge the Commons so that real change could occur. Fairfax had always supported parliament's established role, both as his employer and as the government in the absence of the king. There was no change now; Fairfax deferred to parliament. So Ireton offered his resignation, which Fairfax refused.

The castles and palaces of London and the south-east had fallen into parliament's hands early in the war, and Windsor's turn had come in 1642. It was to this army stronghold that Ireton withdrew, perplexed, late in 1648, to ponder his ideas and strategy. What emerged was his *Remonstrance of the Army*. In it, Ireton had shifted position further. If the king was restored, he might not honour treaties made in captivity and he would have popular support. Therefore, there must be a different basis for government. A supreme council or parliament, elected on a wide franchise, should make law and exercise judicial power. Charles was to be made subject to those laws.

Ireton was turning now to the 'sovereignty of the people', the key Leveller demand, as his basis. This was not a Leveller invention but a key topic among philosophers of the day. In the hands of a senior army commander, it had great force.

While Ireton was puzzling over the constitution at Windsor and Ormond was in Ireland attempting to unite all factions against the Puritans, others were making plans for a settlement. To strengthen their position and align their aims, probably at the suggestion of Cromwell, the army began talks with the Levellers. At first, a few soldiers and Agitators joined the Leveller meetings at the Nag's Head. Some were uncompromising, announcing that the first thing to do 'was to cut off the king's head'. Others were uncertain, unwilling to act or wrestling with the complex legal arguments.[14]

From September until late November, Charles was in Newport, staying at the mayor's house while negotiating with parliament's commissioners. His options had narrowed. Ireland might rise but Scotland had already fallen in his cause. He agreed to many of parliament's demands but still held out over bishops and the penalties to be imposed on his supporters. The Independents began to fear that Charles would be removed from Newport and reinstated as king before any of their plans came to fruition. The Treaty of Westphalia was signed that month, bringing the Thirty Years War to an end. That would relieve France of pressure and Mazarin might now send aid to Charles, although France was still at war with Spain and was facing a rising of its own, the Fronde. Despite Henrietta-Maria's urgent efforts, Mazarin found no spare resources for her English husband. Still, to the Independents, France now seemed a threat.

However, the negotiations in Newport dragged on and the time allowed was twice extended. If agreement was reached parliament would restore the king to power, but they were concerned that Charles still had an army in Ireland under Ormond's command and demanded that the king disown it. Charles had already warned Ormond not to accept commands which he made under duress and in captivity, but in any case he stalled with the commissioners on this point. All sides became exhausted and tensions rose.

When Ireton emerged from Windsor, he had composed his *Remonstrance*. It addressed the army's dilemma directly. For men who had fought for the rule of law, the solution to their nation's woes must be legal. But there was no way to bring the king to justice within English law – justice was dispensed by the crown and any attack on the king would be treason. Ireton found an argument to outweigh that. He said that public safety justified the army entering politics, that the judgement of heaven was against the royalists and that the king had broken his covenant to protect the people's rights and liberties. This nullified the duty of his people to obey him. Instead, parliament would be able to declare certain acts illegal, even though they were committed in the past. The main demand of Ireton's *Remonstrance* was that the king must be brought to justice.

When Fairfax called a Council of Officers – not the General Council of the Army which had met at Putney and which incorporated more ranks and more Levellers, but the original army command – the officers were concerned that they would be held responsible for the war, but they urged a settlement, for the peace of the kingdom. Fairfax agreed to support parliament's peace proposals, which were then being finalised with the king. However, the army wanted to make its own overtures to Charles so that it could make sure its position was protected. The officers took a few days to confer.

Meanwhile, the Nag's Head meetings had developed into more serious and high-level discussions. Ireton met the Levellers on 15 November and accepted that the *Remonstrance* should be modified to include some of their aims. A committee was to be set up with four representatives each from the Levellers, the army, London Independents and MPs. Ireton's *Remonstrance* was approved by the Council of Officers and sent to the Commons. The army was demanding the king be brought to justice.

Cromwell was still in Yorkshire. His protracted absence in the north was only partly explained by military demands. After he left Edinburgh, he put down residual royalist action in the north and set up garrisons there. He then took command of the siege of Pontefract but even when Lambert arrived there in mid-November, Cromwell delayed going south, even though the future of the army and the kingdom were being decided. He delayed because one of his periods of indecision had engulfed him.

For the radicals in the south, much now depended on Colonel Robert Hammond, in whose custody Charles remained and whose allegiances were mixed. Would he obey parliament or the army? Cromwell wrote two letters to the governor of Carisbrooke, dated 6 and 25 November. Hammond was related to Cromwell through the Hampdens, but also to Charles's chaplain, and had already left active service due to unease over army action. Cromwell was very fond of the young man and the letters are affectionate, in Cromwell's customary vein. On the 6th he told Hammond that 'peace is only good when we receive it out of our Father's hand, most dangerous to go against the will of God to attain it. War is good, when led to it by our Father; most evil when it comes from the lusts that are in our members.'[15] Cromwell was mulling over the factions in parliament and how to make a workable accord with the Presbyterians and made no indication of an Independent solution by the army.

The Council of Officers sent its demands to the king on 16 November. These, unlike other proposals put to him, required permanent changes to the constitution: parliament would be reformed and Charles would lose control of both the army and the militia, as well as appointment of officials for ten years which would stop his nullifying the settlement – the army's main fear. The king was unlikely to accept these terms and in fact, he rejected them the following day. Having approached the king and been rebuffed, the officers felt increasingly free to act.[16]

Ireton's *Remonstrance* was presented to the Commons on 20 November. If Cromwell had not seen it, he certainly knew that the army was against the Newport Treaty and looking for justice because he wrote to Fairfax that 'I find a very great sense in the officers of the regiments of the sufferings and the ruin of this poor kingdom, and in them all a very great zeal to have impartial justice done upon Offenders; and I must confess, I do in all, from my heart, concur with them'.[17]

When he wrote to Hammond again five days later, the tone was still sympathetic, advising Hammond to 'seek to know the mind of God in all that chain of Providence, whereby God brought thee thither, and that person to thee' – meaning, it seems, the king. Cromwell continues, 'And then tell me, whether there be not some glorious and high meaning in all this, above what thou hast yet attained? And, laying aside thy fleshy reason, seek of the Lord to teach thee what this is; and He will do it. I dare be positive to say, it is not that the wicked should be exalted.'

Then he asks whether their institutions truly are in accordance with God. Is *Salus Populi* – the safety of the people – a sound principle? Will the expected Newport Treaty bring that safety or throw everything away? Hammond should consider 'whether this Army be not a lawful power, called by God to oppose and fight against the King'. He asks Hammond to 'look into providences ... they hang so together; have been so constant'. He writes of 'malice against God's people, now called Saints', yet the saints in arms have been blessed by providence and 'in this poor Army, wherein the great God has vouchsafed to appear'.[18] The letter puts forwards dilemmas – spiritual and political – which both Cromwell and Hammond must resolve. 'We in this northern army were in a waiting posture, desiring to see what the Lord would lead us to. And a Declaration is put out, at which many are shaken: although we could perhaps have wished the stay of it till after the treaty', for many wanted parliament to conclude their pact with the king before the army published its manifesto. Cromwell was mulling over his moral position, waiting to see how politics played out and struggling with his conscience until some action showed him the will of God. He was also testing Hammond.

Meanwhile, after the Prince of Wales returned to France, his cousin Prince Rupert took over the fleet. Several forces were undermining the position of the New Model Army: Rupert, Ireland and the Newport Treaty. Irish forces were coming together under Ormond, and at any moment parliament might restore the king.

There were signs that Charles was planning to escape, and Rupert's presence with the fleet made this more possible and more threatening. Ireton and his allies wrote to Robert Hammond demanding that he prevent parliament taking possession of the king. The Commons had pushed aside the army's *Remonstrance* with its demand for justice; they would consider the army's political theories later, when they had dealt with the king's answer to their own proposals for a settlement.

Pressure was mounting on Fairfax. On 15 November, the Commons voted to bring Charles to London for a personal treaty. On 22 November, the army moved from St Albans to Windsor and, in those tense winter days, Fairfax issued orders to Hammond to return to army HQ. Hammond was torn between his duty to his general and his duty to parliament; he offered to resign his post but not to change the terms of the king's imprisonment and he reiterated his duty to parliament. Soldiers were sent to the Isle of Wight to escort Hammond back to army HQ. Reluctantly, he left Charles at Carisbrooke with orders to his juniors to prevent the removal of the king, and set out for Windsor. At Farnham he received an order from parliament to return to Carisbrooke, but before he could comply he was arrested by the army. Once more the struggle for the constitution had become a tussle over the custody of the king.

Ireton and Lilburne too were tussling. There was to be a committee – Lilburne thought Ireton had agreed but Ireton was in bed with his wife, Bridget, when the message was delivered. Later there seemed to have been a misunderstanding. One thing about which there was no misunderstanding was men with arms. Now that matters were coming to a head, troops were sent to the Isle of Wight to take control of the monarch.

When he had arrived breathlessly at Holmby that summer's day two years earlier, Cornet Joyce had been courteous and they had set off in good humour to a royal lodge. This time the treatment of the king was to be very different.

28

The Death of the King

The army would wait no longer. They intended to prevent parliament's treaty with Charles and to take custody of the king. Ireton had determined to bring the king to justice, although Fairfax and Cromwell were ambivalent, the latter still delaying in the north. For Charles, the stay in Newport had been pleasant – he had been able to ride out and had his trusted friends and chaplains – but the negotiations were painful; either he must concede most of his powers or he should try once more to escape. He knew the army was restless and his safety increasingly threatened. When he at last came to an agreement with the parliamentary commissioners and parted from them on 27 November, he had conceded to thirty-eight of their demands in return for four points of his own – under the Treaty of Newport, the king's powers would be much reduced.

The commissioners returned to London and Charles was taken back to Carisbrooke Castle. Robert Hammond, the governor, had become sympathetic to the king, but he had been arrested by the army on 28 November, in contravention of orders from parliament, and taken to army headquarters at Windsor. Fairfax was being pushed by strong voices among his men, notably Henry Ireton who now sent troops to Carisbrooke. Cromwell was lingering in Yorkshire, ostensibly leading the siege of Pontefract despite Lambert's presence there. On 28 November, Fairfax ordered his lieutenant general to come south but still Cromwell delayed, spending a week travelling, unlike his swift journeys when moving into battle.

On 29 November, two radical officers with 2,000 infantrymen arrived on the Isle of Wight and surrounded Carisbrooke. The king and his attendants were alarmed and Charles was urged to escape but he refused, saying he had given his word and the attempt would fail. Like Hammond, the garrison commanders at Carisbrooke and their men had confused loyalties and some were sympathetic to the king. It made no difference, as the soldiers who arrived with Cobbett and Merryman knew their orders and were soon within the building where the king lodged. From now on Charles would have little privacy or safety, as the army was passing beyond patience and respect into a revolutionary frame of mind.

At daybreak on 1 December, soldiers pushed into the king's rooms, told Charles that he was leaving for Hurst Castle and hurried him to a waiting carriage before he could eat breakfast. Rolph, an ardent Leveller and one of the new officers, tried to get into the coach but Charles pushed him back. 'It has not come to that yet,' he told Rolph as his own attendants climbed in. He was taken to a boat which made the three-hour crossing to the Hampshire coast. Hurst Castle is a fortress on a spit of land, built by Henry VIII to guard the Solent. It was a grim place without grounds or domestic comfort. As a harbinger of his future, his arrival there on a winter morning must have seemed bleak, but now that his opponents were closing in on him Charles kept his bearing with growing grace and fortitude. His life was now threatened and his mind was shifting as he prepared himself. The governor was rude to him but was reprimanded by one of the new officers. The king's rooms were small and so dark he needed candles at midday. His only exercise was along the stony beach with his two companions, Sir Thomas Herbert and James Harrington.

Getting control of the king was only the first step for the army. They could break off contact between Charles and parliament but the country needed a government and a settlement. Ireton had demanded the king be brought to trial. New constitutions had been discussed the year before, and since his release from prison Lilburne had been loudly promoting the *Agreement of the People*, but in reality a constitution existed, a long-established one, at the apex of which was the king. If he was to be brought to trial, what body could do so and how was the king's power to be redistributed? Parliament was the obvious institution to use but the army wanted parliament dissolved, while the Commons was trying to reinstate the king. There was a stagnation of power which threatened to turn into a breakdown.

The situation was critical, a decision was urgently needed and the officers were pressing for action. Yet Cromwell was still on his way back from Yorkshire. When the newsbooks speculated on the army's bid for power, Fairfax was not mentioned – the suspect was always Cromwell, Lieutenant General of Horse and the triumphant victor of Naseby and Preston. Yet at this crucial moment he delayed, allowed his son-in-law Ireton to drive the arguments in the Council of Officers and was careful to arrive in London only after the army had acted. In that week between the king's removal to Hurst Castle and Cromwell's arrival in London, both parliament and the army made their decisions.

In Scotland, Argyll had given an example that the army planned to follow. Once he controlled the Committee of Estates again, the marquis ordered the dissolution of parliament and new elections, but in England parliament had awarded itself the power over its own dissolution. However, the army was increasingly radical; not only Leveller views but expectations of the Second Coming were growing. Colonel Thomas Harrison, a leading millenarian, told Lilburne quite plainly that the army had made up its mind to put the king to death, either under martial law or by uprooting parliament.

It was inevitable that the most radical groups would come together at this moment. The army had possession of the king and was threatening parliament; now the informal talks between the Levellers and army officers became concrete. The discussions picked up the ideas discussed in Putney the year before but now there was no talk of preventing the king's negative voice – now there was no mention of a king. The question was how to create a new executive, structure parliament and achieve a separation of powers.

Lilburne had influence in the army and he wanted the people's rights guaranteed by a new constitution first – before parliament was dissolved or martial law imposed. Otherwise, he would not trust the army. Lilburne wanted the *Agreement of the People* put to a popular vote. Harrison and Ireton seemed to agree but really everything was in flux. The Levellers could not hammer down a firm agreement. The proposed constitutional committee – of officers, City Independents, MPs and Levellers – did meet but was never properly formed. The Levellers wanted irrevocable clauses in any new constitution – if it could be tinkered with by future parliaments, it was not worthwhile – but the committee refused to bind the whole electorate indefinitely.

The Commons had two different and important documents before it: Ireton's *Remonstrance* and their Newport Treaty with the king. It chose the latter. This angered the army and once more Fairfax led his men on a march into London while issuing a demand that corrupt members withdraw. On 1 December, as radical officers removed the king from Carisbrooke, the Commons rejected Ireton's *Remonstrance* and intensively debated the terms agreed with Charles at Newport. Troops were already marching towards London; by the evening of 1 December, Fairfax had 7,000 men formed up in Hyde Park. The following day, troops filled the streets from Westminster to Ludgate. Fairfax demanded £40,000 in arrears of assessment from the City and set up his headquarters in Whitehall. The army had taken over the capital and this time they were not leaving.

Yet the Commons continued their business. After a twenty-four-hour session, on 5 December they voted in favour of the Newport Treaty with the king. Lilburne had been at Windsor negotiating with his committee, but when the army marched into London he moved to Whitehall to continue discussions. At last the struggle for power had come to the centre of government and shown its hand. In those few highly charged December days, the army took control of parliament and reshaped it.

The army officers were determined to prevent the Newport Treaty and the reinstatement of the king. They had power now and they planned a new constitution. While it was being agreed, parliament must be either purged or dissolved. The army officers wanted a dissolution – a purge was utterly illegal and parliament had forfeited its trust – but a dissolution would leave a power vacuum. They therefore agreed to purge parliament, retaining only members who were sympathetic to their aims.[1]

Without any authority from Fairfax, soldiers moved into the Palace of Westminster early on the morning of 6 December. By seven o'clock they were in Westminster Hall and at the entrance to the House of Commons. In the lobby stood Colonel Pride with a list in his hand. Beside him was Lord Grey of Groby to identify the members whom the army had decided to exclude.

Some MPs were allowed to enter, some were turned back and others were detained. The two latter groups were identified by their record – if their votes had been obnoxious to the army they were purged. The detained members were taken to a tavern that night where they slept on benches and chairs. After several days, most were released but some were held for two weeks. Forty-five members were held and another ninety-six refused entry – 143 in all were subject to Pride's Purge. When the king had come to arrest five members, there had been uproar at his abuse of parliament; now that the army was the arresting officer, less resistance was offered. Many members, although not purged, absented themselves anyway out of either fear or disapproval, so that over the next few days business was difficult as there were too few MPs to make a quorum.

Late on 6 December, just after the purge had been completed, Cromwell rode into London. He said he had not 'been acquainted with this design; yet, since it was done, he was glad of it, and would endeavour to maintain it' – or so it was recorded in Ludlow's *Memoirs*, which were not always reliable.[2] Cromwell took his seat in the Commons and was thanked for his victories, as this was his first appearance in the House since the battle of Preston. Fairfax meanwhile extracted the £40,000 from the City of London, partly by removing it from various guild buildings and partly by quartering troops on the citizens.

Parliament had been reduced to a small group who agreed with the army's aims. The king was in a fortress on a sandbar in Hampshire. The army had power, but even now the officers were in a quandary, especially Commander-in-Chief Fairfax and his lieutenant general, Oliver Cromwell. It was essential to hold the army together because if it fractured they would lose all they had gained and England might break into anarchy.

The officers had little time. Leveller ideas made their own men restive. Parliament had been purged, leaving only a Rump of members, and English hearts and minds had not been won. Argyll and the Whiggamores might hold Scotland but their loyalty to the New Model leaders was weak; they disliked and distrusted the religious diversity of the Independents. In Ireland, Colonel Michael Jones held Dublin for parliament but most of the other forces were coalescing behind Ormond, with Catholics hoping to regain their positions of influence. To a godly English eye, Ireland looked utterly perilous. Decisions had to be made and action taken. Prince Rupert had been put in charge of the royalist fleet and was widely expected to combine with Ormond's growing land forces in Ireland. If Charles retained any of his powers, he would soon build on those to regain all. Ireton, the senior officers and the Levellers drew up their blueprint for a form of government in which there was no king.

In reality, Ormond's task was not easy. Inchiquin's officers were Protestant and feared a Catholic revival; the rift between Catholic and Protestant was a hard chasm to bridge. Ormond, however, had an authority which reached beyond sects, and when messages arrived from the Pope they were not as uncompromising as Rinuccini. Irish forces were coming together.

To the army leaders in London, the situation was threatening and urgent. In taking possession of the king and purging parliament, they had taken a forward position from which there was no viable retreat.

The *Agreement* was nearing completion. On 10 December, after intense debates between Ireton and Lilburne, their text was agreed and sent to the Council of Officers for their consideration. On 15 December, Lilburne published the text and was furious when the officers spent three weeks altering it before presenting it to parliament. But these were strange, highly charged days. Within the Palace of Westminster, soldiers kept guard until 12 December to make sure no delinquent members crept in. Within the palace, the Commons was a small, nervous group. They sent a message to Fairfax asking him to justify the purge but they received no reply.

The army had turned its attention to the man they held responsible for the conflict. On 15 December, the Council of Officers resolved to bring Charles to justice; two days later Colonel Thomas Harrison rode down to Hurst Castle to fetch the king. News of the colonel's arrival alarmed Charles and his gentlemen; Harrison had previously threatened assassination, so the king was pleased to discover that he was to be moved to Windsor. He would escape the forbidding darkness of Hurst, ride out along the highways and arrive at one of the royal castles, although it was now army headquarters. The Duke of Hamilton was already there, held at the army's pleasure.

At Winchester, Charles was welcomed by the mayor and citizens before moving on to Farnham and Bagshot, from whence he came to Windsor. He was housed in his old rooms and seemed strangely unconcerned about the plans of his captors, keeping melon seed to plant in the spring. He still hoped that Ormond had the military strength to overcome 'the rebels', but at Hurst he had written that he expected the worst and at Windsor he spent his mornings at prayer or attended church services in St George's Chapel. Until very recently, Charles had always negotiated with the expectation that his enemies would squabble, or that his supporters would triumph in war, but now one enemy had full control. The core of Charles's character began to strengthen, showing a quiet courage and providing him with the dignity he had always feared he lacked. Beneath his rigid self-control, some quality showed which was deeper than his royal training and infused with faith.

The army had driven out its enemies, those who had denigrated it or invited in the Scots; those whose voting record the army deplored. The Commons, although reduced to around one-fifth of its membership, was composed of the army's allies and only three or four peers were still in the Lords. Parliament was docile but decisions had to be made – about the form of government and about the fate of the king. Ireton had made his position clear, but now that the time to try Charles came near men began to prevaricate. We lack evidence for all the conversations and suppositions which passed between people over that midwinter, even among the principal instigators of what followed. Historians have speculated about Cromwell and Ireton – how much they too prevaricated and why finally they took action. The evidence is unclear. Cromwell in particular had a recurrent pattern of withdrawal and indecision, with long searches in his conscience or for God's providence, which also gave him time for slow political calculation. But once he decided to act, he was swift and implacable. So it proved this time.

Cromwell was a sturdy countryman who thought slowly and in depth but then moved with speed, as a cavalryman and as a politician. He was no Leveller; he liked tradition and lived comfortably in the social order of the England of his time. He hoped for better justice, a competent legislature, and he hungered, as his companions did, for a godly England in which those who were to be saved under God's judgement would build a pure state in preparation for the imminent holy one. He was a complex mixture of plain gentleman and millenarian, but the experience of war had defined him. He was always among his relatives, many of whom were fellow soldiers and MPs, but the army had become his first priority and probably his first love. He led it and moulded it, but essentially Cromwell put the army first and as it worked out its demands on the rest of the country, taking ever more power, Cromwell rose on its back like a surfer on a wave. He was already sleeping 'in one of the king's rich beds in Whitehall' but had not yet made it his own.[3]

In December 1648, the army had power but was faced with choice. They made that choice gradually. On 21 December, at a meeting of the Council of Officers, a proposal for the king's death was overturned by four votes, with Cromwell leading those who opposed. A last deputation was sent to the king, led by Lord Denbigh, but Charles would not see him. If the Puritans despaired of Charles, he was utterly weary of them. At the core of Charles were beliefs which he held stubbornly, and a raw courage which he had already displayed in war. At some time amid the long captivity and endless negotiations, he began to prepare himself for a martyr's end. He knew better than anyone what his opponents wanted and had found by hard discussion how his sense of duty conflicted with those aims.

Once Denbigh was rejected, Cromwell made up his mind. Ireton too had delayed but now the lieutenant general and his son-in-law were set on their course. Only the difficulty of creating the court and finding officers for it stood in the way of the army now. The Rump had been picked for its sympathies and it did as required. On 28 December the Commons introduced an ordinance, setting up a High Court of Justice to try the king, and on the first day of 1649 it was passed. The Lords rejected it, so the Commons passed an act giving themselves the supreme power 'in this nation' and by so doing gave themselves full control of the kingdom once the king was removed.

However, finding officers for the court was a scramble. The central court judges refused to sit and the Commons finally fell back on John Bradshaw, Chief Justice of Chester, who was a republican and a friend of Milton. A total of one hundred and thirty-five commissioners were chosen by name but fifty-five of them never appeared. Fairfax was among them; he came to the preliminary hearing but nothing more. Attendance remained low throughout the meetings over procedure, but nonetheless a date was set for the trial to begin – 20 January 1649.

On the day before the trial was to start, the king's coach, drawn by six horses, was outside Windsor Castle. The road was lined with soldiers, pikes and muskets at the ready to prevent any attempt at escape. Charles was coming back to his capital, which he had not seen since he left London early in January 1642 to escort Henrietta-Maria to the coast. If he could see the approaches to Westminster through his carriage windows, London could not see him. The city was full of soldiers, men who had survived years of warfare, who smoked but seldom drank and whose days were marked by long periods of preaching and prayer. Special days were given over to fasting before the men gathered to pray. They were tough and disciplined; the inhabitants of London were intimidated by them and increasingly unsure of each other in this radically altered city. It was a bleak homecoming for the captured king. The journey was kept secret but, in any case, no crowds could approach him through the long lines of soldiers. Charles was brought into the city and taken to St James's Palace.

Scottish commissioners had arrived in London. They had worried about the Newport Treaty, which held nothing for Scotland; but now, more worryingly, the English parliament had been whittled down to friends of the army, London was infested with soldiers and the trial of the king was about to begin. Charles was King of Scotland but the northern kingdom had not been consulted and everything that was happening breached the Covenant. The Scots' position was complex and legalistic but, in any case, they were unable to make any impact on the process which was relentlessly rolling forward.

The Scots had been recently beaten, but the Irish forces were gathering. On 17 January, Ormond signed an agreement with the Confederates by which 18,000 of their troops would join his own. The army's *Remonstrance* and their animus against the king had galvanised Ireland. The position in Ulster had changed, for after Monro joined Hamilton, Major General George Monck had taken Carrickfergus and Belfast for parliament. The Scots were out of Ulster, parliament held the north-eastern seaboard but Ormond controlled most of the rest of the island. Only the irreconcilable Owen Roe O'Neill held out for the Gaelic Catholic interest there.

This coalescing of forces in Ireland had an equally galvanising effect on the army and the Rump in London. They had subdued Scotland for now, but the threat from Ireland was growing. Ormond's dealings with the Confederates were known in London and may have hurried the army into action. By the time that confirmation arrived of Ormond's treaty, the king had been brought into London for judgement.

The trial was to be held in Westminster Hall, that great meeting place within the palace. It was prepared for the trial which was to be open to the public. Bradshaw acquired a shot-proof hat. John Cook was prosecutor and the appointed commissioners were to hear the evidence and judge the king.

Normally, the great hall had booksellers and benches where two law courts sat but now the great chamber had been cleared. Instead, a wooden platform had been erected with seats at the back for the commissioners, a table for the president, and below him a table for the clerks where the mace and sword of state lay. On either side were two galleries for the gentry. A seat covered in crimson velvet was set in front of the judging panel, ready for the prisoner.

The crowds could come into the main body of the hall to watch the proceedings. This was separated from the dignitaries by a gangway lined by pikemen and musketeers while guards were stationed behind the king's chair.

On the afternoon of 20 January, the roll was called and sixty-eight commissioners affirmed their presence to judge the king. Cromwell was among them, as was Ireton. When Fairfax was called, the only response was from a masked lady in the gallery who cried, 'He has more wit than to be here.' This was Lady Fairfax.[4]

The Agreement of the People was brought into parliament on the same day that the king was brought to trial. The officers had discussed the *Agreement* and amended it. On this day of all days it was introduced to the Commons, who said they would consider it when their present weighty business would permit.

King Charles was brought from St James's Palace by sedan chair, taken by boat and landed in Cotton Garden, which fronted the river. Sir Robert Cotton's house was between the Painted Chamber and the banks of the

Thames. At Windsor, the king's rooms had been suddenly searched, after which communication with his wife and friends had been cut off. Now in London, among the revolutionary army, he was given little peace. The guards smoked in his presence and barged into his rooms without knocking, while the king's attendants attempted to preserve some respect and privacy. But Charles had dignity of his own which the hastily assembled court only accentuated. It could hardly be legal since all justice in England was undertaken by the crown, but it had a wider significance which everyone present felt. Charles arrived wearing black with a tall black hat which he did not take off, signalling his disrespect for the proceedings. In the great hall, with its magnificent roof, and his people crowding forward behind the gruff soldiers, the black-clad king, seated on the crimson chair, was a small man but a figure of central and intense majesty.

Cook read the charge: that Charles Stuart, King of England, having been 'trusted with a limited power to govern by and according to the laws of the land, and not otherwise, had attempted to erect an unlimited and tyrannical power to rule according to his will, and in pursuance of this design, had levied war against the present parliament, and the people therein represented'. Cook impeached Charles Stuart 'as a tyrant, traitor, murderer, and a public and implacable enemy of the Commonwealth of England'.[5]

When Bradshaw called the king to answer the charge, on behalf of the Commons and good people of England, Lady Fairfax interrupted again – 'it is a lie, not a half, not a quarter of the people of England. Oliver Cromwell is a traitor.' Lady Fairfax was hustled out of the hall.

The court, and the people who had assembled it, stood on shaky ground, as was obvious to all. The court had been set up by a parliament already purged by the army. By what authority had he been brought here, Charles asked. Bradshaw answered that it was by the authority of the people of England, by whom he had been elected king. Charles answered that he was king by inheritance, not election, and refused to answer the charge. Amid cries of 'justice' from the soldiers and 'God save the King' from the crowd, Charles was removed to Cotton House.

When he returned to the court two days later, the king made his point. The court was illegal. If he could be tried by such a process in which power overrode the law and made its own, then the freedom and liberty of the people of England were in jeopardy.

Because the king would not plead, the court adjourned to the Painted Chamber to hear evidence. It was here, two days later and in the prisoner's absence, that they condemned him to death. On the 27th, Charles was brought into Westminster Hall to hear his sentence. He asked to be heard by the Lords and Commons in the Painted Chamber, which would have been a political assembly, but this was refused. Bradshaw read out the sentence, the commissioners all stood to show their assent, and the king, despite repeated attempts to speak, was not allowed to answer. After his first day in court, he had been heard little as he was not permitted to speak, but onlookers remarked that he never stammered. This time Bradshaw made certain that the king was not heard. Immediately after the sentence, as Charles demanded his right to reply, Bradshaw denied it and the guards began to hustle the king from the hall. Some blew smoke in his face; one is said to have spat at him. 'I am not suffered to speak,' the king called out. 'Expect what justice other people will have.'[6]

The trial was over. Charles was taken to his old room in Whitehall Palace, where he was allowed a letter from Prince Charles. Then he was moved back to St James's Palace as men began work on the scaffold in Whitehall. He burned his papers and spent his last hours with Juxon, Bishop of London, either in prayer or listening to Juxon's preaching.

Two of his children were still in England, living as captives in St James's Palace. Here they saw their father for the last time. Princess Elizabeth was a pretty and learned girl who had been captured when she was six. She was now thirteen and in poor health. Her brother Henry, Duke of Gloucester was nine. Charles feared that the Rump would make Henry a puppet king, to thwart the claims of Princes Charles and James to the thrones. Since the king had come south as a prisoner in 1647, he had been able to see his children several times, although James had subsequently escaped. Although held under difficult conditions, their meetings had been warm and gentle occasions, lacking the pomp of their earlier lives. A description of this last meeting was recorded by Elizabeth herself.[7]

The children knew what was happening when they were brought to their father's room; they were crying and Elizabeth became hysterical but Charles comforted her until the children's grief agitated him too. He told them to obey their mother and Prince Charles, who would become sovereign. The king said he was going 'to a Glorious Death ... for the laws of the land and for maintaining the true Protestant religion'. It was important to Charles that Henry should understand the position. He took the boy on his lap and told him that 'my enemies will cut off my head', and warned the child that they might try to make him king but that he must not be king, for then they would cut off the heads of his brothers Charles and James too, and likely enough Henry's own. The boy vowed that he would be torn to pieces first – he was a brave child who grew up to be a soldier. His speech pleased and reassured the king.

Both children were crying and the king, upset, turned aside. Then turning back, he held them closely to him before they were led away.

The rest of his life was spent in prayer. He slept, and on the morning of 30 January 1649, Charles dressed carefully and told Thomas Herbert, his attendant, that he 'feared not death'. It was a second marriage day, he said, on which he would be espoused to Jesus. Around 10 a.m., he was escorted across St James's Park to Whitehall Palace, where he and his attendants waited for several hours. The Commons was passing an act against proclaiming another monarch which they wanted in place before they executed the king.

It was a bitterly cold day. Charles and his bishop were taken to the Banqueting House on Whitehall, which had been built for King James and had a ceiling painted by Rubens. The scaffold had been erected outside the central window. Charles stepped out of the window onto the scaffold and into the presence of an awed crowd. The platform was draped in black but beyond it the densely packed people had gathered to see the act carried out. Only Bishop Juxon and two guards stepped out to join the executioner and his assistant.

Preparations had been physically straightforward but legally difficult. The original death warrant had been dated the 26th, the day before the sentence. Signatures had been collected on it, but as it stood the document was illegitimate and more signatures were needed; it had been difficult to get enough. By altering the date on the warrant and using a certain amount of coercion, fifty-nine signatures had been obtained, giving it some force.

Cromwell is quoted as insisting that any members of the High Court who were in the Commons that day should come out to sign the warrant without delay: 'Those that are gone in shall set their hands,' he said. 'I will have their hands now.'[8] The warrant lay for signature on a table in the Painted Chamber and tensions rose through the day, infecting Cromwell himself. He had a tendency to horseplay, which on this occasion prompted him to draw a line in ink across Henry Marten's face; Marten inked him in return. When, much later, the signatories were on trial, some regicides said they were frightened into assenting to the judgement in the court but not into signing the warrant. The document itself is now in the House of Lords library. Irregular procedures had been used to make the execution seem legal. Now, on a bleak January afternoon, it was carried out.

Ranks of soldiers and cavalrymen were drawn up around the scaffold, making it impossible for Charles to make himself heard by the crowd. So, he spoke primarily to Juxon and his words were later published.[9] He said that parliament, not he, had originated the war and he protested against the subjection of the country to rule by the sword. He desired the liberty and freedom of his people and the security of their property, but he did not believe in their having a share in government: 'A subject and a sovereign are clean different things.' He prayed that his enemies might be forgiven and affirmed that he was dying in the profession of the Church of England.

Then he prepared for death. His hair was tucked up into a white satin nightcap. He made sure that the executioner knew the signal. Juxon he admonished to 'Remember' whatever last tasks he had given him. The block was unusually low and the king had to lie, not kneel, to put his head on it. Then he made the signal and the axe fell. The executioner picked up the head and held it aloft. 'Behold the head of a traitor,' he intoned.

The packed crowd groaned in horror. The king embodied the nation; now the king had been dismembered. The mood was hostile, and the troops of horse were ordered to move the people quickly away.

Charles's body was put in a coffin and taken to his chamber in Whitehall. Ten days later, Juxon led the group who took the king's body to Windsor where it was buried in St George's Chapel. The following day a book was published, comprised of writings supposedly by the late king. *Eikon Basilike* was a best-seller and went through edition after edition. As a ruler, Charles had been high-handed and inept, and his enemies hated him for his stubbornness and political duplicity. But latterly, Charles's patience, his dignity and graciousness throughout his imprisonment had won many over. The spectacle of his trial and death were images which stuck in people's minds with great force; the small king who upheld his beliefs and died courageously made many forget their grievances against him – and indeed many of his people had never been sure what the war was all about. The nation was shocked, which was followed by grief and then fear.

News of the execution spread from Whitehall across England into Scotland, Ireland and continental Europe. Henrietta-Maria was at the Louvre when one of her English courtiers brought her the news. Two weeks had passed since Charles's execution and rumours had reached Paris, but definite confirmation shocked the queen so much that she was silent and frozen for many hours. She retired to a convent but her chaplain reminded her that she must attend to her family. Then Henrietta-Maria roused herself, a small intense widow in black who began to rally the leading royalists and to send advice to her son, who had been in Holland since the aborted naval mission of the previous year.

The parliament in Edinburgh proclaimed Charles II as King of Great Britain, France and Ireland on 5 February. The Earl of Ormond proclaimed Charles II from his house in Carrick-on-Suir, County Tipperary, on the 17th. He spoke afterwards of the loss of 'my great and good master, King Charles I' as something he found hard to bear.[10]

The impact of the king's execution was profound; it was said 'that the shock proved fatal to humble folk'. It was certainly a destabilising event which cut through all legal and emotional certainties. Many English gentry were abroad in exile. Letters carried the news across the continent. Sir Roger Burgoyne was a strong parliamentarian but before the king's death, early in January, he wrote, 'I could be content to be a monke or hermit, rather than a statesman at the present conjunction of affairs ... What will become of us in England God only knows.' Mr Cockram wrote from Rouen to young Ralph Verney in February:

I doubt not but ere this you have heard the dolefull news of our king's death, whoe was beheaded laste teusday was seven nighte, at two of the clock, afternoon, before Whitehall, the moste barbarous Ackt, and lamentable sight that ever any Christians did beholde. The Numerous guarde of horse and foote of Armed Tygers did binde the hands and stop the mouths of many thousand beholders, but could not keep their eyes from weeping, for none but harts of flinte could forbeare.

Mr Cockram considered the execution 'the beginning of England's grater Miserie than ever hath bin hitherto'.[11]

Intellectual reaction was more measured. Hobbes's *Leviathan*, published the following year, was concerned with preventing revolution and argued for a strong state. Marvell's *Horatian Ode*, also written in 1650 and a masterpiece of taut ambiguity, ostensibly lauding Cromwell's military campaign in Ireland, had a few verses reflecting on the execution of the king:

> That thence the royal actor borne
> The tragic scaffold might adorn,
> While round the armed bands
> Did clap their bloody hands.
>
> He nothing common did or mean
> Upon that memorable scene,
> But with a keener eye
> The axe's edge did try.
>
> Nor call'd the gods with vulgar spite
> To vindicate his helpless right;
> But bowed his comely head
> Down as upon a bed.[12]

John Milton was jubilant at the king's death. For him the regicide was 'such a solemn and for many ages unexampled act of due punishment', 'an action ... worthy of heroic ages'.[13] Even Marchamont Nedham, changing position once more, wrote of it as a deliverance. He dwelt on the malice of the Presbyterians who would betray the cause to the Scots and thought that in purifying parliament the army was commendable for the justice of its proceedings. The army had delivered the Commonwealth from slavery and ruin. Milton published *The Tenure of Kings and Magistrates* later that year, in which he gave praise to the army for extirpating tyranny and saving the nation's liberty.

Power had irrevocably shifted. Although the army had made the decisive move, with the death of the king the inheritor of power was parliament. With the execution safely behind them, those MPs who deplored the illegality of the act but who accepted a state with no monarch began to drift back into the

Commons. At first those who voted for the Newport Treaty were excluded, but to get the numbers up they were allowed to register their dissent and then come in. Men like Arthur Hazelrig and Sir Henry Vane returned to sit in the House. Both became increasingly influential over the following years. Still, the Commons was only around half its previous size.

Acts were passed to abolish the office of king and the House of Lords. To create a new executive, an act instituted a Council of State. A committee was set up to define its powers and to propose its forty-one members. Fairfax, Cromwell and Skippon were the only members from the army.

The new revolutionary government had much business before it, but perhaps its most urgent task – as it saw things – was to regain control of Ireland. In the absence of the king, the English parliament assumed the sovereignty over Ireland which the crown had previously held. The Commons were in a hurry to act. Money had been raised seven years earlier to subdue Ireland and the Adventurers were clamouring for the deal to be honoured – until Ireland was retaken, they could not claim the confiscated land they had been guaranteed.

Scotland was a different issue. The government there had proclaimed Charles II as king but Scotland was sovereign, and was not in arms. Ireland was. The army which Ormond now commanded was already making gains. The new Council of State made plans to send troops and Fairfax was asked to choose which regiments should go. The General Council of the Army asked Cromwell to command the expedition but he prevaricated and sought God. He wanted to be sure that the expedition would be properly equipped and not fail for lack of supplies. Once satisfied, he said 'that the worke was a greate worke' and accepted. The Council of State approved his appointment.

So it was Cromwell, not Fairfax, who began to gather men, supplies and money to take to Ireland and to begin the work of reconquest. In due course this would lead to the extinguishing of the three kingdoms as separate entities and their amalgamation into a single godly state. The War of the Three Kingdoms was over, and the three states were about to enter their first union.

The main points from Selected documents of negotiation or proposals for constitutional change

Abridged by Jane Hayter-Hames

The Newcastle Propositions[1]

On behalf of the parliament of England (also speaking for Ireland) and the parliament of Scotland:

All declarations made against the two parliaments and other recent ruling bodies be declared null and void.

King to swear and sign Solemn League and Covenant.

King to pass acts to make all subjects in all three kingdoms swear the Covenant.

Pass acts to abolish bishops and other church officers in England and Ireland, such act to conform to the treaty of 1643.

Assembly of Divines to be established by act of parliament.

Reformation of religion to be established by act of parliament in consultation with the assembly of divines.

An oath to be imposed on Catholics to renounce main tenets of their faith and forswear the Pope's supremacy.

Penalties of recusancy to be imposed on all Catholics who do not take the oath and their children to be raised by Protestants.

Parliament to control the armed forces for twenty years.

Treaties between England and Scotland to be confirmed by act of parliament.

The cessation in Ireland to be declared null and void.

Parliament in England to nominate all officers of state and judges in England and Ireland in perpetuity.

Parliament in Scotland to nominate all officers of state and judges for Scotland.

The militia of the City of London to be under the command of the Lord Mayor and Common Council, along with command of the Tower of London.

Those documents passed under the Great Seal by the commissioners appointed by parliament of England to be confirmed and the Great Seal to be controlled by parliament.

Includes a list of royalists to be excluded from pardon, others to be excluded from court and public office.

All active royalists to lose part of their estates.

The Case of the Army Truly Stated[2]

Proposed by the agents of five regiments to Sir Thomas Fairfax and the whole army (15 October 1647)

Complains that the grievances of the army have been put to parliament over several months but nothing has been done, either for them or for 'the poore oppressed people of the nation'.

Parliament declared the army as enemies of the state and has not recanted.

There has been no provision for apprentices, widows, orphans and wounded soldiers, nor any redress of grievances.

None of the public burdens or oppressions by arbitrary committees have been removed.

'The rights of the people in their Parliaments concerning the nature and extent of that power, are not cleared and declared.'

The Engagements and Representations of the army have been declined and the army warned not to make demands, although the soldiers have not been paid.

The agitators have been discouraged and not been properly consulted.

The soldiers are going to be sent to Ireland or disbanded before any arrears are settled.

The soldiers took up arms for the rights and liberties of the people but now are being treated as if they were simply servants of the state, 'and may not as free Commons claime their right and freedome as due to them'.

The soldiers' rights were to be addressed before any rights of the king were restored but now he will regain his powers, including his negative voice, so the soldiers will depend on him for redress.

The King's evil councillors are freely admitted to the army and confer there.

Delinquent MPs have not been purged although it was insisted on at Kingston

Therefore the promises by the army to stand for the national interest have not been fulfilled.

Because of free quarters and heavy taxation, the people resent the army more and more.

Demands:
Parliament should be dissolved within 9-10 months.

Members must be purged from parliament who have forfeited trust or sat while the Speaker was absent.

Parliament to confirm Fairfax's remonstrance from Kingston.

Elections to be held once in every two years, 'all the freeborn at the age of 21 years and upwards, be the electors' and the parliament have a certain time limit.

All power is originally and essentially in the whole body of the nation. The Commons have the supreme right to make law but also to call into account all officers of the nation for neglect or treachery. The people's right to choose their representatives must be confirmed. The king has contended against the power of the Commons and the people have defended it with their blood.

The Excise on beer, cloth and English 'manufactures' should be removed and all other excise better regulated.

People have spent vast sums of money through tax, yet the costs of the war have not been met. Proper accounts must be made throughout the kingdom, including the City of London.

Parliament men have bought bishops' lands cheaply and received their arrears but little money has been brought to the treasury. The sales must be reviewed and if necessary held again on a proper basis.

Before the king has his rights, the people's needs must be addressed:

- All prohibitions on petitioning to be removed.
- Useless officers of the court removed and the money used to pay the armed forces.
- Investigation to be held into stocks and lands held by the City of London which are not paying their just share of tax.
- Forest lands as well as dean & chapter lands should be set aside to pay the army.
- Arrears of assessments must be collected.
- Fees paid to Receivers of Customs and Excise must be investigated.
- The cost of the army should be calculated and published. The tax required to pay should be charged uniformly across the whole country.
- No monopolies.
- Prisoners not to be held indefinitely who have no real estate to pay or who have not been brought to trial.
- No compulsion to go to church or use the Book of Common Prayer.
- No statutes against 'conventicles' or to prevent prayer meetings.
- No compulsion to pay tithes.
- No-one to be forced to take oaths. No-one obliged to answer 'Interrogatories' about themselves in court.
- Committee to look into injustices in the law.
- No-one to be exempt from the law.
- Ancient rights and donations of the poor to be restored.
- Indemnity for the soldiers to prevent them having to spend money coming to London to wait on committees
- Security for arrears.
- Those who have had estates sequestered but did not fight for the king to have their property back and those who compounded not to have to pay because their estates sequestered for so long. Those who fought for the king must compound but not be ruined.

'In case the union of the Army should be broken…ruine and destruction will breake in upon us like a roaring sea…'

The Heads of the Proposals Offered by the Army

(1 August 1647)[3]
Parliament should set an end date for its sitting. New parliaments to be called every two years, to sit for '120 days certain' and no parliament to sit past 240 days'.

Between parliaments, the king may call an extraordinary parliament but not interrupt the regularity of meetings.

Representation should be equal and constituencies made proportional to the rates they bear. Members should be free to speak and not be censured for what they say in the house.

Parliament to control the armed forces for ten years.

Parliament to manage the finance of the armed forces and the public debts of the kingdom for ten years.

Those who fought against parliament may not hold public office for five years without consent of parliament.

Parliament to chose the officers of the army. County commissioners to control the local militia.

There shall be a Council of State, whose members serve for not more than seven years, to control the armed forces of England and Ireland, as well as foreign relations, but which requires parliament's consent to make war or peace.

Parliament to appoint the chief officers of state and judges in both kingdoms for ten years, then the king to choose between three candidates.

Peers created after 1643 may not sit in the House of Lords nor vote in parliament without consent of both houses.

Grants made under the Great Seal since it was removed from parliament to be made void and those made under parliament's Great Seal confirmed.

Treaties made between England and Scotland to be confirmed.

Cessation in Ireland to be made void.

The coercive power, authority and jurisdiction of the bishops to end.

The Book of Common Prayer to be permitted but not compulsory; no penalties to be imposed for not attending church but other methods to be found to restrict papists.

Taking of the Covenant not to be enforced.

The king, queen and royal family to be restored without diminution of their personal rights.

Five Englishmen and persons involved in the Irish rebellion will be reserved to the judgement of parliament but all people excepted [from pardon] to be remitted.

Rates for composition [compounding] to be reduced.

There shall be a general Act of Oblivion.

Reform Issues
The people shall have the right to petition.

Excise on basic commodities on which poor people live to be abolished.

Oppressions and encroachments of forest laws to be prevented.

Monopolies to be abolished.

Rates of tax between counties to be equalised.

People not to be imprisoned for debt who have no way to pay, other means to be found.

People not to be compelled to incriminate themselves.

Length and cost of legal proceedings to be reduced.

The power of county committees and deputy-lieutenants to be limited and regulated.

Accounts to be properly taken for the vast sums levied.

The soldiers to be paid their arrears.

Four Bills

(Passed by both houses of parliament in Westminster, 14 December 1647)[4]

  I. Parliament to have full control of all land and sea forces for twenty years and the finance to support them. After that, the king may not raise or use armed forces without the consent of both houses of parliament.

 II. Annulment of all oaths, declarations, proclamations and judicial proceedings made against parliament since the start of the war.

III. All peerages granted since May 1642 to be cancelled.

 IV. Parliament has the right to adjourn to any place in England of its own choosing for as long as it considers necessary. This does not constitute a determination of parliament.

With further propositions regarding confirmation of recent acts passed by parliament, restoring MPs to jobs from which they have been removed, making void the cessation in Ireland, indemnity, abolition of the Court of Wards and feudal dues, confirmation of the treaty with Scotland, payment of arrears to the army from bishops' lands forfeitures and forest lands, the abolition of bishops deans chapters and vicars.

A list appended of those whose property is to be forfeited and who are excepted from pardon but not more than seven to lose their lives.

Presbyterian government and the directory to be established in England and Ireland but there shall be no compulsion or penalties over conforming. No toleration of the popish religion or use of the Book of Common Prayer. Everyone to attend service on the Lord's Day.

The king to assent to these bills under the Great Seal but as this conflicts with safety and security, the king to give consent to the two speakers to warrant any three of several named peers to give assent to the said Bills, after which they will send their committee to treat with the king in the Isle of Wight.

The Engagement between the King and the Scots

(26 December 1647)[5]

The king will confirm the Solemn League and Covenant in both kingdoms for the security of those who take it, but there shall be no compulsion to take it.

The king will confirm Presbyterian church government, the directory for worship and Assembly of Divines in England for three years. He and his household will use his accustomed form of worship. After three years, discussion between the Church of England and Scottish divines will settle future church government. The Sects will be suppressed.

The King to ratify the acts of the Scottish parliament passed 1644-47.

Since the army under Fairfax has taken over London and purged parliament, and has sent bills to the king without the consent of the Scots and against the terms of their treaty with the English parliament, the kingdom of Scotland will endeavour to bring the king to London to make a treaty, with parliament and the Scottish commissioners.

All armies should be disbanded.

The English parliament should have an end date set and the army must withdraw.

In case this is not granted, an army will be sent into England from Scotland to preserve religion and the king's position. Any person from England or Ireland may join the army and will be given protection by the Scots.

The king will not make an agreement with the English parliament or any treaty, cessation or agreement with any parties in Ireland, without the consent of the kingdom of Scotland.

Once there is peace, there will be an Act of Oblivion.

The king and the prince will visit and reside in Scotland as frequently as possible.

The King is to settle the debts due to Scotland from the English parliament under the Brotherly Assistance and the treaty made with parliament.

The king to create a union of the two kingdoms or at least free trade.

That subjects of both countries should have mutual capacity and privilege in both countries.

Ships will be provided to protect Scottish trading vessels.

The Remonstrance of the Army to the House of Commons

(dated 16 November 1648)[6]
This document is based on our regard for the 'Privileges and Freedom of Parliament'.

The justification for the army entering politics is – *salus populi suprema lex* – the safety of the people is the supreme law. This is not to be used lightly but remembering all that has happened, it applies.

Reminds parliament of their Vote of No Addresses to the king of January 1648. During the 2nd Civil War, the judgement of heaven was against the royalists. Yet parliament has re-opened negotiations with the king.

Instead of reconciliation, offenders should be called to account, even if they have not broken the law as it then stood. If the public interest has been violated, justice is required and no person is exempt.

The king's crime was in breaking his covenant to protect the people's rights and liberties.

The king was guilty of all the blood spilt.

God would be appeased if judgement was executed against him.

The king is in prison; as soon as he is restored, he can renounce any concessions as having been extracted under duress.

There is danger in bringing the king to London, as people believe he has sought peace. Should he start another war, they are likely to support him to preserve peace, rather than support parliament in making war.

The Solemn League and Covenant bound its signatories to preserve the king's person and authority. However, the king did not sign it and should not be protected by it. The over-riding duty was to defend religion and the public interest.

The king has committed treason and must be brought to justice.

The Prince of Wales and Duke of York must come in and be declared incapable of holding office, then exiled. Their estates must be used to pay off debt and for the benefit of poor people.

Other delinquents must be brought to justice.

Arrears and debts must be paid.

To Settle the Kingdom
Parliament must set a date to end its sitting.

There must be an equal distribution of elections to make parliament an equal representation 'of the whole people electing'.[7]

There should be annual or biennial elections.

No-one who has opposed parliament may vote for some years.

Parliament has the supreme authority in making law, constitution and offices.

No rights or liberties conferred by this document can be removed by parliament.

There should be no more kings unless they are elected.

Parliament should give effect to the whole programme, to be finalised in a contract or Agreement of the People.

Submitted by John Rushworth, on behalf of the Lord General and his Council of Officers.

Agreement of the People

Presented to the General and the Council of the Army (11 December 1648)[8]
Parliament to be dissolved on or before 30 April next.

The next representative (parliament) to be composed of 300 people. Each town and county to be proportionally represented.

Voters to be natives of England who have subscribed this agreement, pay poor rates and are not servants. They shall be men of twenty-one or over who are house-keepers dwelling in the constituency. Those who supported the king cannot vote for seven years.

For fourteen years, the king's supporters cannot sit in parliament.

If men vote or sit who are ineligible, either their estates will be confiscated or they will be imprisoned.

A minimum of one hundred and fifty people must be present to pass laws.

Each parliament shall elect a Council of State to manage public affairs. They will act on instructions from parliament.

No officer of state or of the army may be a member of the Council of State.

Parliament may not over-turn this agreement.

Parliament may not penalise people or legislate for their religion but it may instruct and direct, as long as there is no compulsion, or support for popery.

Parliament may not force people to serve in war.

People cannot be questioned for actions taken in the recent wars, except the present Commons can question the king's supporters and parliament must settle the accounts.

No-one can be exempted from the process of the law by virtue of birth or any grant or charter. Such exemptions are null and void.

Parliament is not to interfere with the execution of the laws.

No M.P. is to be a receiver or treasurer.

No parliament may remove the foundations of common liberty or level men's estates, destroy property or make all things common.

Between parliaments, the Council of State may call an extraordinary one for no longer than forty days.

All securities on public faith must be paid before the next parliament, except that the next parliament can negate gifts made by the present Commons to their own members or the Lords.

An army officer who resists the orders of future parliaments shall lose the protection of the law and 'die without mercy'.

Endnotes

1 On the Fault Line of the Islands

1. Byrne, K., *Colkitto* (Colonsay: House of Lochar, 1997); Stevenson, D., *Alasdair MacColla and the Highland Problem in the 17th Century* (Glasgow: John Donald, 1980)
2. Williams, R., *The Lords of the Isles* (Colonsay: House of Lochar, 1997)
3. Caldwell, D. H., *Islay, Jura and Colonsay, A Historical Guide* (Edinburgh: Birlinn, 2011)

2 Inheriting Three Kingdoms

1. Quoted in D. H. Willson, *King James VI and I* (London: Cape, 1956), p. 165
2. Quoted in Willson, *King James*, p. 313
3. James VI, *The Trew Law of Free Monarchies* (1598), quoted in Willson, *King James*, p. 132
4. C. Russell, *King James VI and I and his English Parliaments* (Oxford University Press: 2011), pp. 145-6; G Burgess, *Absolute Monarchy and the Stuart Constitution* (New Haven and London: Yale University Press, 1996), p. 28, 33, 96
5. Russell, *King James VI and I*, p. 149
6. Gardiner, S. R., *History of England from the Accession of James I to the Outbreak of the Civil War 1603-1642*, Vol II (London: Longman, Green & Co., 10 vols), p. 67
7. Burgess G., *Absolute Monarchy and the Stuart Constitution*, pp. 28, 33, 96; Daly, J., 'The Idea of Absolute Monarchy in Seventeenth-Century England', *The Historical Journal*, Vol. 21, No. 2 (June, 1978), pp. 227-250; Coke, Sir E., *The Institutes of the Laws of England* (London, 1628-1644); Coke, Sir E., *The Reports of Sir Edward Coke* (London: from 1600)
8. Lee, M., *Great Britain's Solomon: James VI & I in his Three Kingdoms* (Urbana: University of Illinois Press, 1990), p. 51
9. MacDonald, F. A., *Mission to the Gaels* (Edinburgh: John Donald, 2006), p. 2

10. Lee, *Solomon*, p.51
11. *Calendar of State Papers Venetian, Vol 10, p. 513-14,* quoted in Lawrence D. R., *The Complete Soldier* (Leiden Boston: Brill, 2009), p. 107

3 The King James Version
1. Elizabeth I, *Collected Works*, Marcus, L. S. Mueller, J., Rose, M. B. (University of Chicago Press, 2002) p 364
2. Willson, D. H., *King James VI and I* (London: Cape, 1956), p. 123
3. Willson, *King James*, p. 38
4. Willson, *King James*, p. 314; Patterson, W. B., *King James VI and the Reunion of Christendom* (Cambridge University Press, 1997) p 12; Stevenson, D., *The Scottish Revolution 1637-44* (Newton Abbot: David and Charles, 1973), pp. 23-24
5. Stone, L., 'The educational revolution in England, 1560-1640,' *Past and Present*, No. 28 (July, 1964); Cressy, D., *Literacy and the Social Order; Reading and writing in Tudor and Stuart England* (Cambridge University Press, 1980); MacLean, G., *Literacy, Class, and Gender in Restoration England,* Text, Vol. 7 (Indiana University Press, 1994), pp. 307-335
6. Donne, J., *Complete Verse and Prose,* Hayward, J., Ed. (London: Nonesuch, 1962), p. 433
7. Nicholls, M., 'Strategy and Motivation in the Gunpowder Plot', *Historical Journal* vol. 50, no. 4 (Dec, 2007) pp 787-807
8. *A Discourse of the Maner of the Discovery of this Late Intended Treason* (London, 1605)
9. Howell, T. J., Cobbett, W., Jardine, D., *A Complete Collection of State Trials and Proceedings for High Treason and Other Crimes and Misdemeanors from the Earliest Period to the Year 1783: 1640-49* (1816), p. 497
10. Parker, G., Smyth, L. M., eds. *The General Crisis of the Seventeenth Century* (London: Routledge & Kegan Paul, 1978); Cunningham, A., Grell, O. P., *Four Horsemen of the Apocalypse: religion, war, famine and death in reformation Europe* (Cambridge University Press, 2000)
11. Raleigh, Sir W., *An Abridgement of Sir Walter Raleigh's History of the World* (London: Gillyflower, 1698), p. 33
12. Donne, J., *Complete Verse and Selected Prose*, Sermon XXXVI, p. 619
13. Johnson, S., *Lives of the Poets: Milton* (London: Macmillan, 1906), p. 35
14. Silke, 'Primate Lombard and James I', Cal. S.P. Ire., 1611-14, pp. 131-3, quoted in Moody, T. W., Martin, F. X., Byrne, F. J., *A New History of Ireland,* Vol III (Oxford: Clarendon Press, 1978), p. 217. *Cor unum et viam unam* means one heart and one way, comes from Jeremiah 32: 39 and had been commented on by Calvin.
15. Marshall, R. K., *The Winter Queen, The Life of Elizabeth of Bohemia 1596-1662* (Edinburgh: Scottish National Portrait Gallery, 1998), p. 31

4 Men of Influence

1. See Russell, C., *James and English Parliaments* (Oxford University Press, 2011)
2. Willson, *James,* p. 175
3. *Commons Journal,* Vol I, p171, in Gardiner, S.R., *History England 1603-1642,* Vol III, p. 176
4. Willson, *James,* P 249-255
5. Shohet L., 'Interpreting "The Irish Masque at Court" and in Print,' *Journal for Early Modern Cultural Studies,* Vol. 1, No. 2 (Fall – Winter, 2001), pp. 42-65
6. Connolly S. J., *Contested Island, Ireland 1460-1630* (Oxford: University Press, 2007), p. 390
7. Cuddy N., *The King's Chambers: the bedchamber of James I in administration and politics, 1603–1625,* D. Phil thesis, University of Oxford, 1987, p81
8. Cuddy, *King's Chambers,* pp. 85, 93
9. Macdonald, A.R., 'Consultation and Consent under James VI', *The Historical Journal,* 54, 2 (2011), pp. 287-306
10. Noppen, J. G., *Royal Westminster* (London: Country Life, 1937); Saunders, H. St G., *Westminster Hall* (London: Michael Joseph, 1951); Port, M. H., *The Palace of Westminster on the Eve of Conflagration 1834* (London Topographical Society, 2011); Thurley, S., *Whitehall Palace: an architectural history of the royal apartments, 1240-1698* (New Haven and London: Yale University Press, 1999)
11. Sayles, G.O., *The King's Parliament of England, 1975* (London: Edward Arnold, 1975); Jones, C., *A Short History of Parliament* (Woodbridge: Boydell Press, 2009)
12. Willson, *King James,* p. 191
13. From Beckett, J. C., *Cavalier Duke* (Belfast: James Camlin, 1990) p 1
14. 'Hamilton, James 1st Duke', *Oxford Dictionary National Biography* (Oxford: University Press, 2004)

5 Money and Land

1. Ashton, R., *The Crown and the Money Markets, 1603-1640* (Oxford: Clarendon Press, 1960), p. 20
2. Scott, W. R., *Joint-Stock Companies to 1720,* Vol. 1 (Cambridge: University Press, 1912), pp. 129-149; Cramsie J., *Kingship and Crown Finance under James VI and I 1603-1625* (Woodridge: RHS & Boydell Press, 2002), pp. 35-40; Ashton, R., *The City and the Court, 1603-1643* (Cambridge: University Press, 1979), pp. 93-7, p. 103-6; Cramsie, J., 'Commercial Projects and the Fiscal Policy of James VI and I' in *The Historical Journal,* Vol. 43, No. 2 (Jun., 2000), pp. 345-364
3. Judges, A. V., 'The Origins of English Banking', *History,* Jan, 1931, Vol. 16, p. 142
4. Ashton, *The City and the Court,* p177
5. Quoted in Gardiner, S. R., *The History of England 1603-1641,* Vol I, p. 177

6. Dodgshon, R. A., *From Chiefs to Landlords* (Edinburgh: University Press, 1998), pp. 44-45

7. Caldwell, D. H., *Islay, Jura and Colonsay*; Mackie, R.L., *A Short History of Scotland* (Edinburgh: Oliver and Boyd, 1962)

8. Ohlmeyer J. H., *Civil War and Restoration in the Three Stuart Kingdoms, The career of Randal MacDonnell, marquis of Antrim, 1609-1683* (Cambridge: University Press, 1993) p 33

9. Connolly, *Contested Island*, p. 320-1

10. Connolly, *Contested Island* p 289-308

11. Willson, D.H., *King James*, p. 244; Cramsie, *Kingship and Crown*, p. 81

12. Willson, *James*, p. 348-9; Gardiner, *History of England 1603-1641*, Vol II, p. 251-3

13. *Holinshed Chronicles*, Vol III (London, 1808), p. 824

14. Myers, A. R., *Parliaments and Estates in Europe to 1789* (London: Thames and Hudson, 1975); Van Zanden, J. L., Buringh, E., Bosker, M., 'The rise and decline of European parliaments, 1188—1789', *Economic History Review*, Vol. 65, No. 3 Aug 2012, pp. 835-861

6 Multiple Kingdoms

1. Wormald, J., The Creation of Britain: Multiple Kingdoms or Core and Colonies?' *Transactions of the Royal Historical Society* (1 January 1992, Vol.2), pp.175-194

2. Russell, C., 'Composite Monarchies in early modern Europe' in Grant, A., Stringer K., *Uniting the Kingdom? The Making of British History* (London, New York: Routledge, 1995)

3. Hansard, T., Cobbett's Parliamentary History of England from the Earliest Period to the Year 1803, Vol I (London: Black Parry and Co., 1806) pp 972-989

4. Levack B. P., *The Formation of the British State* (Oxford: Clarendon Press, 1987) pp 1-2

5. Gardiner S. R, *History of England 1603-1642*, Vol I, p. 324-340

7 The Heir

1. James I, *Speech to the Privy Council*, 1617, quoted in Carlton, C., *Charles I, The Personal Monarch* (London: Routledge & Kegan Paul, 1983) p 23

2. Willson, *King James*, p. 412

3. Ibid, p. 428

4. Gardiner, *History of England 1603-1642*, Vol III, p. 307

5. Gardiner, *History of England 1603-1642*, Vol V, p. 5

6. Willson, *King James*, p. 433

7. Clarendon, E., Earl of, *The History of the Rebellion and Civil Wars in England*, Macray W. D., ed. Vol I (Oxford: Clarendon Press, 1888), p. 28

8. Halliwell, J. O., *Letters of the Kings of England*, Vol II (London: H. Colburn, 1848) p 232-6

8 *The New Reign*

1. Meade to Stutevalle, July 2, Birth, T., ed., *Court and Times of Charles I*, Vol. I (London: H. Colburn, 1848) p 39
2. Clarke, A 'Selling Royal Favours, 1624-32', Moody, Martin, Byrne, *A New History of Ireland*, Vol III, p. 234
3. Ibid, p. 238
4. Cust, R., *Charles I, A Political Life* (Harlow: Pearson Education, 2007), pp. 82-103; Tyacke, N., *Anti-Calvinists: the rise of English Arminianism c.1590-1640* (Oxford: Clarendon Press, 1987)
5. Harleian Ms. 4771, fol, 15, Quoted in Gardiner, *History of England 1603-1642*, Vol VI, p. 233
6. Gardiner, *History of England 1603-1642*, Vol. VI pp 230-237
7. Woolrych, A., *Britain in Revolution* (Oxford: University Press, 2002), p. 57

9 *The Political Nation*

1. 'William Laud', *Dictionary of National Biography* (Oxford: University Press, 2004)
2. Reid, C. J., 'The Seventeenth Century Revolution in English Land Law,' *Cleveland State Law Review*, 221 (1995), pp. 221-301; Tawney, R. H., *Religion and the Rise of Capitalism* (London: John Murray, 1936), p. 172; Trevor-Roper H. R., *Archbishop Laud* (Basingstoke: Macmillan, 1988), pp. 166-170
3. Hirst, D., *The Representative of the People? Voters and Voting in England under the Early Stuarts* (Cambridge: University Press, 1975); Plumb, J., 'The Growth of the Electorate in England 1600 to 1715,' *Past and Present*, Nov 1969, pp. 90-116
4. Providence Island was one of the earliest to use African slave labour. See Pestana, C. G., *The English Atlantic in the Age of Revolution 1640-1661* (Cambridge, Mass.: Harvard University Press, 2004), p. 190
5. *Victoria County History, Huntingdonshire*, Vol. II (Folkestone: University of London Institute of Historical Research, 1974)
6. Kupperman, K.O., *Providence Island 1630-1641* (Cambridge: University Press, 1993)
7. Curtis, M.H., *Oxford and Cambridge in Transition 1558-1642* (Oxford: Clarendon Press, 1959)
8. https://www.historyofparliamentonline.org/volume/1604-1629/member/wentworth-sir-thomas-1593-1641; Wedgwood, C. V., *Thomas Wentworth, First Earl of Strafford 1593-1641, A Revaluation* (London: Jonathan Cape, 1961)
9. Zagorin, P., 'Did Strafford Change Sides?' *The English Historical Review*, Vol. 101, No. 398 (Jan., 1986), pp. 149-163
10. 'Hamilton, James, first duke of Hamilton', *Oxford Dictionary National Biography* (Oxford University Press, 2005)
11. Ohlmeyer, *Civil War and Restoration*, p. 18
12. Pestana, *English Atlantic*; McFarlane, A., *The British in the Americas 1480-1815* (London: Longman, 1994)

10 Without Parliament

1. Gardiner, *History of England 1603-1642*, Vol. VII, pp. 176-9; Carlton, *Charles I*, p. 48
2. Ingrao, C.W., *Habsburg Monarchy 1618-1815* (Cambridge: University Press, 2000) p 6
3. Gardiner, *History of England 1603-1642*, Vol VII, p. 176-9; Carlton, *Charles I*, p 173
4. *Proceedings in Parliament 1628*, Vol 2 (New Haven: Yale University Press, 1977-83) p 58; pp 324-5
5. National Archives, C 115/M35/8387
6. *Charles I, King and Collector* (London: Royal Academy of Arts, 2018)
7. Gardiner, *History of England 1603-1642*, Vol VII, p. 125
8. Quoted in Tawney, *Religion and the Rise of Capitalism*, p. 172
9. Calvin J., *Sermons on Deuteronomy*, 1 (Deut. 16:18-19). *Opera*, XXVII, 410-11. See McNeill J. T., 'The Democratic Element in Calvin's Thought' in *Church History*, Vol. 18, No. 3 (Sep., 1949), pp. 153-171
10. Quoted in Greaves R. L., 'Traditionalism and the Seeds of Revolution in the Social Principles of the Geneva Bible' in *The Sixteenth Century Journal*, Vol. 7, No. 2 (Oct., 1976), pp. 94-109

11 Charles, King of Scotland

1. Terry, C. S., *The Scottish Parliament; Its Constitution and Procedure 1603-1707* (Glasgow: James MacLehose and Sons, 1905), p. 12
2. Firth, C.H., *The House of Lords during the Civil War* (London: Longman, Green and Co., 1910), p. 17
3. Stevenson, *The Scottish Revolution 1637-44*, pp. 18, 35-40
4. Kerr, Rev. J., *The Covenants and the Covenanters* (Edinburgh: R. W. Hunter, 1895), p. 16
5. Gardiner, S.R., ed., *The Constitutional Documents of the Puritan Revolution 1625-1660* (Oxford: Clarendon Press, 1968), p. 132-3
6. Carlton, *Charles I*, p. 208

12 Thomas Wentworth in Ireland

1. Kearney, H.F., *Strafford in Ireland 1633-41* (Manchester: University Press, 1959), p. 35
2. McCafferty, J., *The Reconstruction of the Church of Ireland: Bishop Bramhall and the Laudian Reforms, 1633-1641* (Cambridge: University Press, 2007)
3. Knowler, W., ed., *Letters and dispatches of the Earl of Strafforde* (London: W. Bowyer, 1739). Wentworth's correspondence with Laud is an important source for studying both men. Knowler published a selection of Strafford's papers in 1739. The full Strafford papers were deposited in Sheffield Central Library in the late 1940s and are available on microfilm.
4. Kearney, *Strafford in Ireland*, p. 40
5. Wedgwood, *Strafford. A Revaluation*, p. 140
6. Kearney, *Strafford in Ireland*, p. 69-70

7. Morgan, H., review of Pawlisch, H. S., *Sir John Davies and the Conquest of Ireland: A Study in Legal Imperialism* (Cambridge: University Press, 1985) in *The International History Review*, Vol. 8, No. 3 (Aug., 1986), pp. 490-492.
8. Wedgwood, W*entworth. A Revaluation*, p. 169
9. Little, P., 'Blood and Friendship': The Earl of Essex's Protection of the Earl of Clanricarde's Interests, 1641-6', *The English Historical Review*, vol. 112, no. 448 (Sept, 1997) pp. 927-941
10. Kearney, *Strafford in Ireland,* Ch 12, esp. p 183
11. Wedgwood, *Strafford. A revaluation*, p. 254
12. Ibid, p. 249
13. Ibid, p. 250

13 The Great Men of the North Channel

1. Wedgwood, *Strafford. A Revaluation*, p. 254
2. Ohlmeyer, *Civil War and Restoration*, p. 18
3. Ibid, p. 80
4. Ibid, p. 79
5. Wedgwood, *Strafford. A Revaluation*, p. 254-5
6. Macinnes, A. I., *The British Confederate, Archibald Campbell, Marquess of Argyll c.1607-1661* (Edinburgh: John Donald, 2011), p. 73
7. Yorke P, Earl of Hardwicke, ed., *Miscellaneous State Papers from 1501to 1726,* Vol. II (London: W. Strahan & T. Cadell, 1778), p. 113-121

14 The Great Men of the North Channel

1. Stevenson, *The Scottish Revolution 1637-1644*, p. 143
2. Carlton, *Charles I*, p. 206; Gardiner, *History of England 1603-1642*, Vol. IX, p. 38
3. Knowler, W., ed., *The Earl of Strafford, Letters and Despatches*, Vol. II (London: W. Bowyer, 1739) p 374
4. Woolrych, *Britain in Revolution*, p. 125
5. Gardiner, *History of England 1603-1642*, Vol IX, p. 98; Woolrych, *Britain in Revolution*, p. 132-3
6. See Cust, *Charles I: A Political Life*, pp. 82-103 for a discussion of James I's *Declaration of Sports*, R. Montagu's *A New Gagg for an Old Goose* (1624) and *Appello Caesarem* (1625); Charles I's proclamation of 'utter dislike'...of new opinions differing from...true religion...established in the Church of England (1626); Hall, *Via Media* (1619) and Caroline policy.
7. The Thomason Tracts 1640-1661, the originals of which are in the British Library, are a full collection of these. See Fortescue, G. K., *The Catalogue of the Pamphlets, Books, Newspapers, and Manuscripts Relating to the Civil War, the Commonwealth, and Restoration, Collected by George Thomason, 1640-1661* (London: British Museum, 1908; reprinted 1977)
8. Hist. Mss. Comm., 3rd Report (London: HMSO, 1873) p 3

9. Rushworth, J., *The Tryal of Thomas, Earl of Strafford* (London: R. Chiswell, 1700), Article 23 of the Impeachment

15 The Long Parliament Meets

1. Clarendon, E. Earl of, *The History of the Rebellion and Civil Wars in England*, Mackray, W. D., ed., Vol. I (Oxford: Clarendon Press, 1888), p. 220
2. *Journals of the House of Commons: Volume 2, 1640-1643* (London: H.M.S.O., 1802) p 20: 3 November 1640
3. Strafford to Radcliffe, in *The life and original correspondence of Sir George Radcliffe*, Whittaker, T. D., ed. (London, 1810), p. 214
4. Gardiner, *History of England 1603-1641*, Vol IX, p. 234
5. Stevenson, *The Scottish Revolution 1637-44*, pp. 193-195
6. Kearney, *Strafford in Ireland*, p. 202
7. Warwick, Sir P., *Memoirs of the Reign of King Charles I., with a continuation to the happy restoration of King Charles II* (London, 1701), p. 247
8. *Journals of the House of Lords*, Vol IV (London, 1771), p. 142
9. Hast, A., 'State Treason Trials during the Puritan Revolution, 1640-1660', *The Historical Journal*, Vol. 15, No. 1 (Mar., 1972), p. 42
10. Knowler, *Strafford's Letters*, Vol II, p. 416
11. Wedgwood, *Strafford, a Revaluation*, p. 374-5
12. Firth, C., *Oliver Cromwell and the Rule of the Puritans in England* (London: G. P. Putnam, 1900) pp 53-56
13. Stevenson, *Scottish Revolution 1637-44*, p. 234
14. *Journals of the House of Commons: Volume 2, 1640-1643*, p. 300

16 The Irish Rebellion of 1641

1. Corish, P., 'The Rising of 1641 and the Confederacy, 1641-5' in Moody, Martin, Byrne, *A New History of Ireland*, Vol. III; Connolly, S. J., *Divided Kingdom, Ireland 1630-1800* (Oxford: University Press, 2008), p5
2. Castlehaven, J. Touchet, Earl of, *The Earl of Castlehaven's Memoirs of the Irish Wars, 1684, with The Earl of Anglesey's Letter from a person of honour in the countrey.* (New York: Delmar, 1974), p. 13
3. Ibid, pp. 10-14
4. Corish, 'The Rising', *New History Ireland*, p. 291
5. Woolrych, *Britain in Revolution*, p. 196
6. Connolly, *Divided Kingdom*, p. 39
7. Percival-Maxwell, *The Outbreak of the Irish Rebellion of 1641* (Dublin: Gill and Macmillan, 1994), p. 218
8. Connolly, *Divided Kingdom*, p. 50
9. Corish, 'The Rising', p. 293; Woolrych, *Britain in Revolution*, p. 199; Connolly, *Divided Kingdom*, p. 43
10. Connolly, *Divided Kingdom, p. 43*
11. Firth, *The House of Lords during the Civil War*, pp. 92, 107

12. Gardiner, *Constitutional Documents*, p. 233-6
13. Perceval-Maxwell, *Outbreak of the Irish Rebellion*; Fennell, B., 'Dodgy Dossiers: Hearsay and the 1641 Depositions', *History Ireland*, Vol. 19, No. 3 (May/June 2011), pp. 26-29; Read, J. M., 'Atrocity Propaganda and the Irish Rebellion', *The Public Opinion Quarterly*, Vol. 2, No. 2 (April 1938), pp. 229-244
14. Woolrych, *Britain in Revolution*, p. 206; Shagan, E. H., 'Constructing Discord: Ideology, Propaganda, and English Responses to the Irish Rebellion of 1641', *Journal of British Studies*, Vol. 36, No. 1 (Jan., 1997), pp. 4-34
15. Corish, 'The Rising', p. 292
16. Ohlmeyer, J. *Civil War and Restoration*, p. 92
17. Connolly, *Divided Kingdom*, p. 39
18. Plowden, A., *Henrietta-Maria, Charles I's indomitable queen* (Stroud: Sutton, 2001), p. 167
19. Bottigheimer, K. S., *English Money and Irish Land: The 'Adventurers' in the Cromwellian Settlement of Ireland* (Oxford University Press, 1971), pp. 70, 179

17 Taking Positions
1. A pamphlet published by Parliament, 9 June 1642, *Journals of the House of Commons*, Vol. II, 1640-1642 (London: House of Commons, 1803) p 618
2. Durston, C. & Eales, J., *The Culture of English Puritanism 1560-1700* (Basingstoke: Macmillan, 1996), p. 212
3. Capp, B., *England's Culture Wars* (Oxford: University Press, 2012), p. 196
4. Gardiner, *Constitutional Documents*, pp. 249-5
5. Parker, H., *Observations upon some of His Majesties Late Answers and Expresses* (1642)
6. 'Robert Devereux, 3rd Earl of Essex', Oxford Dictionary of Biography (Oxford: University Press, 2014)
7. Stevenson, D., *Alasdair MacColla and the Highland Problem in the Seventeenth Century* (Edinburgh: John Donald, 1980), pp. 74-91

18 Civil War in England – Royalists Ascendant
1. Plowden, *Henrietta-Maria*, p. 177
2. *Letters of Queen Henrietta-Maria*, Green, M. A. E., ed. (London, 1857 – facsimile by Bibliolife), p. 128
3. Ibid, p. 167
4. Holmes, C., *The Eastern Association in the English Civil War* (London: Cambridge University Press, 1974), pp. 34-5
5. Cromwell, O., *The Letters and Speeches of Oliver Cromwell*, Carlyle, T., commentator, Lomas, S.C., ed., Vol II (London: Methuen, 1904), p. 417
6. Carte, T., The *Life of James, Duke of Ormonde*, Vol. V (Oxford: University Press, 1851), pp. 368-70
7. Clarendon, *History of the Rebellion*, Vol III, p. 510 (Bk VIII, 264)

8. Kenyon, J. & Ohlmeyer, J., *The Civil Wars: A Military History of England Scotland and Ireland 1638-1660* (Oxford: University Press, 1998), see pp 195-210
9. Plowden, *Henrietta-Maria,* p. 186
10. Woolrych, *Britain in Revolution*, p. 271; Rowe, V. A., *Sir Henry Vane the Younger* (London: Athlone Press, 1970), p. 24
11. Cust, R., *Charles I, a Political Life* (Harlow: Pearson Education, 2007) p 373
12. Ohlmeyer, *Civil War and Restoration*, p. 129-30
13. Cust, *Charles I*, p. 382
14. Rowe, *Vane*, p. 33
15. Plowden, *Henrietta-Maria*, p. 194

19 The Emergence of Oliver Cromwell

1. 'Montagu, Edward, second earl of Manchester', *Oxford Dictionary of National Biography* (online version, 200)
2. *Victoria County History, Huntingdonshire,* Vol 2 (Folkestone: for the University of London, 1974), pp. 14-31
3. Healy S, 'The Unmaking of Oliver Cromwell', in Little, P., ed., *Oliver Cromwell, New Perspectives* (Basingstoke: Palgrave Macmillan, 2009)
4. Cromwell, *Letters and Speeches*, Carlyle, Lomas, Vol I, p. 90
5. Coward, B., *Oliver Cromwell* (Harlow: Longman, 1991) pp 19-20
6. Ibid p 21
7. Holmes, *The Eastern Association*, p. 7
8. Marshall, A., *Oliver Cromwell Soldier: the military life of a revolutionary at war* (London: Brassey's, 2004), p. 27
9. Buchan, J, *Oliver Cromwell* (London: Hodder and Stoughton, 1934), p. 163
10. Cromwell, *Letters and Speeches*, 'A Letter from Cromwell to Sir William Spring', Sept. 1643.
11. Coward, *Cromwell,* p. 26
12. Little, P., *Lord Broghill and the Cromwellian Union with Ireland and Scotland* (Woodbridge: Boydell, 2004), pp. 33-41

20 Cromwell and Montrose Win Victories

1. *Calendar of State Papers Domestic, 1644–5* (London: HMSO, 1890), p. 152
2. Cromwell, *Letters and Speeches*, Carlyle, Lomas, Vol. I, p. 176
3. Patrick Gordon in particular refers to Alasdair's troops as 'Irishes'. Gordon of Ruthven, P., *Britane's Distemper* (Aberdeen: Spalding Club, 1844)
4. Woolrych, *Britain in Revolution*, p. 293. There are only small discrepancies between authors on the numbers of troops. See Gardiner, S. R., *History of the Great Civil War 1642-1649*, Vol. II (London: Longman, Green and Co, 1889), p. 87

5. Buchan, J., *Montrose* (London: Thomas Nelson and Sons, 1928), p. 200; Gardiner, *Great Civil War*, Vol. II, p. 90-98; Stevenson, *Alasdair McColla*, p 134-6
6. Stevenson, *Alasdair MacColla*, p. 148
7. See Edwards, D., Lenihan, P., Tait, C., *The Age of Atrocity* (Dublin: Four Courts, 2007) for a discussion of accepted violence in the period and the unusual levels of atrocity in Ireland.
8. Ibid, p. 163
9. Ibid, p. 158

21 The Creation of the New Model Army

1. Woolrych, *Britain in Revolution*, p. 300
2. Ibid
3. Tawney, *Religion and the Rise of Capitalism*, p. 173; Yerby, G., *The English Revolution and the Roots of Environmental Change* (London: Routledge, 2016), p. 234; Trevor-Roper, H., *Archbishop Laud*, p. 170
4. Donagan, B., 'Codes and Conduct in the English Civil War', *Past & Present*, No. 118 (Feb., 1988), pp. 65-95
5. *Calendar of State Papers Domestic, 1644–5* (London: HMSO, 1890), p. 159
6. Rushworth. J., *Historical Collections of Private papers of State*, Vol. VI (London: Thomason, 1721), p. 4
7. Gentles, I., *The New Model Army* (Oxford: Blackwell, 1992), pp. 21-23
8. Ibid p 26
9. Holmes, *The Eastern Association*, p. 220

22 Naseby and Philiphaugh – Royalist Collapse

1. Castlehaven, *Memoirs*, pp. 14-15
2. Gentles, *New Model Army*, p. 39
3. Gardiner, *Constitutional Documents*, p. 289
4. Ibid, p. 290
5. Woolrych, *Britain in Revolution*, p. 276
6. Gentles, *The New Model Army*, pp. 34-36
7. Ibid, p. 94
8. Stevenson, *Alasdair MacColla*, p. 191
9. Dodgshon, R.A., *From Chiefs to Landlords: Social and Economic Change in the Western Highlands and Islands, c. 1493-1820* (Edinburgh: University Press, 1998), pp. 46-50
10. Clarendon, *History of the Rebellion*, Vol. III, p. 450
11. Buchan, *Oliver Cromwell*, p214
12. Woolrych, *Britain in Revolution*, p. 318
13. Stevenson, *Alasdair MacColla*, p. 203-207
14. Carlton, *Charles I*, p. 288
15. Ibid, p. 298

23 The War of Ideas

1. Bruce J, ed., *Charles I in 1646: Letters of King Charles the First to Queen Henrietta-Maria*, p. 45 (10 June)
2. Raymond, J., *Making the News: an anthology of the newsbooks of revolutionary England, 1641-1660* (Moreton-in-the-Marsh: Windrush, 1993), p. 2
3. Ibid
4. Robertson, R., *Censorship and Conflict: the subtle art of division* (Pennsylvania: State University Press, 2009), pp. 46-47
5. Stone, L., 'The Educational Revolution in England, 1560-1640', *Past and Present*, 1964, p. 45
6. Clegg, C. S., *Press Censorship* (Cambridge: University Press, 2008), pp. 208-9
7. O'Hara, D. A., *English Newsbooks and the Irish Rebellion 1641-1649* (Dublin: Four Courts Press, 2006), p. 85
8. *Mercurius Hibernicus, or a Discourse of the Late Insurrection in Ireland*, Bodleian, Ashmole 991, no. XII
9. Ibid
10. *Mercurius Britanicus*, 29 July – 5 Aug 1644
11. *Mercurius Britanicus* 53 (7–14 October 1644), p. 415
12. Frank, J., *The Beginnings of the English Newspaper* (Cambridge Mass.: Harvard University Press, 1961), p. 209
13. Clarendon, *History of the Rebellion*, Vol I (1888), p269
14. Cressy, D., *England on Edge: Crisis and Revolution 1640-1642* (Oxford: University Press, 2006), pp. 296-309
15. Robertson, *Censorship*, p. 100
16. Milton, J., Sonnet VIII, *When the Assault Was Intended to the City*, composed 1642
17. 'Nedham, Marchamont', *Oxford Dictionary of National Biography* (Oxford: University Press, 2004)
18. Lilburne, J., *The freeman's freedom vindicated* (16 June 1646)
19. Lilburne, J., *A remonstrance of many thousand citizens and other freeborn people of England to their own House of Commons* (1646)
20. Worden, B., *Literature and Politics in Cromwellian England* (Oxford: University Press, 2007), p. 18
21. Capp, *England's Culture Wars*, p. 196-7

24 Negotiations and the Sale of the King

1. 'Letter 28 May 1646', *Charles I in 1646: Letters of King Charles to Queen Henrietta-Maria*, p. 41-2
2. Ohlmeyer, *Civil War and Restoration*, pp. 167-190; McDonnell, H., and Ohlmeyer, J., 'New Light on the Marquis of Antrim and the 'wars of the three kingdoms',' *Analecta Hibernica*, No. 41 (2009), pp. 11, 13-66, with thanks for Hector McDonnell for this reference

3. Burghclere, Lady, *The Life of James First Duke of Ormonde*, Vol I (London: John Murray, 1912), p. 280
4. Stevenson, D., *Revolution and Counter-Revolution, 1644-51* (Edinburgh: John Donald, 2011), p. 50
5. '9 October 1646,' *Letters of Queen Henrietta-Maria*, p. 326
6. '1 December 1646,' *Letters of Queen Henrietta-Maria*, p. 335
7. '17 October 1646,' *Charles I in 1646: Letters of King Charles the First to Queen Henrietta-Maria*, p. 71
8. Ibid, '30 November 1646,' p 80
9. Ibid, '28 November 1646,' p 76-77
10. McDonnell & Ohlmeyer, 'New Light on the Marquis,' p 19
11. Carlton, *Charles I, the Personal Monarch*, p. 313
12. Cromwell, *Letters and Speeches*, Vol I, p. 252
13. Woolrych, *Britain in Revolution*, p. 351; Kenyon & Ohlmeyer, *Civil Wars*, p. 148
14. Stevenson, *Revolution and Counter-Revolution*, p. 69
15. Ibid, p. 69-70

25 The Army Makes Its Move

1. Woolrych. A., *Soldiers and Statesmen* (Oxford: University Press, 1987) p 4
2. Holles, D., *Memoirs of Denzil Lord Holles, Baron of Ifield in Sussex, from the year 1641, to 1648* (London: Goodwin, 1699)
3. Buchan, *Oliver Cromwell*, pp. 237-8, quoting Ludlow
4. Cox, Sir R., *History of Ireland* (London: Joseph Watts, 1689), p. 197
5. '11 May 1647,' *Letters of Queen Henrietta-Maria*, p. 343
6. Text in Rushworth, J., *Historical Collections*, Vol VI (8 vols, London: Robert Boulter, 1680-1701), pp. 468-70. Rushworth was Fairfax's secretary but became Oliver Cromwell's in 1649
7. Woolrych, *Soldiers and Statesmen*, p. 57
8. Bodleian, *Clarendon Ms*, 26 April 1647 quoted in Gardiner, *History of the Great Civil War,* Vol. III, p. 61
9. *Old Parliamentary History,* XV 390, quoted in Woolrych, *Soldiers and Statesmen,* p 103
10. Clarke, W., *The Clarke Papers*, Firth, C., Woolrych, A., eds. (London: R.H.S., 1992) Preface by Firth, p. xxiii
11. Gardiner, *Great Civil War*, Vol. III, p. 96-7
12. Ibid, pp. 91-2; Woolrych, *Soldier and Statesmen,* pp. 10-114
13. Clarke Papers, Vol. I, p. 119-120; Woolrych, *Soldiers and Statemen,* pp. 112-113
14. Gardiner, *Great Civil War,* Vol. III, pp. 98-99
15. Gardiner, *Great Civil War,* Vol. III, p. 117-9; Woolrych, *Soldiers and Statesmen,* p. 126. The original of the *Declaration (or Representation)* is in Worcester College, Oxford, *Clarke pamphlets*, AA.1.19 (43)

16. Clarendon, *History of the Rebellion*, Vol X, p. 104
17. Carlton, *Charles I*, p. 317
18. Clarendon, *History of the Rebellion*, Vol. X, 103; Carlton, *Charles I*, p. 317
19. Berkeley, Sir J., *Memoirs,* p. 3-10, quoted in Gardiner, *Great Civil War*, Vol III, p 145
20. De Retz, *Memoires* III, 1859, p. 242, quoted in Gardiner, *Great Civil War,* Vol. III, p. 143
21. Berkeley, *Memoirs* II p 360, quoted in Woolrych, *Soldiers and Statesmen,* p. 146
22. Gardiner, *Great Civil War*, Vol. III, p. 188
23. Gardiner, *Great Civil War*, Vol. III, p. 149-150
24. Ibid, p. 156
25. Clarke, *Clarke Papers,* Vol. I, p. 179
26. Ibid, p. 193, 16 July 1647
27. Ibid, p. 213, 17 July 1647
28. Berkeley J., *Memoirs of Sir John Berkeley* (London, 1702 – Ecco facsimile), p. 34
29. Woolrych, *Soldiers and Statesmen,* p177-8

26 The Putney Debates

1. Quoted in 'John Lilburne', *Oxford Dictionary of National Biography* (online, 2006)
2. Foxley, R., 'Lilburne and the Citizenship of Free-Born Englishmen, *The Historical Journal*, Vol. 47, No. 4 (Dec., 2004), pp. 849-874
3. Lilburne et al, *England's Birthright Justified* (London: Larner's Press, 1645)
4. Prall, S.E., *The Agitation for Law Reform during the Puritan Revolution 1640-1660* (The Hague: Martinus Nijhoff, 1966) p 44
5. Overton, R., *An Arrow against all Tyrants* (London, 1646)
6. Quoted in Carlton, *Charles I*, p. 319
7. *Mercurius Pragmaticus*, 11 January 1648, p. 8
8. *Mercurius Pragmaticus,* 14-21 September 1647
9. Woolrych, *Soldiers and Statesmen*, p. 192
10. Wolfe, D.M., *Leveller Manifestoes* (London: Cass, 1967), pp. 198-222
11. Clarke, *The Clarke Papers* (London: Royal Historical Society, 1992), Vol. I, p. 236
12. Ibid, p. 255-6
13. Ibid, p. 272-3
14. Ibid, p. 280
15. Ibid, p. 296
16. Ibid, p. 299-311
17. Ibid, p. 326-7
18. Ibid, p. 336
19. Ibid 339-340
20. Ibid, p. 373, 383
21. Quoted in Carlton, *Charles I*, p. 322

27 *The Second Civil War*

1. Brailsford, H.N., *The Levellers and the English Revolution* (London: Cresset Press, 1961) p 418-9
2. Capp, B., *England's Culture Wars* (Oxford: University Press, 2012), pp. 87-92
3. Donagan, B., 'Codes and Conduct in the English Civil War,' *Past & Present*, No. 118 (Feb., 1988), pp. 65-95; Edwards, Lenihan, Tait, *Age of Atrocity* (Dublin: Four Courts Press, 2010)
4. The most quoted text is Spencer, E., *A View of the State of Ireland* (1596). In the 17th century, both sides used scorched earth, see Earl of Castlehaven's *Memoirs;* Murphy, J. A., 'The Sack of Cashel', *Journal of the Cork Historical and Archaeological Society*, No. 76, 1971, pp. 1-20
5. For troop numbers, Gardiner, *Great Civil War*, Vol. III, p. 32; Woolrych, *Britain in Revolution, p. 403*
6. Stevenson, *Revolution and Counter-Revolution 1644-5*, p. 84
7. *Mercurius Pragmaticus*, Thomason Tracts, E. 457, 11. (quoted in Gardiner, *Great Civil War,* vol III, p. 428)
8. Buchan, *Oliver Cromwell*, pp. 277-283 has a good account of the Battle of Preston
9. Cromwell, *Letters and Speeches*, Carlyle, Lomas, Vol. I, Letter LXIV, p. 336
10. Cromwell, *Letters and Speeches*, Carlyle, Lomas, Vol. I, p. 342
11. Buchan, *Oliver* Cromwell, p. 283; 'James Hamilton, 1st Duke of Hamilton', *Oxford Dictionary of National Biography* (online, 2004)
12. Adams, S., 'The Making of the Radical South-West', in Young, J. R., *Celtic Dimensions of the British Civil Wars* (Edinburgh: John Donald, 1997)
13. Gardiner, *Great Civil War,* Vol. III, p. 486
14. Ibid, p. 500
15. Clarke, *Clarke Papers*, Vol. II, p. 50
16. Gardiner, *Civil War,* Vol. III, p. 507
17. Fraser, A., *Oliver Cromwell* (London: Phoenix, 2008), p. 331, quoting Cromwell from Abbott, W. C., *Writings and Speeches of Oliver Cromwell*, Vol I (Cambs., Massacusetts: Harvard University Press, 1937-47), p. 691
18. Cromwell, *Letters and Speeches*, Carlyle, Lomas, Vol. I, pp. 393-400

28 *The Death of the King*

1. Lilburne, J, *Legal Fundamental Liberties* and Ludlow E., *Memoirs of Edmund Ludlow*, Vol I (London: A. Millar, 1751), p. 229; Gardiner *Great Civil War,* Vol III, pp. 536-7
2. Ludlow, Vol I, pp. 211-12
3. Buchan, *Oliver Cromwell,* p. 302
4. Clarendon, *History of the Great Rebellion*, Bk IX, p235
5. Gardiner, *Great Civil War*, Vol III, p. 563
6. Gardiner, *Great Civil War,* vol. III, p. 587
7. Included in *Eikon Basilike: The Pourtrature of His Sacred Majestie in His Solitudes and Sufferings* (London, 1649)

8. *State Trials*, quoted in Gardiner, *Great Civil War*, Vol III, p. 590

9. *King Charles his speech made upon the scaffold at Whitehall Gate, immediatly before his execution, on Tuesday the 30. of Jan. 1648. With a relation of the manner of his going to execution* (London, 1649)

10. Burghclere, *Duke of Ormonde*, Vol II, p. 352, from *Carte Mss.* Vol. III, pp. 408-9

11. Verney, F. P. and M. M., *Memoirs of the Verney Family* (London: Longman, Green and Co., 1925), pp. 444-5

12. Marvell, A., *An Horatian Ode upon Cromwell's Return from Ireland* (1650, publ. 1681)

13. Worden, *Literature and Politics in Cromwellian England*, p. 182-3

Appendices

1. Gardiner, S. R., *Constitutional Documents of the Puritan Revolution 1625-1660* (Oxford: Clarendon Press, 1968) p 290

2. 'The Case of the Army Truly stated', Wolfe, D. M., *Leveller Manifestoes of the Puritan Revolution* (London: Cass, 1967)

3. Gardiner, *Constitutional Documents, p. 316-326*

4. Gardiner, *Constitutional Documents*, pp. 335-347

5. Gardiner, *Constitutional Documents*, pp. 347-352

6. *The Parliamentary or Constitutional History of England,* Vol XVIII (London, J. & R. Tonson, 1762-3), pp. 162-238; Gentles, I., *The New Model Army* (Oxford: Blackwell, 1992), p. 274-6

7. *Parliamentary History*, p. 233

8. Rushworth, J., *Historical Collections*, Vol VII (London: D. Browne, 1721), pp 1358-61

Bibliography

Manuscript Sources
Bodleian Library, Oxford
The Carte Papers, 20, 21, 57
Rawlinson Ms. A.1.5
Tanner Ms. 53, 55, 58, 60
Ashmole 991, no. XII

National Records of Scotland
Hamilton Papers, GD 406
Campbell, Duke of Argyll, GD 45
Mackay, Baron Rea papers, GD 84
Douglas, Earl of Morton papers, GD 150

National Library of Ireland
Lismore Papers Ms. 43, 266
Orrery Papers Ms. 32–36

Guildhall Library, London
Honourable Artillery Company Archives 1611–1682

Printed Primary Sources
A Discourse of the Maner of the Discovery of this Late Intended Treason (London, 1605)
Berkeley, Sir J., *Memoirs of Sir John Berkeley* (London, 1702 – facsimile)
Borlase, *History of the Execrable Irish rebellion* (London, 1662)
Charles I in 1646: Letters of King Charles The First to Queen Henrietta-Maria, Bruce, J., ed (Camden Society, 1856 – Kessinger facsimile)
Clarke, W., *The Clarke Papers*, Firth, C.H., ed. Vols I & II (London: RHS, 1992)

Bibliography

Correspondence of the Scots Commissioners in London 1644-46, Meikle, H. W., ed. (Edinburgh, 1917)

Cox, R., *History of Ireland* (London: H. Clark, 1689)

Cromwell, O., *Memoirs of the Protector Oliver Cromwell and his sons Richard and Henry* (London: Longman, Hurst, 1820)

Firth, C. H., Rait, R. S., *Acts and Ordinances of the Interregnum 1642-1660* (England: HMSO, 1911)

Gilbert, J. T., *A Contemporary History of Affairs in Ireland 1641-1652* (Dublin, 1879)

Gordon, P. of Ruthven, *A Short Abridgement of Britane's Distempers from the Year of God 1639 to 1649* (Aberdeen: Spalding Club, 1844)

Gookin, V., *The Great Case of Transplantation Discussed* (1655)

Historical Manuscripts Commission Reports: Egmont, Inchiquin, Ormond, Portland

Letters of Queen Henrietta-Maria, Green, M. A. E. ed. (London: Richard Bentley, 1857 – Bibliolife facsimile)

Knowler, W., ed., *Letters and dispatches of the Earl of Strafforde* (London: W. Bowyer, 1739)

Mercurius Britanicus

Mercurius Hibernia

Mercurius Pragmaticus

Mercurius Veridicus

Moderate Intelligencer

'Letters Monroe to Leslie', *A True Relation of the proceedings of the Scottish Armie now in Ireland* (1642)

'Letters Monroe to Leslie', *A True Relation of the proceedings of the Scottish Armie now in Ireland* (1642)

Milton, J., *Political Writings* (Cambridge: University Press, 1991)

Nedham, M., *The Case of the Kingdom Stated* (London, 1647 – facsimile)

Perfect Occurrences of Parliament

Rushworth, J., The Tryal of the Earl of Strafford (London, 1680)

Rushworth, J., *Historical Collections* (London: George Thomason, 1659)

Thomason Tracts

Walker, C., *The Compleat History of Independency upon the Parliament Begun 1640* (London, 1661)

Winthrop, J., *Life and Letters of John Winthrop* (Boston, 1867)

Secondary Sources

Ashton, R., *The City and the Court, 1603-1643* (Cambridge: University Press, 1979)

Ashton, R., *The Crown and the Money Markets, 1603-1640* (Oxford: Clarendon Press, 1960)

Barnard, T., C., *Cromwellian Ireland* (Oxford: University Press, 1975)

Barnard, T. C., 'Planters and Policies in Cromwellian Ireland', *Past & Present*, No. 61 (Nov., 1973), pp. 31-69

Beckett, J.C., *Cavalier Duke* (Belfast: James Camlin, 1990)

Bellings, R., Gilbert, J. T., *History of the Irish Confederation and the war in Ireland, 1641 [-1649]* (Dublin: M. H. Gill and Son, 1882-1891)

Beier, A. L., Finlay, R., *London 1500-1700, the Making of the Metropolis* (London: Longman, 1986)

Bottigheimer, KS., *English Money and Irish Land, The 'Adventurers' in the Cromwellian Settlement of Ireland* (Oxford: University Press, 1971)

Braddick, M. J., *The Nerves of State: taxation and the financing of the English state, 1558-1714* (Manchester: University Press, 1996)

Brown, K., M., *Kingdom or Province? Scotland and the Regal Union* (Basingstoke: Macmillan, 1992)

Brunton, D. & Pennington D. H., *Members of the Long Parliament* (London: Allen & Unwin, 1954)

Buchan, J., *Montrose* (London and Edinburgh: Thomas Nelson and Sons, 1928)

Buchan, J., *Oliver Cromwell* (London: Hodder and Stoughton, 1934)

Burgess G., *Absolute Monarchy and the Stuart Constitution* (New Haven and London: Yale University Press, 1966)

Burleigh, H. S., *A Church History of Scotland* (London: Oxford University Press, 1960)

Byrne, K., *Colkitto* (Colonsay: House of Lochar, 1997)

Caldwell, D.H., *Islay, Jura and Colonsay, A Historical Guide* (Edinburgh: Birlinn, 2011)

Calendar of State Papers Venetian, Vol 10 (London: HMO, 1900), p. 513-14

Canny, N., 'The 1641 Depositions: A Source for Social &Cultural History,' *History Ireland*, Vol. 1, No. 4 (Winter, 1993), pp. 52-55

Capp, B., The Fifth Monarchy Men (London: Faber, 1972)

Carlin, N., 'The Levellers and the Conquest of Ireland in 1649,' *The Historical Journal*, Vol. 30, No. 2 (Jun., 1987), pp. 269-288

Carlton , C., *Charles I, The Personal Monarch* (London: Routledge, 1995)

Castlehaven, J. Touchet, Earl of, *The Earl of Castlehaven's Memoirs of the Irish Wars, 1684, with The Earl of Anglesey's Letter from a person of honour in the countrey* (New York: Delmar, 1974)

Casway, J. I., *Owen Roe O'Neill and the struggle for Catholic Ireland* (Philadelphia: University of Pennsylvania Press, 1984)

Coke, Sir E., *The Institutes of the Laws of England* (London, 1628-1644)

Coke, Sir E., *The Reports of Sir Edward Coke* (London: from 1600)

Journals of the House of Commons Vols I-6 (London: HMSO, 1802)

Connolly, S.J., *Contested Island: Ireland 1460-1630* (Oxford: University Press, 2007)

Connolly, S.J., *Divided Kingdom: 1630-1800* (Oxford: University Press, 2008)

Coonan, T. L., *The Irish Catholic Confederacy and the Puritan Revolution* (New York: Columbia University Press, 1954)

The correspondence of Elizabeth Stuart, Queen of Bohemia, Akkerman, N., ed. (Oxford: University Press, 2011)

Coward, B., *A Companion to Stuart England* (Chichester: Wiley-Blackwell, 2009)

Coward, B., *Oliver Cromwell* (London: Longman, 1991)

Cox, Sir R., *Hibernia anglicana: or, The history of Ireland* (London: J. Watt, 1689)

Bibliography

Cramsie J., 'Commercial Projects and the Fiscal Policy of James VI and I', *The Historical Journal*, Vol. 43, No. 2 (Jun., 2000), pp. 345-364

Cramsie, J., *Kingship and Crown Finance under James VI and I 1603-1625* (Woodridge: RHS & Boydell Press, 2002)

Cressy, D., *Literacy and the Social Order; Reading and writing in Tudor and Stuart England* (Cambridge: University Press, 1980)

Cromwell, O., *Letters and Speeches*, Carlyle, T., & Lomas, S. C., eds. (London: Methuen & Co., 1904)

Cromartie, A., *Sir Matthew Hale 1609-1676: law, religion and natural philosophy* (Cambridge: University Press, 1995)

Cuddy, N., *The King's Chambers: the bedchamber of James I in administration and politics, 1603 – 1625*, D. Phil thesis, University of Oxford, 1987

Cuddy, N., 'The Revival of the Entourage: the Bedchamber of James I, 1603-1625,' in *The English Court: From the Wars of the Roses to the Civil War*, Starkey, D., ed. (London: Longman, 1987)

Cunningham, A., Grell, O.P., *Four Horsemen of the Apocalypse: religion, war, famine and death in reformation Europe* (Cambridge: University Press, 2000)

Curtis, M. H., *Oxford and Cambridge in Transition 1558-1642* (Oxford: Clarendon Press, 1959)

Cust, R., *Charles I: A Political Life* (Harlow: Longman, 2007)

Daly J, 'The Idea of Absolute Monarchy in Seventeenth-Century England', *The Historical Journal*, Vol. 21, No. 2 (June, 1978), pp. 227-250

Dictionary of Irish Biography (Oxford: University Press, 2004)

Dixon, C. S., Freist, D., Greengrass, M., *Living with Diversity in Early-Modern Europe* (Farnham: Ashgate, 2009)

Dodd, A.H. *Studies in Stuart Wales* (Cardiff: University Press, 1952)

Dodgshon, R.A., *From Chiefs to Landlords* (Edinburgh: University Press, 1998)

Donagan, B., 'Codes and Conduct in the English Civil War,' *Past & Present*, Feb 1988, No. 118, pp.65-95

Donne, J., *Complete Verse and Prose*, J. Hayward, Ed. (London: Nonesuch, 1962)

Durston, C., Eales, J., eds. *The Culture of English Puritanism, 1560-1700* (Basingstoke: Macmillan, 1966)

Elizabeth I, *Collected Works*, Marcus, L.S. Mueller, J., Rose, M.B. (University of Chicago Press, 2002)

Farr, D., *Henry Ireton and the English Revolution* (Woodbridge: Boydell & Brewer, 2006)

Farr, D., *John Lambert, parliamentary soldier and Cromwellian major-general, 1619-1684* (Woodbridge: Boydell, 2003)

Firth, C. H., *The House of Lords during the Civil War* (Longmans, Green & Co., 1910)

Firth, C., *Cromwell's Army: a history of the English soldier during the Civil Wars, the Commonwealth and the Protectorate* (London: Methuen, 1902)

Fraser, A., *Cromwell, Our Chief of Men* (London: Phoenix, 2002)

Furgol, E. M., *A Regimental History of the Covenanting Armies* (Edinburgh: John Donald, 1990)

Gardiner, S. R., *History of the Great Civil War 1642-1649* (London: Longmans, Green and Co., 1886)

Gardiner, S.R., *The History of England from the Accession of James I to the Outbreak of the Civil War 1603-1642,* 10 vols. (London: Longmans, Green and Co., 1895–1899)

Gardiner, S. R., *History of the Commonwealth and Protectorate 1649-1656* (London: Longmans, Green and Co., 1903)

Gaunt, P., *Oliver Cromwell* (Oxford: Blackwell, 1997)

Gentles, I., *The New Model Army, In England, Ireland and Scotland, 1645-1653* (Oxford: Blackwell, 1992)

Gillespie, R., *Reading Ireland: print, reading, and social change in early modern Ireland* (Manchester: University Press, 2005)

Goodare, J., 'The debts of James VI of Scotland,' *Economic History Review,* November 2009, Vol.62(4), pp.926-952

Goodare, J., State and Society in Early Modern Scotland (Oxford: Clarendon Press, 1999)

Greengrass, M., *Conquest and coalescence: the shaping of the state in early modern Europe* (London: Edward Arnold, 1991)

Gorski, P. S., *The Disciplinary Revolution* (Chicago: University Press, 2003)

Hansard, T., *Cobbett's Parliamentary History of England from the Earliest Period to the Year 1803,* Vol I (London: Black Parry and Co., 1806)

Hazlett, H., 'The Financing of the British Armies in Ireland, 1641-9,' *Irish Historical Studies,* Vol. 1, No. 1 (Mar., 1938), pp. 21-41

Helm, P., *John Calvin's Ideas* (Oxford: University Press, 2004)

Hexter, J. H., *The reign of King Pym* (Cambridge, Mass: Harvard University Press, 1941)

Hirst, D., *The Representative of the People* (Cambridge: University Press, 1975)

Holmes, C., *The Eastern Association in the English Civil War* (London: Cambridge University Press, 1974)

Howell T. J., Cobbett, W., Jardine, D., *A Complete Collection of State Trials and Proceedings for High Treason and Other Crimes and Misdemeanors from the Earliest Period to the Year 1783: 1640-49* (1816)

Ingrao, C. W., *The Habsburg Monarchy, 1618-1815* (Cambridge: University Press, 2000)

James VI, *The Trew Law of Free Monarchies* (1598)

Johnson, S., *Lives of the Poets*: Milton (London: Macmillan, 1906)

Johnston of Warriston, A. *Diaries,* 3 Vols (Edinburgh: University Press, 1911-1940)

Jones, C., *A Short History of Parliament* (Woodbridge: Boydell Press, 2009)

Judges, A.V., 'The Origins of English Banking', *History,* Jan,1931, Vol.16, p. 142

Kearney, H. F., *Strafford in Ireland 1633-41* (Manchester: University Press, 1959)

Kelly, P., Young, J. R., eds., *Scotland and the Ulster Plantation* (Dublin: Four Courts, 2009)

Kelsey, S., Inventing a republic: the political culture of the English Commonwealth 1649-1653 (Manchester: University Press, 1997)

Kelsey, S, 'The Death of Charles I,' *The Historical Journal*, Vol. 45, No. 4 (Dec., 2002), pp. 727-754

Kemp, G., McElligott, J., *Censorship and the Press 1580-1720* (London: Pickering & Chatto, 2009)

Kenyon, J. P., *The Stuart Constitution 1603-1688: documents and commentary* (Cambridge: University Press, 1966)

The Knyvett Letters (1620-1644), Schofield, B., ed. (London: Constable & Co. Ltd., 1949)

Lawrence D. R., *The Complete Soldier: Military Books and Military Culture in Early Stuart England 1603-1645* (Leiden Boston: Brill, 2009)

Lee, M., *Great Britain's Solomon: James VI & I in his Three Kingdoms* (Urbana: University of Illinois Press, 1990)

Lee, M., *The Road to Revolution Scotland under Charles I, 1625-37* (Urbana: University of Illinois Press, 1985)

Levack, B. P., *The Formation of the British State* (Oxford: Clarendon Press, 1987)

Little, P., 'The Earl of Cork and the Fall of the Earl of Strafford, 1638-41,' *The Historical Journal*, Vol. 39, No. 3 (Sep., 1996), pp. 619-63

Little, P., ed., *Oliver Cromwell, New Perspectives* (Basingstoke: Palgrave Macmillan, 2009)

Little, P., *Lord Broghill and the Cromwellian Union with Ireland and Scotland* (Woodbridge: Boydell, 2004)

Lynch, K. M., *Roger Boyle, First Earl of Orrery* (Knoxville: University of Tennessee Press, 1965)

Macdonald, A. R., 'Consultation and Consent under James VI', *The Historical Journal*, 54, 2 (2011), pp. 287-306

MacDonald, F. A., *Mission to the Gaels* (Edinburgh: John Donald, 2006)

Mackie, R. L., *A Short History of Scotland* (Edinburgh: Oliver and Boyd, 1962)

MacLean, G., 'Literacy, Class, and Gender in Restoration England', *Text*, Vol. 7 (Indiana University Press, 1994)

Marshall R. K., *The Winter Queen, The Life of Elizabeth of Bohemia 1596-1662* (Edinburgh: Scottish National Portrait Gallery, 1998)

McIlwain, C. H., *The High Court of Parliament and its supremacy* (New Haven: Yale University Press, 1910)

Moody, TW., Martin, FX., and Byrne, FJ., eds., *A New History of Ireland* Vol III (Oxford: University Press, 1973)

Morrill, J., 'The Attack on the Church of England in the Long Parliament, 1640-1642,' in Beales, D. E. D., Best, G., *History, Society and the Churches: essays in honour of Owen Chadwick* (Cambridge: University Press, 1985)

Morrill, J., ed., *Oliver Cromwell and the English Revolution* (London: Longman, 1990)

Morton, A., *Galloway and the Covenanters or The struggle for religious liberty in the south-west of Scotland* (Paisley, 1914)

Murdoch, S., *Scotland and the Thirty Years war: 1618-1648* (Leiden, Boston: Brill, 2001)

Murphy, J. A., 'The Politics of the Munster Protestants, 1641-49,' *Journal of the Cork Historical and Archaeological Society*, Vol 76, 1971, pp. 1-19

Newman, P. R., *The Old Service: Royalist regimental colonels and the Civil War, 1642-46* (Manchester: University Press, 1993)

Nicholls, M., 'Strategy and Motivation in the Gunpowder Plot', *Historical Journal*, Vol 50, No. 4 (Dec, 2007), pp. 787-807

Noppen, J. G., *Royal Westminster* (London: Country Life, 1937)

Ohlmeyer, J., *Ireland from Independence to Occupation* (Cambridge: University Press, 1995)

Ohlmeyer, J., *Civil War and Restoration in the Three Stuart Kingdoms* (Cambridge: University Press, 1993)

O Siochrú, M., *Kingdoms in Crisis* (Dublin: Four Courts, 2001)

O Siochrú, M., *Confederate Ireland 1642-1649* (Dublin: Four Courts Press, 1999)

Oxford Dictionary National Biography (Oxford: University Press, 2004 and online)

Parker, G., Smyth, L.M., *The General Crisis of the Seventeenth Century* (London: Routledge & Kegan Paul, 1978)

Patterson, W. B., *King James VI and the Reunion of Christendom* (Cambridge: University Press, 1997)

Perceval-Maxwell, M., *The outbreak of the Irish rebellion of 1641* (Dublin: Gill & Macmillan, 1994)

Plowden, A., *Henrietta Maria: Charles I's indomitable queen* (Stroud: Sutton, 2001)

Port, M. H., *The Palace of Westminster on the Eve of Conflagration 1834* (London Topographical Society, 2011)

Prall, S. E., *The Agitation for Law reform during the Puritan Revolution 1640-1660* (The Hague: Nijhoff, 1966)

Raleigh, Sir W., *An Abridgement of Sir Walter Raleigh's History of the World* (London: Gillyflower, 1698)

Russell, C., *Crisis of Parliaments: English history 1509-1660* (Oxford: University Press, 1971)

Russell, C., 'Composite Monarchies in early modern Europe', in Grant, A., Stringer K., *Uniting the Kingdom? The Making of British History* (London, New York: Routledge, 1995)

Russell, C., *King James VI and I and his English Parliaments* (Oxford: University Press, 2011)

Russell, C., *The Fall of the British Monarchies 1637-1642* (Oxford: University Press, 1995)

Saunders, H. St G., *Westminster Hall* (London: Michael Joseph, 1951)

Sayles, G. O., *The King's Parliament of England* (London: Edward Arnold, 1975)

Scott, W. R., *Joint-Stock Companies to 1720* (Cambridge: University Press, 1912)

Shagan, E., H., 'Constructing Discord: Ideology, Propaganda, and English Responses to the Irish Rebellion of 1641', *Journal of British Studies*, Vol. 36, No. 1 (Jan., 1997), pp. 4-34

Bibliography

Shohet, L., 'Interpreting "The Irish Masque at Court" and in Print,' in *Journal for Early Modern Cultural Studies*, Vol. 1, No. 2 (Fall – Winter, 2001), pp. 42-65

Stevenson, D., *Alasdair MacColla and the Highland Problem in the 17th Century* (Glasgow: John Donald, 1980)

Stevenson, D., 'The King's Scottish Revenues and the Covenanters, 1625-1651,' *The Historical Journal*, xvii, I (1974) pp 17-41

Stevenson, D., *Revolution and Counter Revolution 1644-51* (Edinburgh: John Donald, 2003)

Stevenson, D., *The Scottish Revolution 1637-44* (Newton Abbot: David and Charles, 1973)

Stone, L., 'The educational revolution in England, 1560-1640,' *Past and Present*, No. 28 (July, 1964)

Tawney, R. H., *Religion and the Rise of Capitalism* (London: John Murray, 1936)

Terry, C. S., *The Scottish Parliament, Its Constitution and Procedure, 1603-1707* (Glasgow: J. MacLehose and Sons, 1905)

Thurley, S., *Whitehall Palace : an architectural history of the royal apartments, 1240-1698* (New Haven, London: Yale University Press, 1999)

Treadwell, V., 'The Irish Customs Administration in the Sixteenth Century,' *Irish Historical Studies*, Vol. 20, No. 80 (Sep., 1977), pp. 384-417

Tyacke, N., *Anti-Calvinists: The Rise of English Arminianism c. 1590-1640* (Oxford: Clarendon Press, 1987)

Underdown, D., *Pride's Purge: Politics in the Puritan Revolution* (Oxford: Clarendon Press, 1971)

Weber, M., *The Protestant Ethic and the Spirit of Capitalism* (London: George Allen, 1952)

Wedgwood, C. V. Thomas Wentworth, first Earl of Strafford, 1593-1641: a revaluation (London: Jonathan Cape, 1961)

Wedgwood, C. V., *The Trial of Charles I* (London: Collins, 1964)

Whitelocke, B., *Memorials of the English Affairs from the beginning of the reign of Charles the First to the happy restoration of King Charles the Second* (Oxford: University Press, 1853)

Williams, R., *The Lords of the Isles* (Colonsay: House of Lochar, 1997)

Willson, D. H., *King James VI and I* (London: Cape, 1956)

Wilson, T., *A Discourse upon Usury* (London: G. Bell, 1925)

Witte, J., *The Reformation of Rights* (Cambridge: University Press, 2007)

Woolrych, A., *Soldiers and Statesmen, The General Council of the Army and its Debates 1647-1648* (Oxford: University Press, 1987)

Woolrych, A., *Britain in Revolution* (Oxford: University Press, 2004)

Wormald, J., The Creation of Britain: Multiple Kingdoms or Core and Colonies?' *Transactions of the Royal Historical Society* (1 January 1992, Vol.2), pp.175-194

Young, J. R., *Celtic Dimensions of the British Civil Wars* (Edinburgh: John Donald, 1997)

Young J. R., *The Scottish Parliament 1639-1661* (Edinburgh: John Donald, 1996)

Acknowledgements

Returning to university as a mature student was a wonderful experience. I would like to thank my tutors and colleagues at the University of Oxford for their generosity and the stimulation of their ideas. The Bodleian Library has become a second home to me and I must thank the staff there for the excellence of the service they provide – and indeed all the Oxford libraries.

I embarked on this project – to provide a narrative of the three kingdoms throughout the convulsions of the seventeenth century until the achievement of a constitutional agreement at the close of the century – a long time ago and the research has overlapped with other projects, so my thanks may, as it were, cross from one book to another and among many archives. I would especially like to thank Boole Library at University College Cork; the British Library; Exeter University Library; the libraries of the universities of Edinburgh, St Andrews and Aberdeen; Trinity College Dublin; and the National Library of Ireland.

Randal, Viscount Dunluce and the Hon. Hector McDonnell were both very generous with pictures and information about the 1st Marquis of Antrim and I am most grateful. I would also like to thank Banbury Town Council, Manchester Art Gallery and Christ's College, Cambridge for their generosity regarding pictures.

I would like to thank Christopher Tyerman for his support and advice throughout my university studies. The following people were very kind in responding to my queries and requests for help: George Southcombe, Toby Barnard, Mark Kishlansky, Mike Braddick and Karl Bottigheimer. William Steen and John Wagstaff of Christ's College, Cambridge were swift and most helpful. I would like to thank John Plumer for his interest and skill while making the maps.

Alice Doyne let me have her thesis. Stephen Terry made careful editorial notes and Tim Wright provided manuscripts and books – thank you.

Many thanks to Mark Beeson and Mary Quicke for reading the full manuscript. I would also like to thank Tony Cammell and Sarah Nevitt for many happy days in Belbroughton Road.

I hope I have not forgotten anyone and thank everyone who showed an interest and asked useful questions.

Index